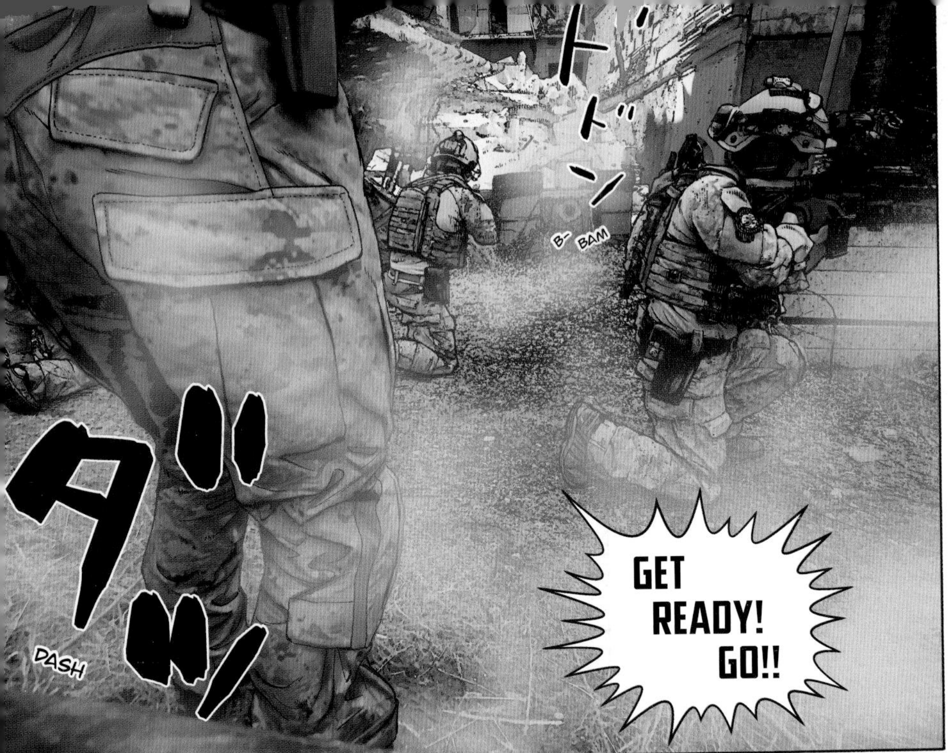
ドドン
B- BAM
GET READY! GO!!
ダッ
DASH

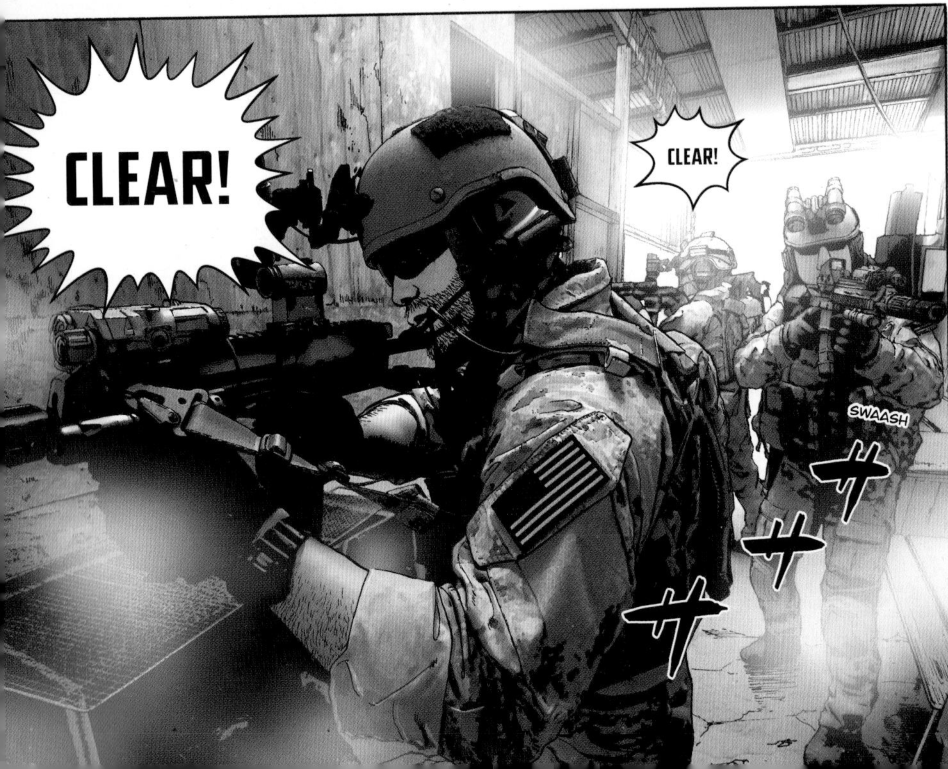
CLEAR!
CLEAR!
SWAASH
ザザザ

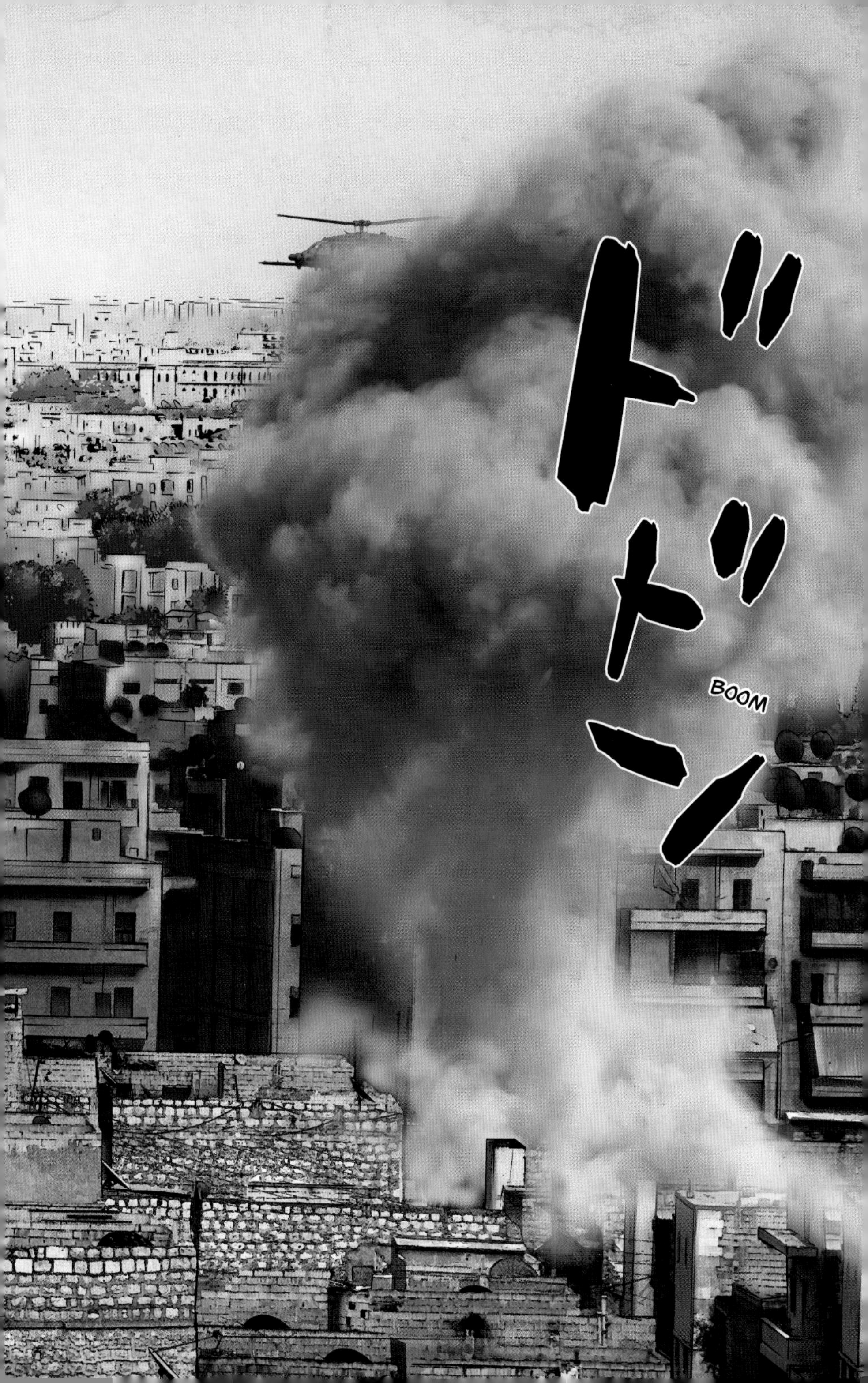
ドドドーン
BOOM

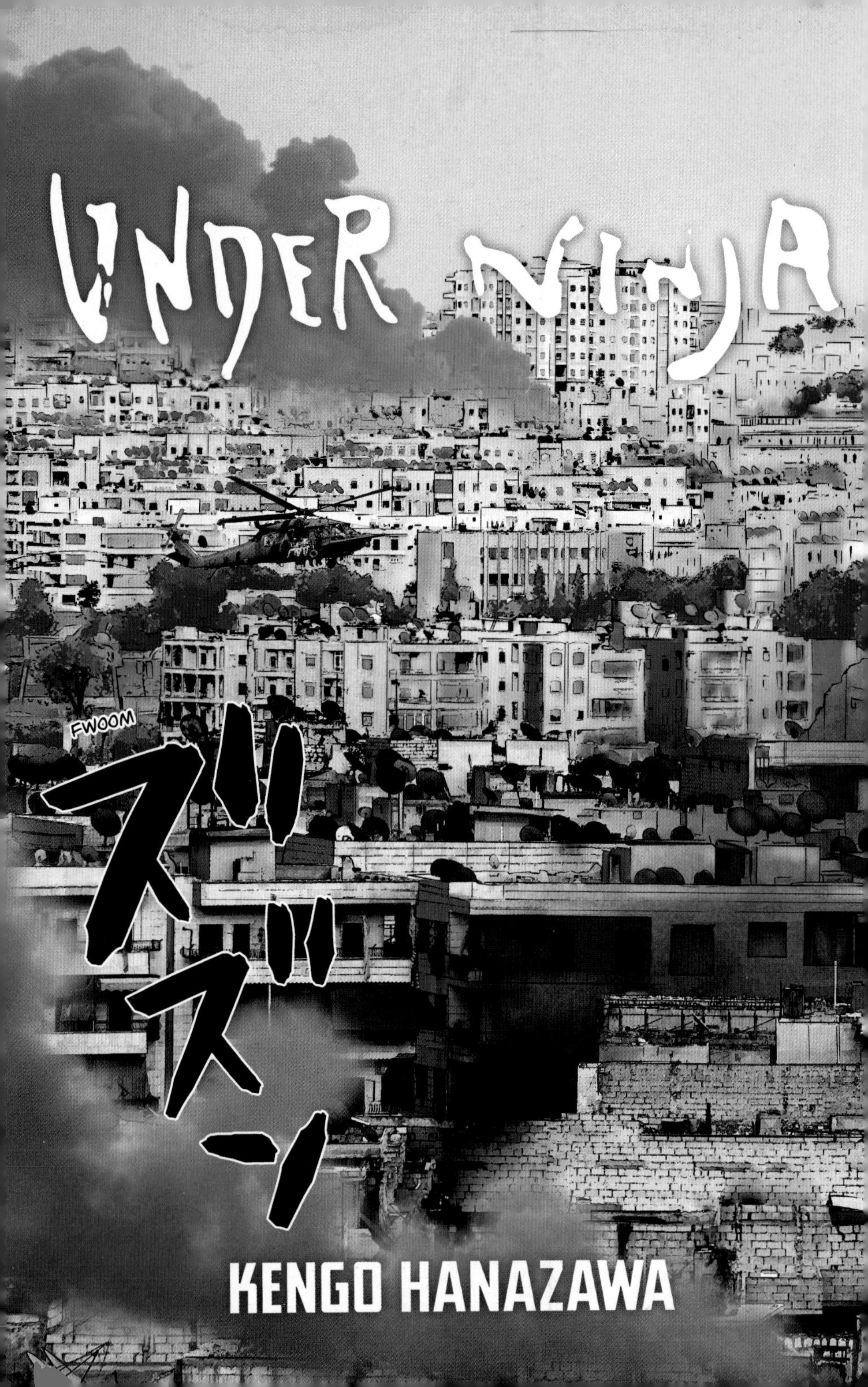
UNDER NINJA
FWOOM
ズズズーッ
KENGO HANAZAWA

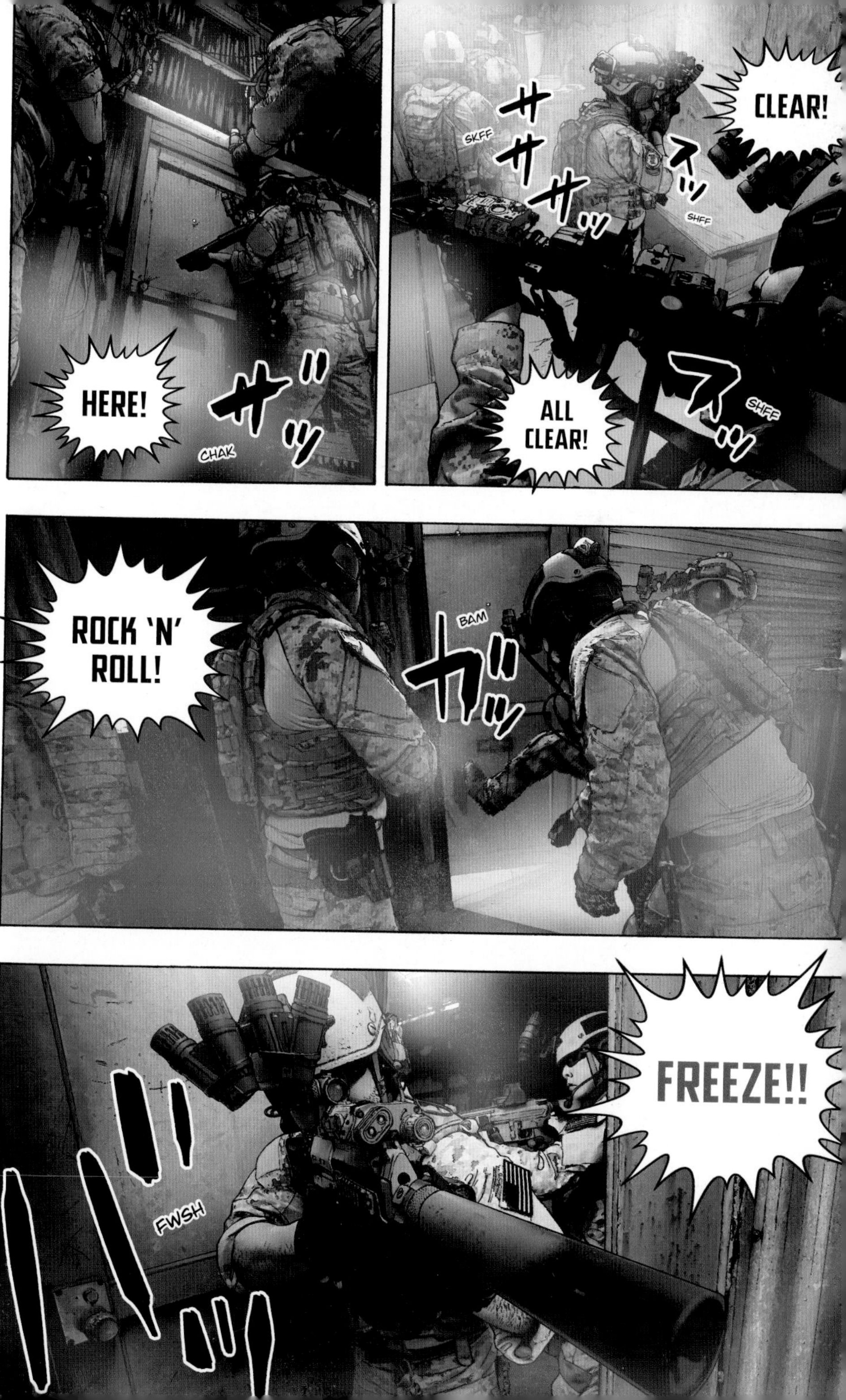
CLEAR!
スッ
SHFF
ササザッ
SKFF
スッ
SHFF
ALL CLEAR!
HERE!
ザッ
CHAK
ROCK 'N' ROLL!
ガッ
BAM
FREEZE!!
FWSH

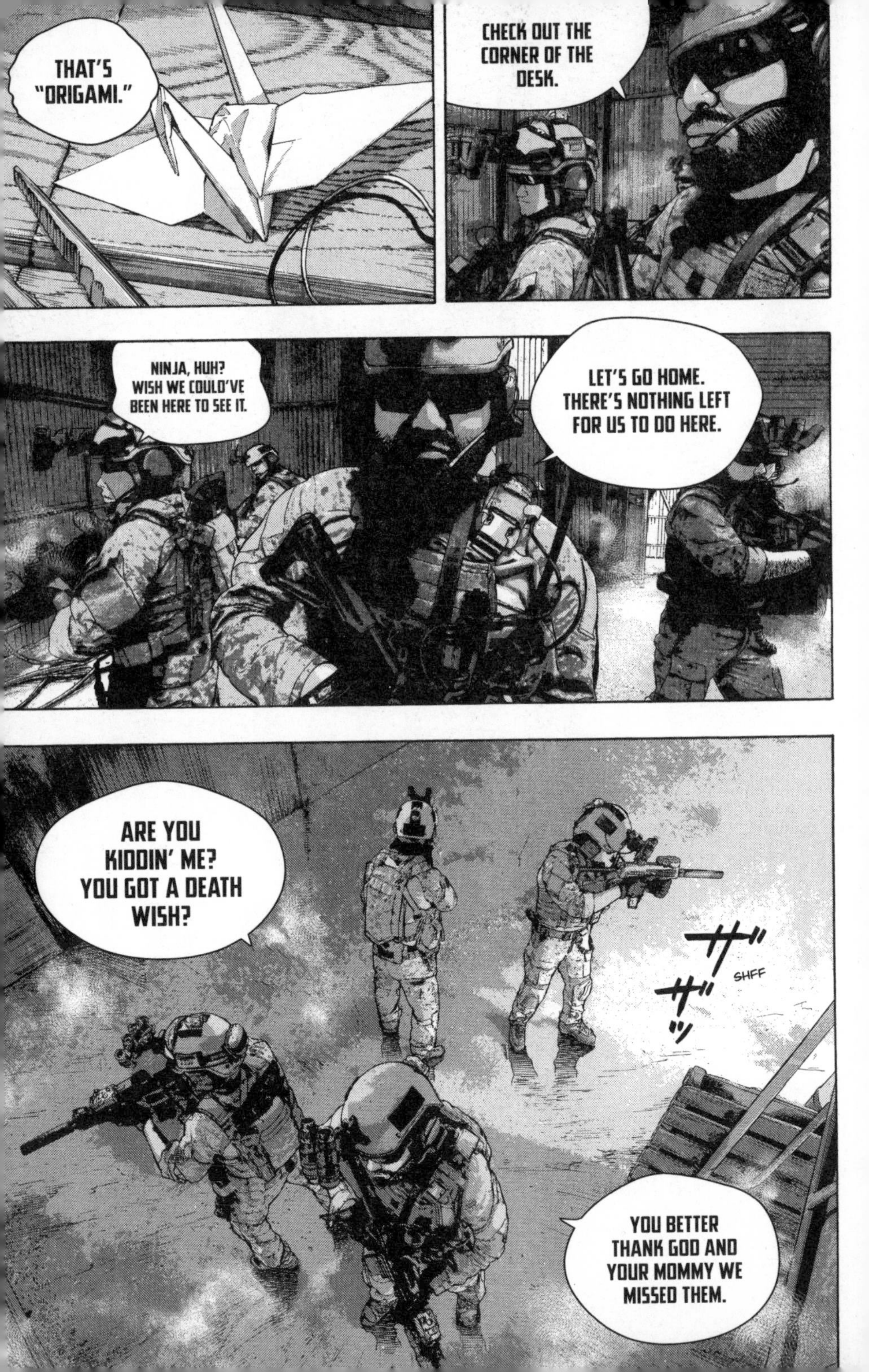
CHECK OUT THE CORNER OF THE DESK.
THAT'S "ORIGAMI."
LET'S GO HOME. THERE'S NOTHING LEFT FOR US TO DO HERE.
NINJA, HUH? WISH WE COULD'VE BEEN HERE TO SEE IT.
ザザッ
SHFF
ARE YOU KIDDIN' ME? YOU GOT A DEATH WISH?
YOU BETTER THANK GOD AND YOUR MOMMY WE MISSED THEM.

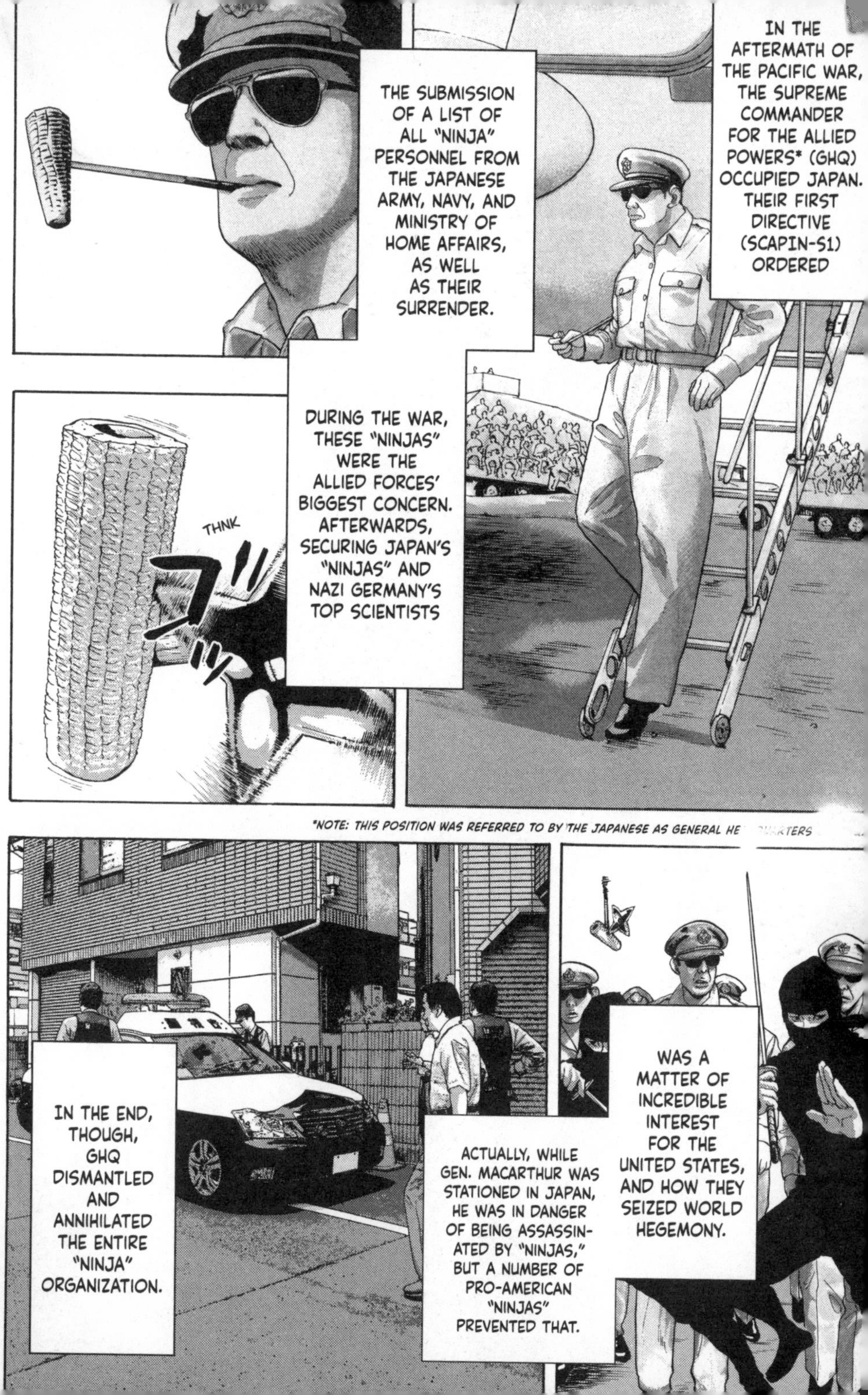
IN THE AFTERMATH OF THE PACIFIC WAR, THE SUPREME COMMANDER FOR THE ALLIED POWERS* (GHQ) OCCUPIED JAPAN. THEIR FIRST DIRECTIVE (SCAPIN-S1) ORDERED
THE SUBMISSION OF A LIST OF ALL "NINJA" PERSONNEL FROM THE JAPANESE ARMY, NAVY, AND MINISTRY OF HOME AFFAIRS, AS WELL AS THEIR SURRENDER.
DURING THE WAR, THESE "NINJAS" WERE THE ALLIED FORCES' BIGGEST CONCERN. AFTERWARDS, SECURING JAPAN'S "NINJAS" AND NAZI GERMANY'S TOP SCIENTISTS
THNK
*NOTE: THIS POSITION WAS REFERRED TO BY THE JAPANESE AS GENERAL HE
WAS A MATTER OF INCREDIBLE INTEREST FOR THE UNITED STATES, AND HOW THEY SEIZED WORLD HEGEMONY.
ACTUALLY, WHILE GEN. MACARTHUR WAS STATIONED IN JAPAN, HE WAS IN DANGER OF BEING ASSASSIN-ATED BY "NINJAS," BUT A NUMBER OF PRO-AMERICAN "NINJAS" PREVENTED THAT.
IN THE END, THOUGH, GHQ DISMANTLED AND ANNIHILATED THE ENTIRE "NINJA" ORGANIZATION.

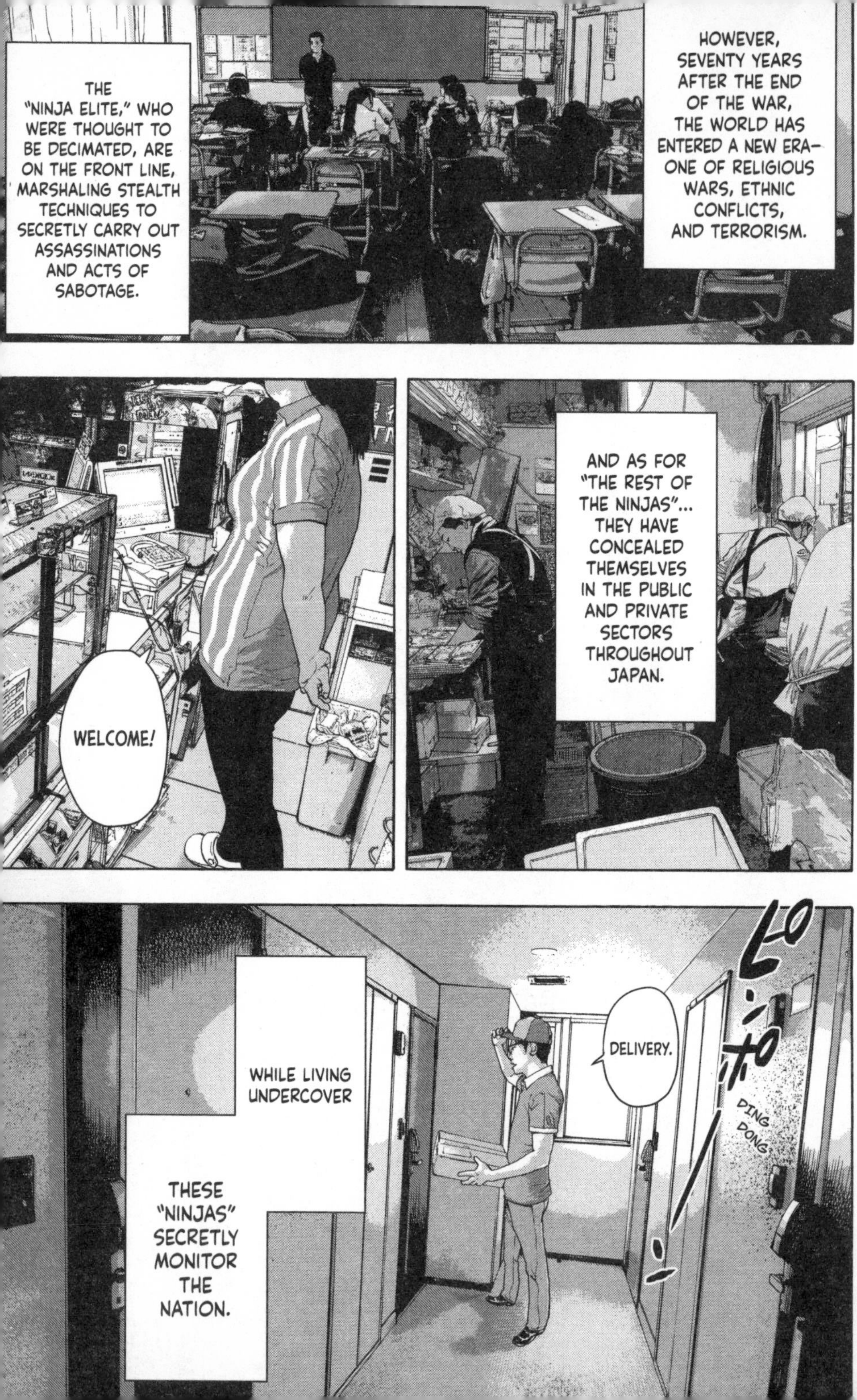
HOWEVER, SEVENTY YEARS AFTER THE END OF THE WAR, THE WORLD HAS ENTERED A NEW ERA—ONE OF RELIGIOUS WARS, ETHNIC CONFLICTS, AND TERRORISM.
THE "NINJA ELITE," WHO WERE THOUGHT TO BE DECIMATED, ARE ON THE FRONT LINE, MARSHALING STEALTH TECHNIQUES TO SECRETLY CARRY OUT ASSASSINATIONS AND ACTS OF SABOTAGE.
AND AS FOR "THE REST OF THE NINJAS"... THEY HAVE CONCEALED THEMSELVES IN THE PUBLIC AND PRIVATE SECTORS THROUGHOUT JAPAN.
WELCOME!
DING DONG
DELIVERY.
WHILE LIVING UNDERCOVER
THESE "NINJAS" SECRETLY MONITOR THE NATION.

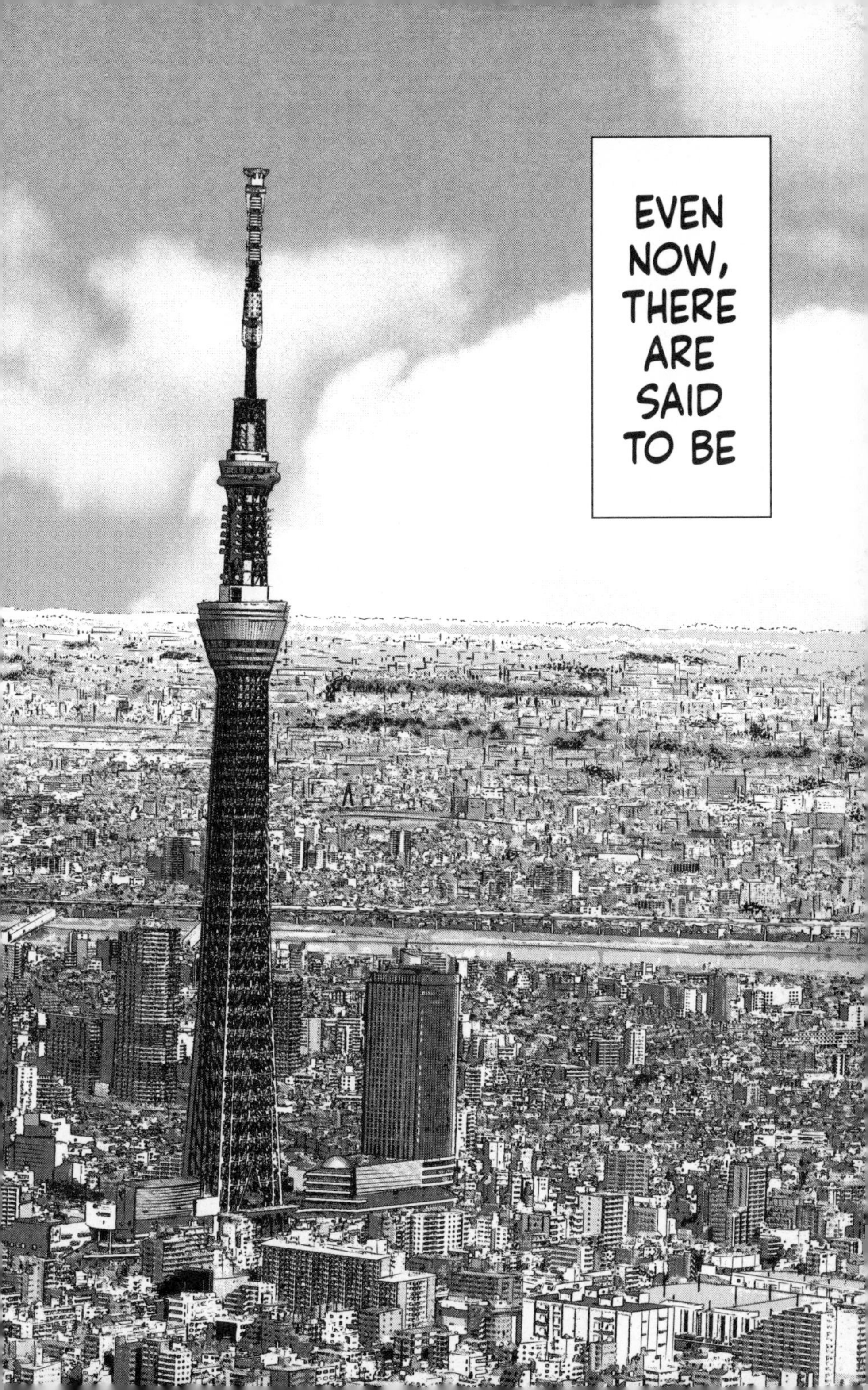
EVEN NOW, THERE ARE SAID TO BE

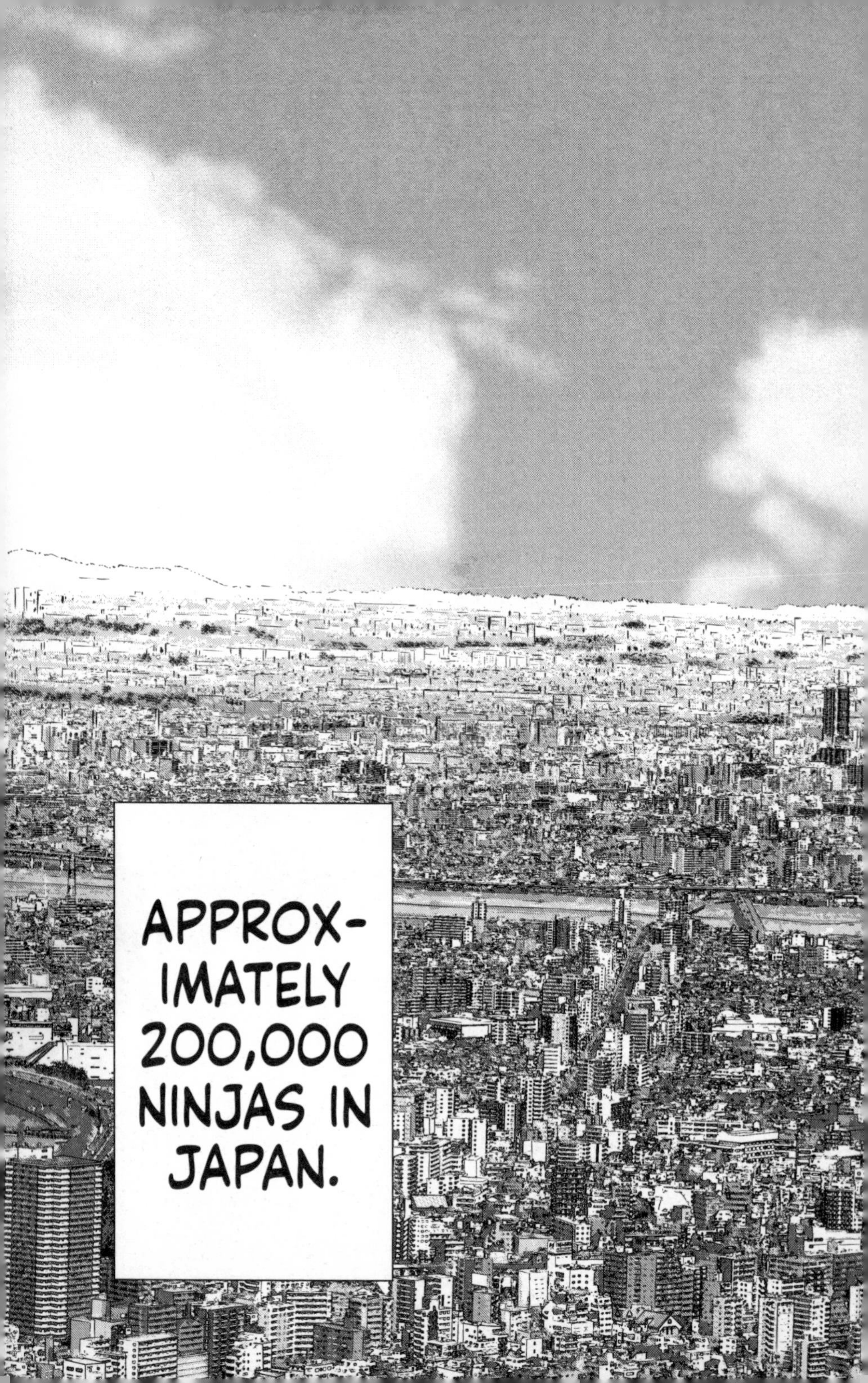
APPROX-
IMATELY
200,000
NINJAS IN
JAPAN.

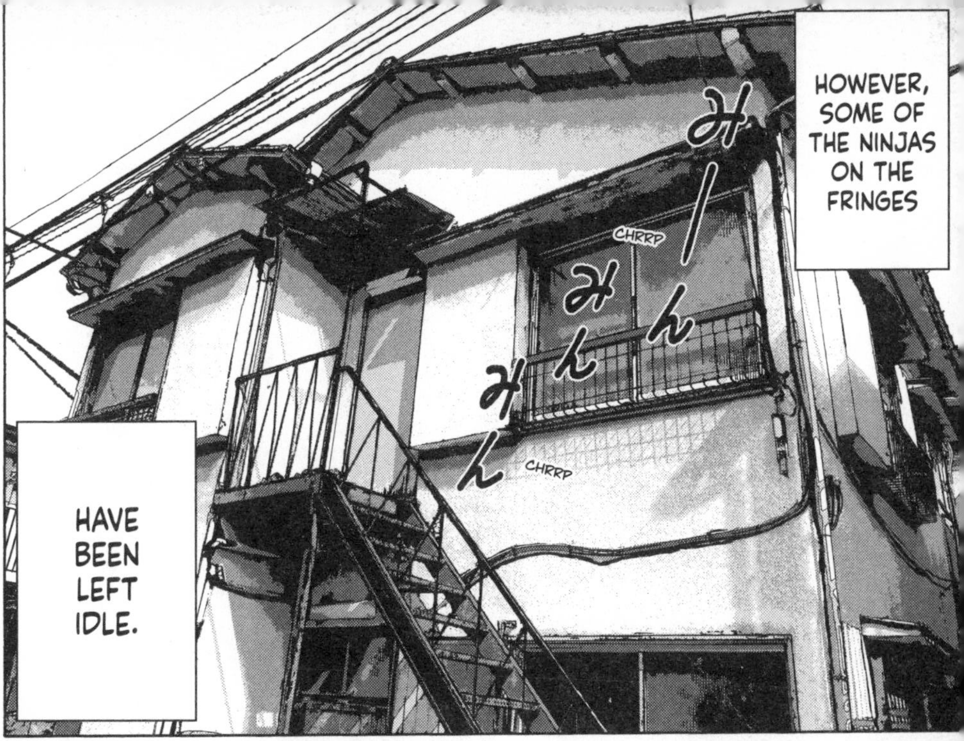
HOWEVER, SOME OF THE NINJAS ON THE FRINGES
みーん
みん
みん
CHRRP
CHRRP
HAVE BEEN LEFT IDLE.

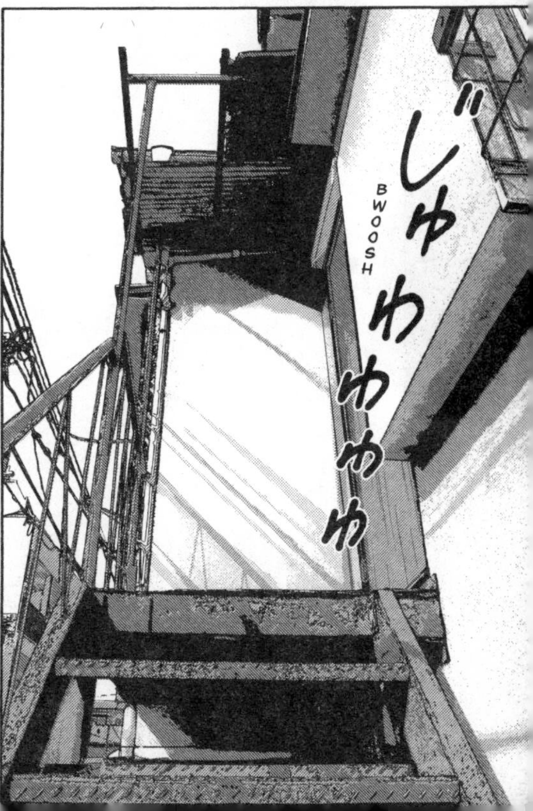
じゅゆゆゆゆ
BWOOSH

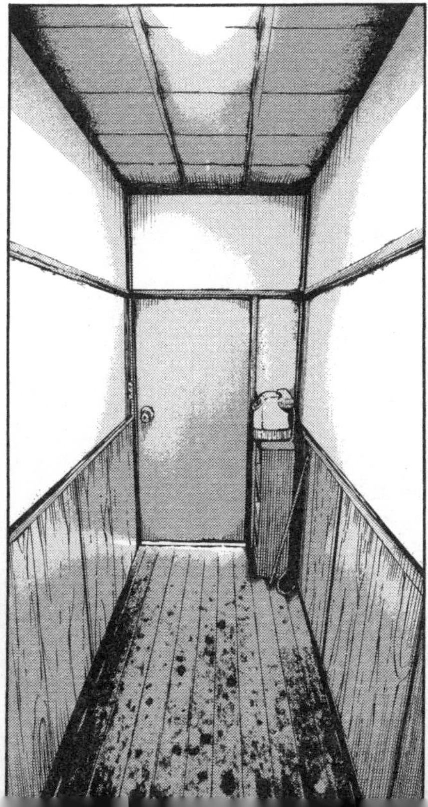

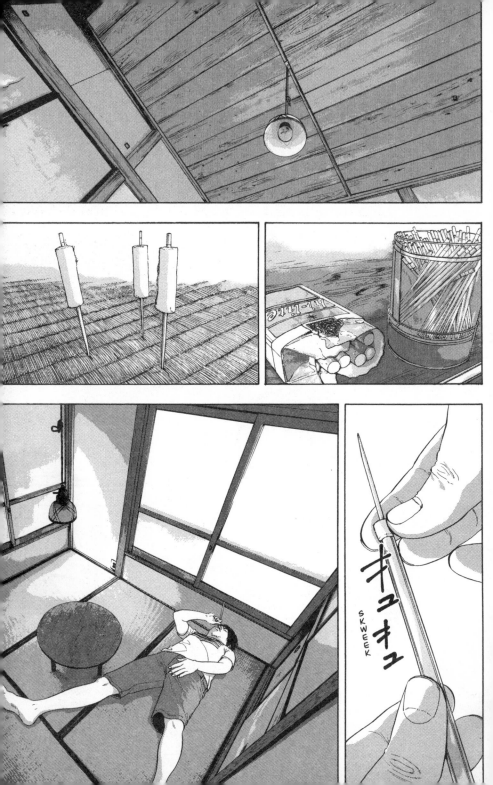

キュ
キュ
SKWEEK

SEVEN
POINTS.

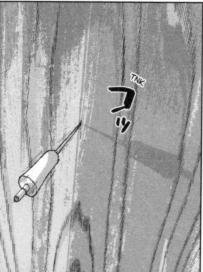

FOUR
POINTS.

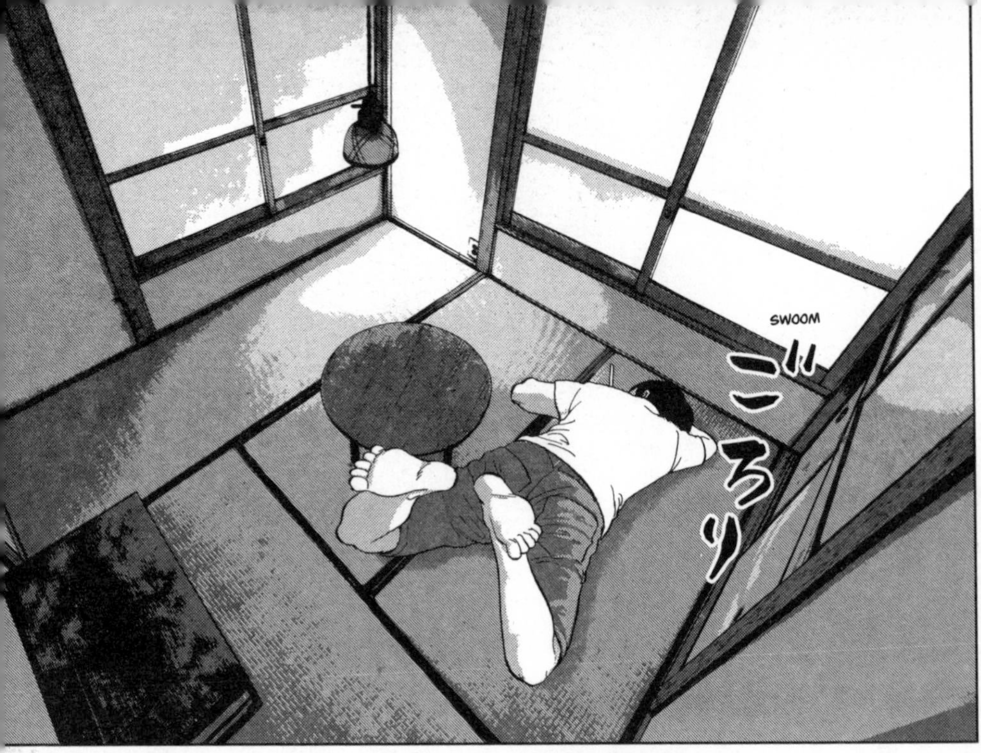
SWOOM
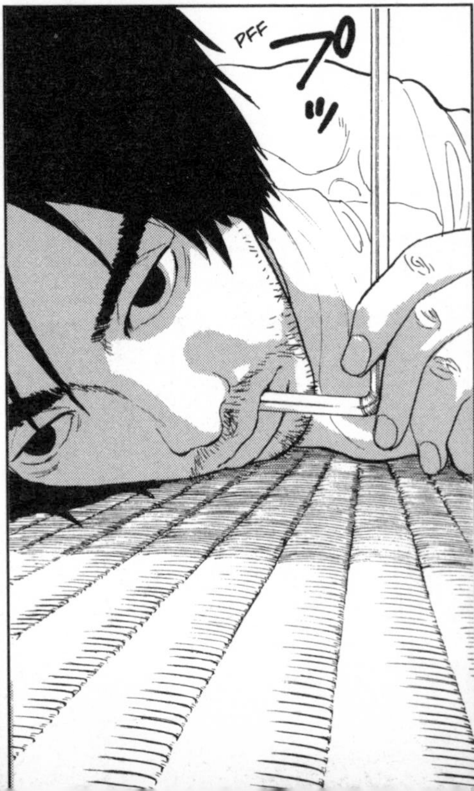
PFF
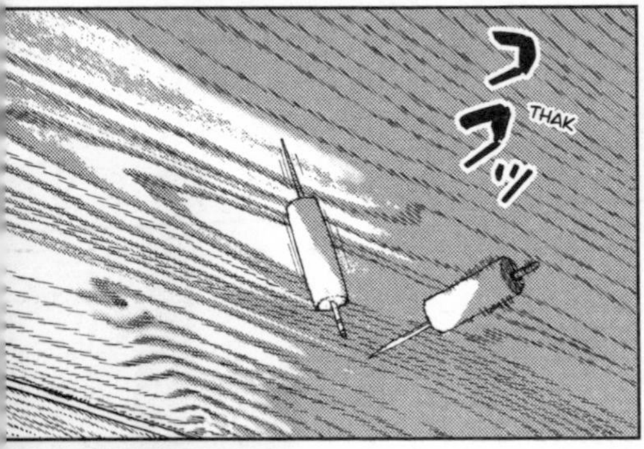
THAK
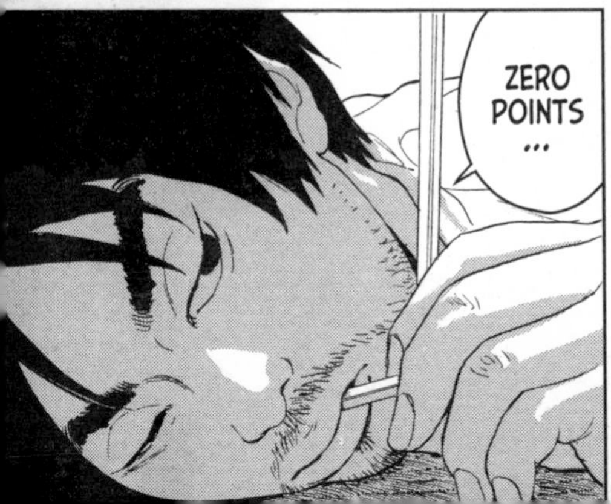
ZERO POINTS ...

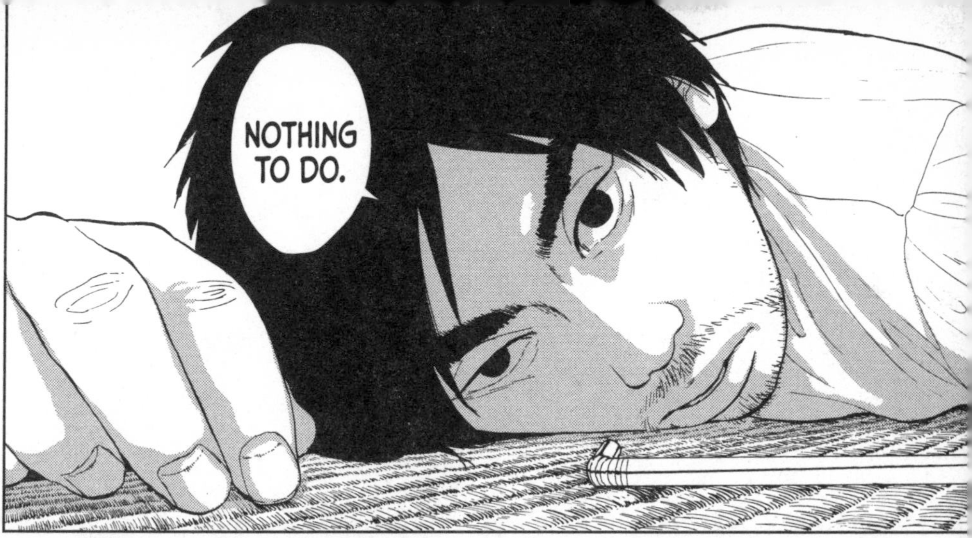
NOTHING TO DO.
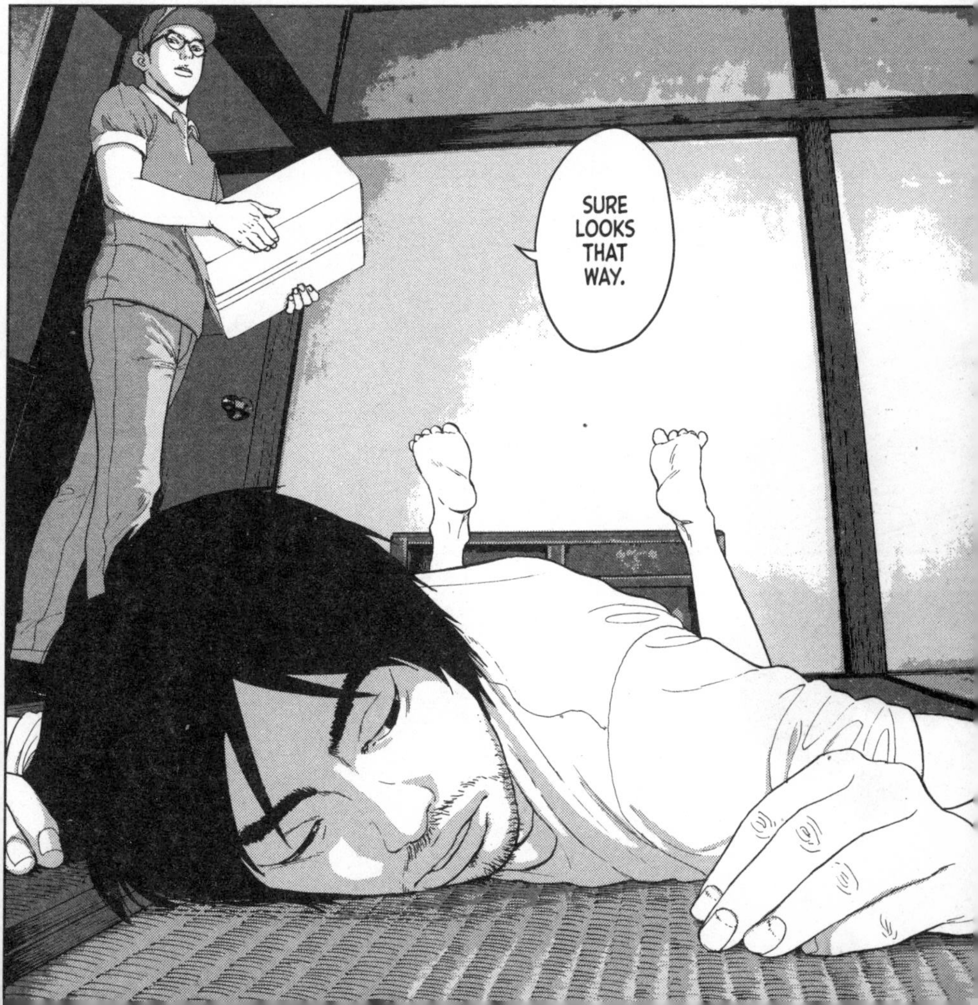
SURE LOOKS THAT WAY.

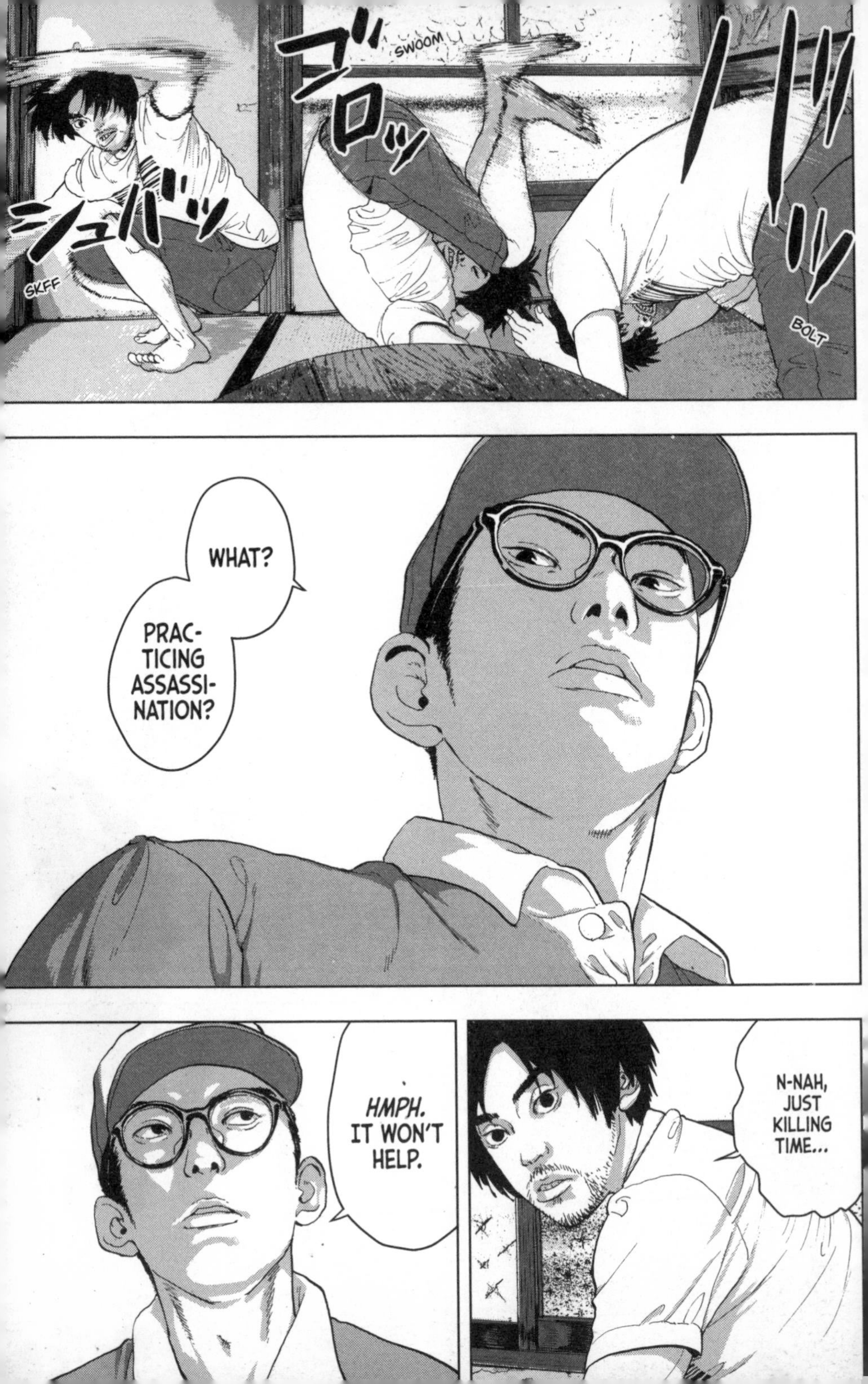
BOLT
ゴロッ
SWOOM
シュバッ
SKFF
WHAT?
PRAC-TICING ASSASSI-NATION?
N-NAH, JUST KILLING TIME...
HMPH. IT WON'T HELP.

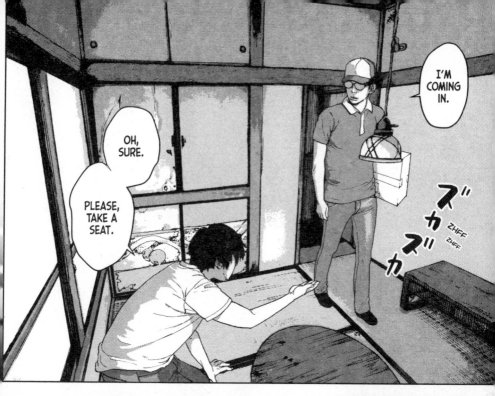

OH, SURE.

PLEASE, TAKE A SEAT.

I'M COMING IN.

ズカズカ ZHFF ZHFF

I DIDN'T NOTICE HIM STANDING THERE. IS HE A CAREER NINJA?*

*NOTE: MID-LEVEL AND ABOVE.

Y- YEAH.

HOT ONE TODAY.

どすっ THMP

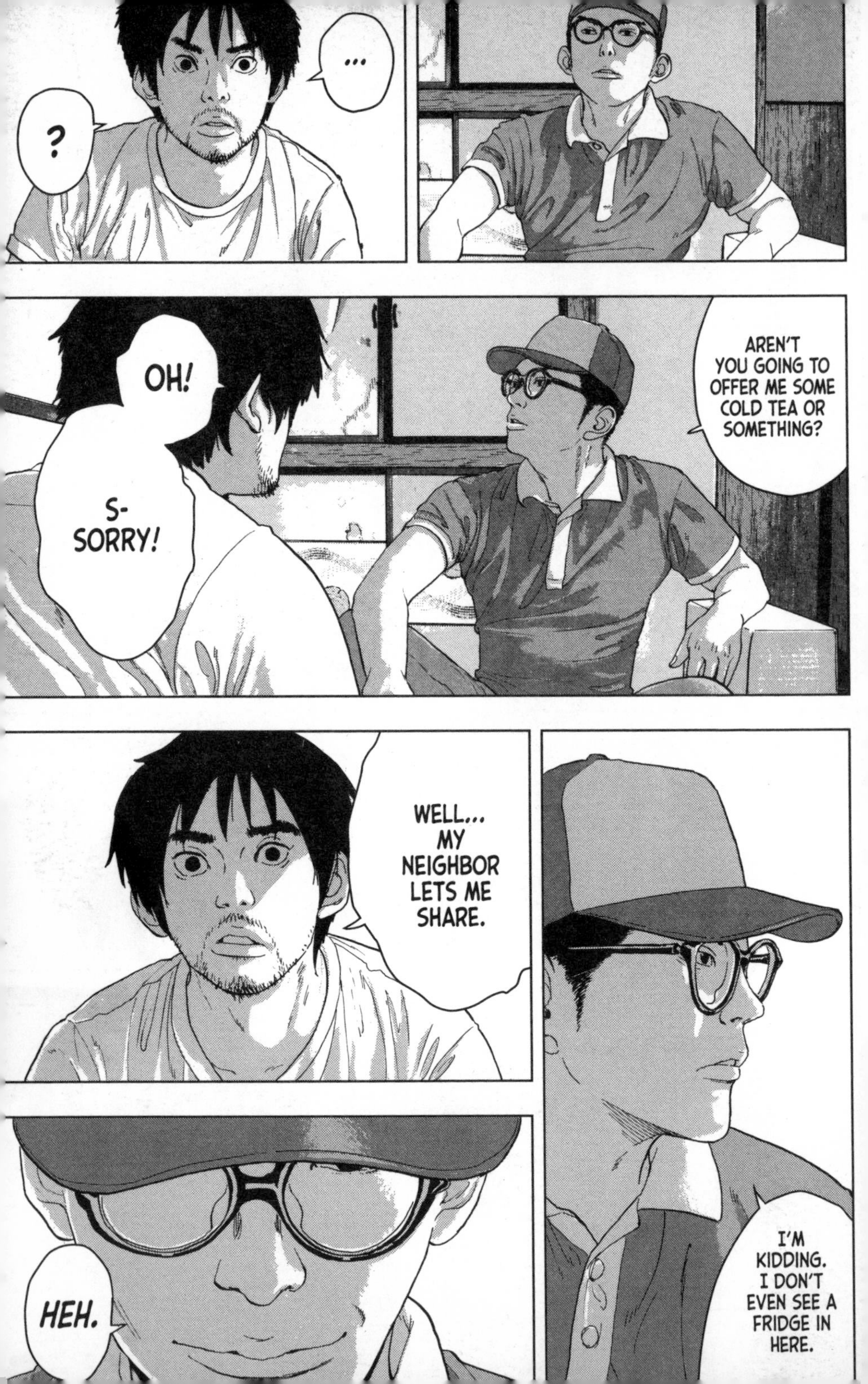
...
?
AREN'T YOU GOING TO OFFER ME SOME COLD TEA OR SOMETHING?
OH!
S-SORRY!
WELL... MY NEIGHBOR LETS ME SHARE.
HEH.
I'M KIDDING. I DON'T EVEN SEE A FRIDGE IN HERE.

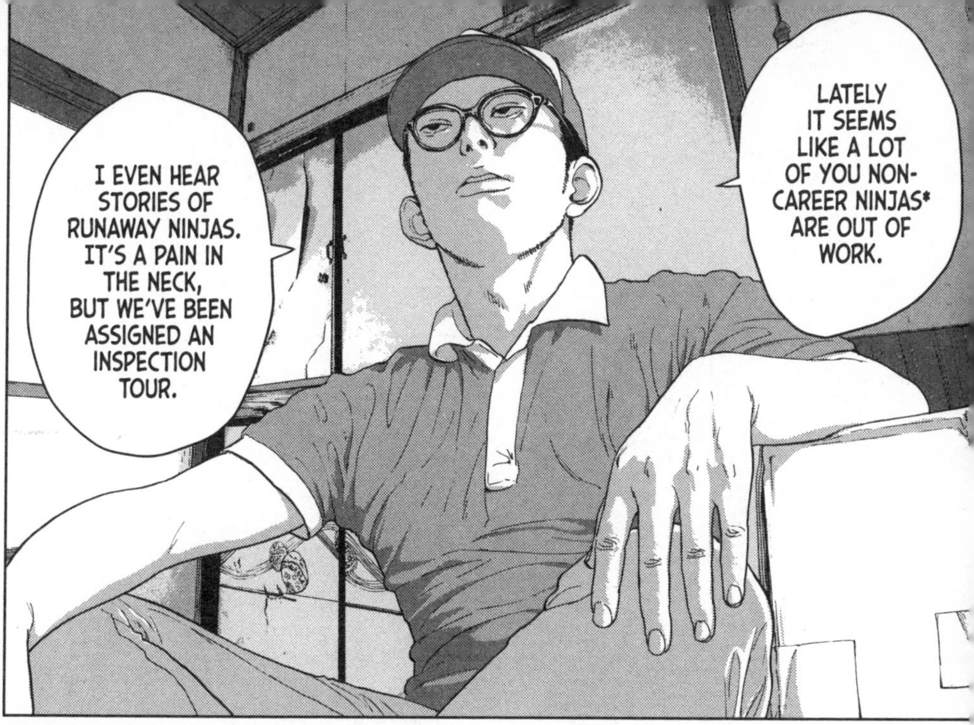
LATELY IT SEEMS LIKE A LOT OF YOU NON-CAREER NINJAS* ARE OUT OF WORK.
I EVEN HEAR STORIES OF RUNAWAY NINJAS. IT'S A PAIN IN THE NECK, BUT WE'VE BEEN ASSIGNED AN INSPECTION TOUR.

*NOTE: LOW-LEVEL NINJAS.

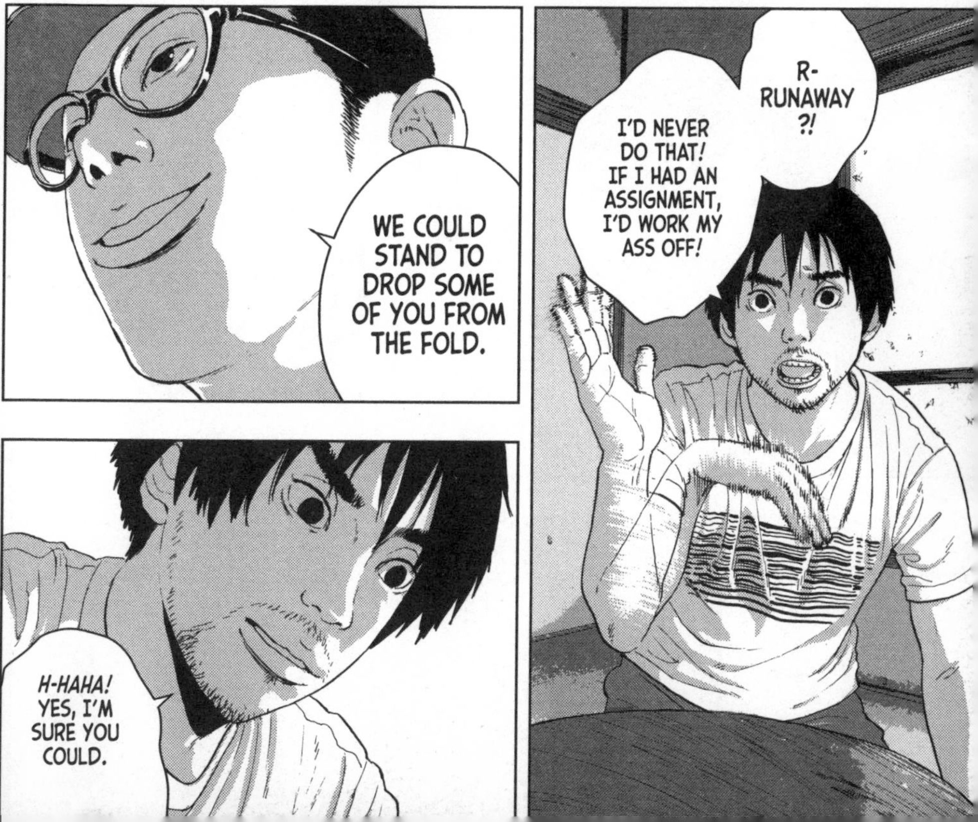
R-RUNAWAY?!
I'D NEVER DO THAT! IF I HAD AN ASSIGNMENT, I'D WORK MY ASS OFF!
WE COULD STAND TO DROP SOME OF YOU FROM THE FOLD.
H-HAHA! YES, I'M SURE YOU COULD.

BUT THERE ARE REGULATIONS. SO JUST REMEMBER THAT ANY NINJA WHO GOES *AWOL* WILL BE *ELIMINATED.*

O-

OF COURSE...

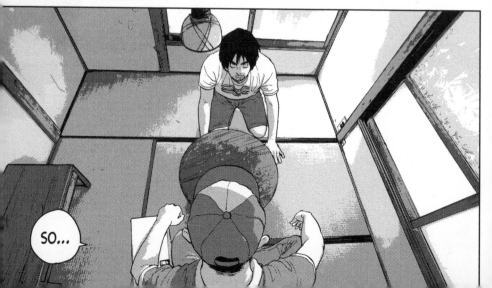

SO...

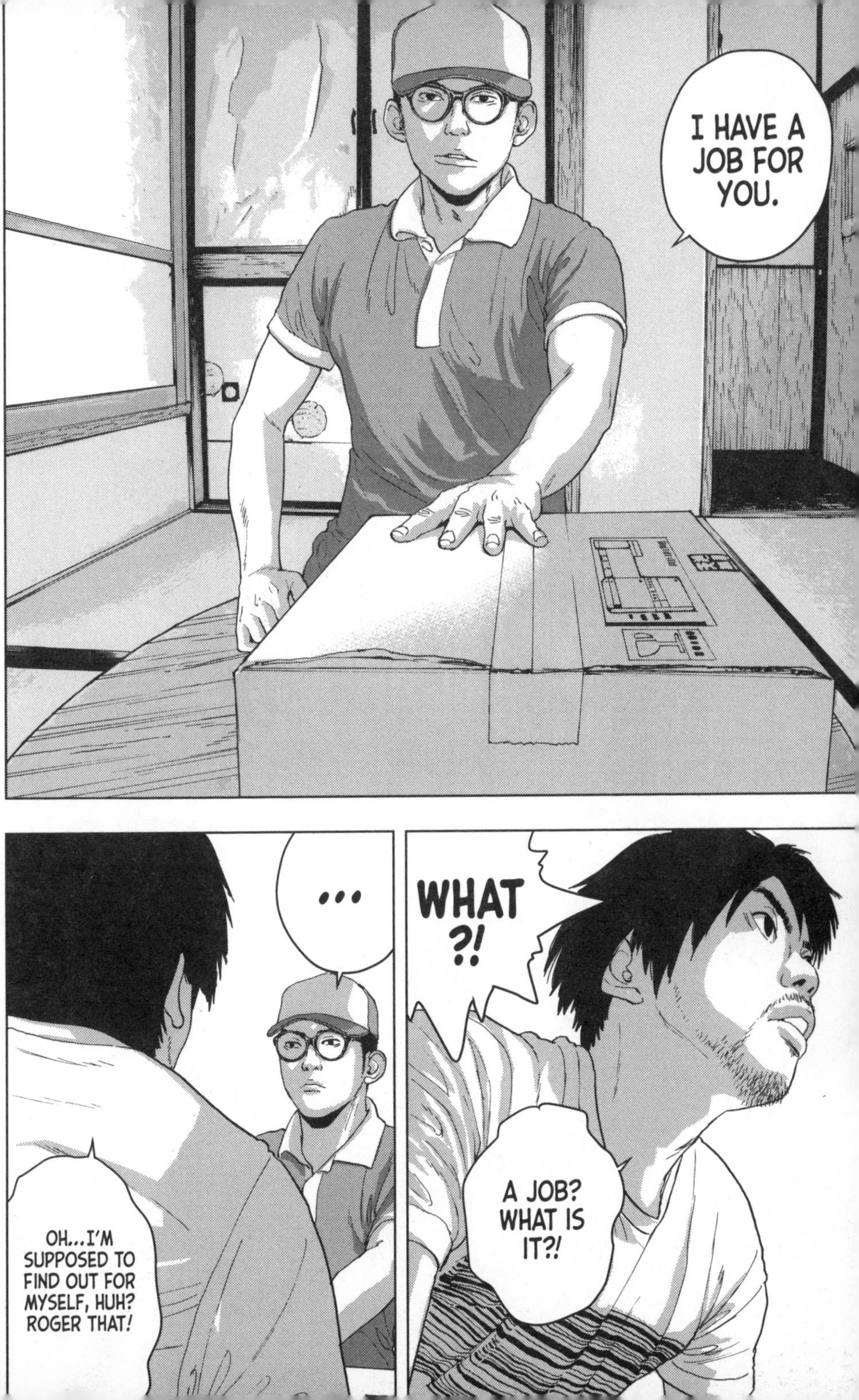
I HAVE A JOB FOR YOU.
WHAT ?!
A JOB? WHAT IS IT?!
...
OH...I'M SUPPOSED TO FIND OUT FOR MYSELF, HUH? ROGER THAT!

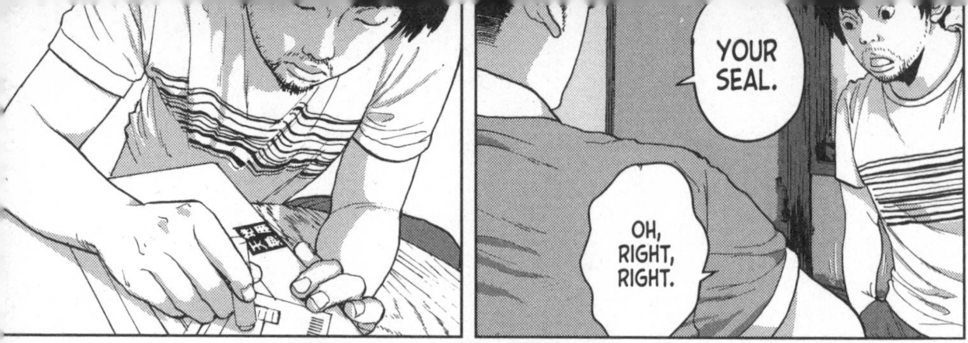
YOUR SEAL.
OH, RIGHT, RIGHT.
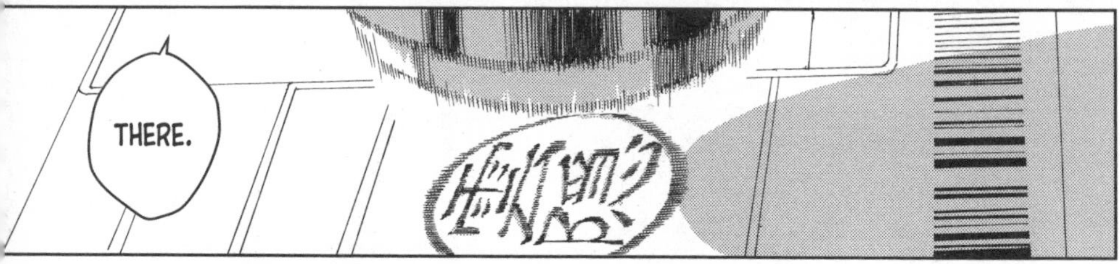
THERE.

*STAMP: KUMOGAKURE

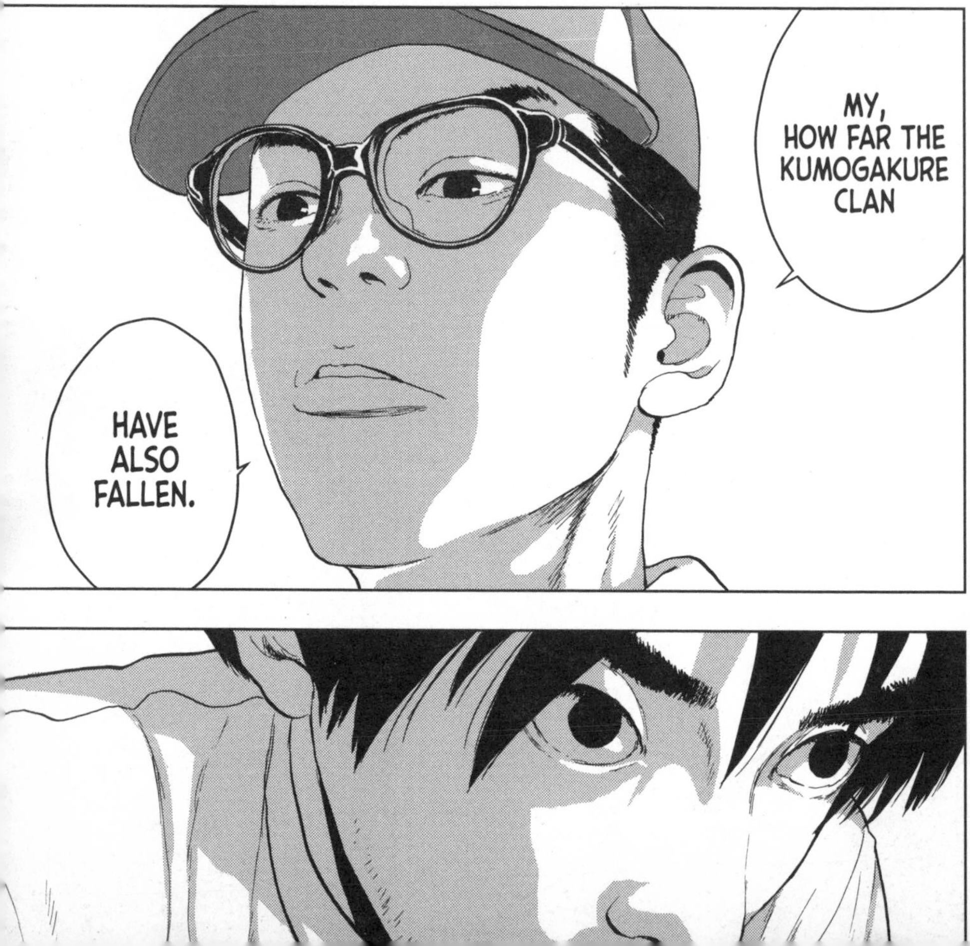
MY, HOW FAR THE KUMOGAKURE CLAN
HAVE ALSO FALLEN.

ポロッ
FWIP

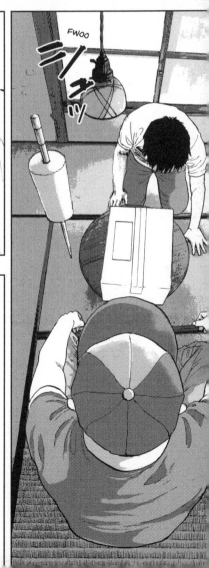

FWOO

シュッ

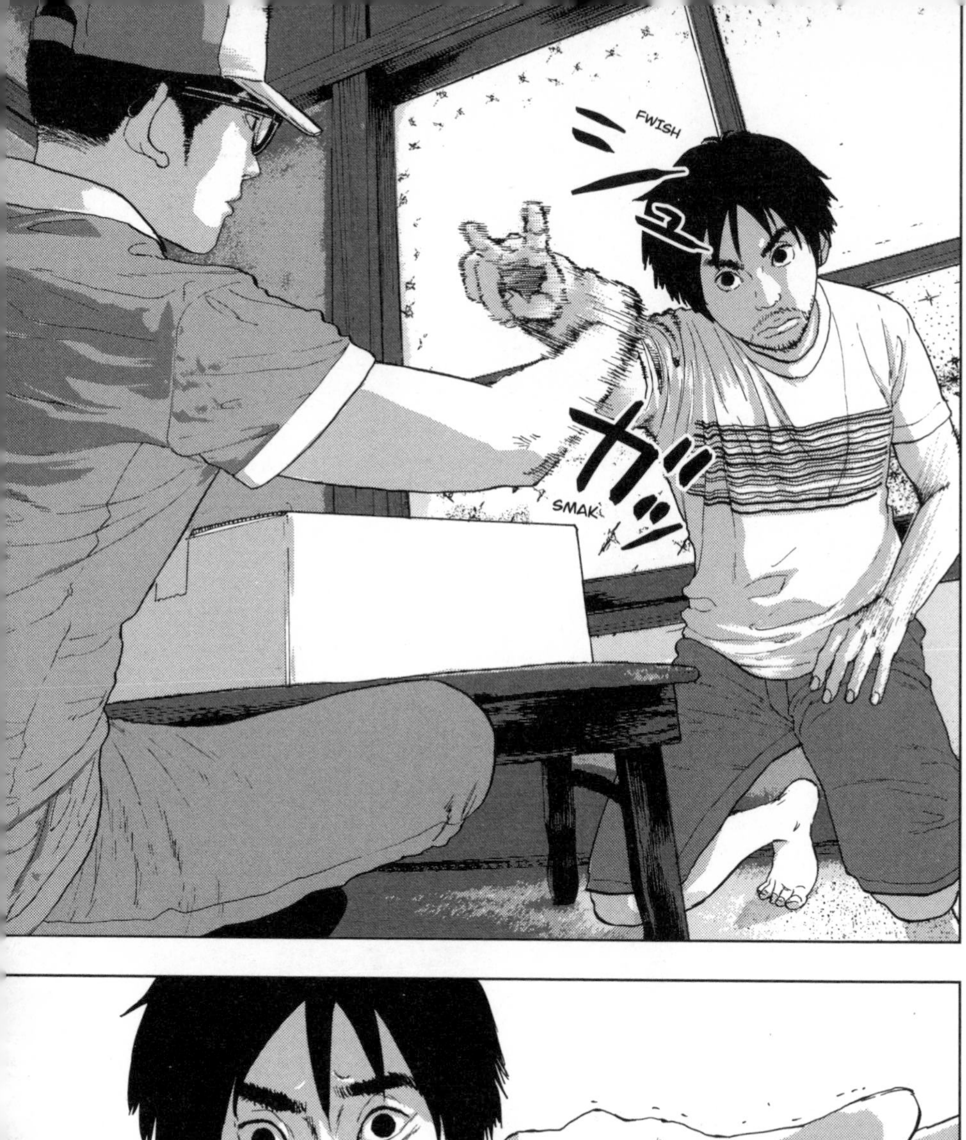
FWISH
SMAK
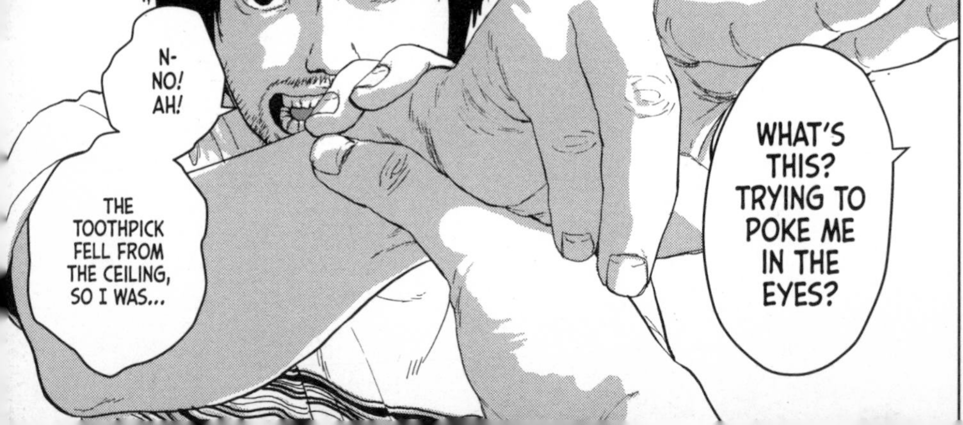
WHAT'S THIS? TRYING TO POKE ME IN THE EYES?
N-NO! AH!
THE TOOTHPICK FELL FROM THE CEILING, SO I WAS...

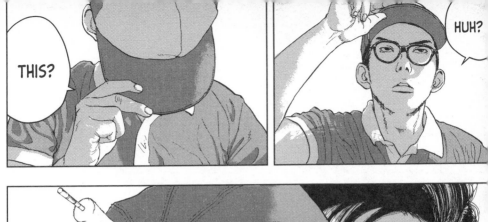

THIS?

HUH?

TEN POINTS... RIGHT?

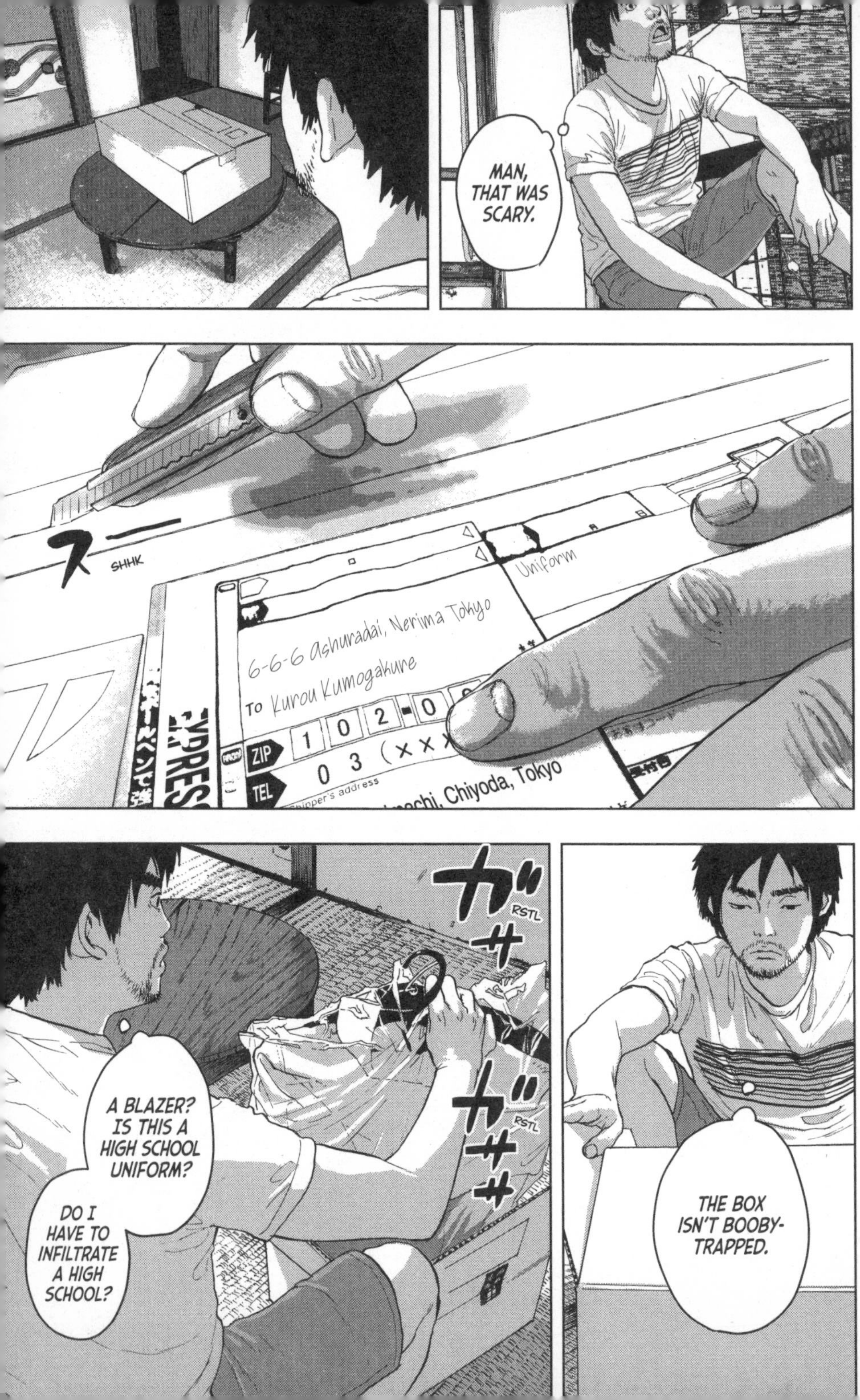
MAN, THAT WAS SCARY.
スー
SHHK
Uniform
6-6-6 Ashuradai, Nerima Tokyo
To Kurou Kumogakure
ZIP
TEL
Shipper's address
Chiyoda, Tokyo
THE BOX ISN'T BOOBY-TRAPPED.
ガサ
RSTL
ガサササ
RSTL
A BLAZER? IS THIS A HIGH SCHOOL UNIFORM?
DO I HAVE TO INFILTRATE A HIGH SCHOOL?

FWAP

A HIGH SCHOOL UNIFORM AND A HOODIE... WHY A HOODIE?

WHAT'S THIS?

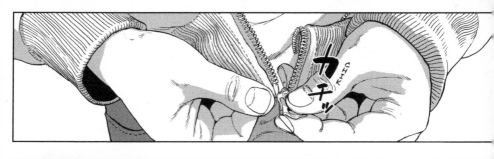

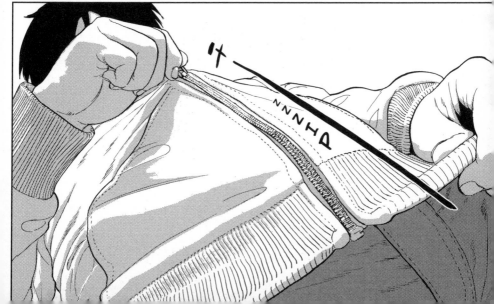

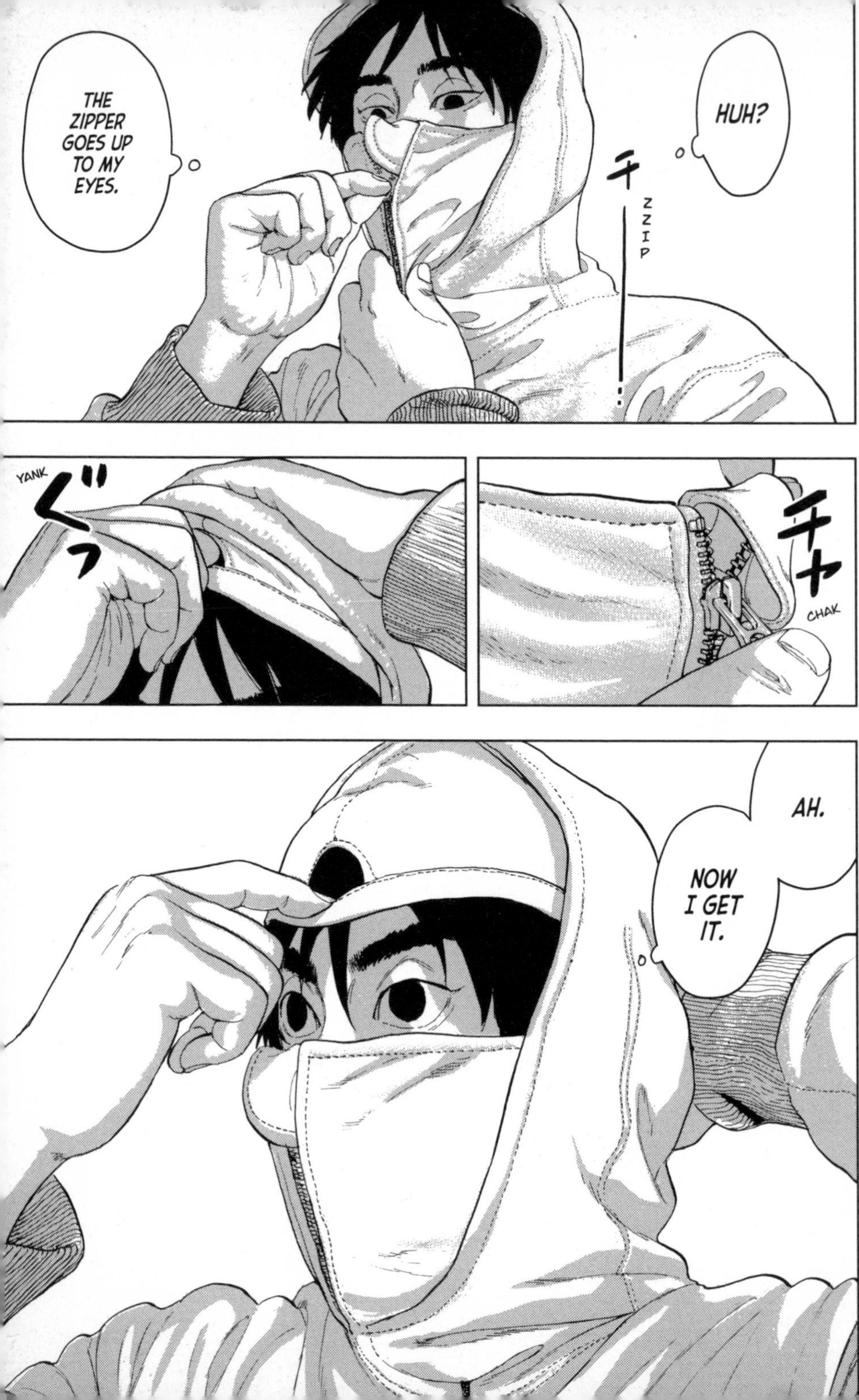

HUH?
チ
ZZIP
THE ZIPPER GOES UP TO MY EYES.
チャ
CHAK
ぐっ
YANK
AH.
NOW I GET IT.

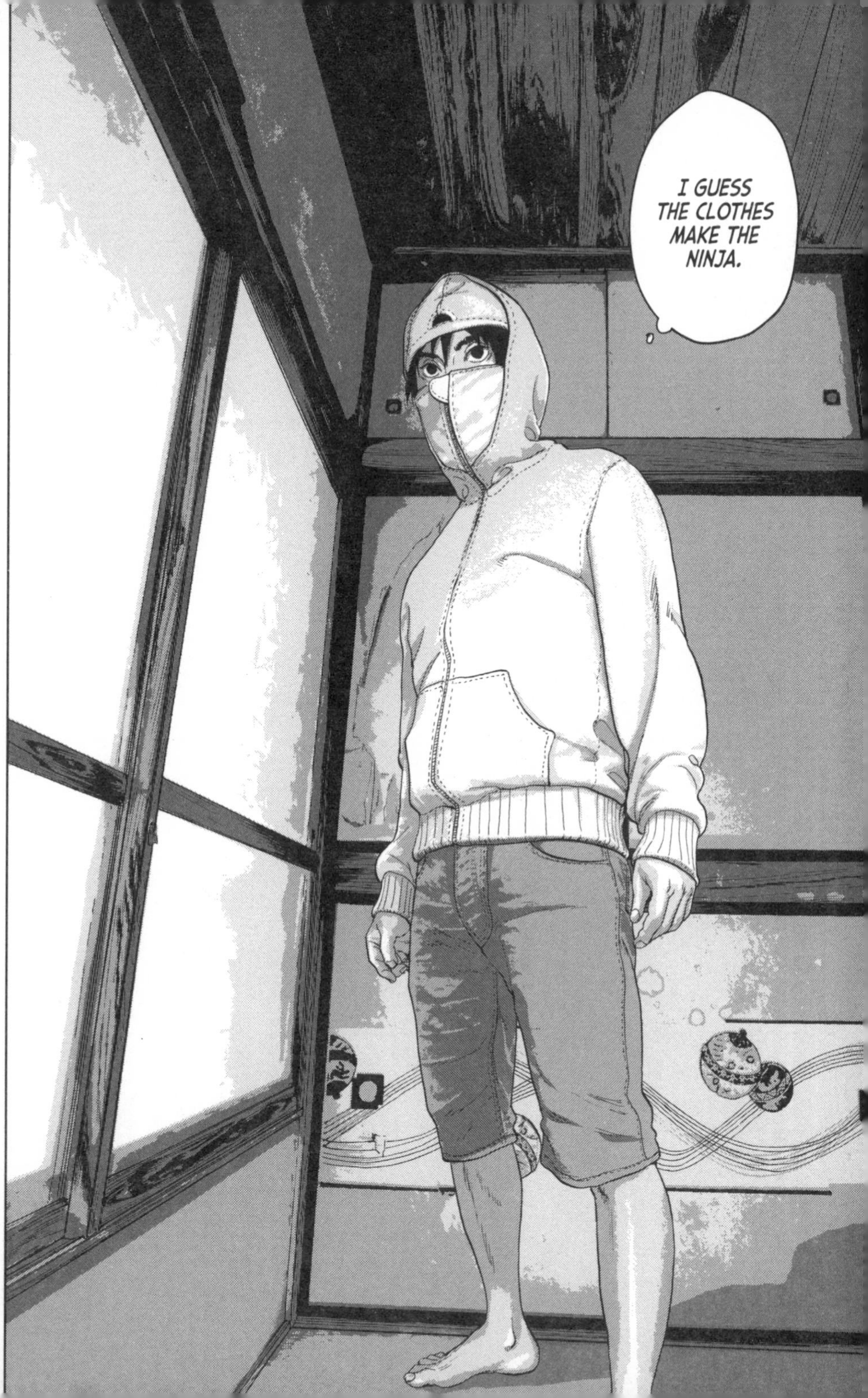
I GUESS THE CLOTHES MAKE THE NINJA.

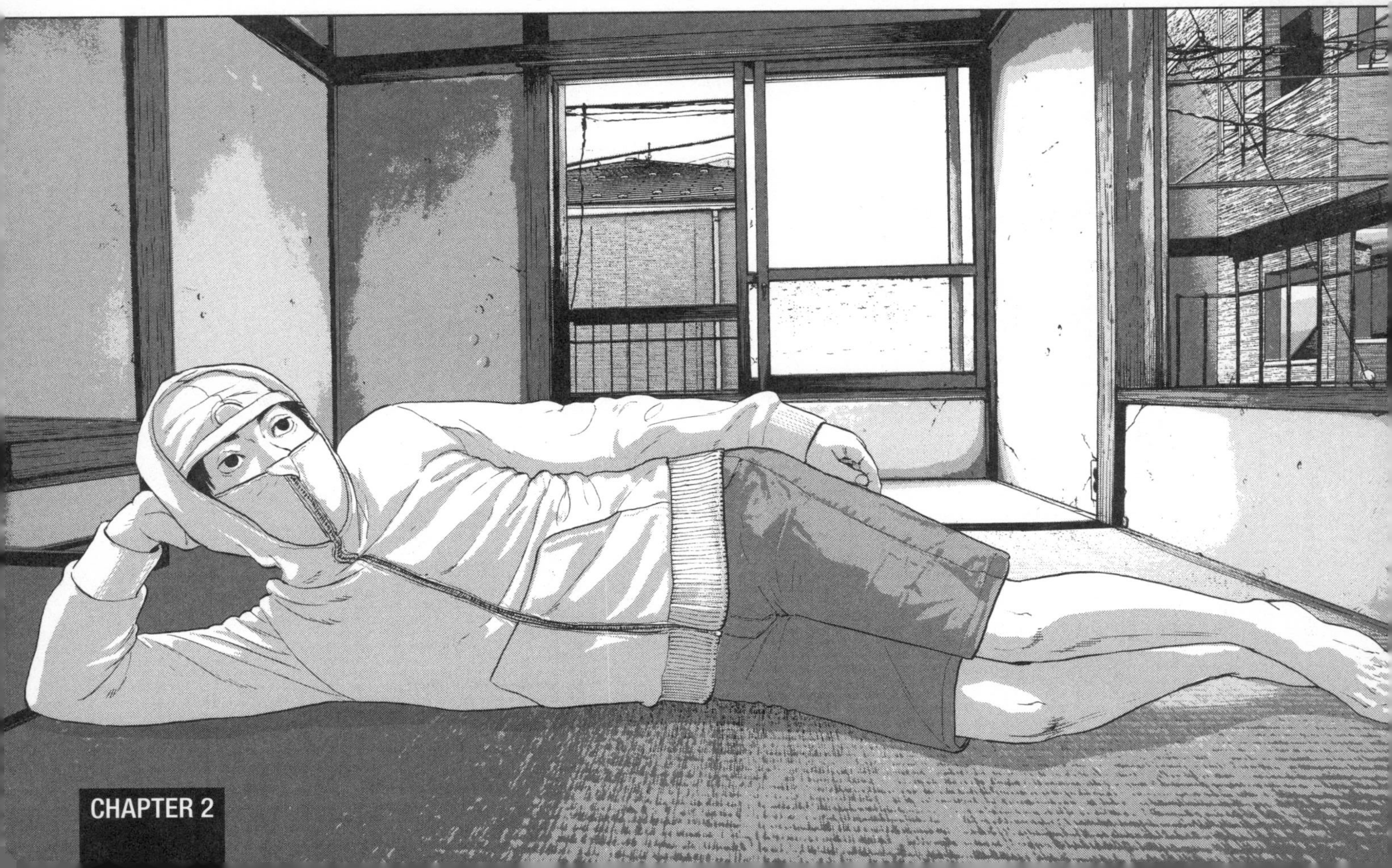
CHAPTER 2

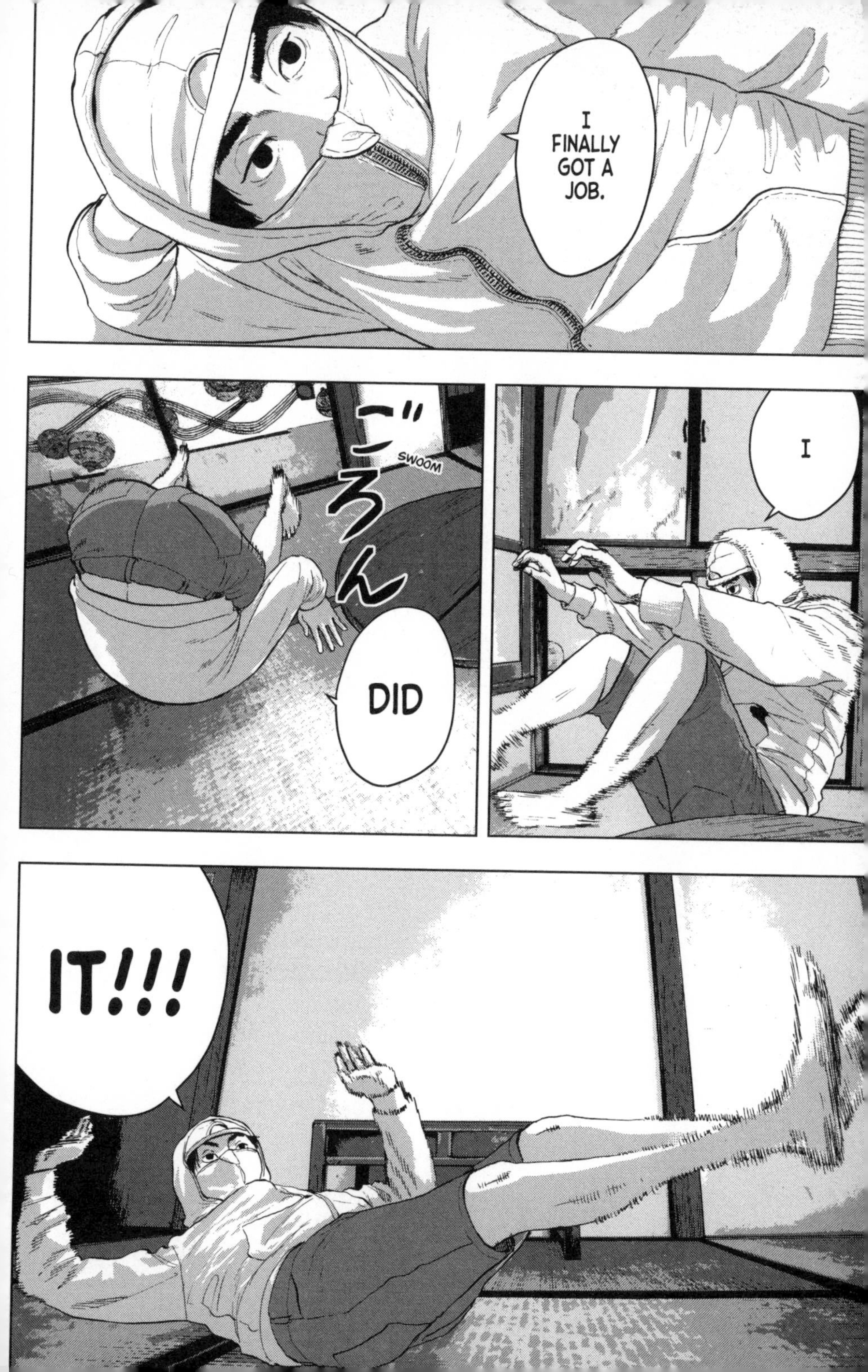
I FINALLY GOT A JOB.
I
ごろん
SWOOM
DID
IT!!!

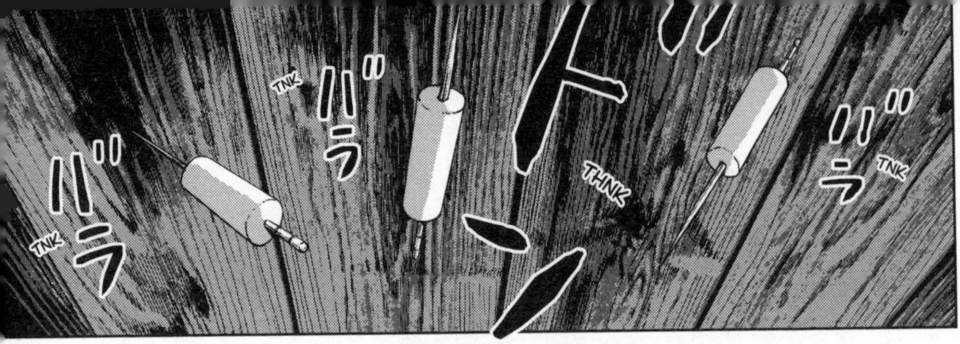
バラ
TNK
THNK
バラ
TNK
バラ
TNK

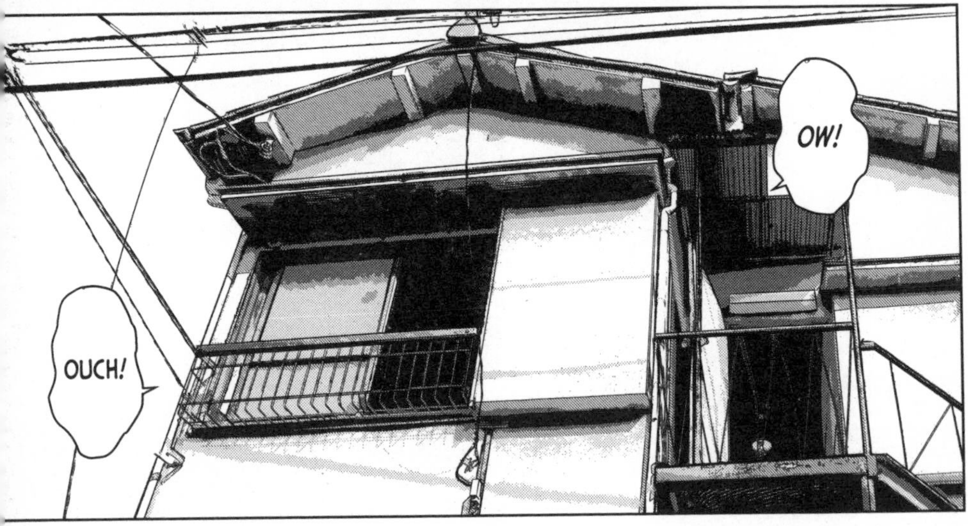
OW!
OUCH!

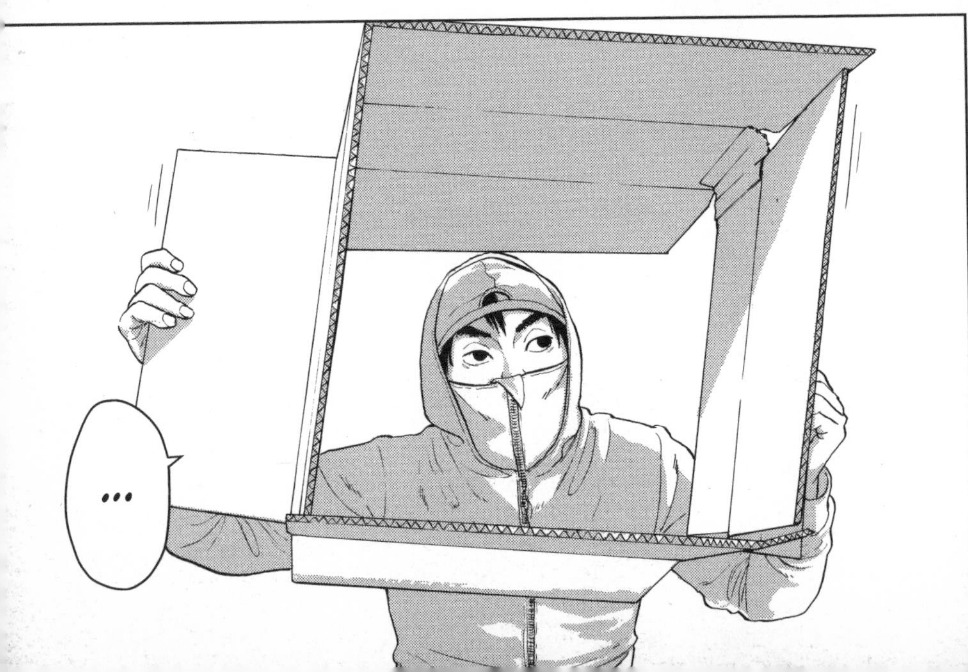
...

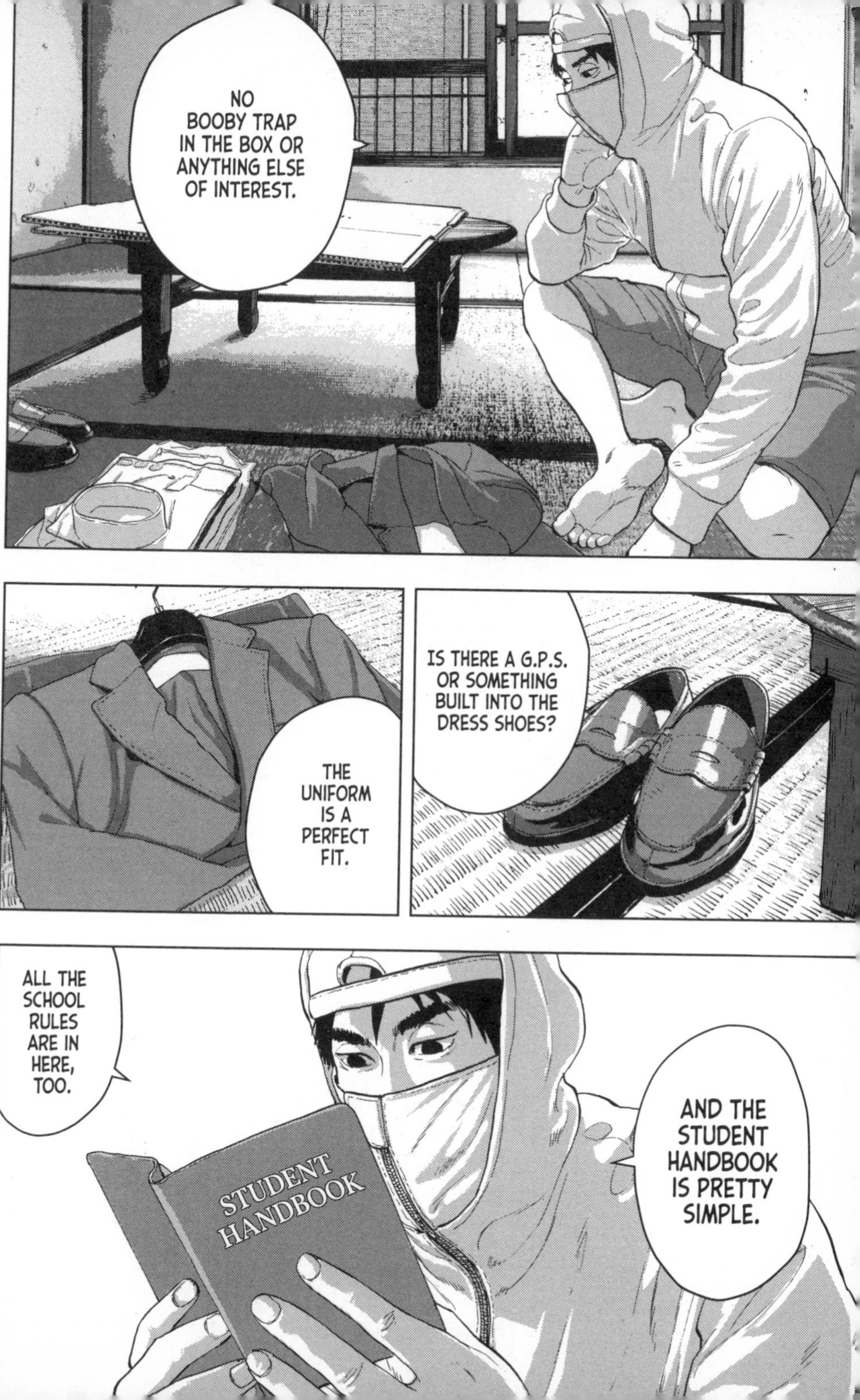
NO BOOBY TRAP IN THE BOX OR ANYTHING ELSE OF INTEREST.
IS THERE A G.P.S. OR SOMETHING BUILT INTO THE DRESS SHOES?
THE UNIFORM IS A PERFECT FIT.
AND THE STUDENT HANDBOOK IS PRETTY SIMPLE.
STUDENT HANDBOOK
ALL THE SCHOOL RULES ARE IN HERE, TOO.

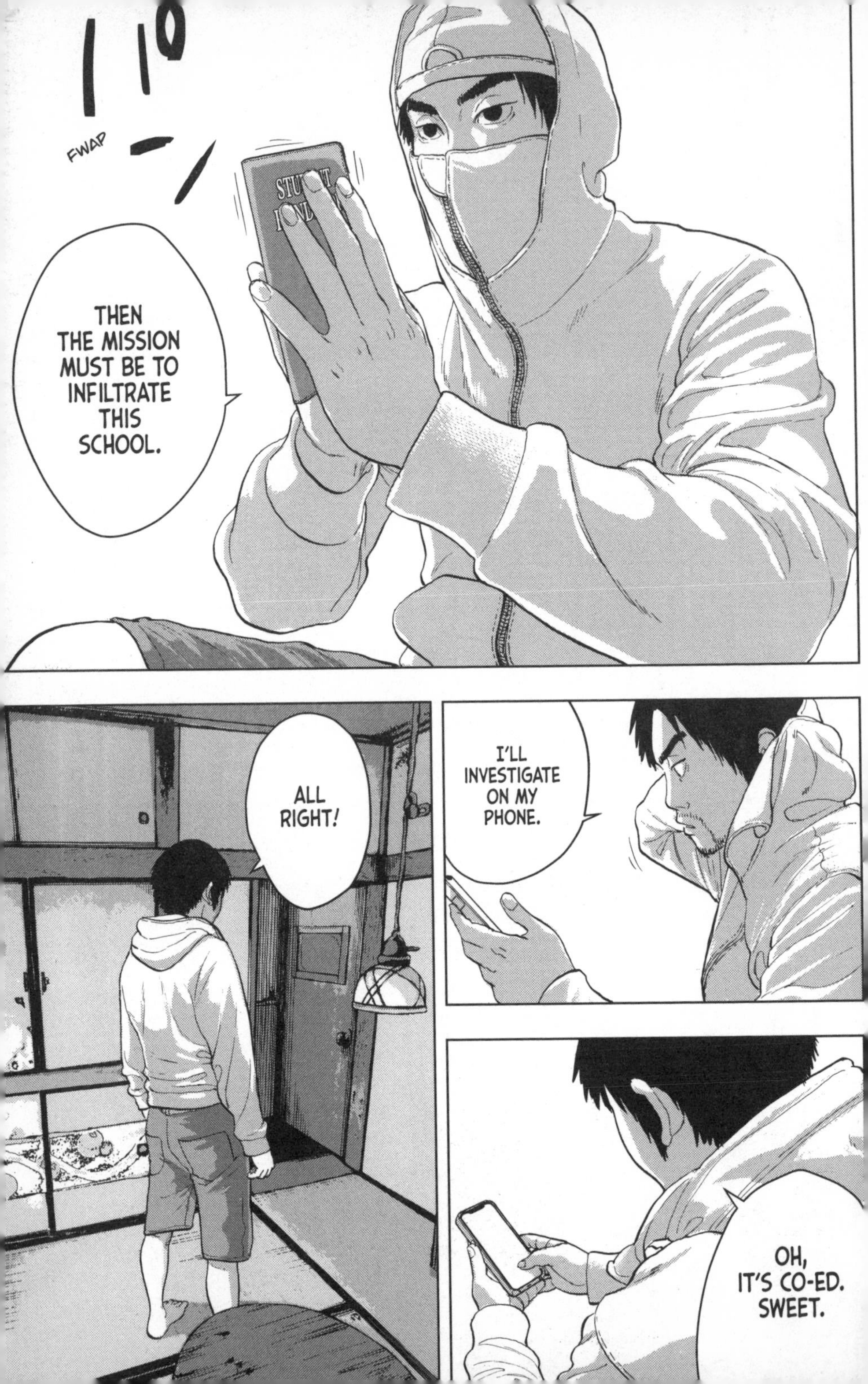
FWAP
THEN THE MISSION MUST BE TO INFILTRATE THIS SCHOOL.
I'LL INVESTIGATE ON MY PHONE.
OH, IT'S CO-ED. SWEET.
ALL RIGHT!

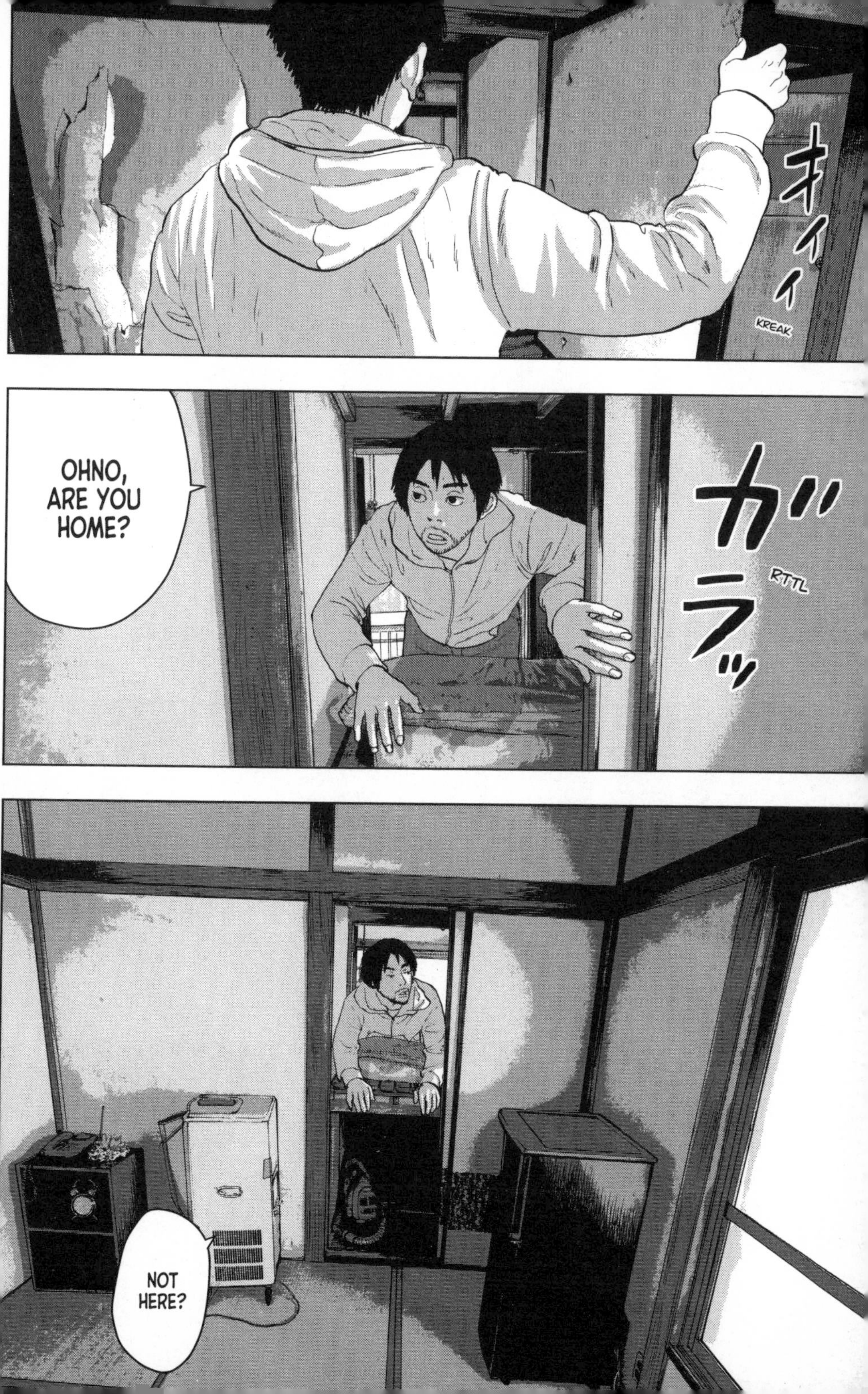
オイイ
KREAK
OHNO, ARE YOU HOME?
ガラッ
RTTL
NOT HERE?

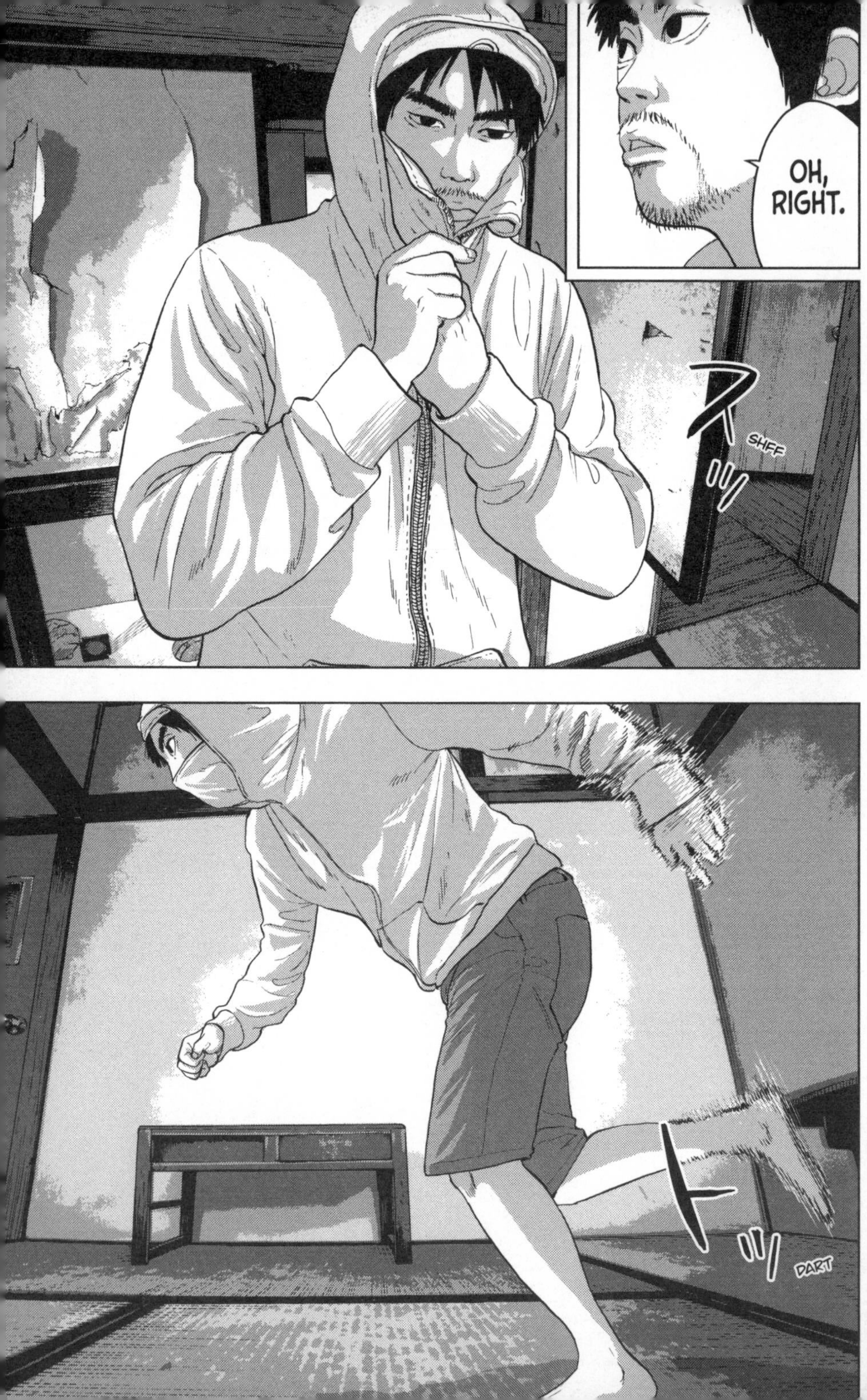
OH, RIGHT.
スッ
SHFF
トッ
DART

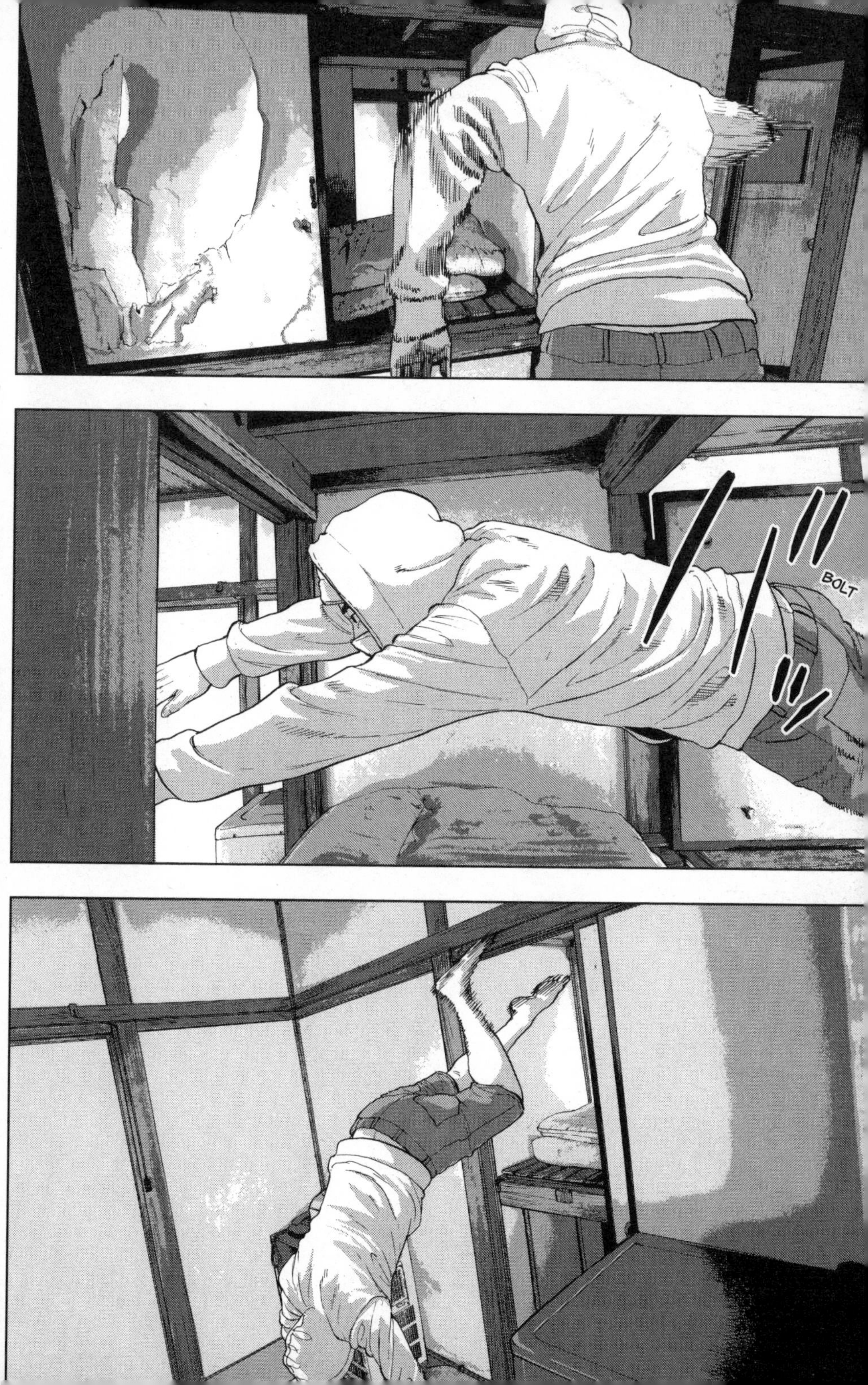
BOLT

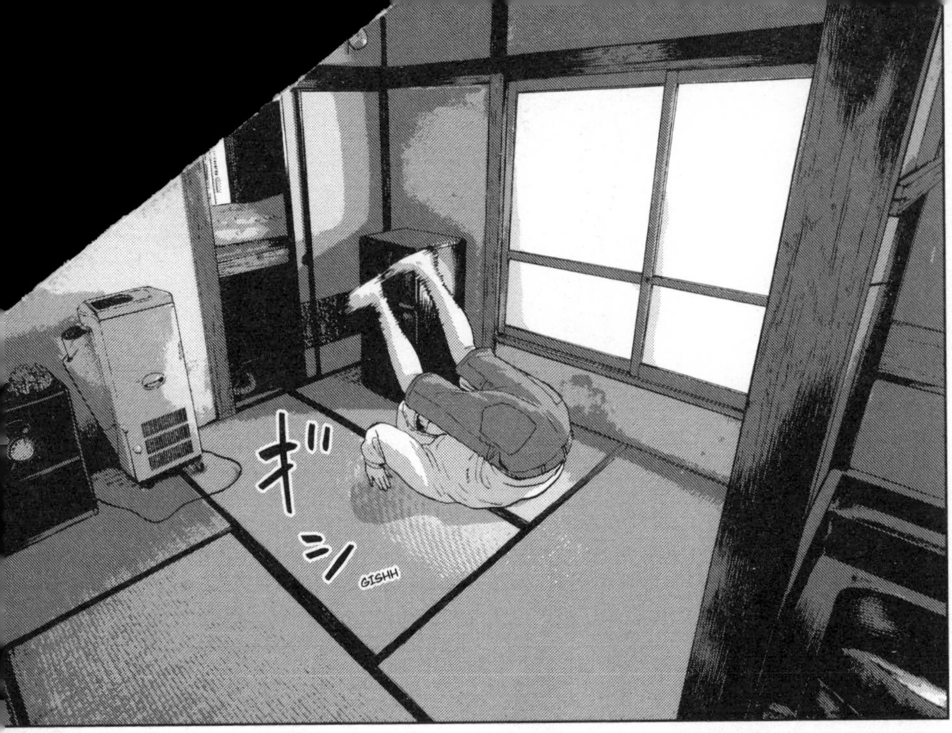
ギシ
GISHH
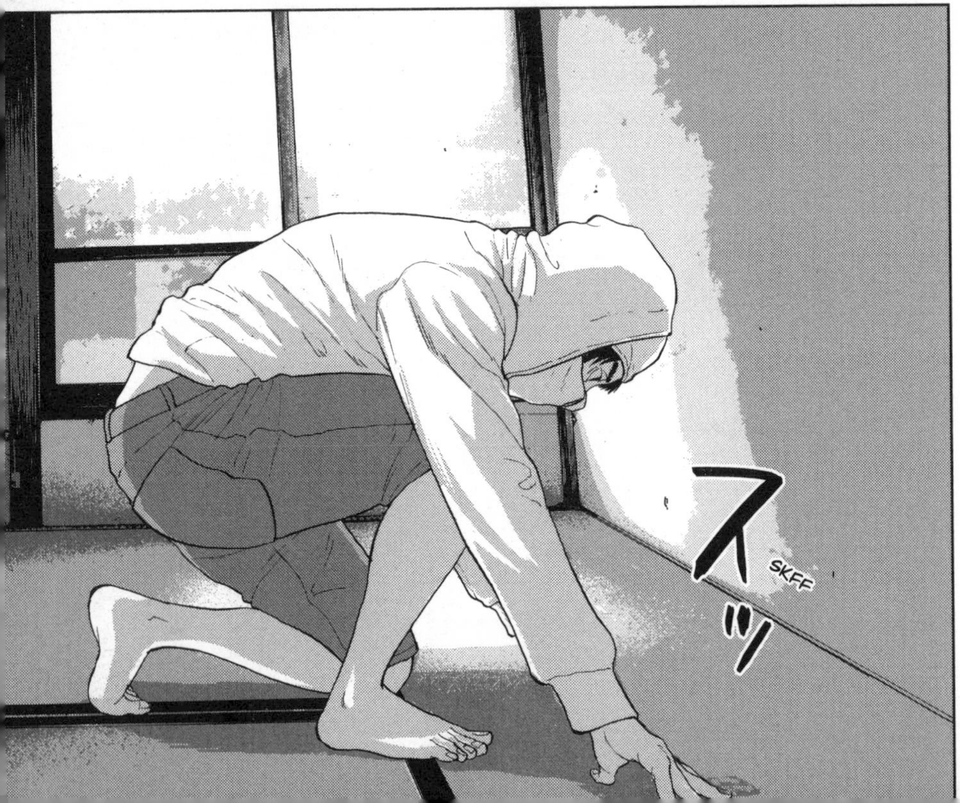
スッ
SKFF

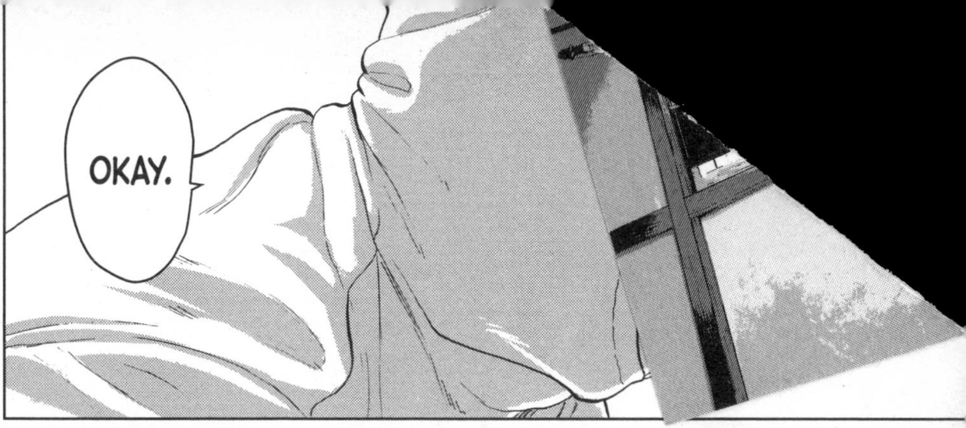
OKAY.
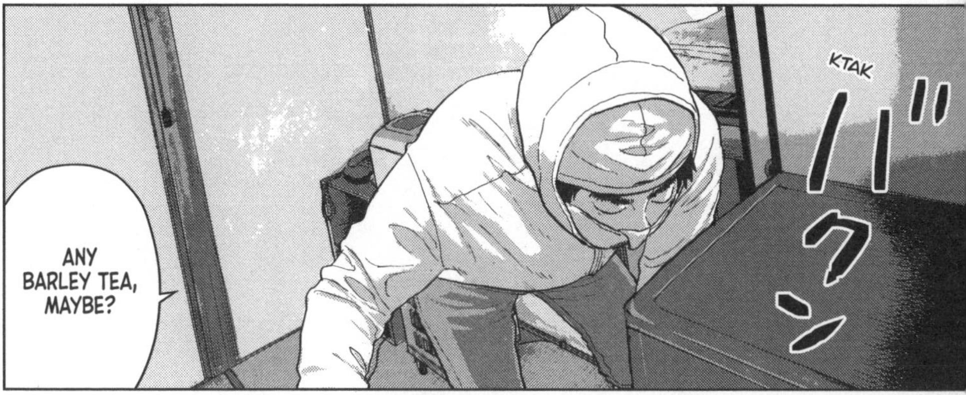
ANY BARLEY TEA, MAYBE?
KTAK
バクン
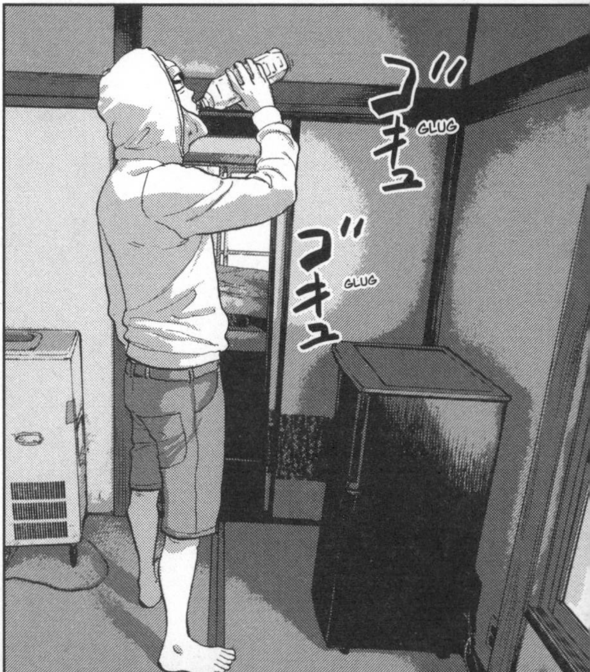
ゴキュ
GLUG
ゴキュ
GLUG
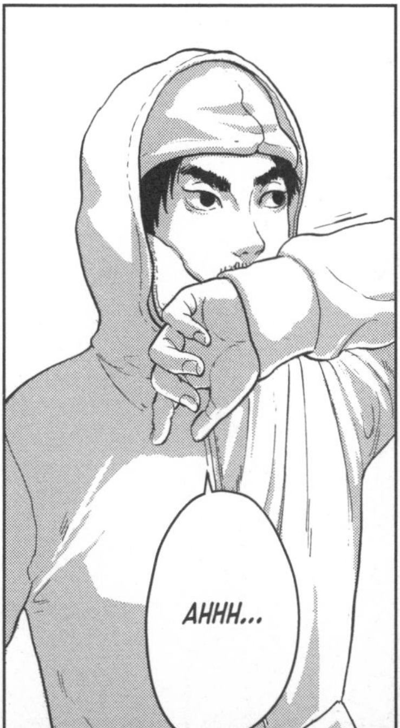
AHHH...

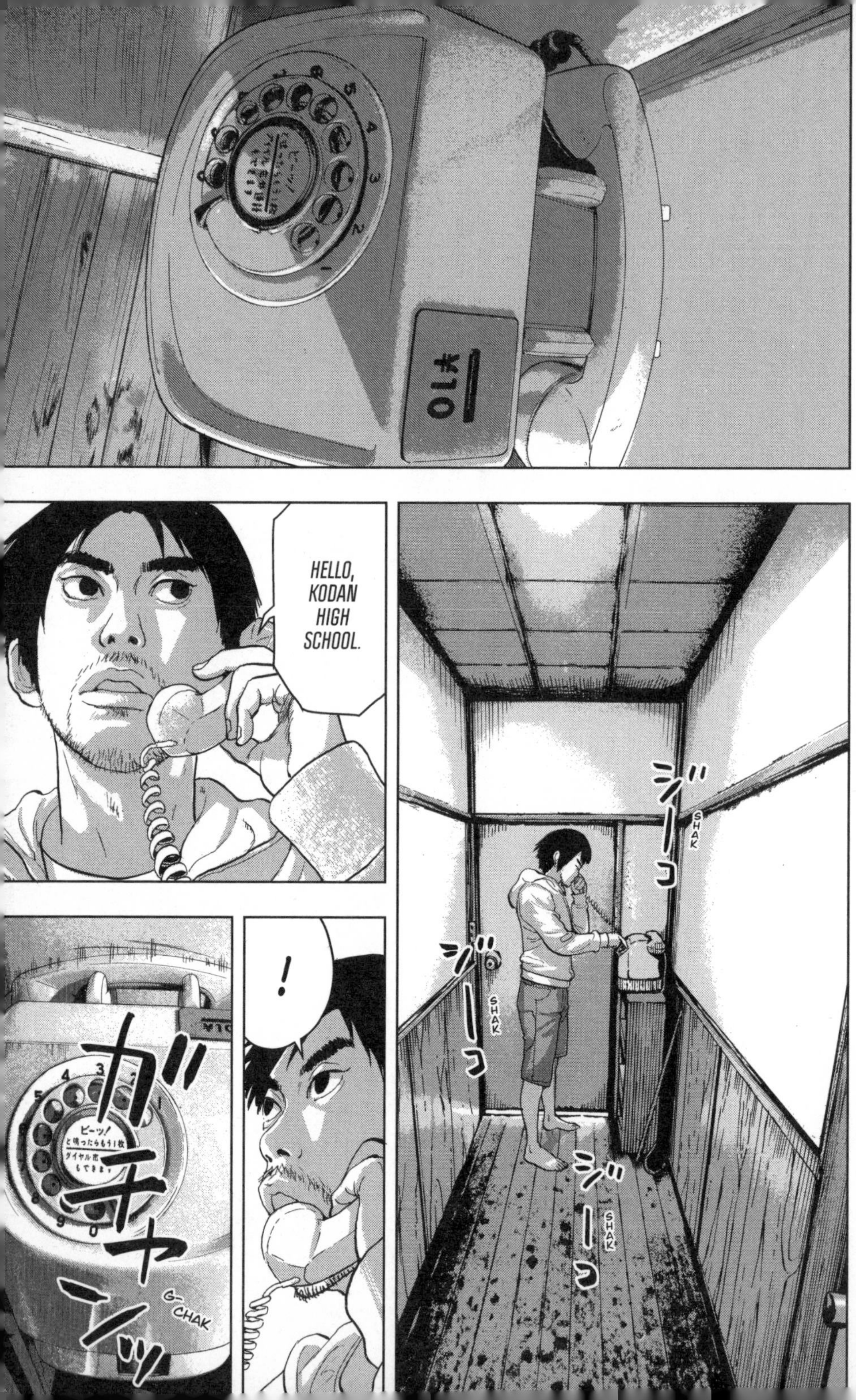
ジーコ
SHAK
ジーコ
SHAK
ジーコ
SHAK
HELLO, KODAN HIGH SCHOOL.
!
ガチャーンッ
G-CHAK

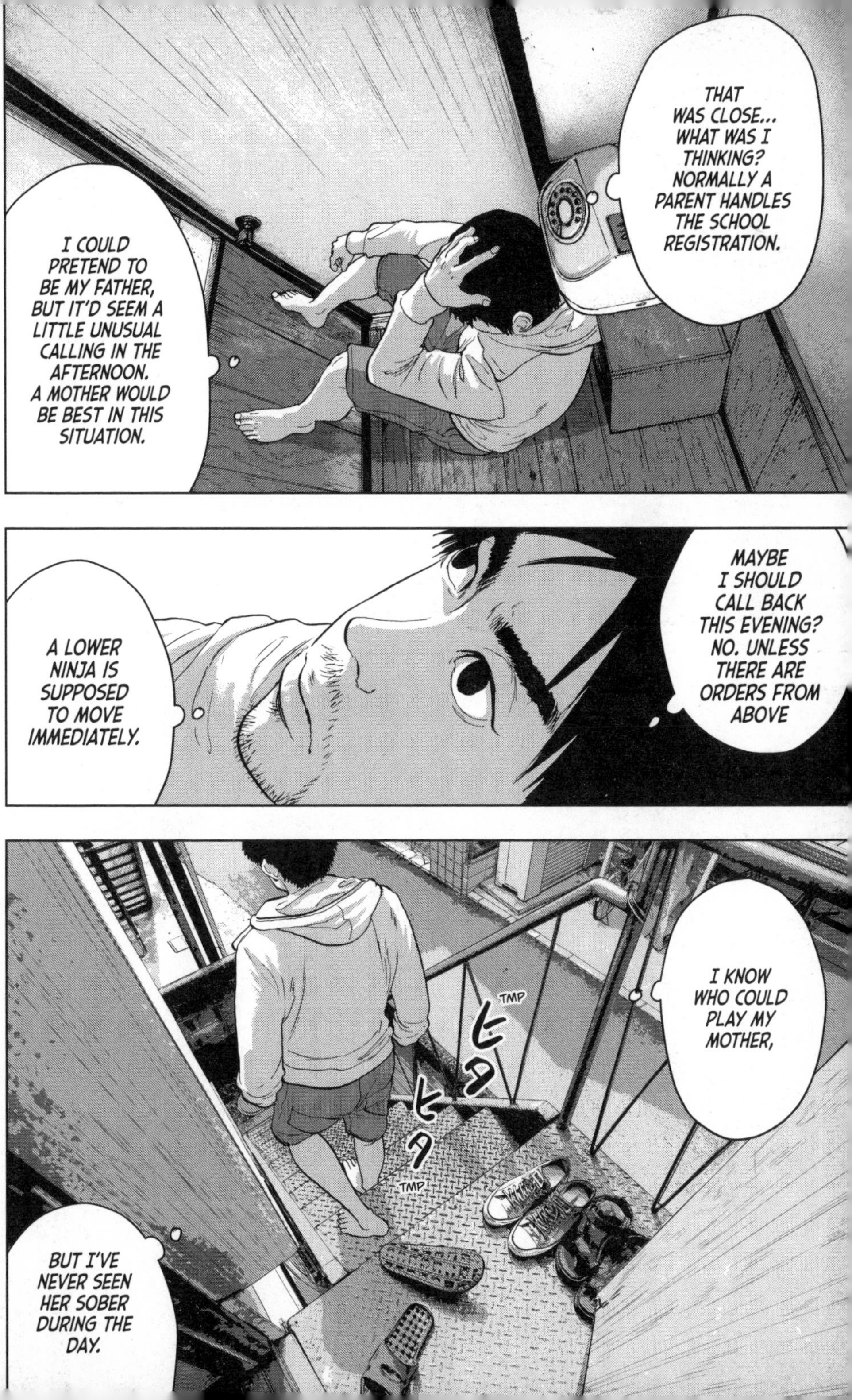
THAT WAS CLOSE... WHAT WAS I THINKING? NORMALLY A PARENT HANDLES THE SCHOOL REGISTRATION.
I COULD PRETEND TO BE MY FATHER, BUT IT'D SEEM A LITTLE UNUSUAL CALLING IN THE AFTERNOON. A MOTHER WOULD BE BEST IN THIS SITUATION.
MAYBE I SHOULD CALL BACK THIS EVENING? NO. UNLESS THERE ARE ORDERS FROM ABOVE
A LOWER NINJA IS SUPPOSED TO MOVE IMMEDIATELY.
I KNOW WHO COULD PLAY MY MOTHER,
TMP
TMP
BUT I'VE NEVER SEEN HER SOBER DURING THE DAY.

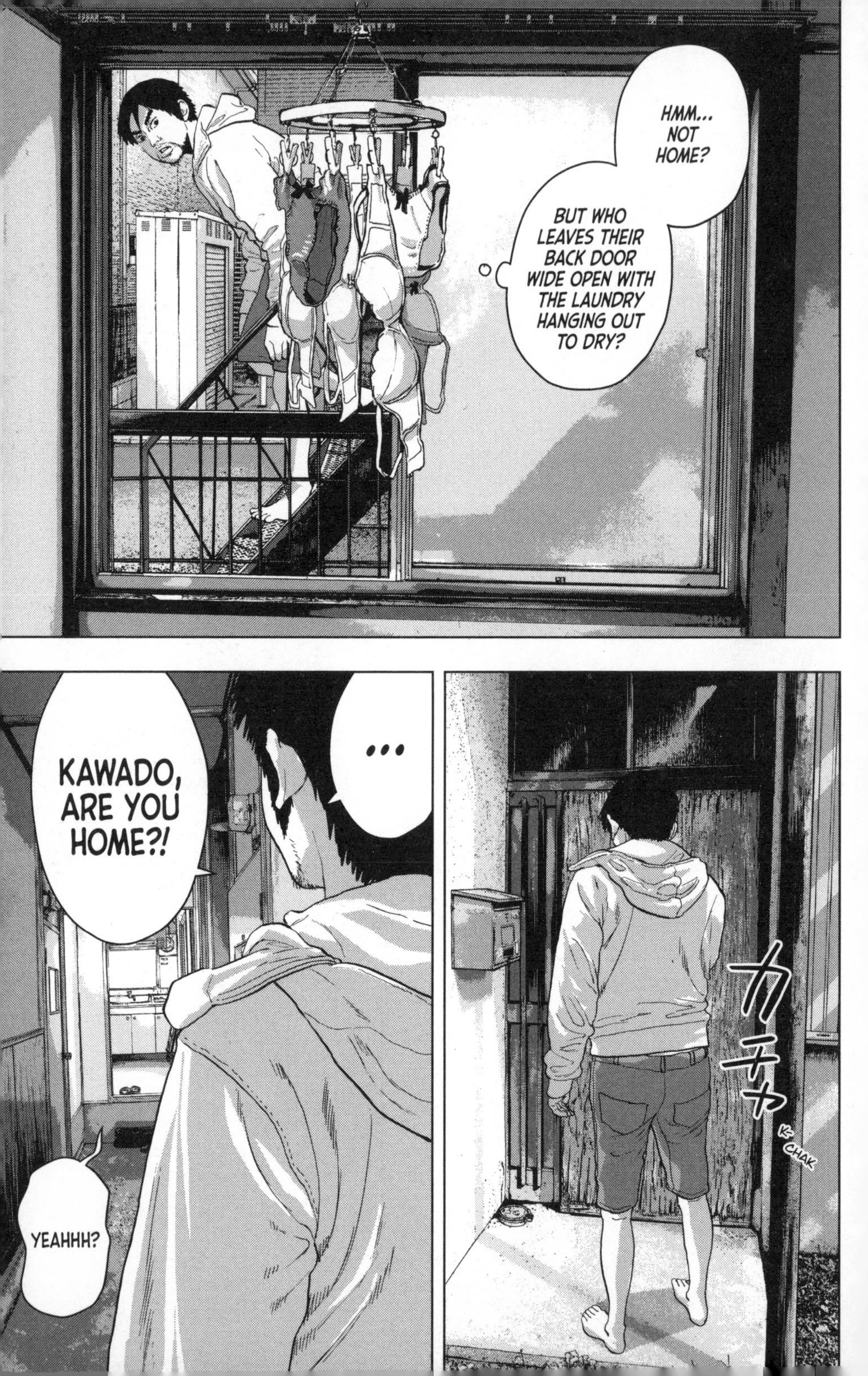
HMM... NOT HOME?
BUT WHO LEAVES THEIR BACK DOOR WIDE OPEN WITH THE LAUNDRY HANGING OUT TO DRY?
カチャ
K-CHAK
...
KAWADO, ARE YOU HOME?!
YEAHHH?

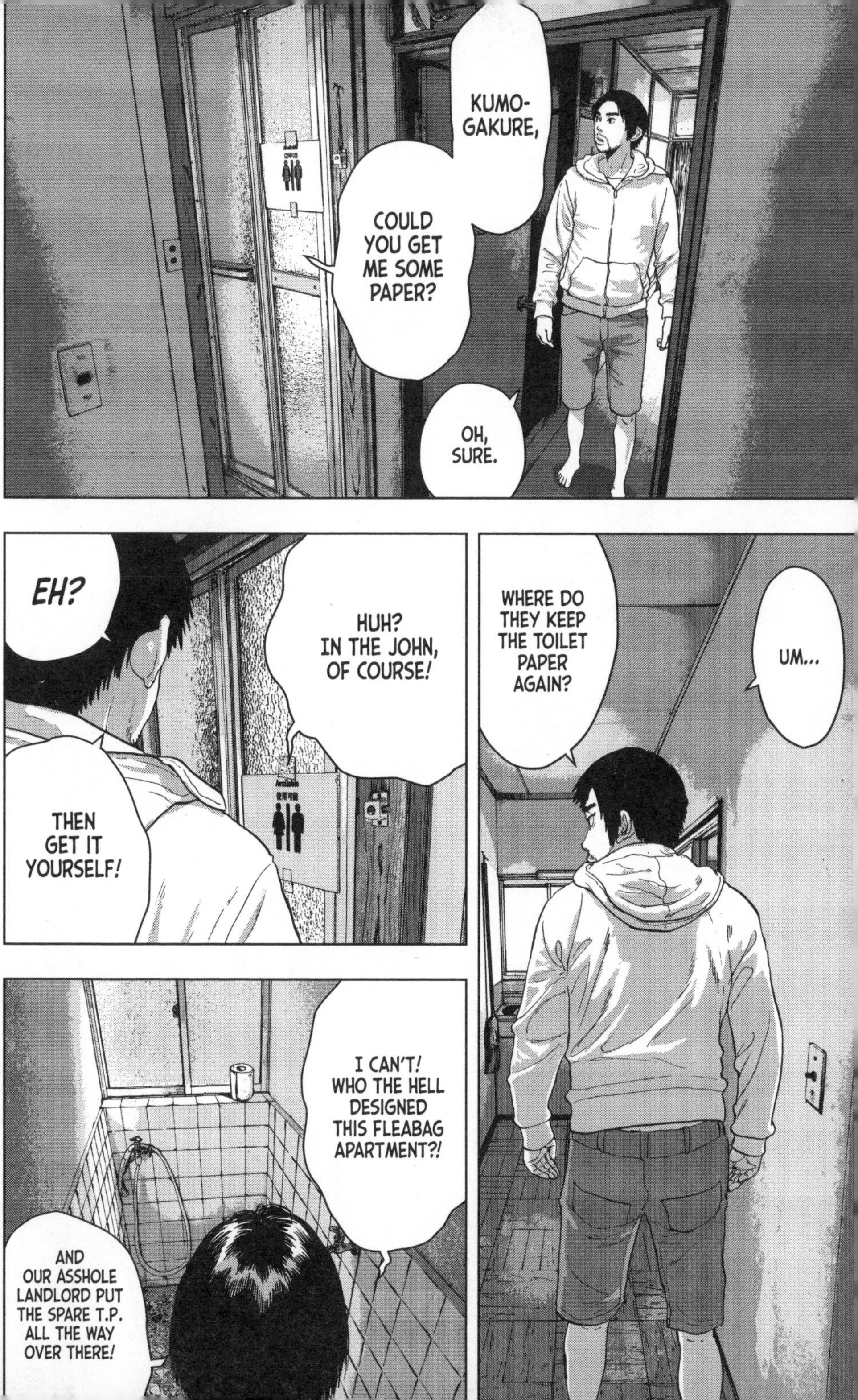
KUMO-GAKURE,
COULD YOU GET ME SOME PAPER?
OH, SURE.
UM...
WHERE DO THEY KEEP THE TOILET PAPER AGAIN?
HUH? IN THE JOHN, OF COURSE!
EH?
THEN GET IT YOURSELF!
I CAN'T! WHO THE HELL DESIGNED THIS FLEABAG APARTMENT?!
AND OUR ASSHOLE LANDLORD PUT THE SPARE T.P. ALL THE WAY OVER THERE!

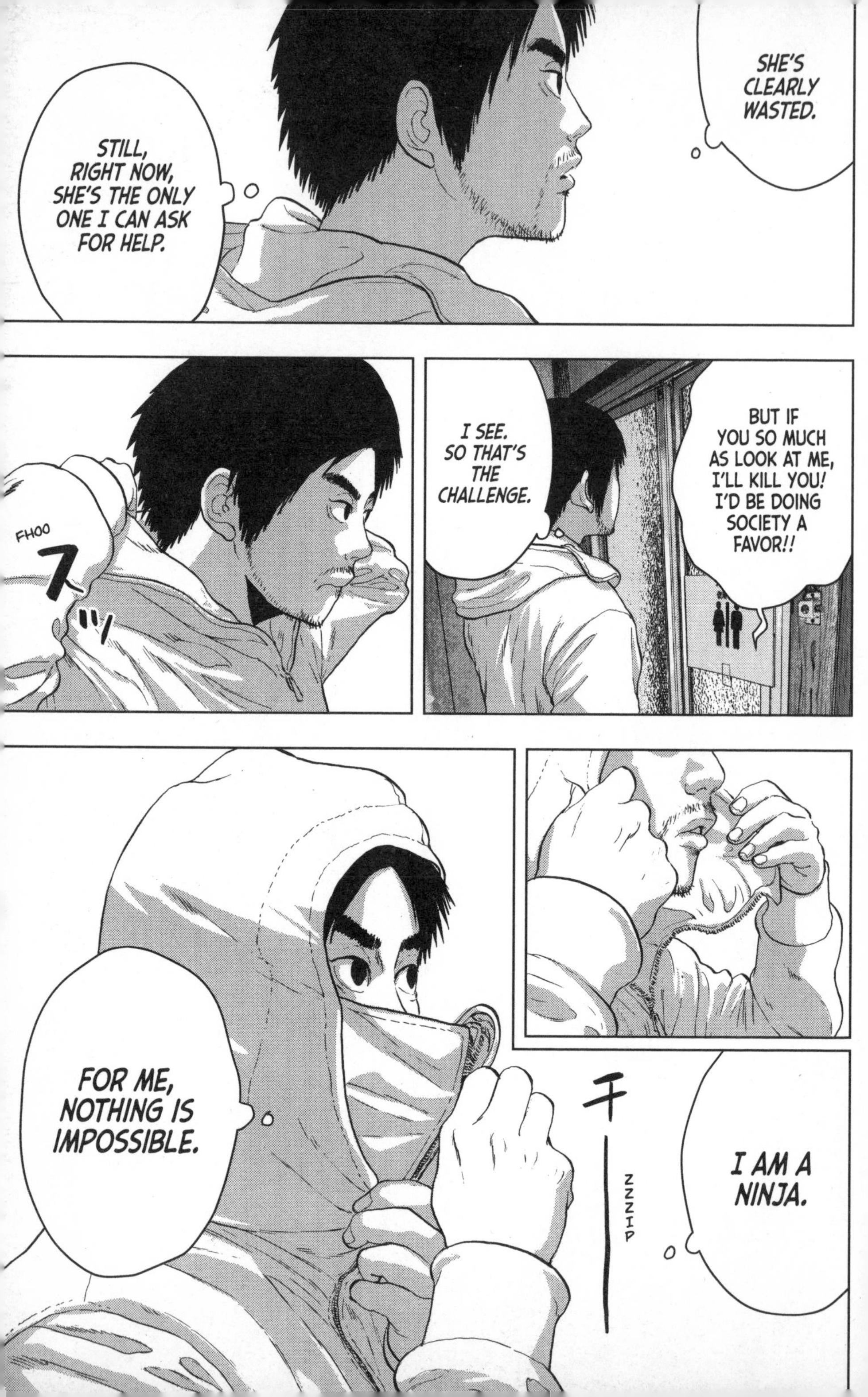
SHE'S CLEARLY WASTED.
STILL, RIGHT NOW, SHE'S THE ONLY ONE I CAN ASK FOR HELP.
BUT IF YOU SO MUCH AS LOOK AT ME, I'LL KILL YOU! I'D BE DOING SOCIETY A FAVOR!!
I SEE. SO THAT'S THE CHALLENGE.
FHOO
スッ
I AM A NINJA.
ZZZIP
チー
FOR ME, NOTHING IS IMPOSSIBLE.

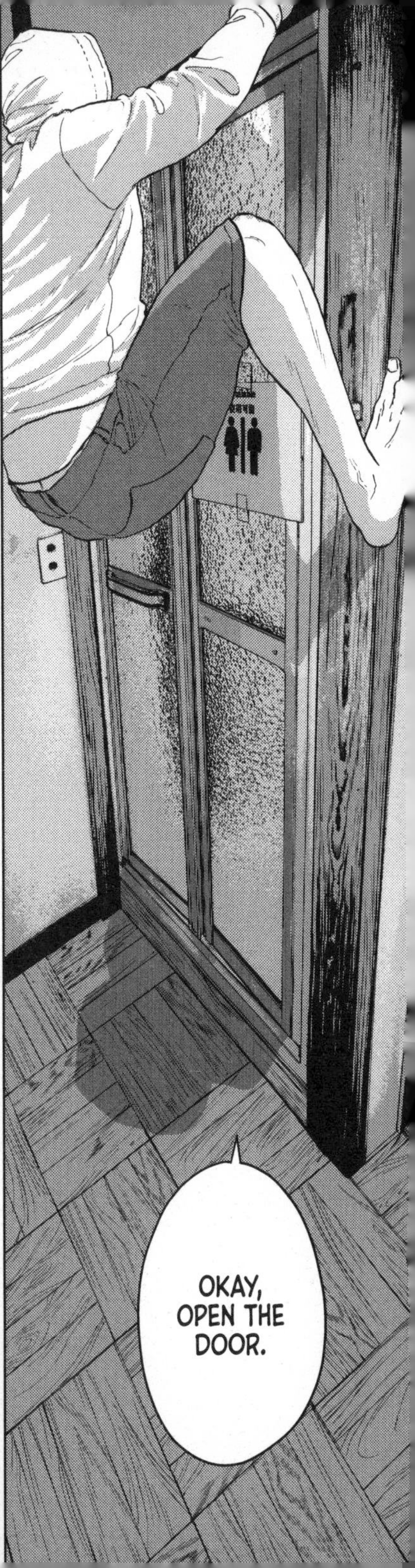
OKAY, OPEN THE DOOR.
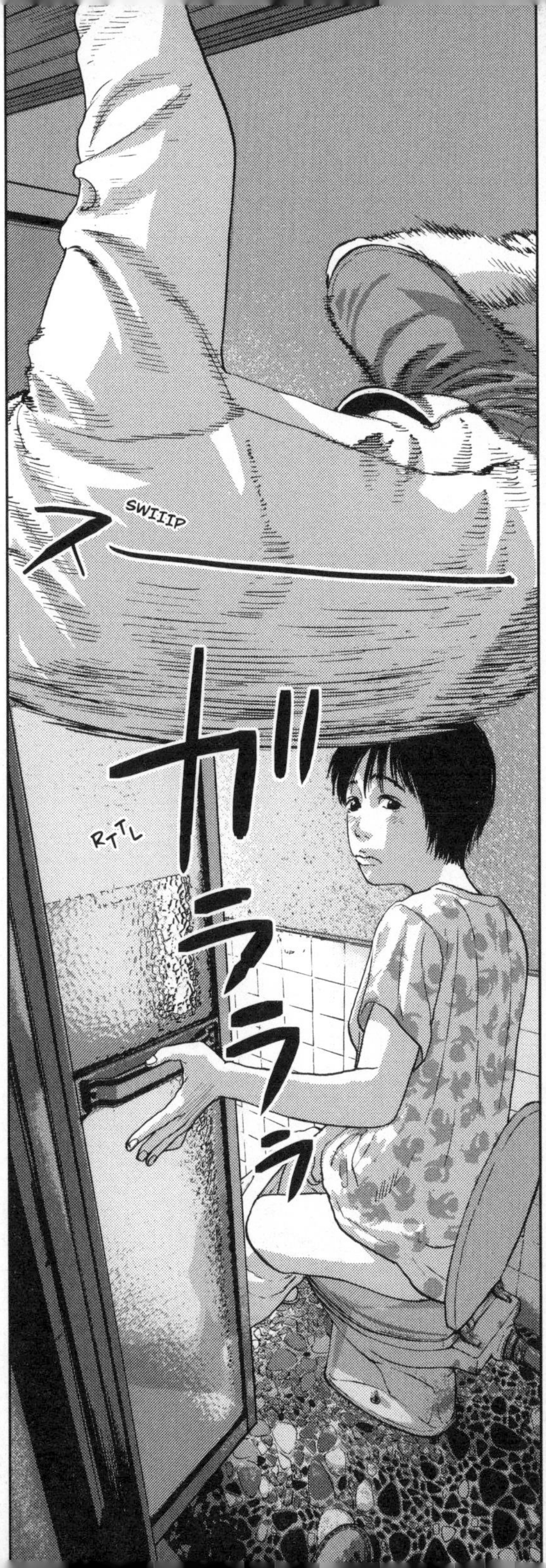
スー
SWIIIP
ガラララ
RTTL

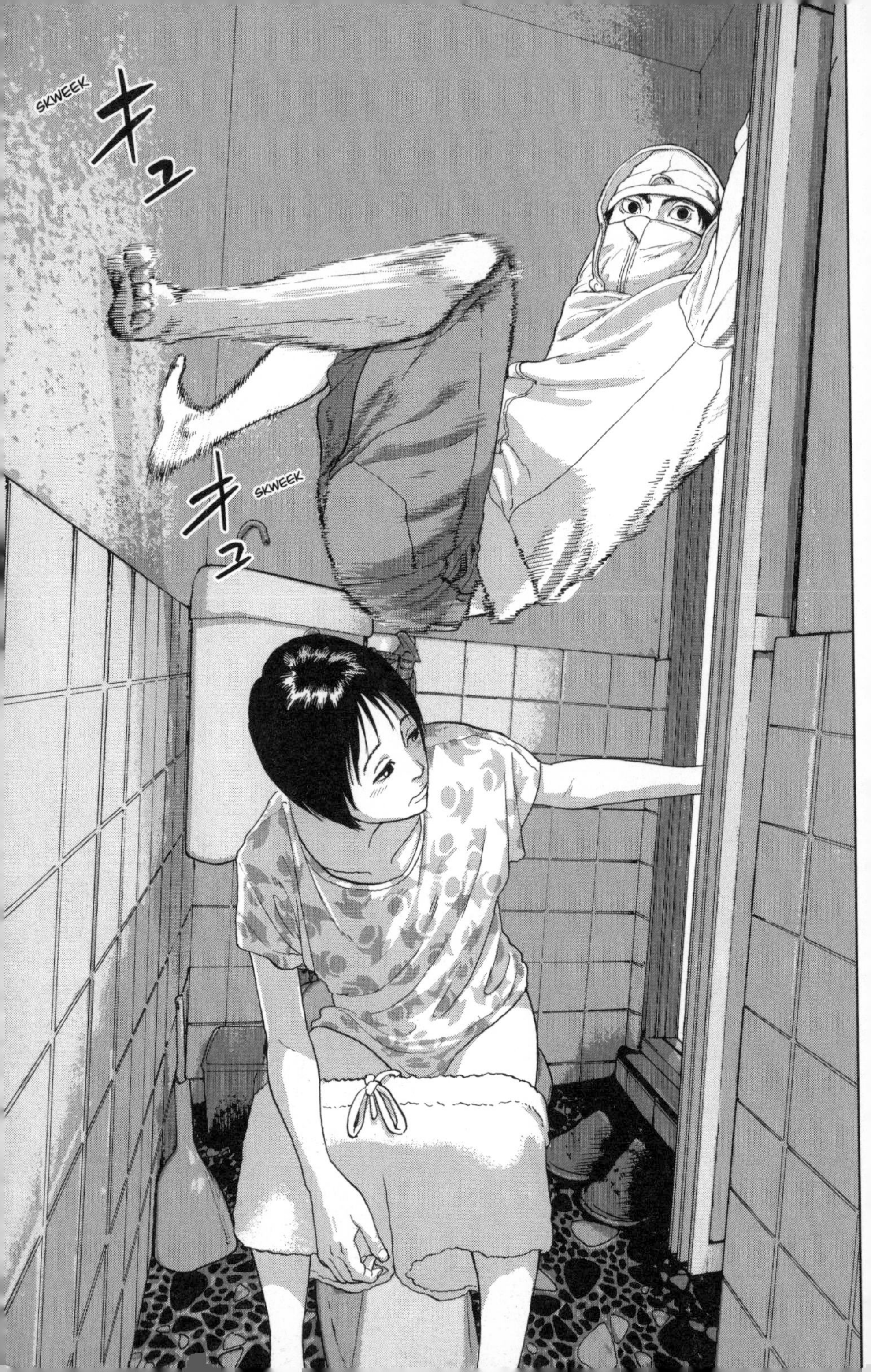
キュ
SKWEEK
キュ
SKWEEK

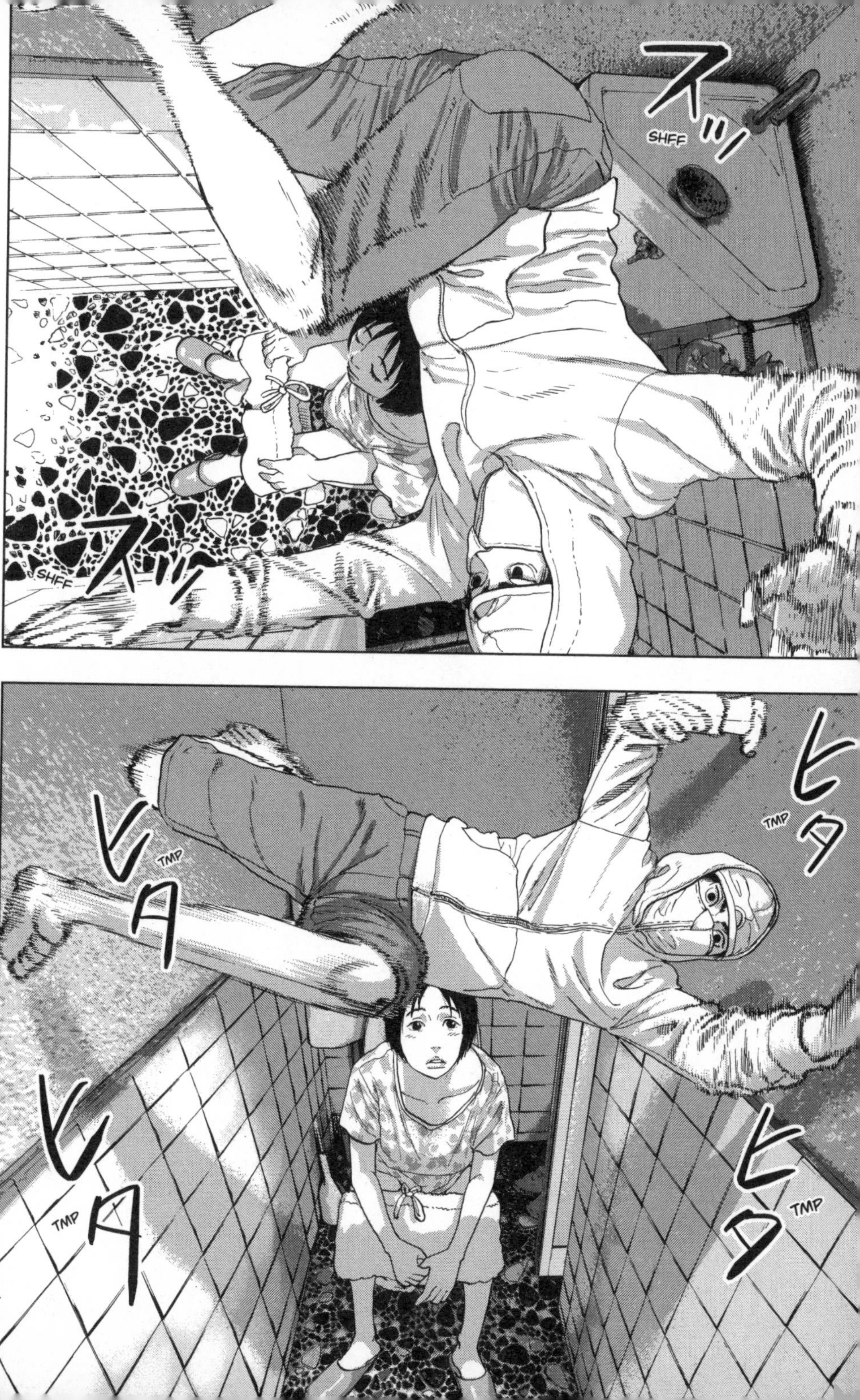
ズッ
SHFF
ズッ
SHFF
ヒタ
TMP
ヒタ
TMP
ヒタ
TMP
ヒタ
TMP

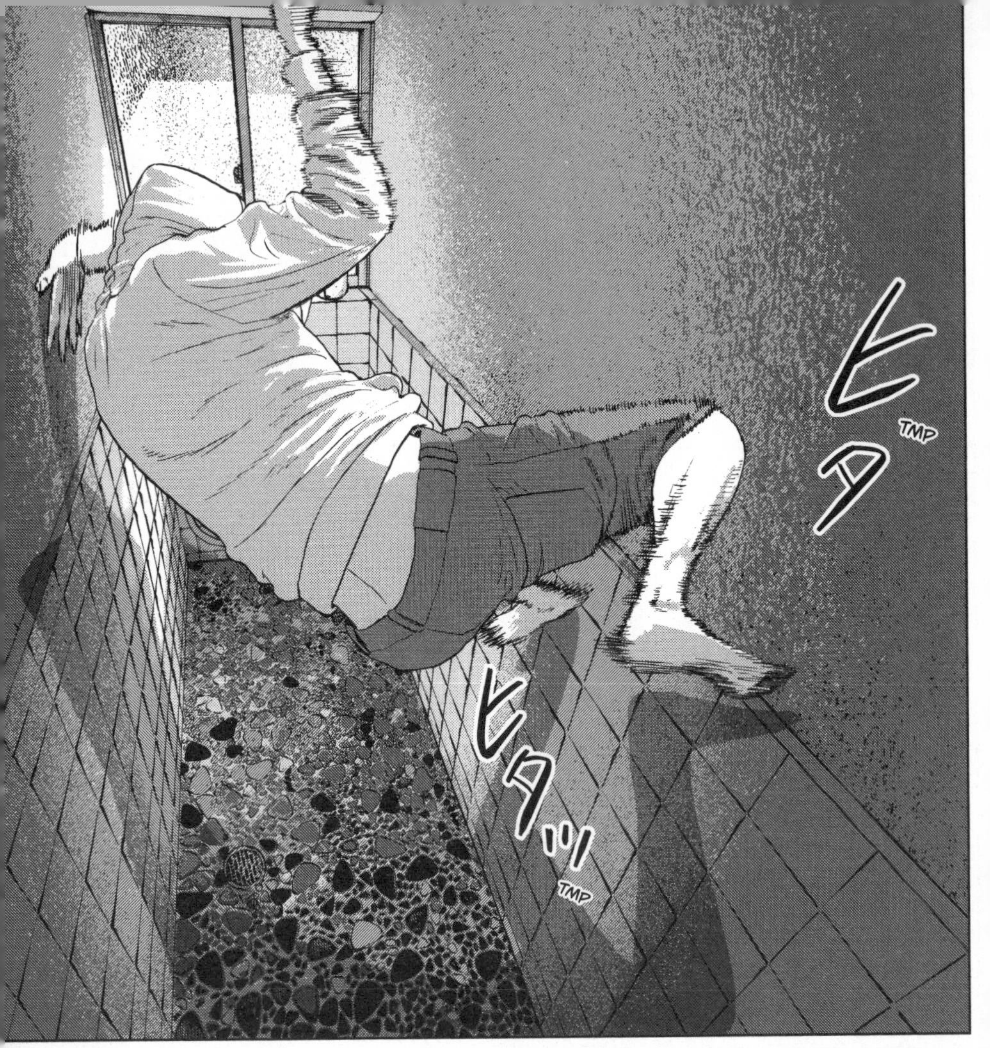
ヒタ
TMP
ヒタッ
TMP
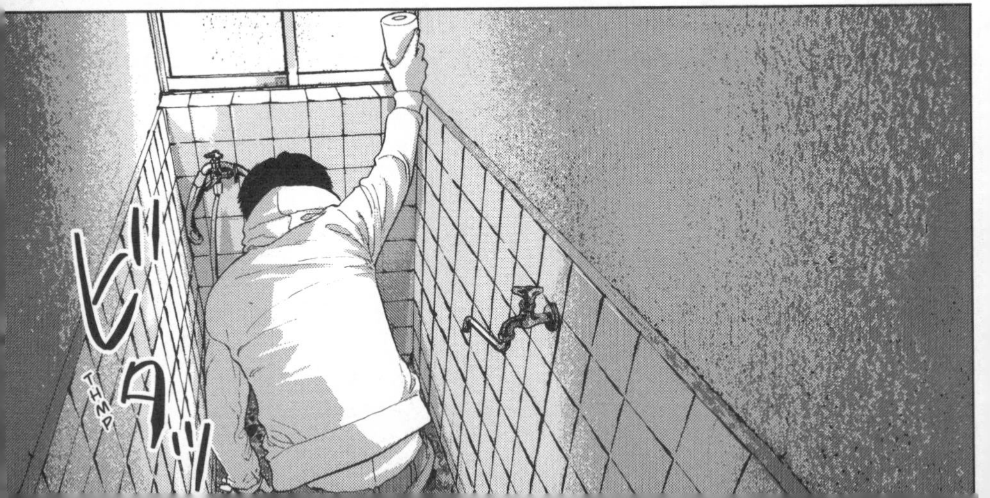
ビタッ
THMP

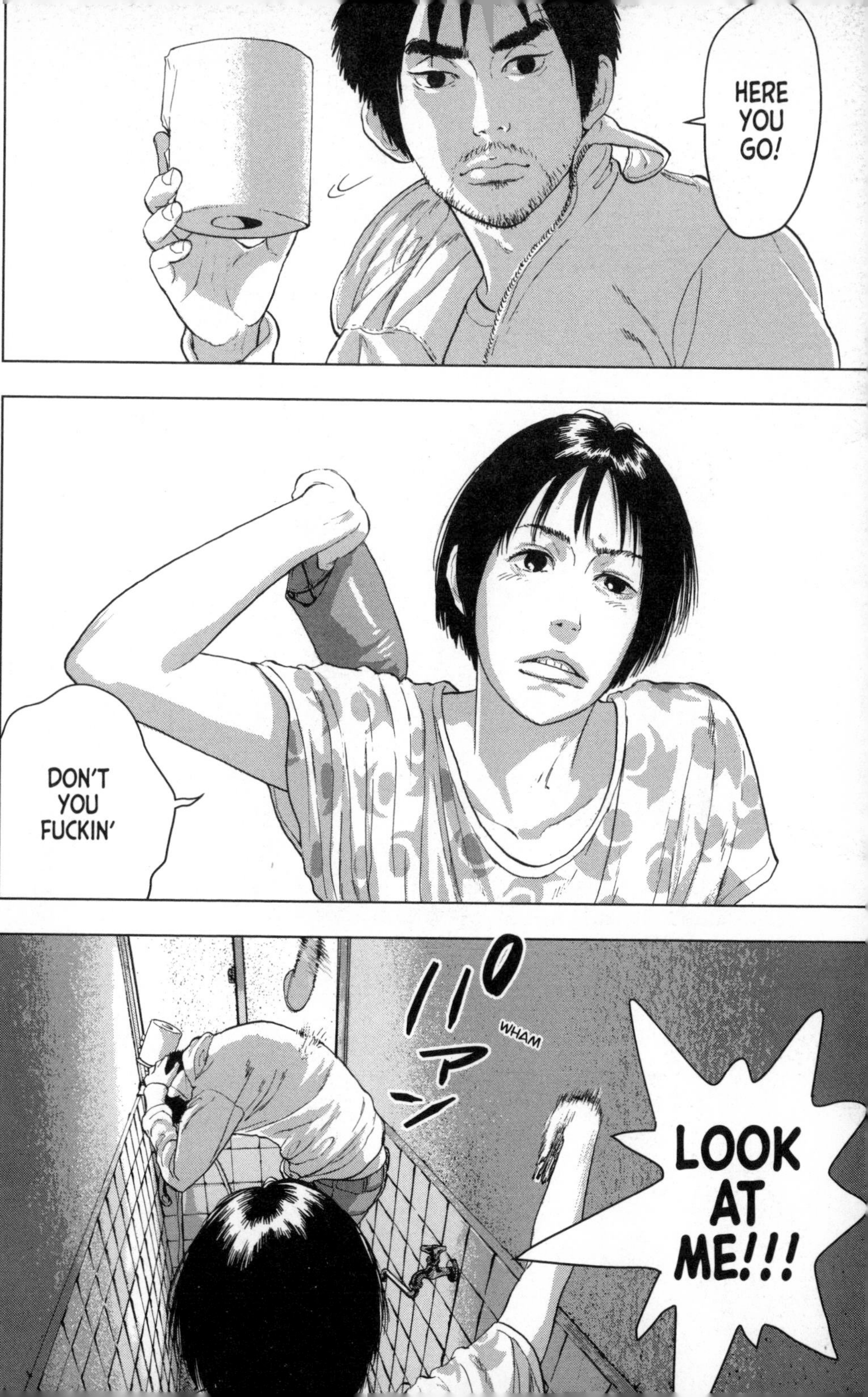
HERE YOU GO!
DON'T YOU FUCKIN'
パァーン
WHAM
LOOK AT ME!!!

CHAPTER 3

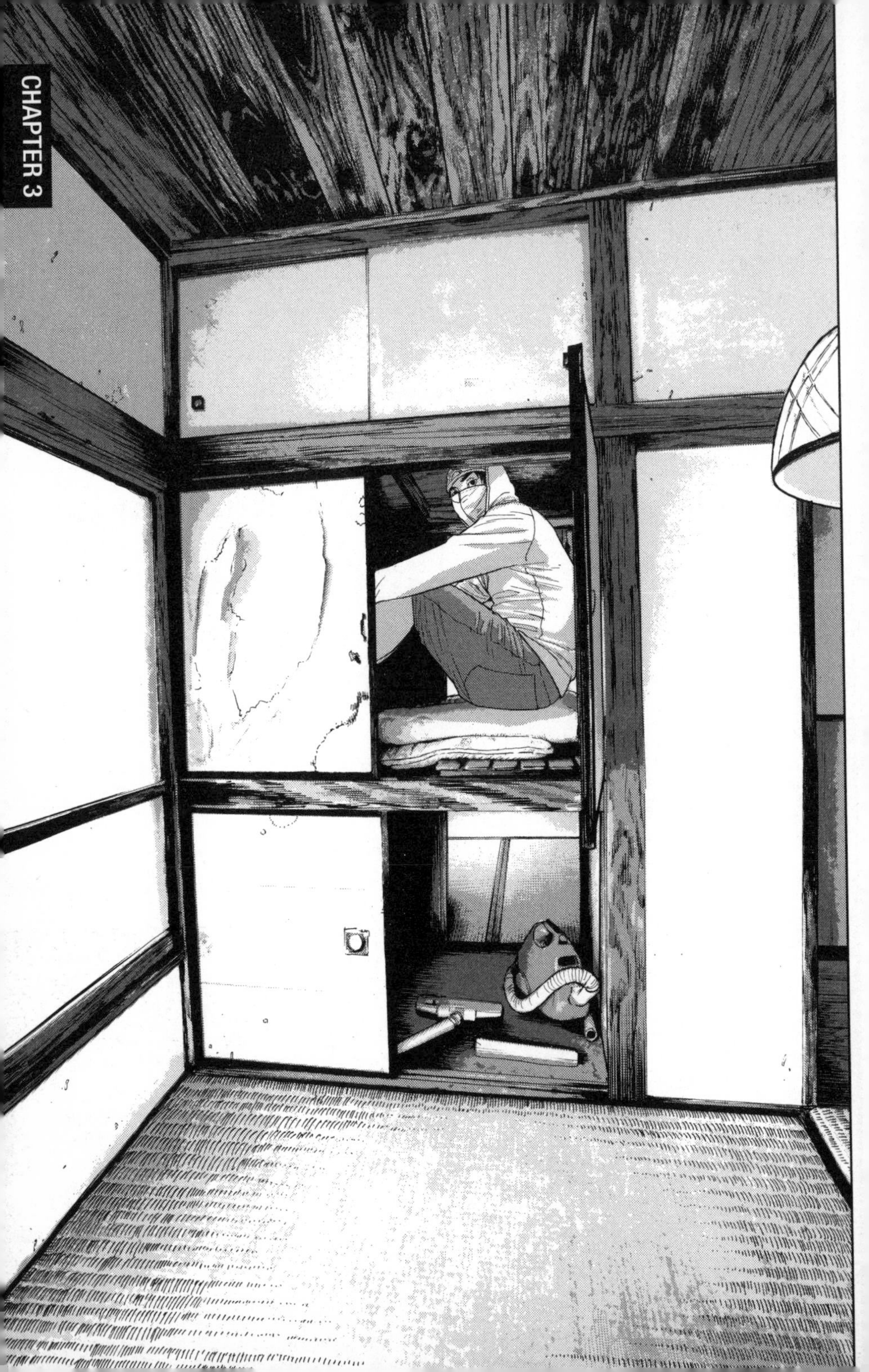

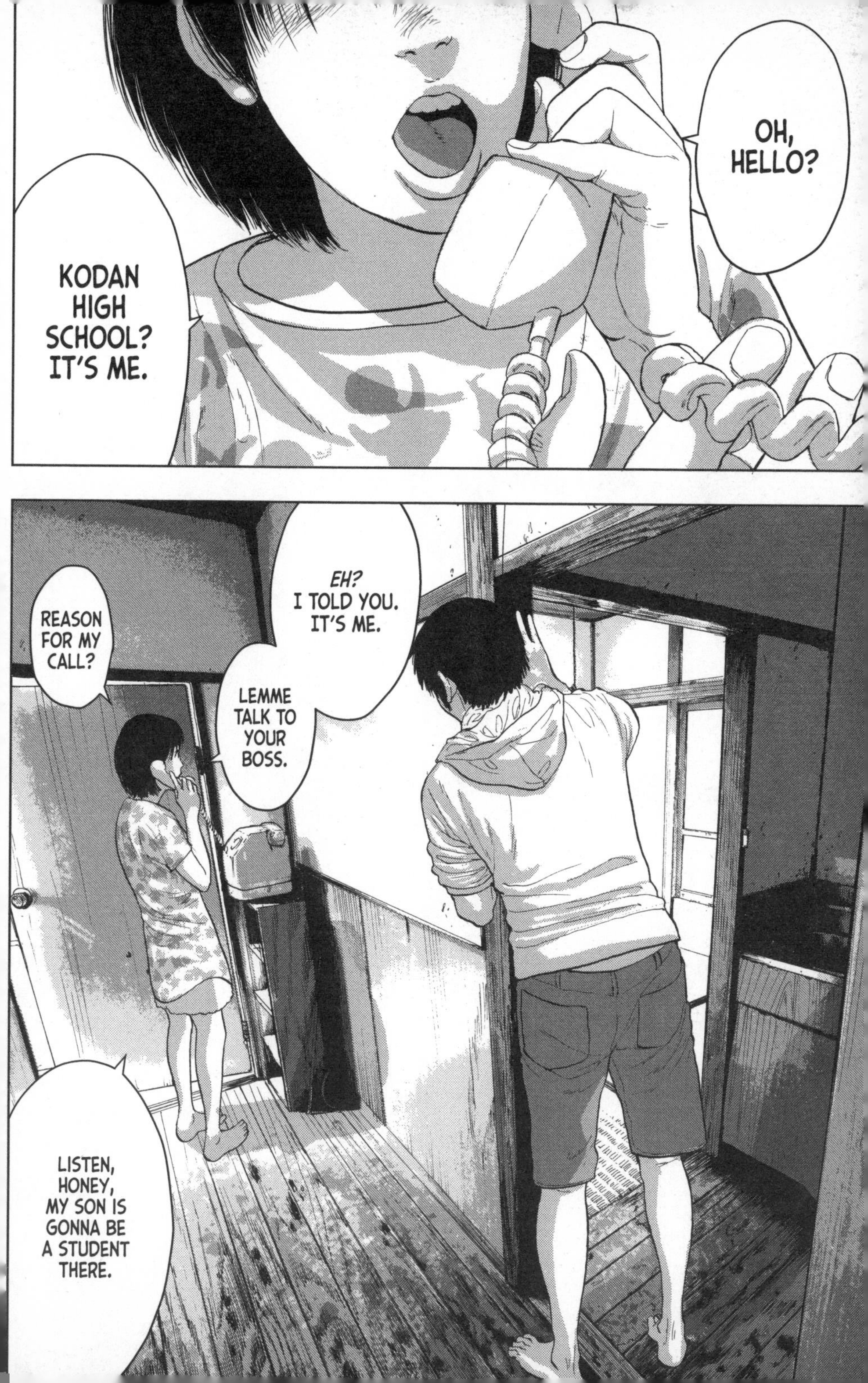
OH, HELLO?
KODAN HIGH SCHOOL? IT'S ME.
EH? I TOLD YOU. IT'S ME.
REASON FOR MY CALL?
LEMME TALK TO YOUR BOSS.
LISTEN, HONEY, MY SON IS GONNA BE A STUDENT THERE.

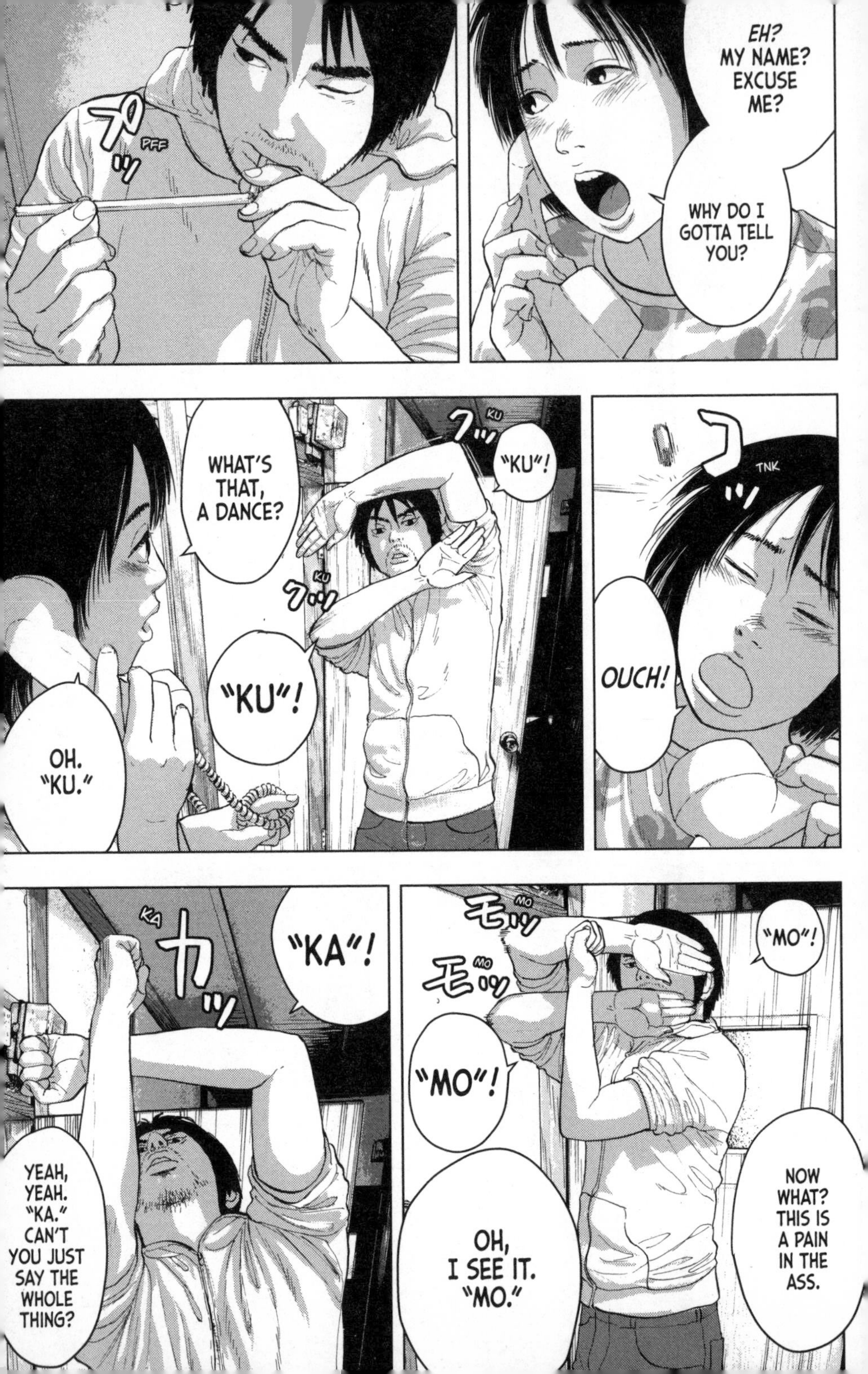
EH? MY NAME? EXCUSE ME?
WHY DO I GOTTA TELL YOU?
PFF
TNK
OUCH!
KU
"KU"!
WHAT'S THAT, A DANCE?
KU
"KU"!
OH. "KU."
MO
"MO"!
MO
"MO"!
NOW WHAT? THIS IS A PAIN IN THE ASS.
OH, I SEE IT. "MO."
KA
"KA"!
YEAH, YEAH. "KA." CAN'T YOU JUST SAY THE WHOLE THING?

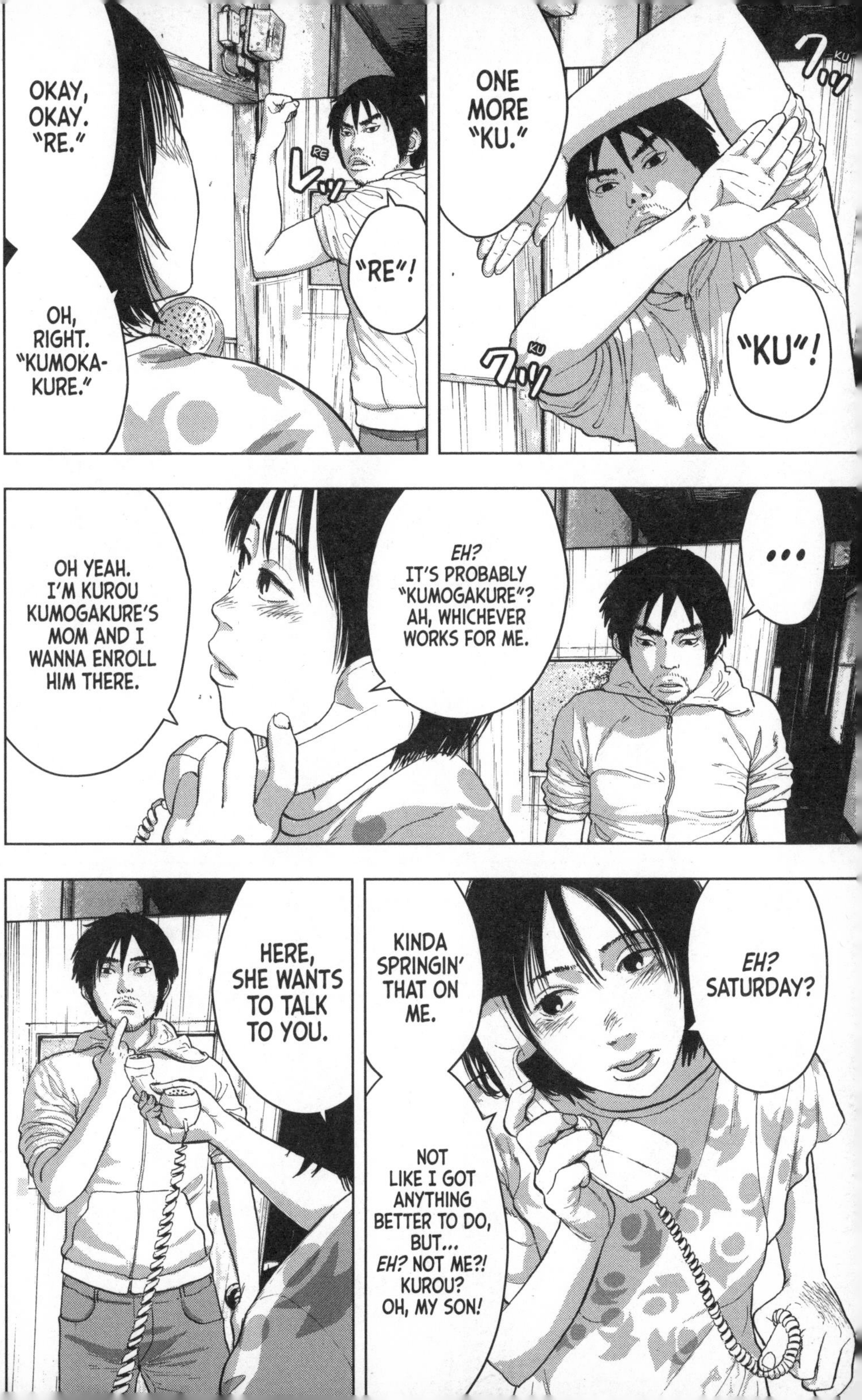
KU
ONE MORE "KU."
"KU"!
KU
OKAY, OKAY. "RE."
RE
"RE"!
OH, RIGHT. "KUMOKAKURE."
...
EH? IT'S PROBABLY "KUMOGAKURE"? AH, WHICHEVER WORKS FOR ME.
OH YEAH. I'M KUROU KUMOGAKURE'S MOM AND I WANNA ENROLL HIM THERE.
EH? SATURDAY?
KINDA SPRINGIN' THAT ON ME.
NOT LIKE I GOT ANYTHING BETTER TO DO, BUT... *EH?* NOT ME?! KUROU? OH, MY SON!
HERE, SHE WANTS TO TALK TO YOU.

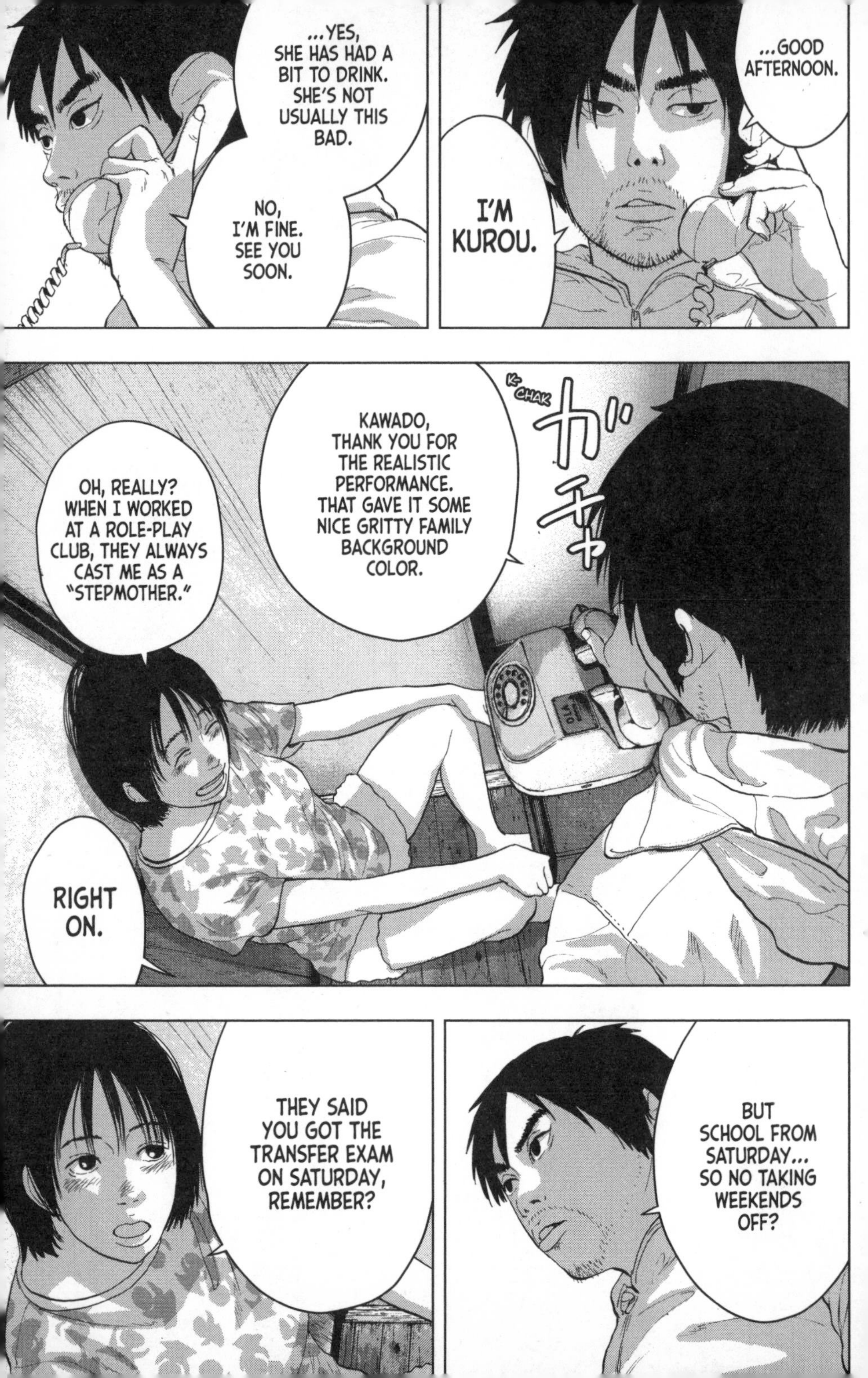
...GOOD AFTERNOON.
I'M KUROU.
...YES, SHE HAS HAD A BIT TO DRINK. SHE'S NOT USUALLY THIS BAD.
NO, I'M FINE. SEE YOU SOON.
K-CHAK
ガチャ
KAWADO, THANK YOU FOR THE REALISTIC PERFORMANCE. THAT GAVE IT SOME NICE GRITTY FAMILY BACKGROUND COLOR.
OH, REALLY? WHEN I WORKED AT A ROLE-PLAY CLUB, THEY ALWAYS CAST ME AS A "STEPMOTHER."
RIGHT ON.
BUT SCHOOL FROM SATURDAY... SO NO TAKING WEEKENDS OFF?
THEY SAID YOU GOT THE TRANSFER EXAM ON SATURDAY, REMEMBER?

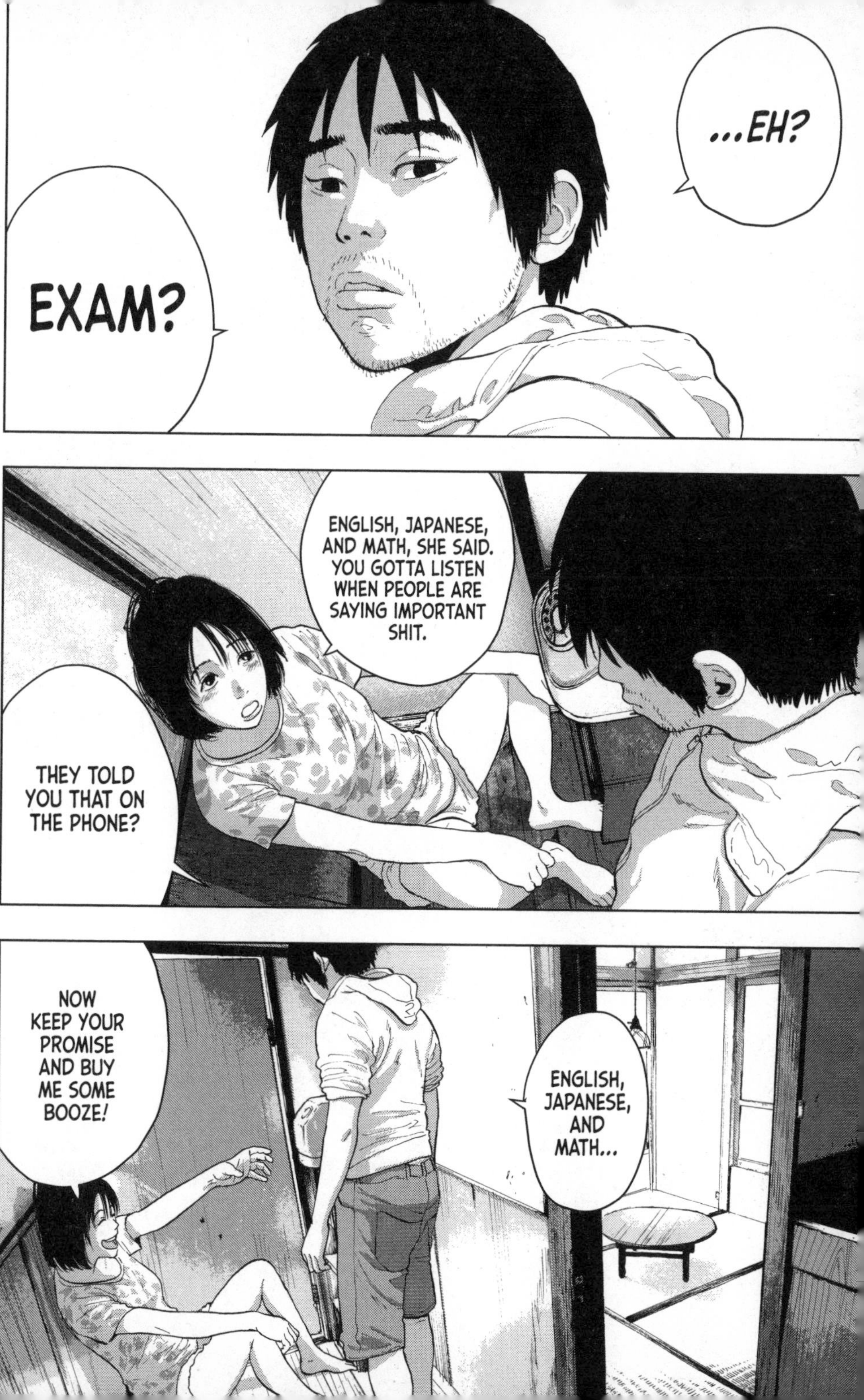
...EH?
EXAM?
ENGLISH, JAPANESE, AND MATH, SHE SAID. YOU GOTTA LISTEN WHEN PEOPLE ARE SAYING IMPORTANT SHIT.
THEY TOLD YOU THAT ON THE PHONE?
ENGLISH, JAPANESE, AND MATH...
NOW KEEP YOUR PROMISE AND BUY ME SOME BOOZE!

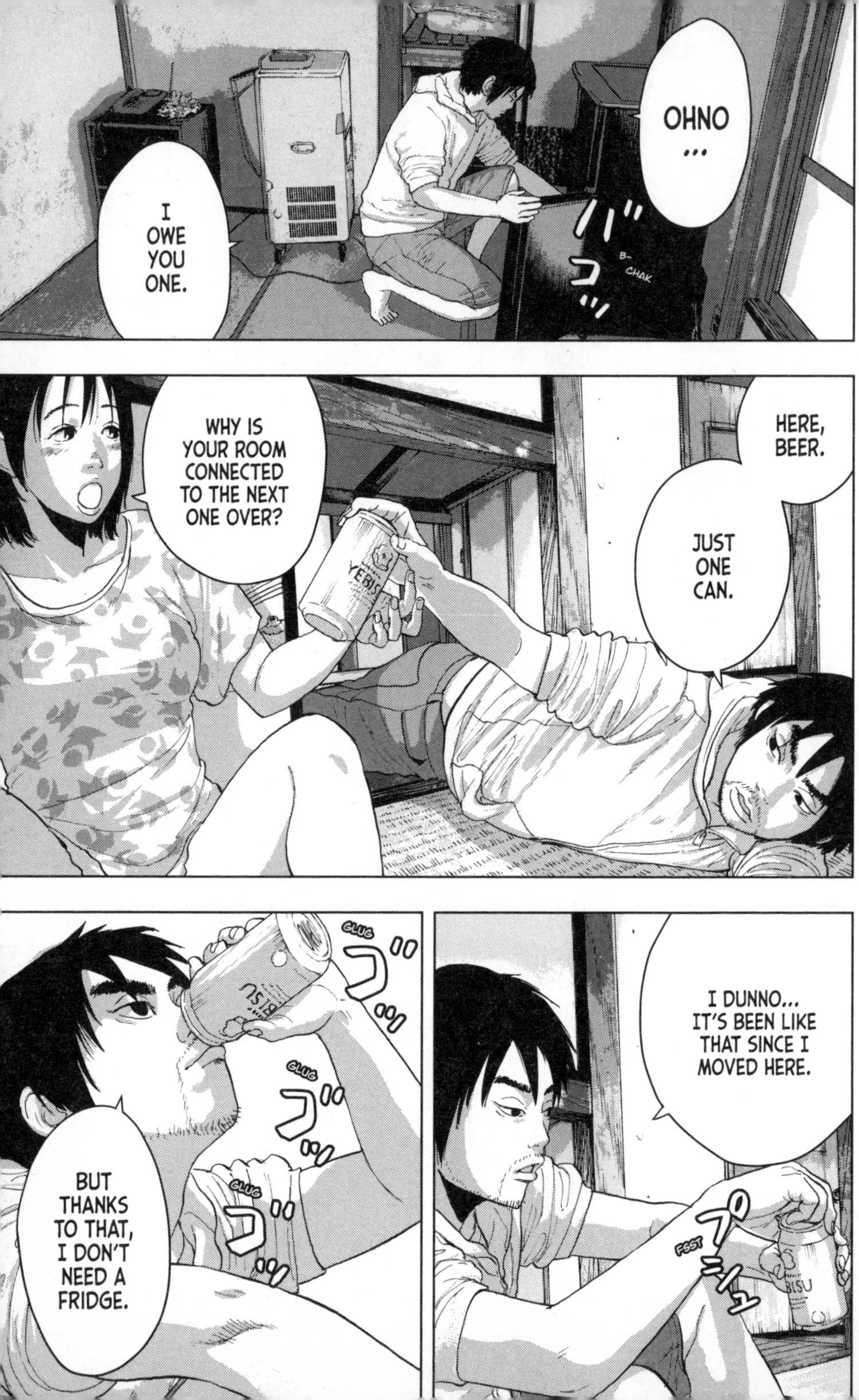
OHNO ...
B-CHAK
I OWE YOU ONE.
HERE, BEER.
JUST ONE CAN.
WHY IS YOUR ROOM CONNECTED TO THE NEXT ONE OVER?
I DUNNO... IT'S BEEN LIKE THAT SINCE I MOVED HERE.
FSST
GLUG
GLUG
GLUG
BUT THANKS TO THAT, I DON'T NEED A FRIDGE.

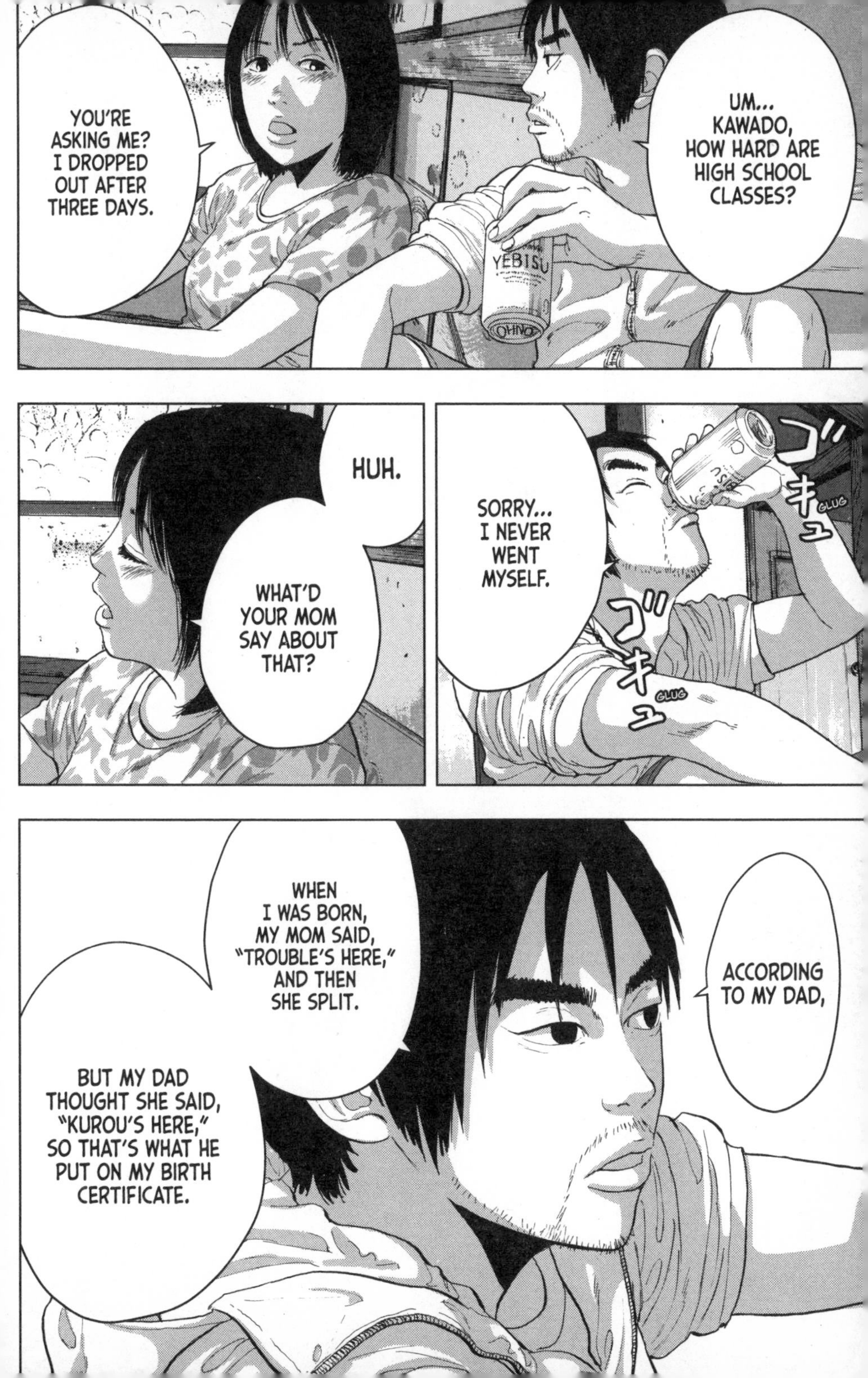
UM... KAWADO, HOW HARD ARE HIGH SCHOOL CLASSES?
YEBISU
YOU'RE ASKING ME? I DROPPED OUT AFTER THREE DAYS.
ゴキュ
GLUG
SORRY... I NEVER WENT MYSELF.
ゴキュ
GLUG
HUH.
WHAT'D YOUR MOM SAY ABOUT THAT?
ACCORDING TO MY DAD,
WHEN I WAS BORN, MY MOM SAID, "TROUBLE'S HERE," AND THEN SHE SPLIT.
BUT MY DAD THOUGHT SHE SAID, "KUROU'S HERE," SO THAT'S WHAT HE PUT ON MY BIRTH CERTIFICATE.

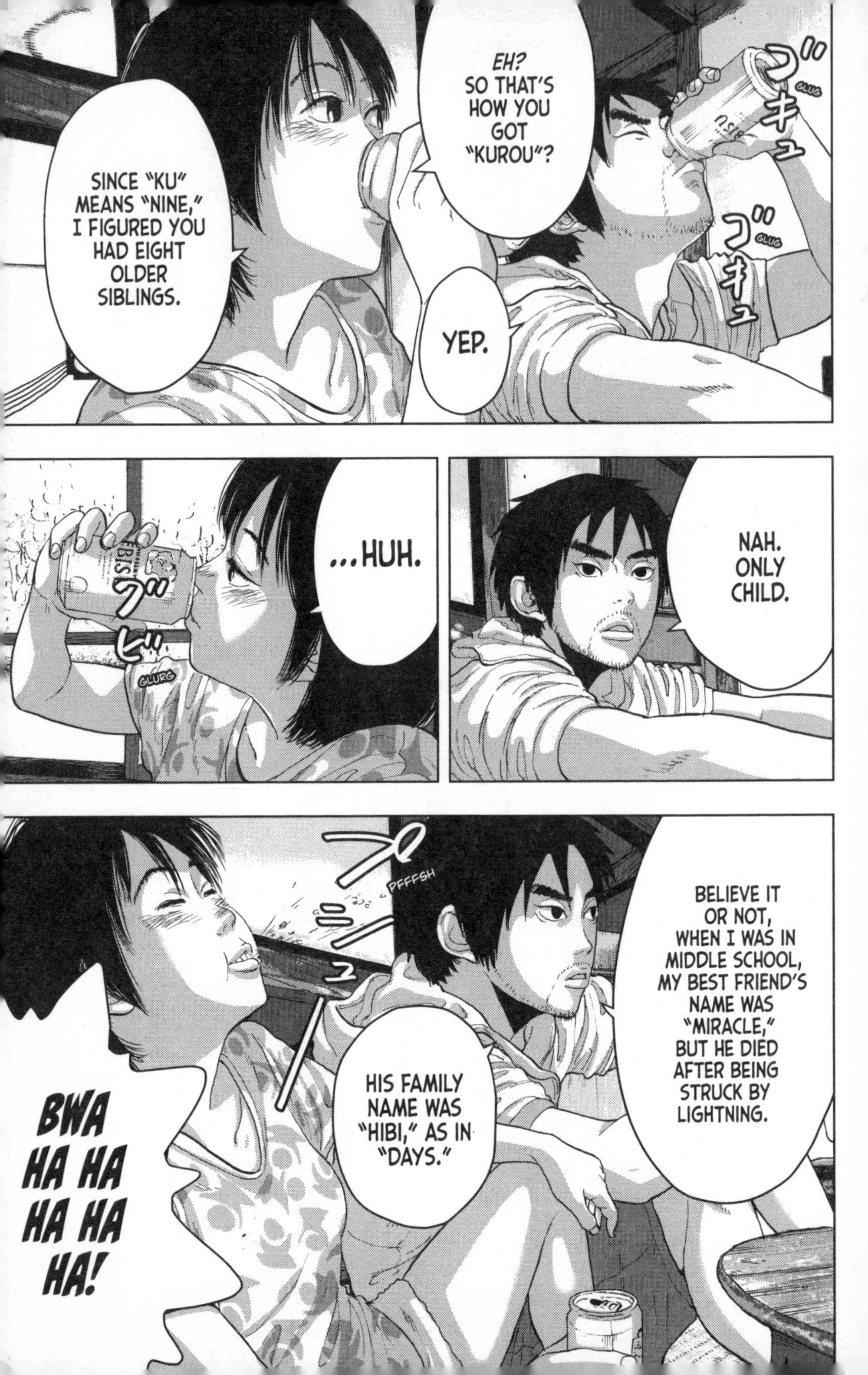
GLUG
GLUG
EH? SO THAT'S HOW YOU GOT "KUROU"?
YEP.
SINCE "KU" MEANS "NINE," I FIGURED YOU HAD EIGHT OLDER SIBLINGS.
NAH. ONLY CHILD.
...HUH.
GLURG
PFFFSH
BELIEVE IT OR NOT, WHEN I WAS IN MIDDLE SCHOOL, MY BEST FRIEND'S NAME WAS "MIRACLE," BUT HE DIED AFTER BEING STRUCK BY LIGHTNING.
HIS FAMILY NAME WAS "HIBI," AS IN "DAYS."
BWA HA HA HA HA HA!

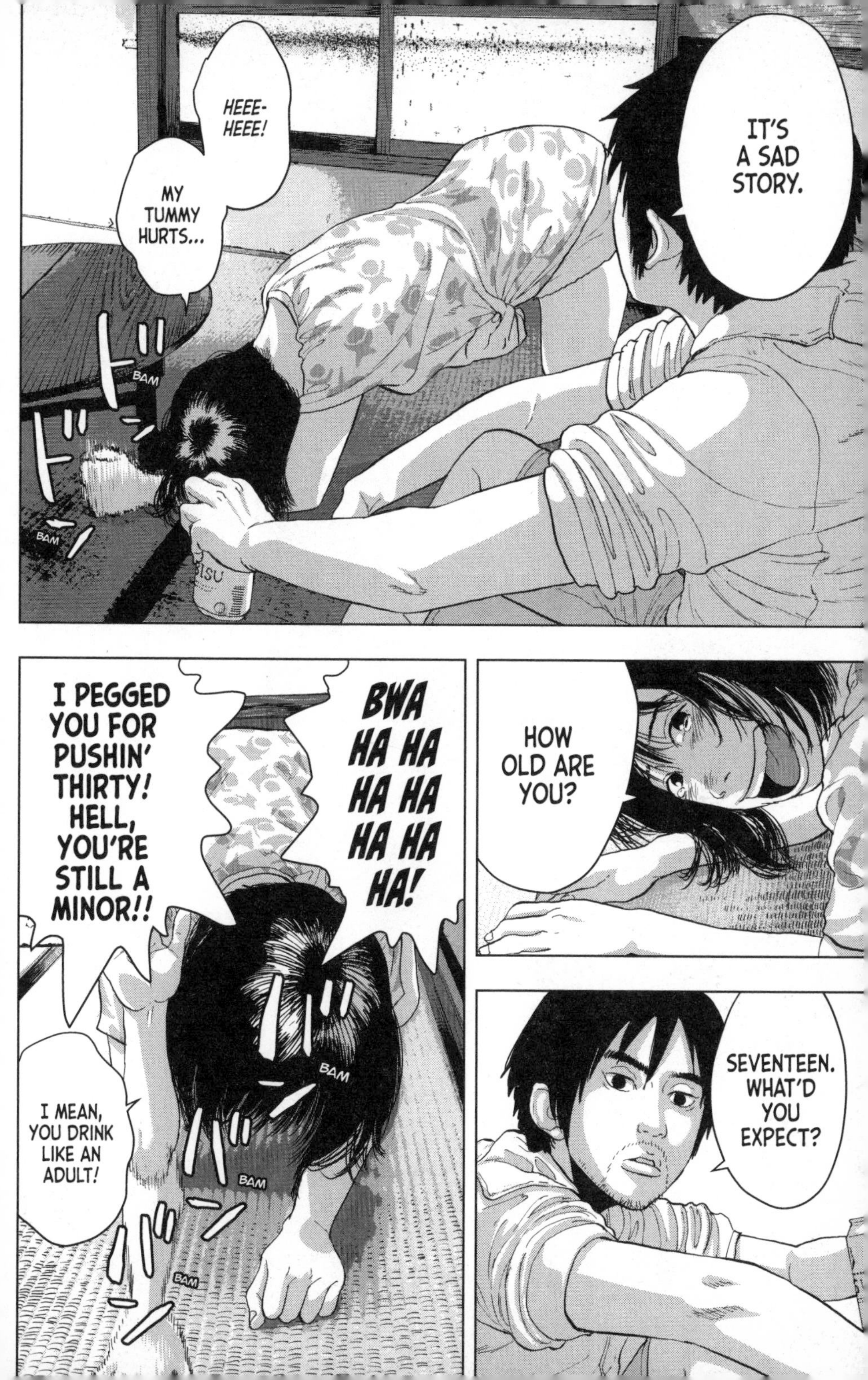
IT'S A SAD STORY.
HEEE-HEEE!
MY TUMMY HURTS...
BAM
BAM
HOW OLD ARE YOU?
SEVENTEEN. WHAT'D YOU EXPECT?
BWA HA HA HA HA HA HA HA HA HA!
I PEGGED YOU FOR PUSHIN' THIRTY! HELL, YOU'RE STILL A MINOR!!
I MEAN, YOU DRINK LIKE AN ADULT!
BAM
BAM
BAM

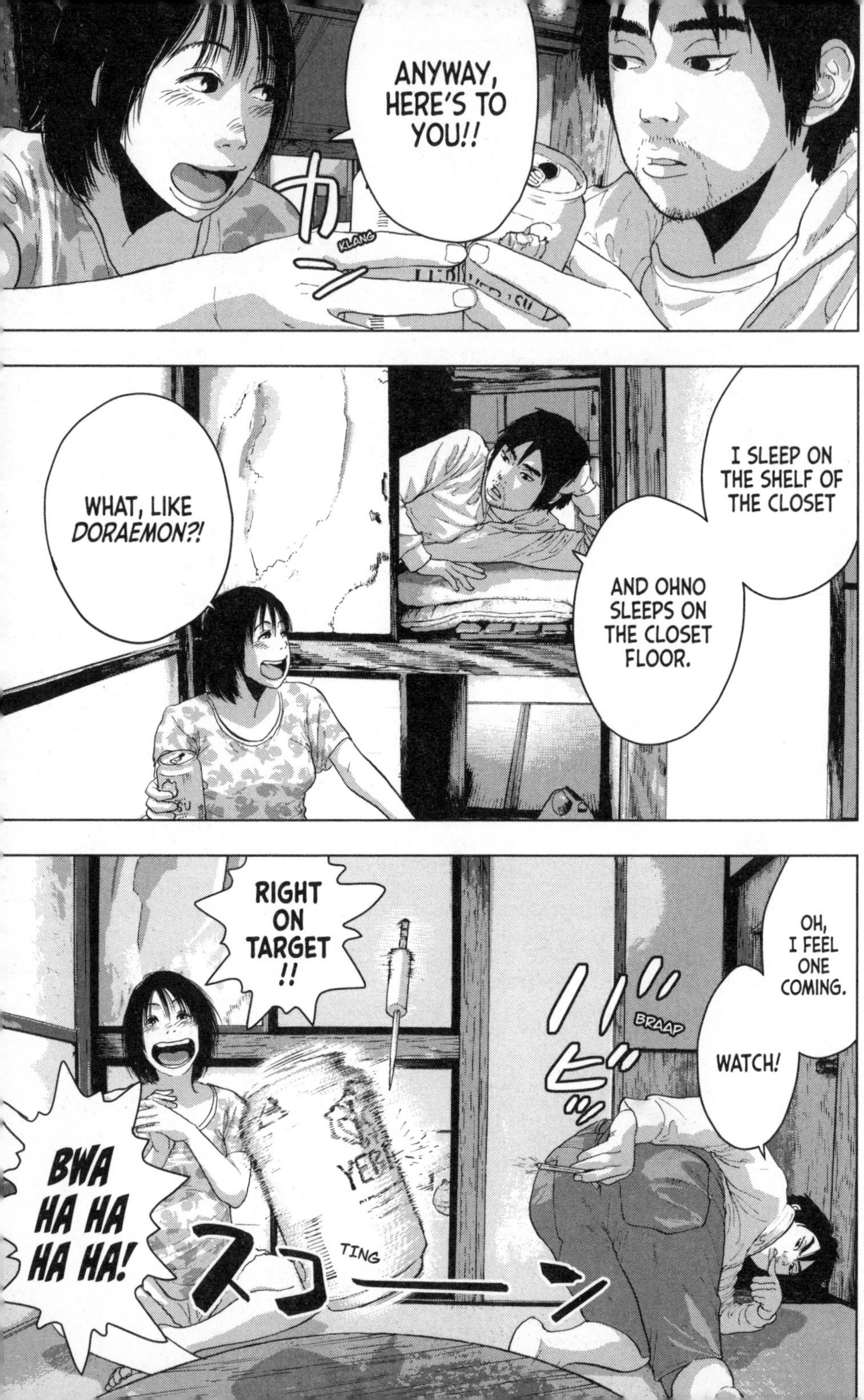
ANYWAY, HERE'S TO YOU!!
KLANG
I SLEEP ON THE SHELF OF THE CLOSET
AND OHNO SLEEPS ON THE CLOSET FLOOR.
WHAT, LIKE *DORAEMON*?!
OH, I FEEL ONE COMING.
WATCH!
BRAAP
RIGHT ON TARGET !!
TING
BWA HA HA HA HA!

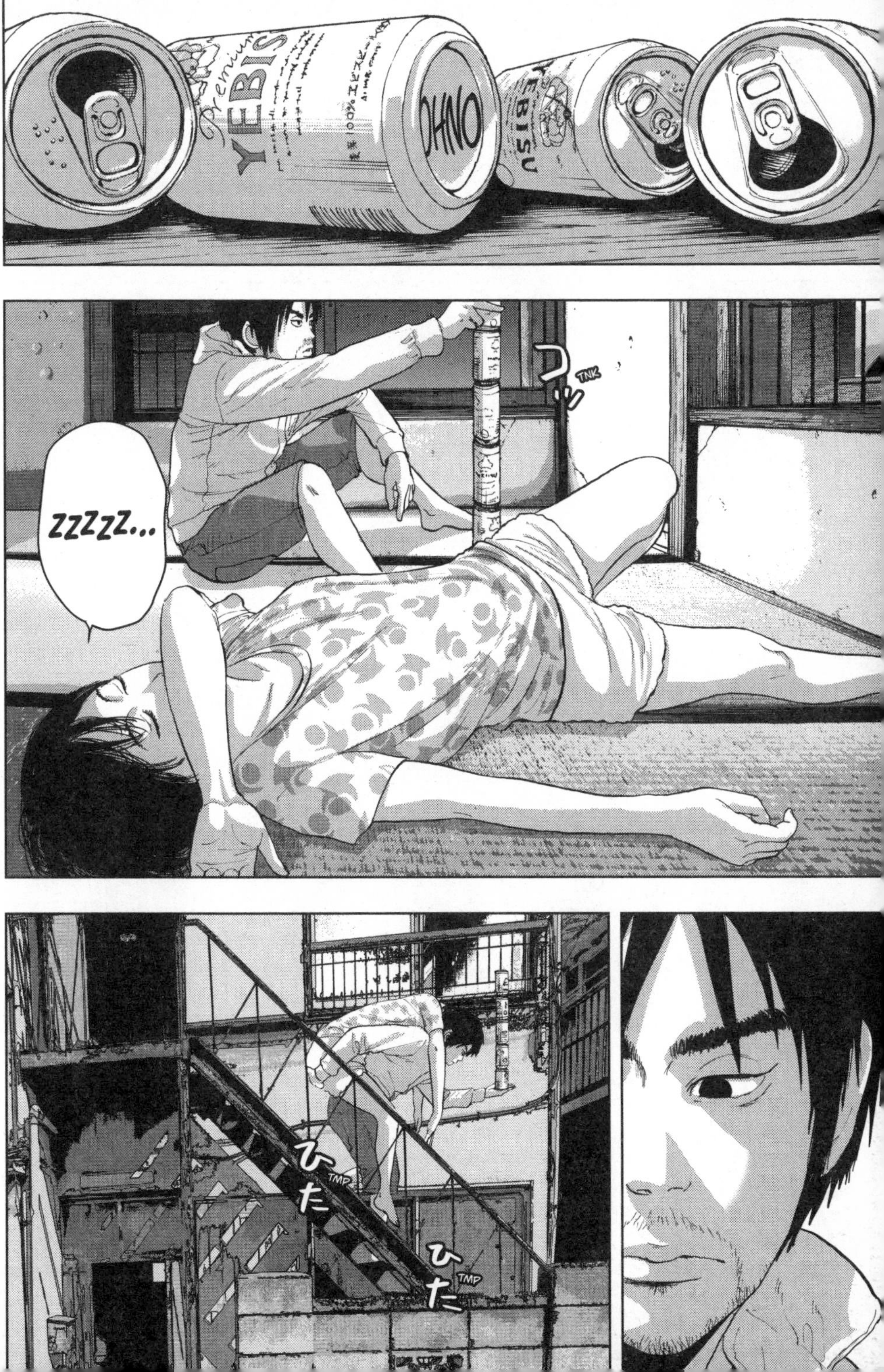
YEBISU
OHNO
YEBISU
コッ
TNK
ZZZZZ...
ひた
TMP
ひた
TMP

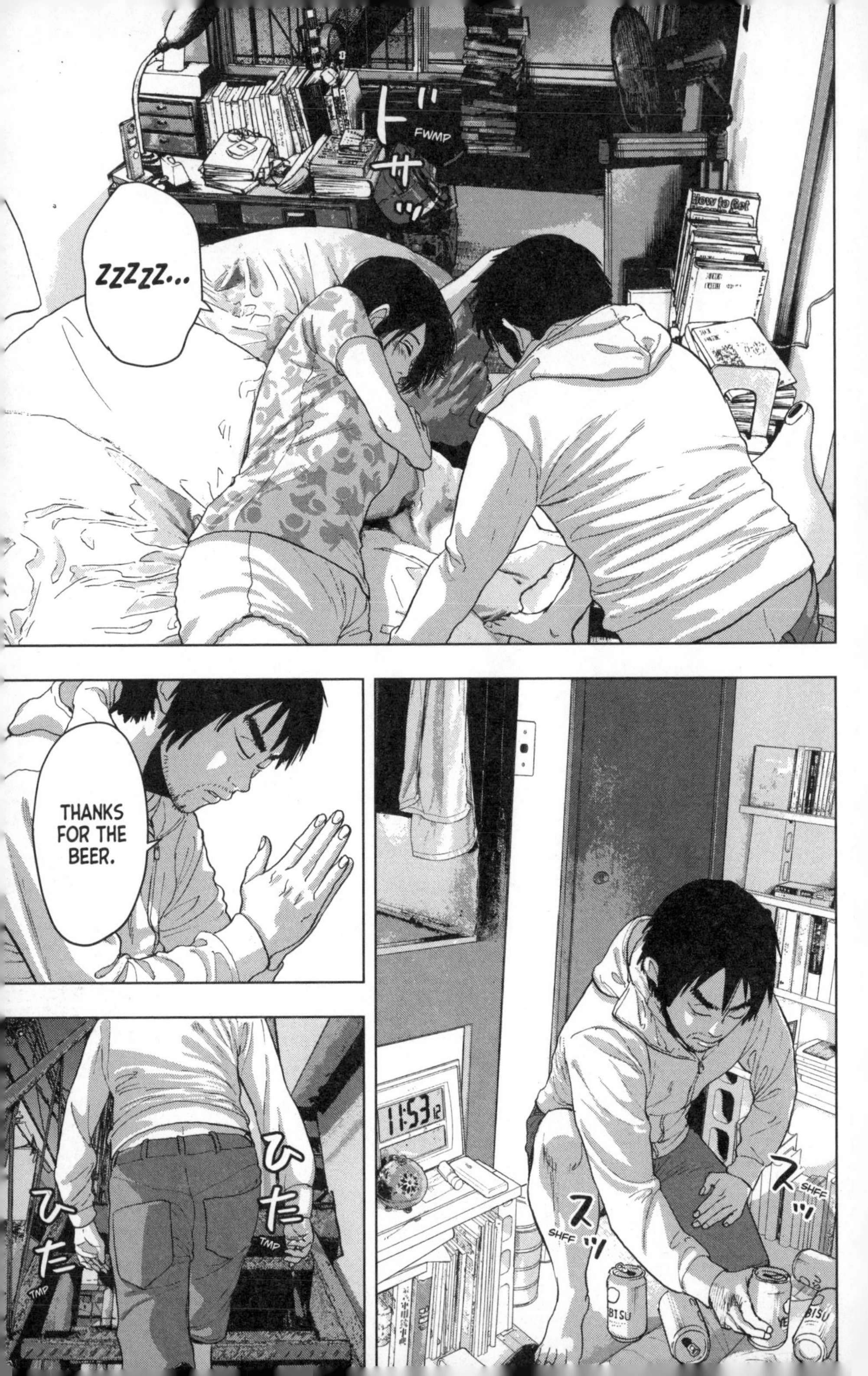
ドサッ
FWMP
ZZZZZ...
スッ
SHFF
スッ
SHFF
11:53 12
THANKS FOR THE BEER.
ひた
TMP
ひた
TMP

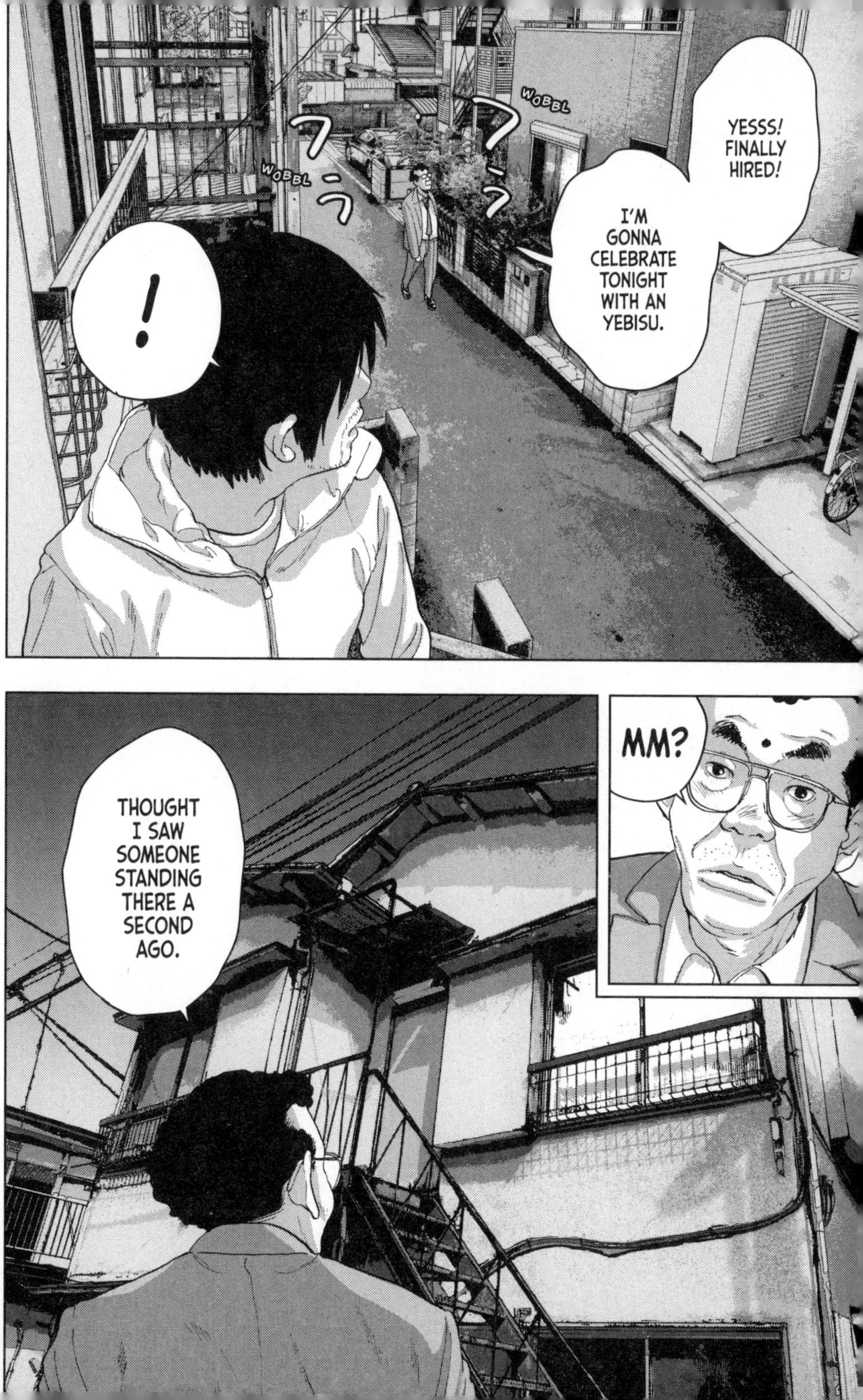
WOBBL
YESSS! FINALLY HIRED!
I'M GONNA CELEBRATE TONIGHT WITH AN YEBISU.
WOBBL
!
MM?
THOUGHT I SAW SOMEONE STANDING THERE A SECOND AGO.

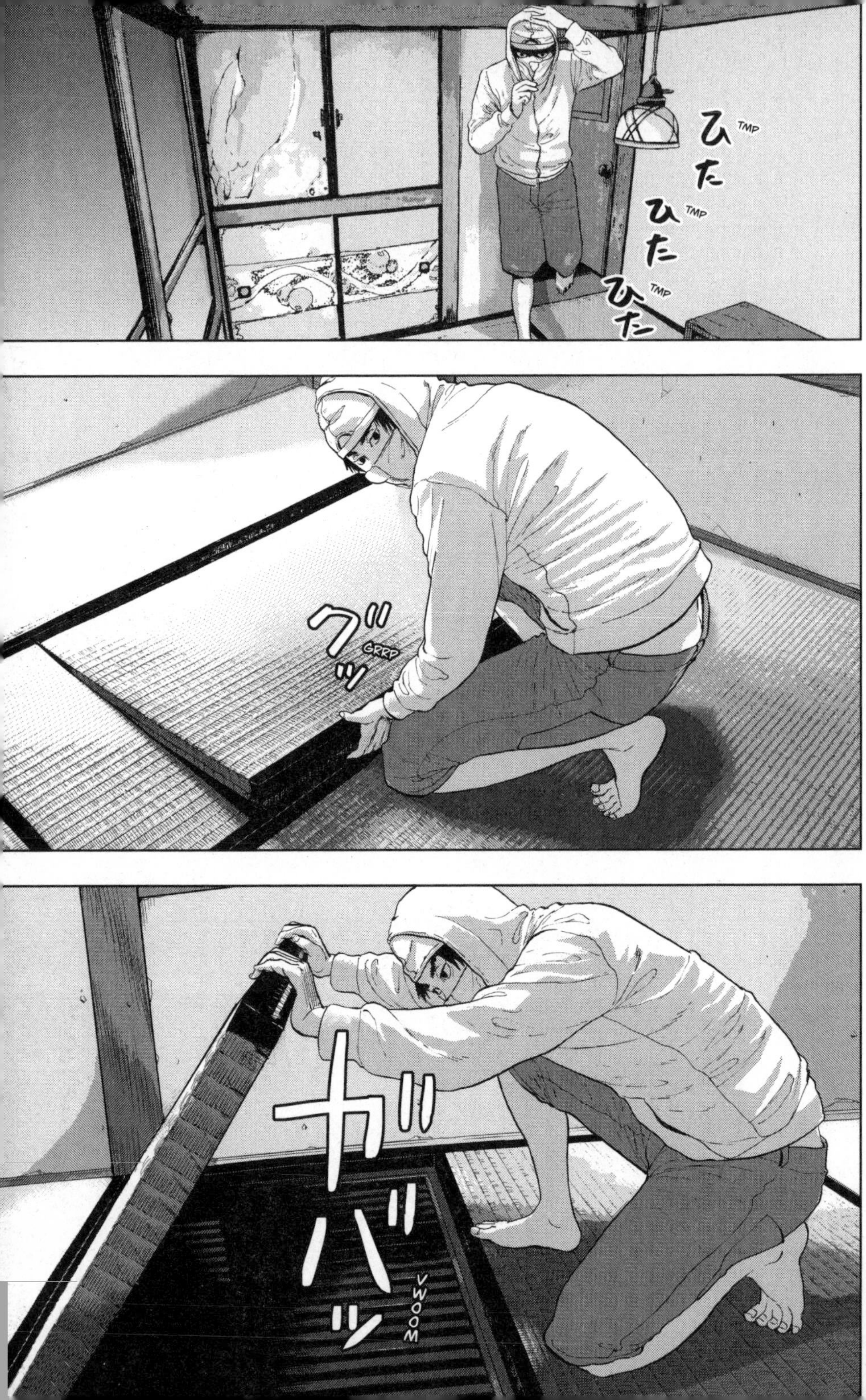
ひた TMP
ひた TMP
ひた TMP
グッ GRRP
ガバッ VWOOM

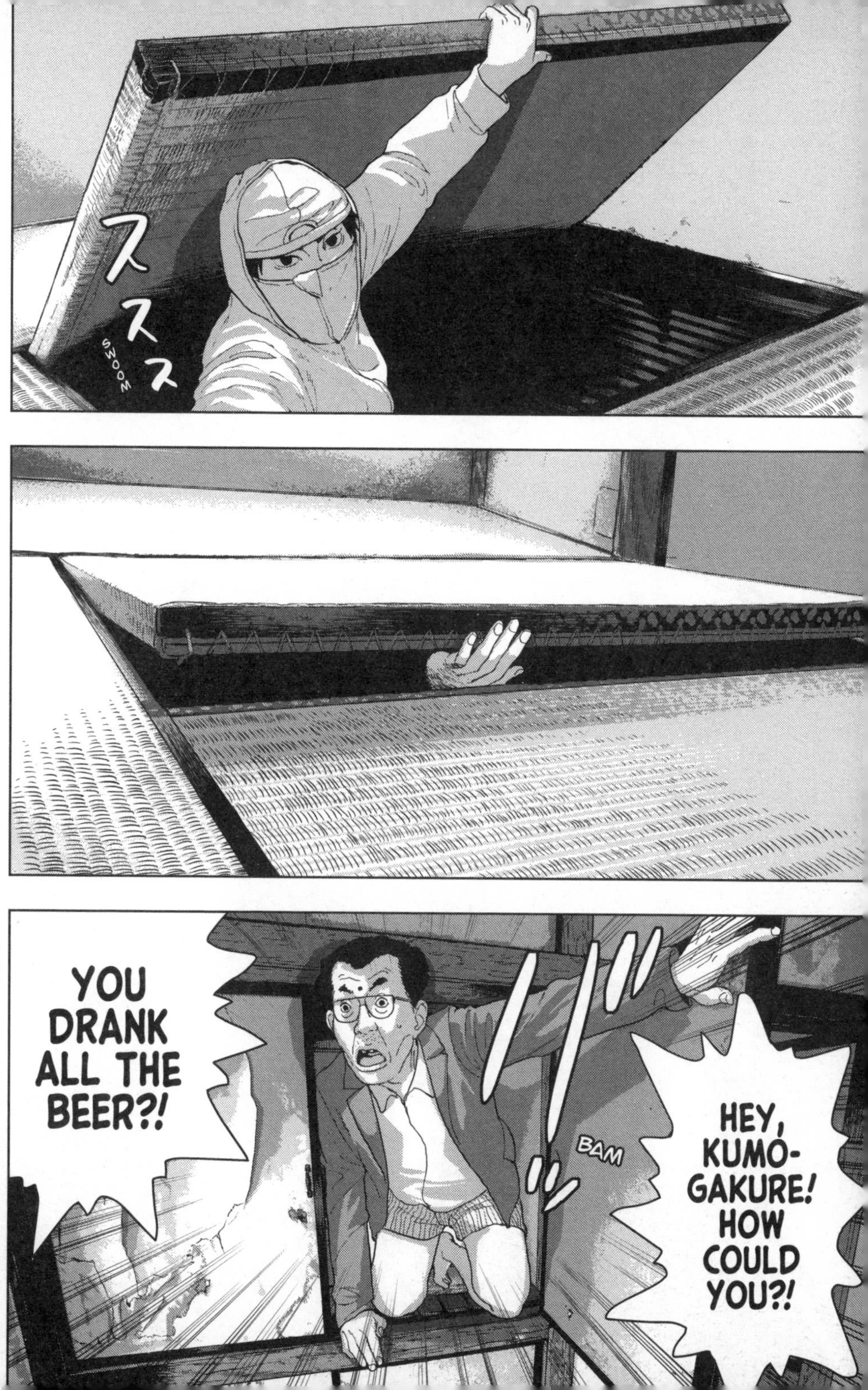
ススス
SWOOM
BAM
HEY, KUMO-GAKURE! HOW COULD YOU?!
YOU DRANK ALL THE BEER?!

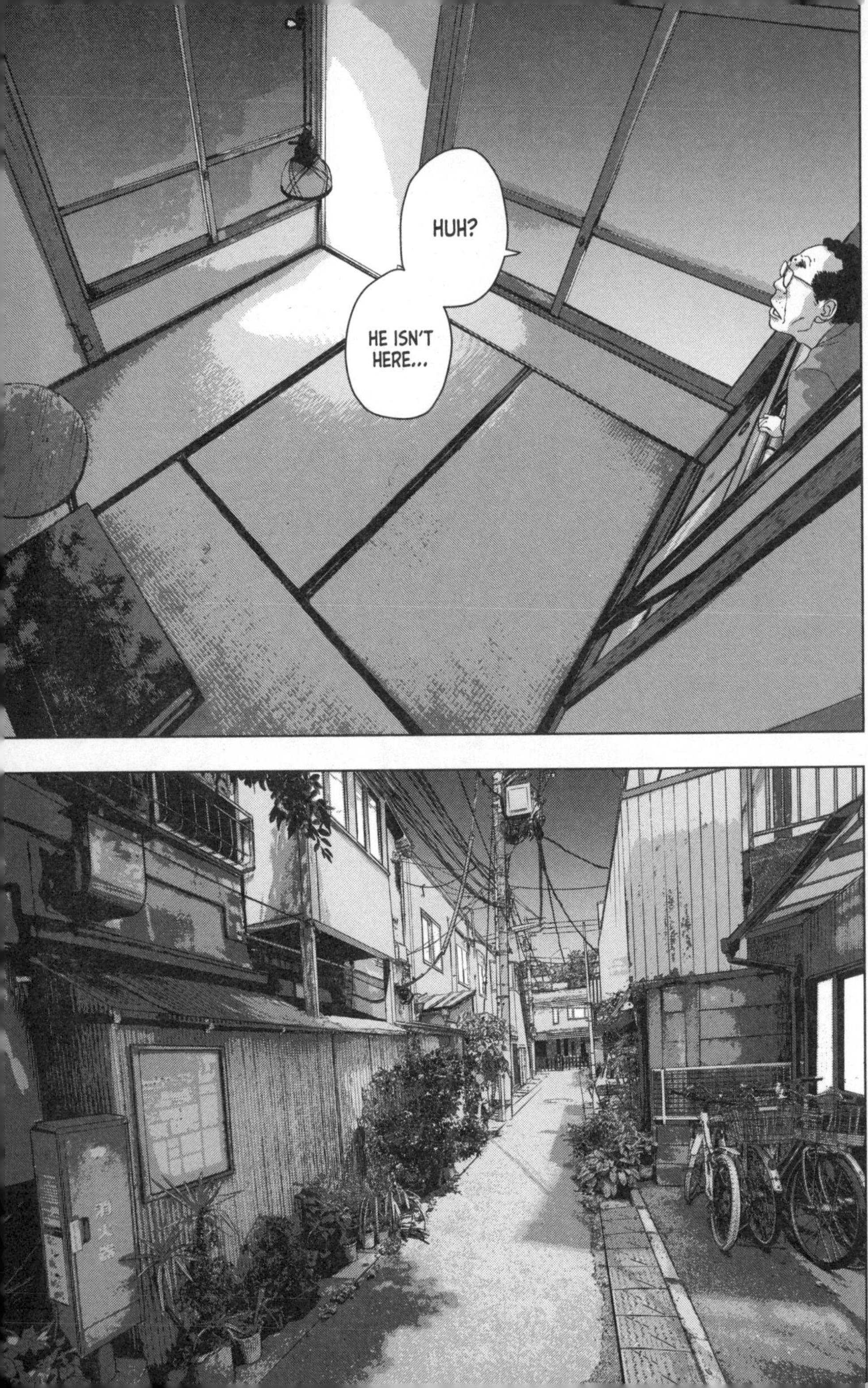
HUH?
HE ISN'T HERE...

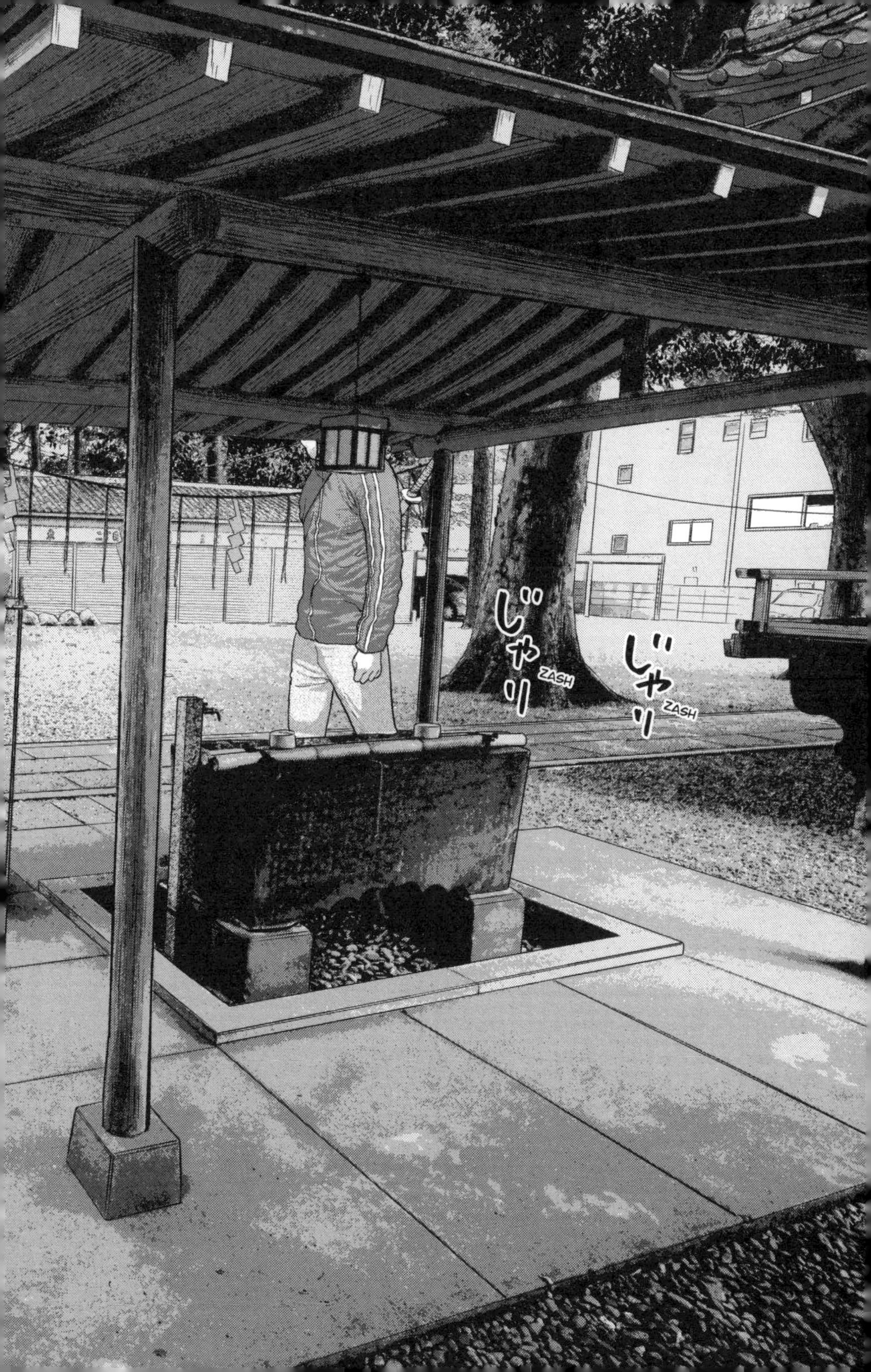
じゃり
ZASH
じゃり
ZASH

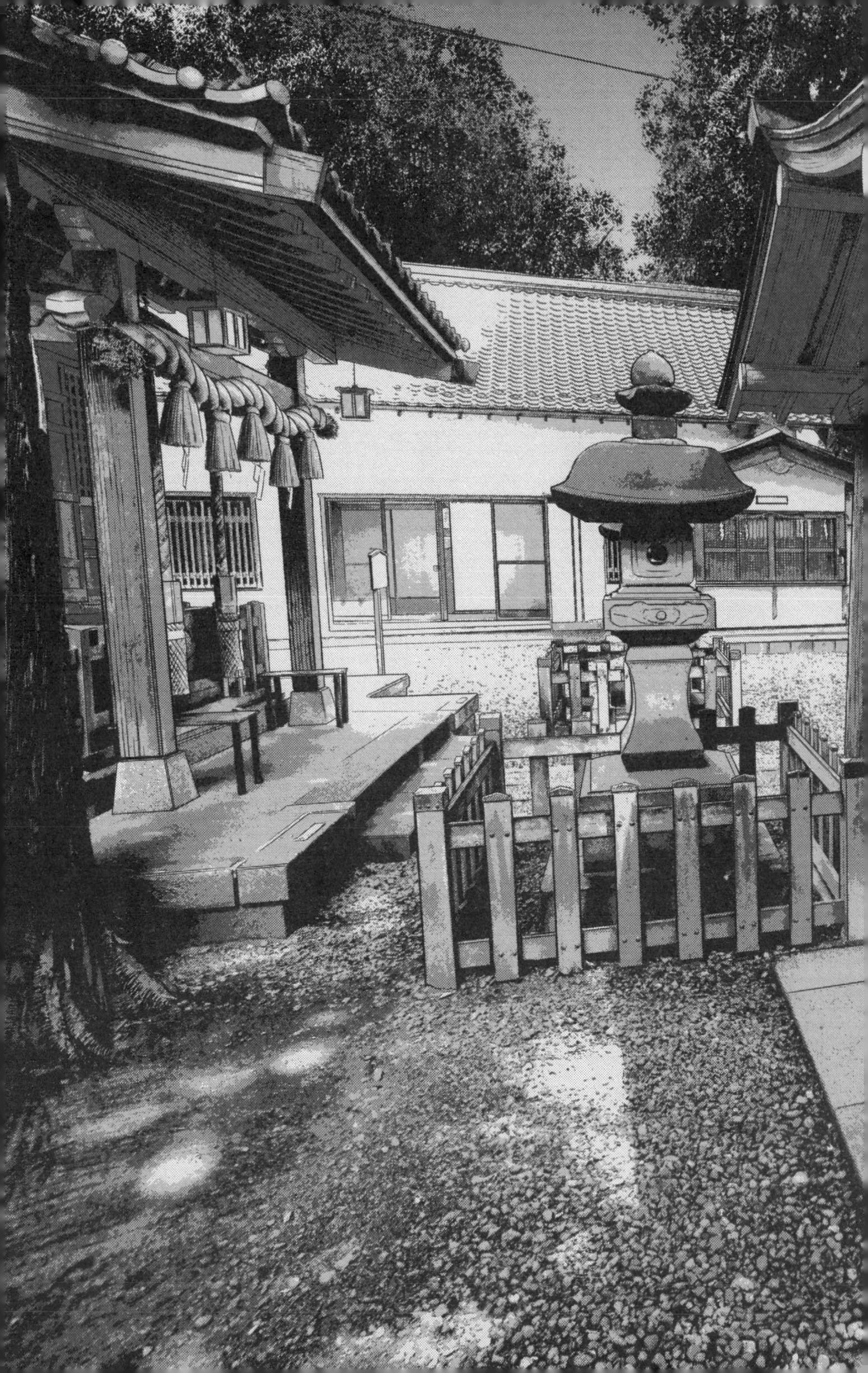

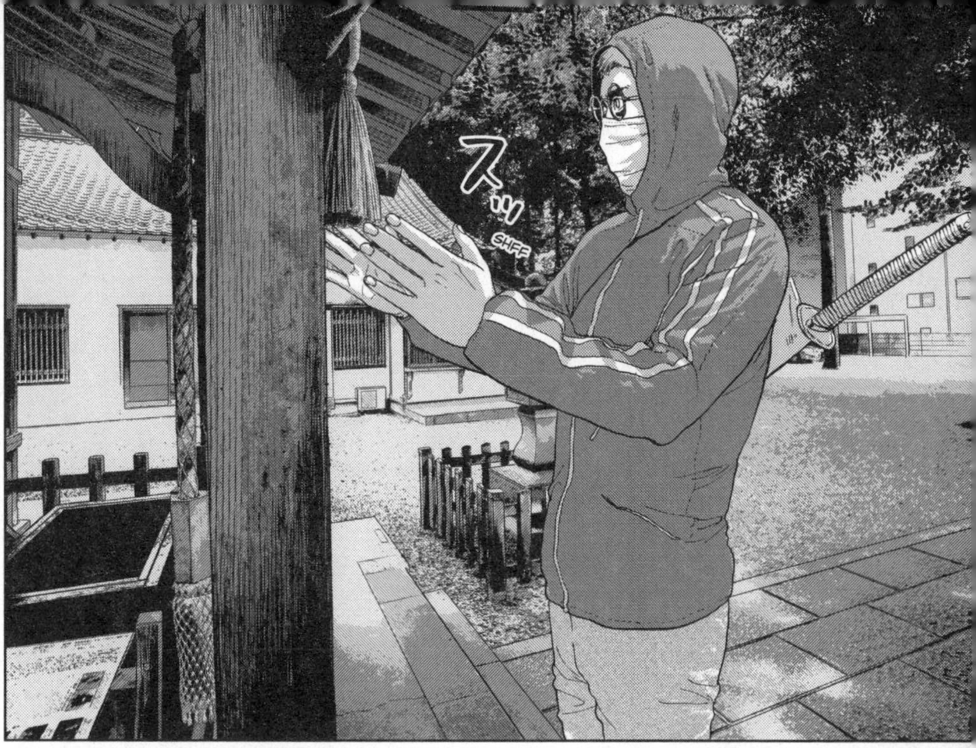
スッ
SHFF
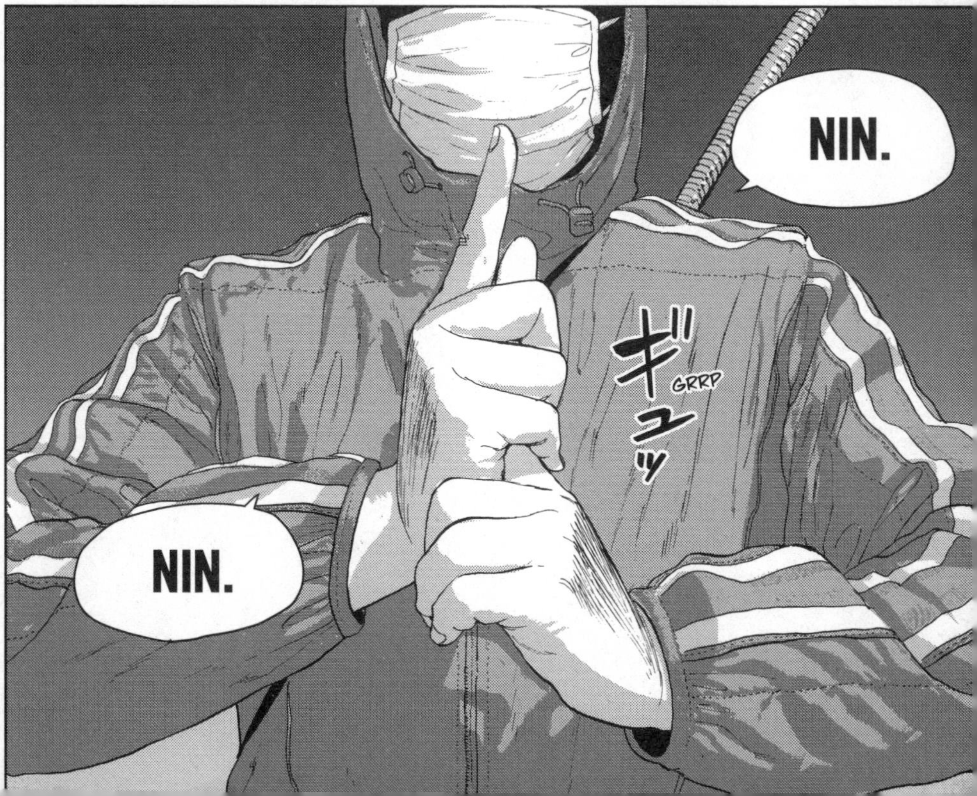
NIN.
ギュッ
GRRP
NIN.

CHAPTER 4

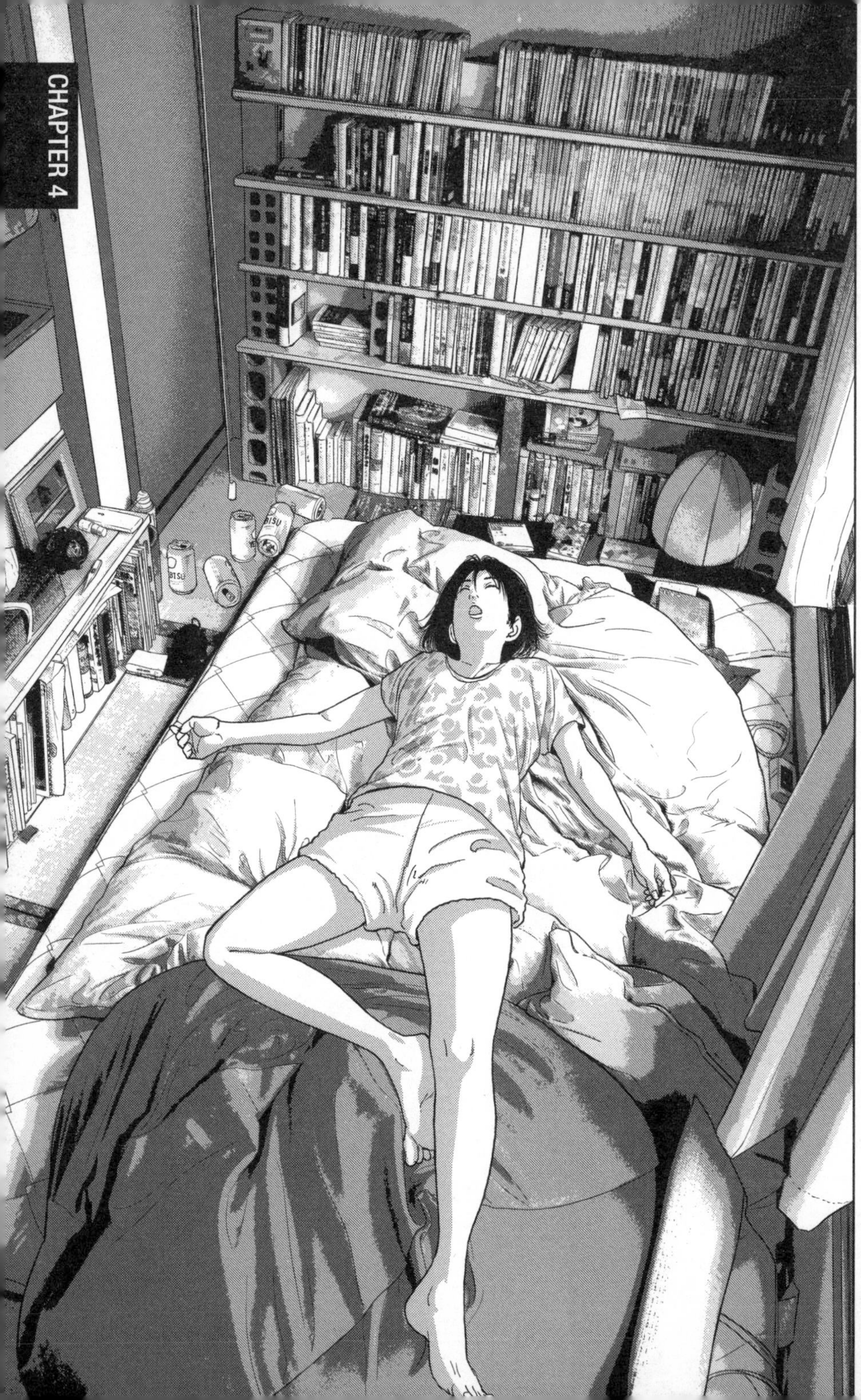
BISU

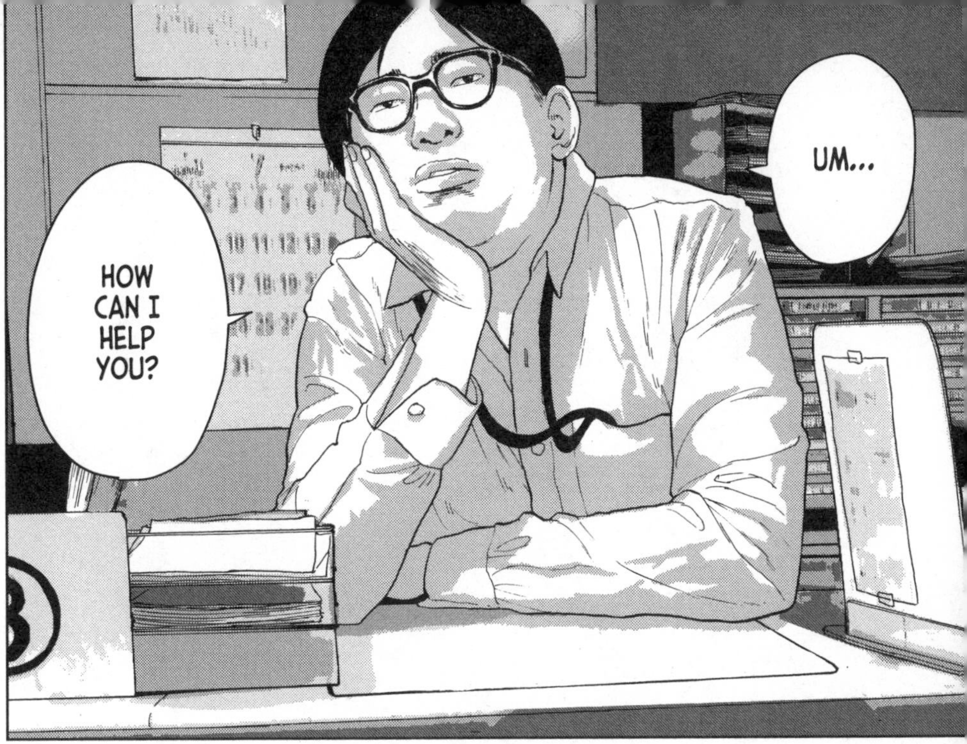
UM...
HOW CAN I HELP YOU?
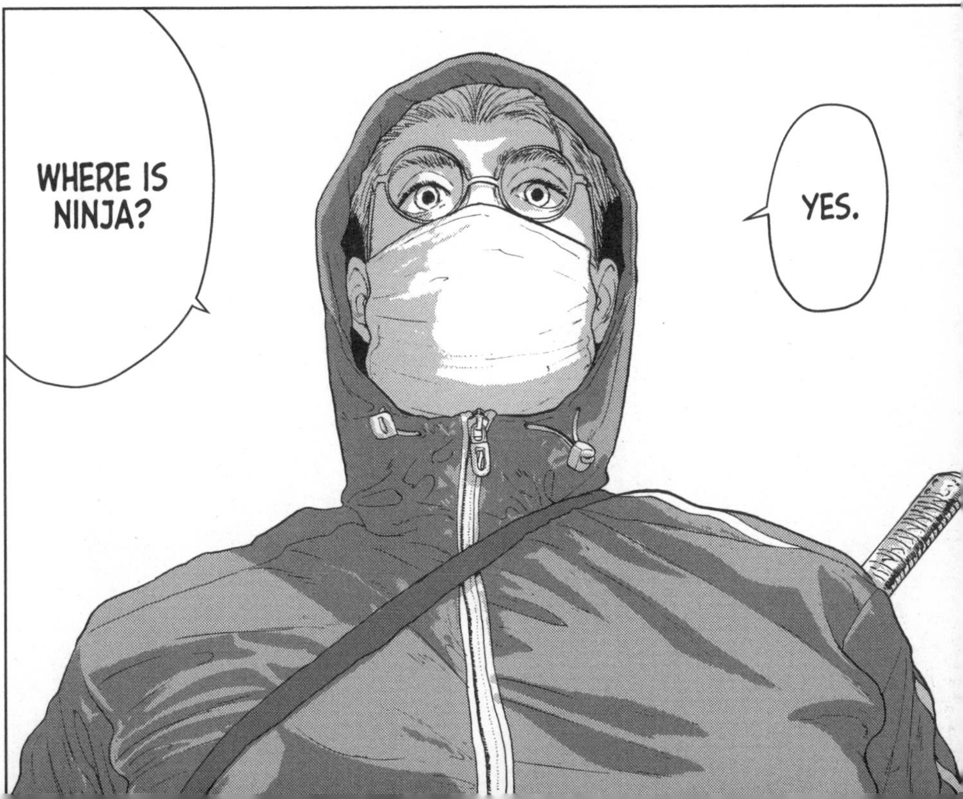
YES.
WHERE IS NINJA?

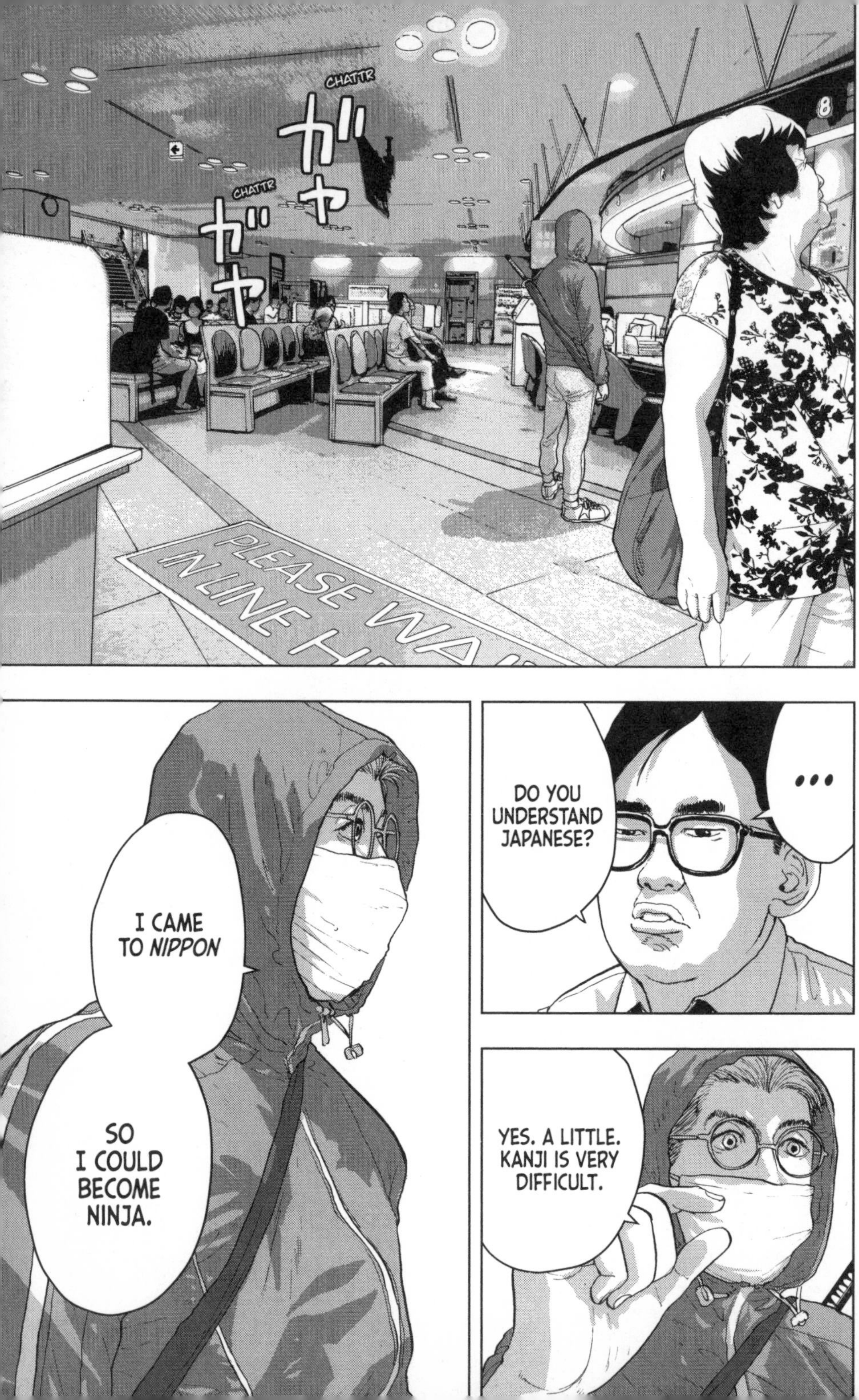
CHATTR
ガヤ
CHATTR
ガヤ
PLEASE
...
DO YOU UNDERSTAND JAPANESE?
YES. A LITTLE. KANJI IS VERY DIFFICULT.
I CAME TO *NIPPON*
SO I COULD BECOME NINJA.

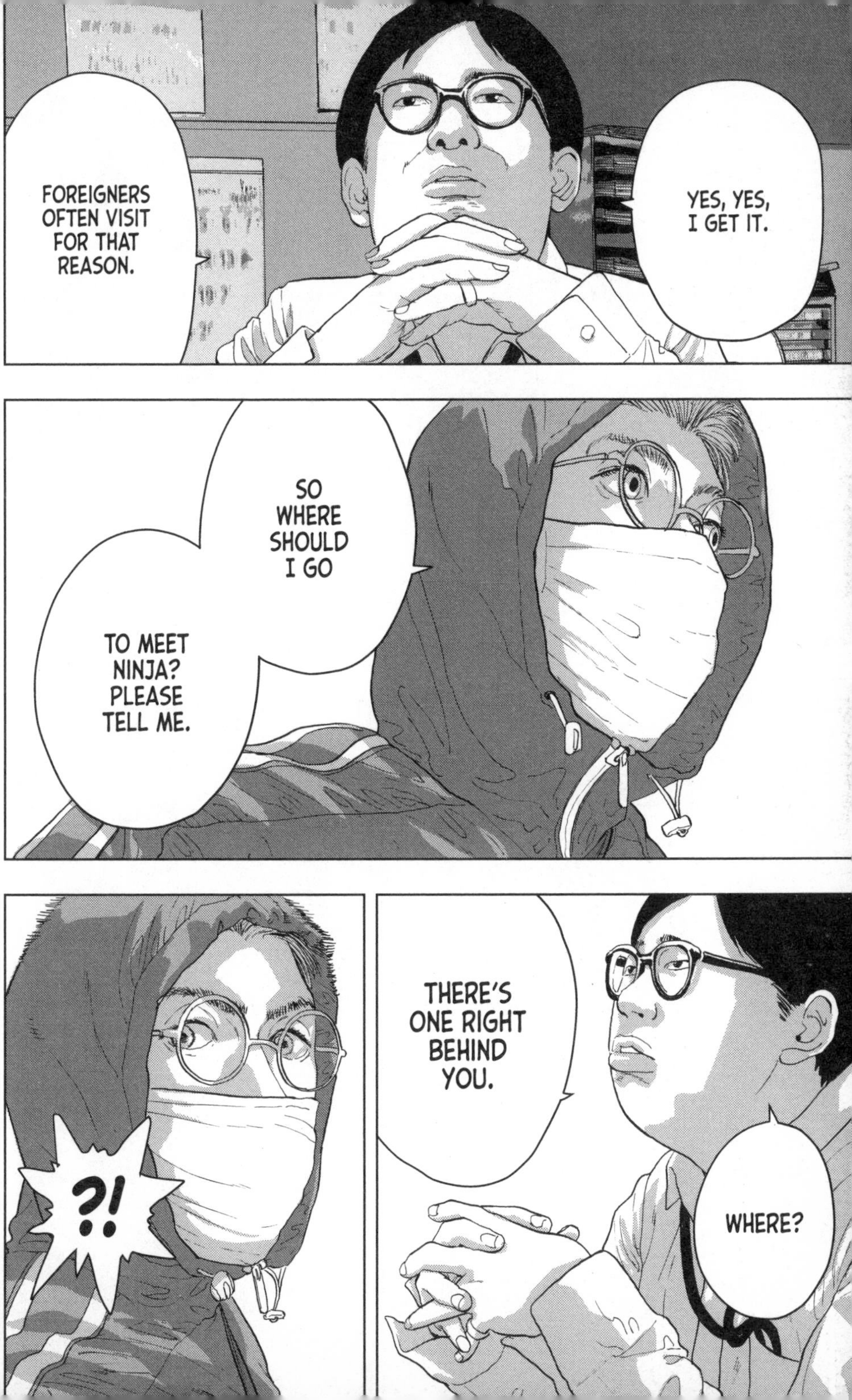
YES, YES, I GET IT.
FOREIGNERS OFTEN VISIT FOR THAT REASON.
SO WHERE SHOULD I GO
TO MEET NINJA? PLEASE TELL ME.
THERE'S ONE RIGHT BEHIND YOU.
WHERE?
?!

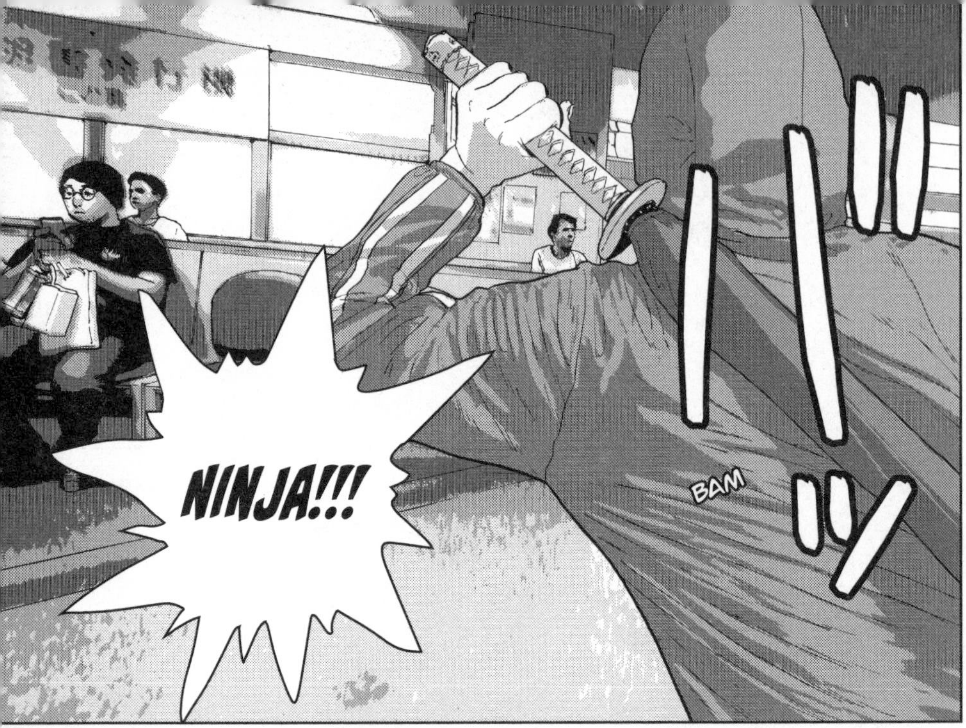
BAM
NINJA!!!

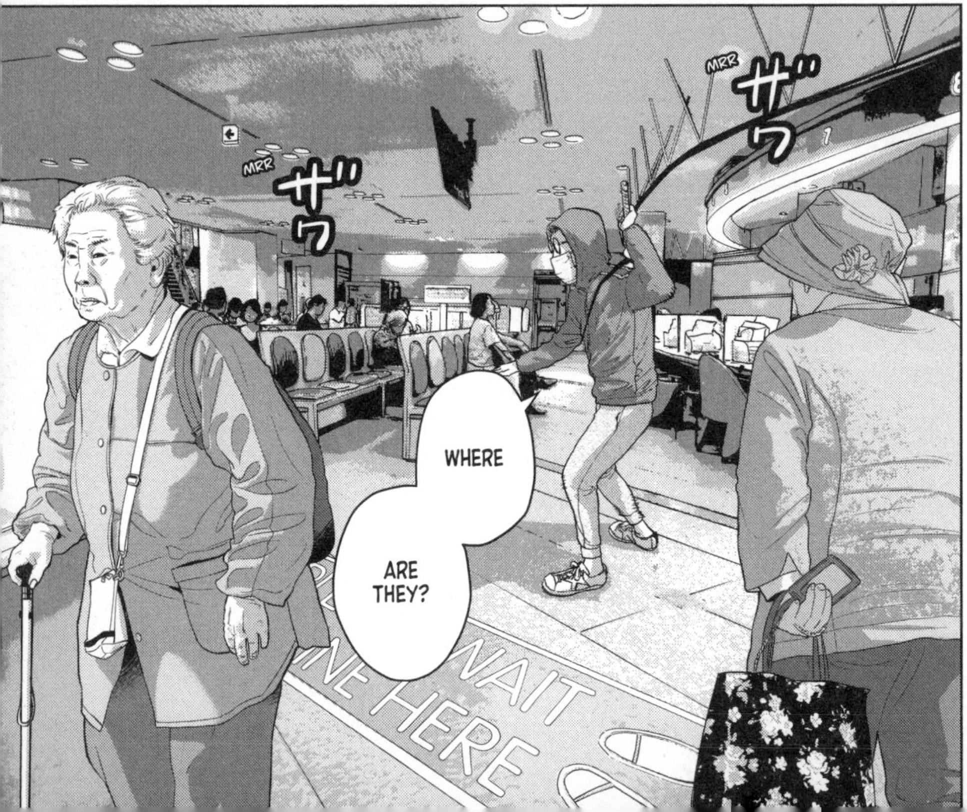
MRR
ザワ
MRR
ザワ
WHERE ARE THEY?

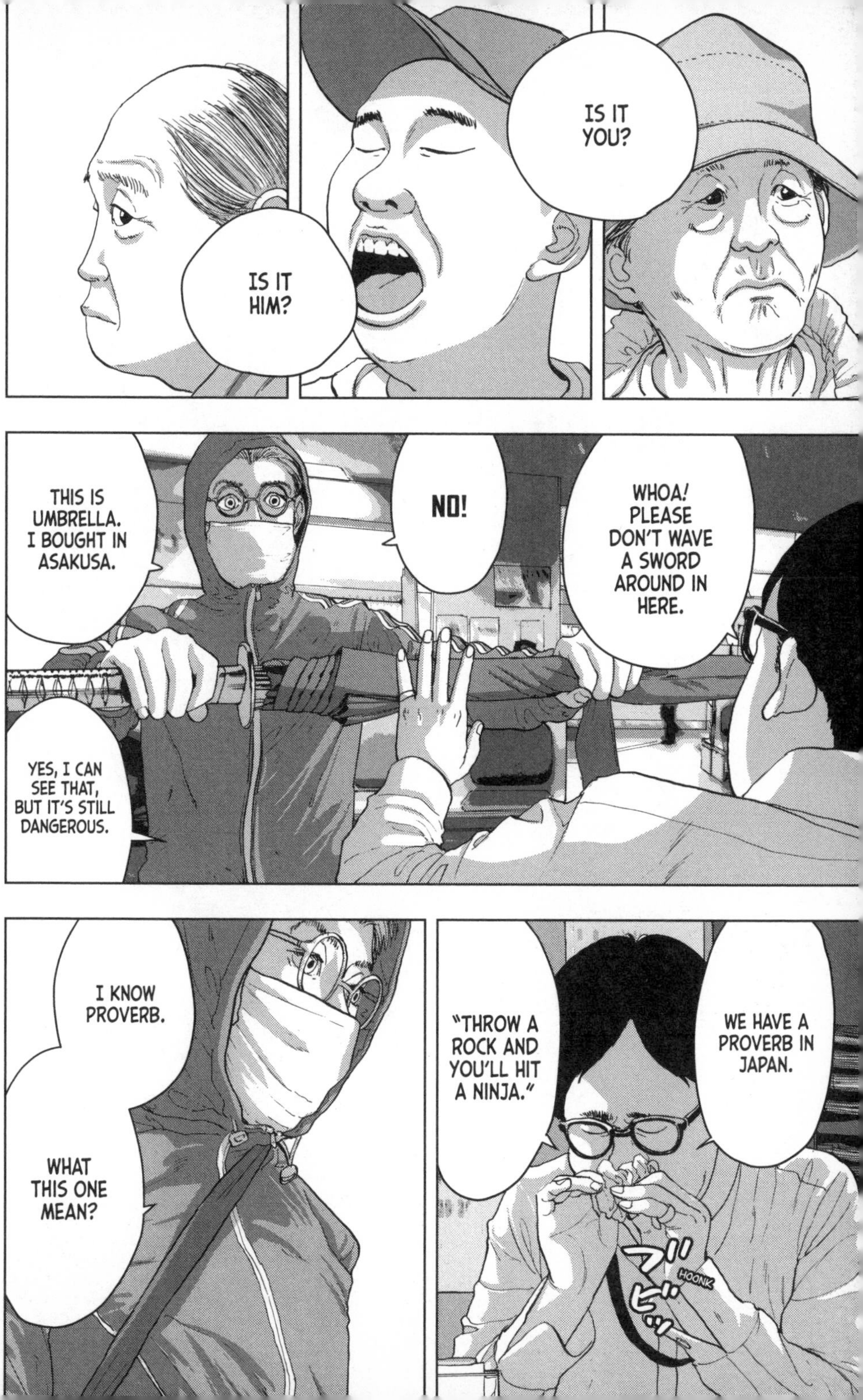
IS IT YOU?
IS IT HIM?
WHOA! PLEASE DON'T WAVE A SWORD AROUND IN HERE.
NO!
THIS IS UMBRELLA. I BOUGHT IN ASAKUSA.
YES, I CAN SEE THAT, BUT IT'S STILL DANGEROUS.
WE HAVE A PROVERB IN JAPAN.
"THROW A ROCK AND YOU'LL HIT A NINJA."
HOONK
I KNOW PROVERB.
WHAT THIS ONE MEAN?

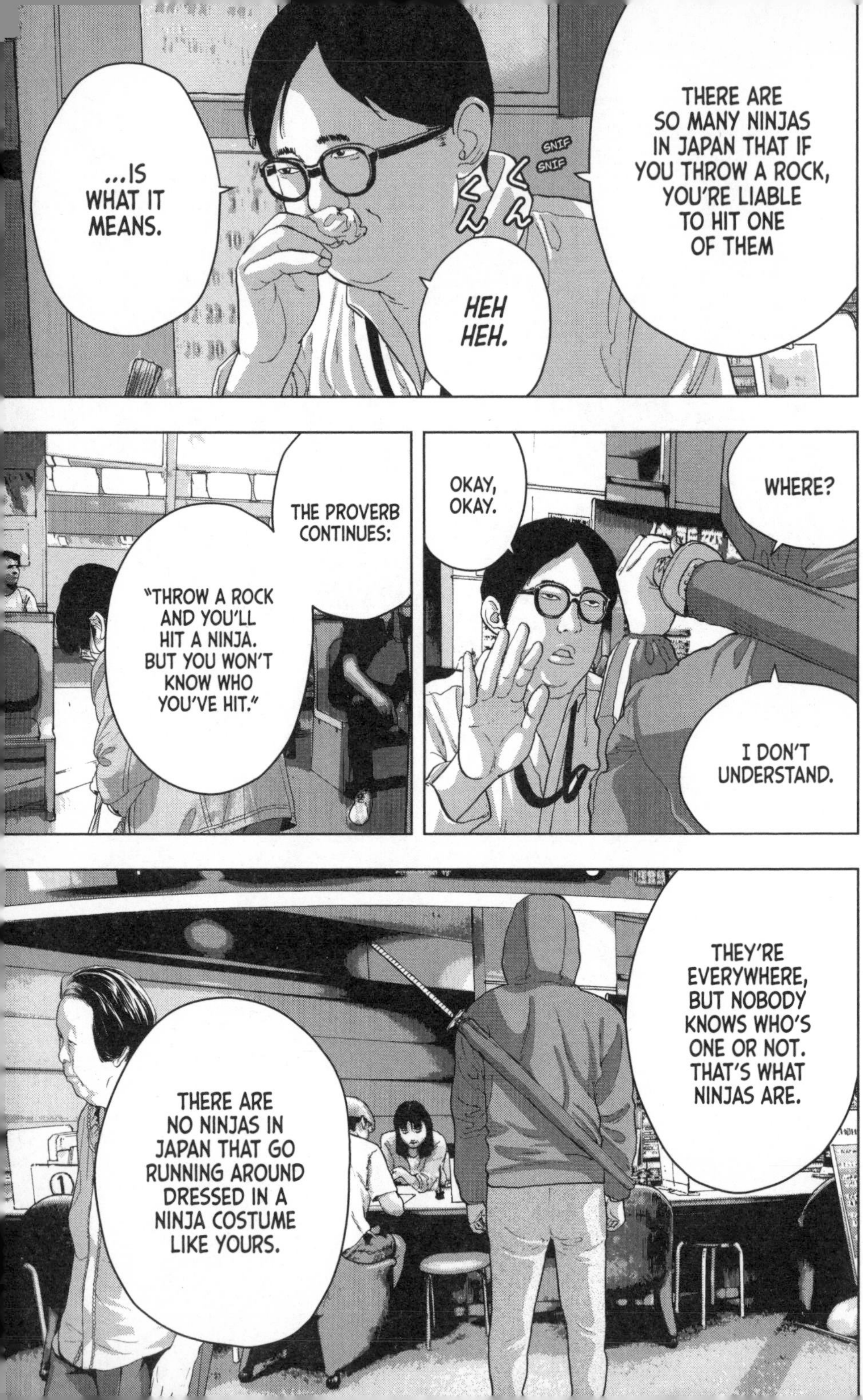
THERE ARE SO MANY NINJAS IN JAPAN THAT IF YOU THROW A ROCK, YOU'RE LIABLE TO HIT ONE OF THEM
SNIF SNIF
くんくん
HEH HEH.
...IS WHAT IT MEANS.
WHERE?
OKAY, OKAY.
I DON'T UNDERSTAND.
THE PROVERB CONTINUES:
"THROW A ROCK AND YOU'LL HIT A NINJA. BUT YOU WON'T KNOW WHO YOU'VE HIT."
THEY'RE EVERYWHERE, BUT NOBODY KNOWS WHO'S ONE OR NOT. THAT'S WHAT NINJAS ARE.
THERE ARE NO NINJAS IN JAPAN THAT GO RUNNING AROUND DRESSED IN A NINJA COSTUME LIKE YOURS.

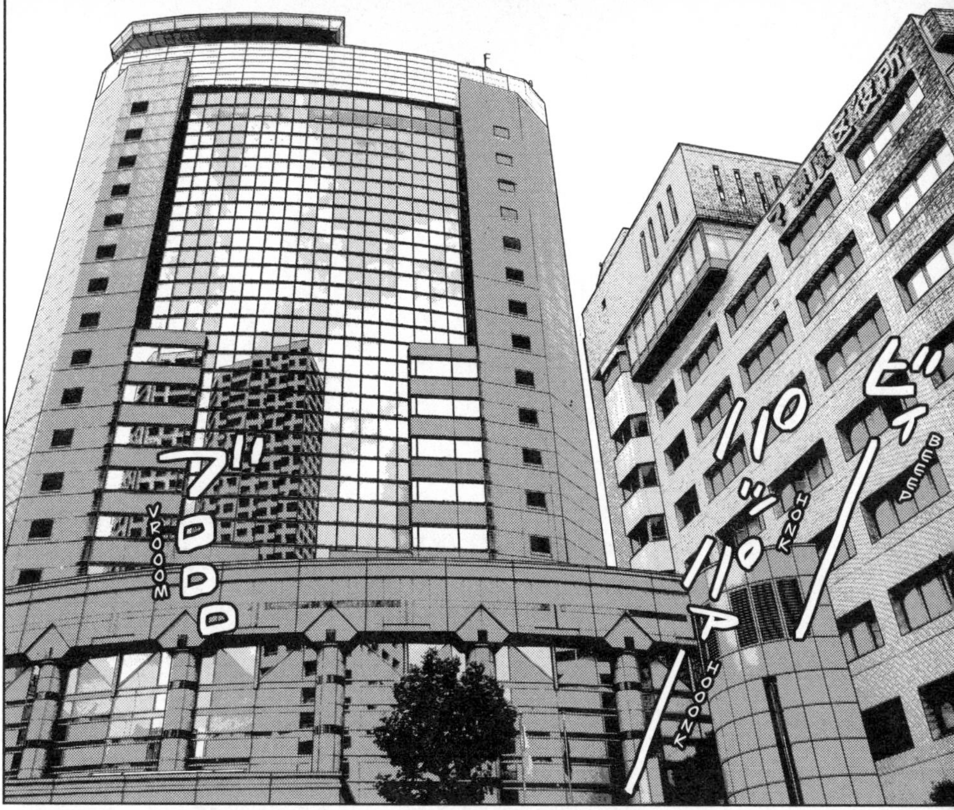
ビィー
BEEEP
パパ
HONK
パー
HOOONK
ブロロロ
VROOOM

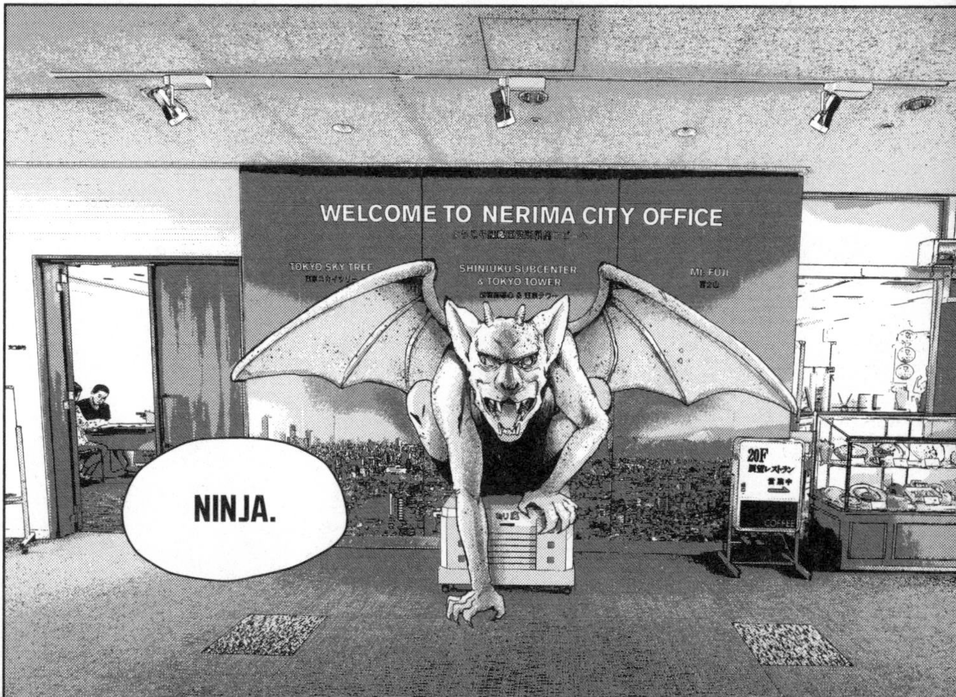
WELCOME TO NERIMA CITY OFFICE
TOKYO SKY TREE
SHINJUKU SUBCENTER & TOKYO TOWER
Mt. FUJI
20F
COFFEE
NINJA.

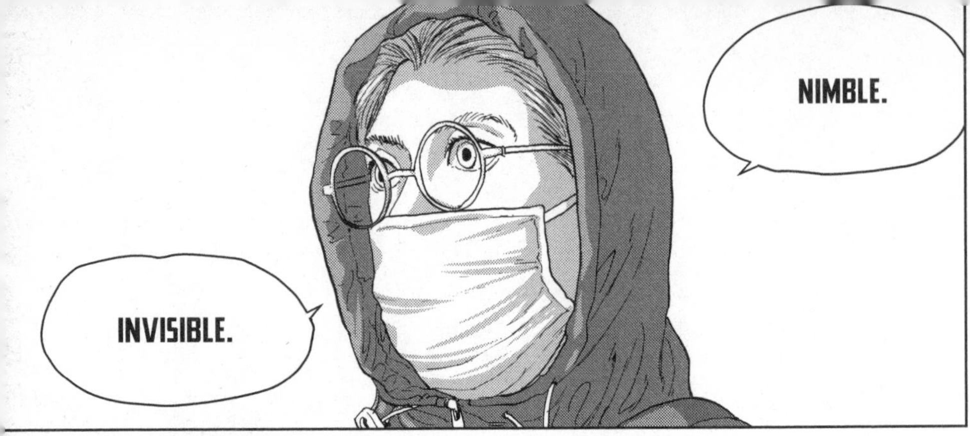
NIMBLE.
INVISIBLE.
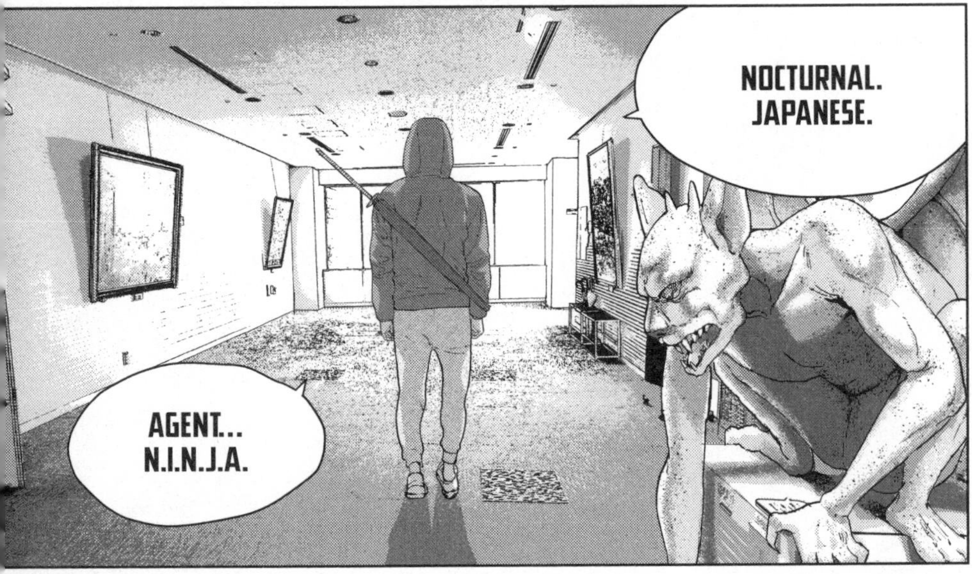
NOCTURNAL. JAPANESE.
AGENT... N.I.N.J.A.
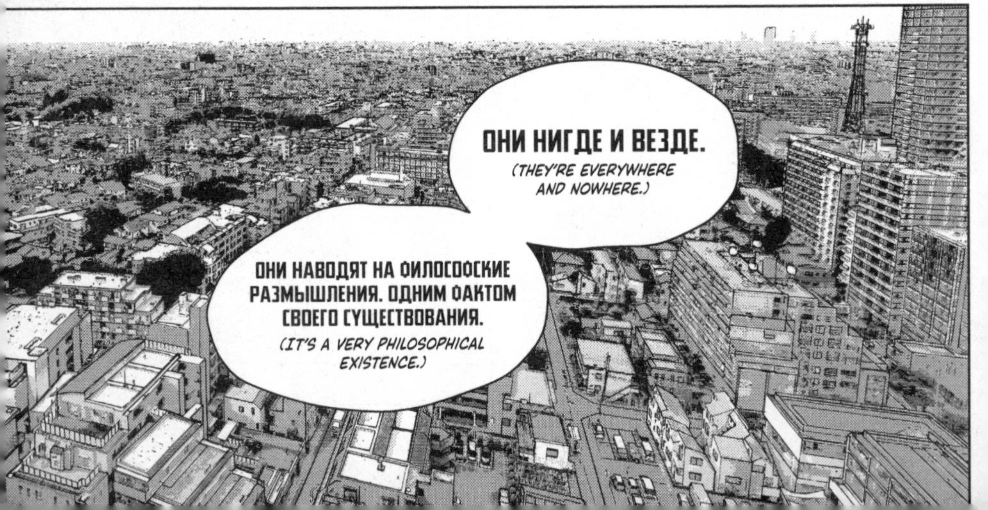
ОНИ НИГДЕ И ВЕЗДЕ.
(THEY'RE EVERYWHERE AND NOWHERE.)
ОНИ НАВОДЯТ НА ФИЛОСОФСКИЕ РАЗМЫШЛЕНИЯ. ОДНИМ ФАКТОМ СВОЕГО СУЩЕСТВОВАНИЯ.
(IT'S A VERY PHILOSOPHICAL EXISTENCE.)

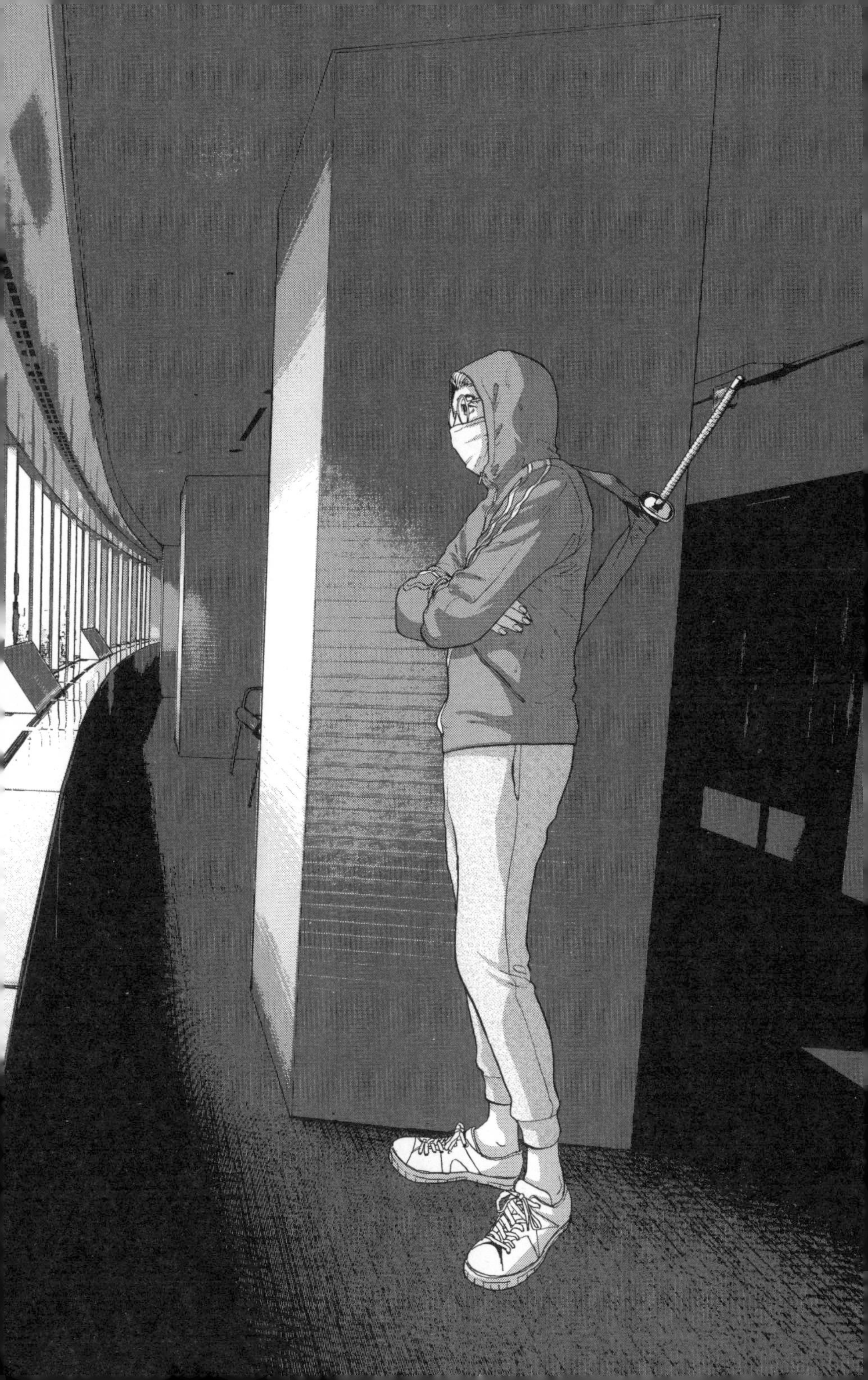

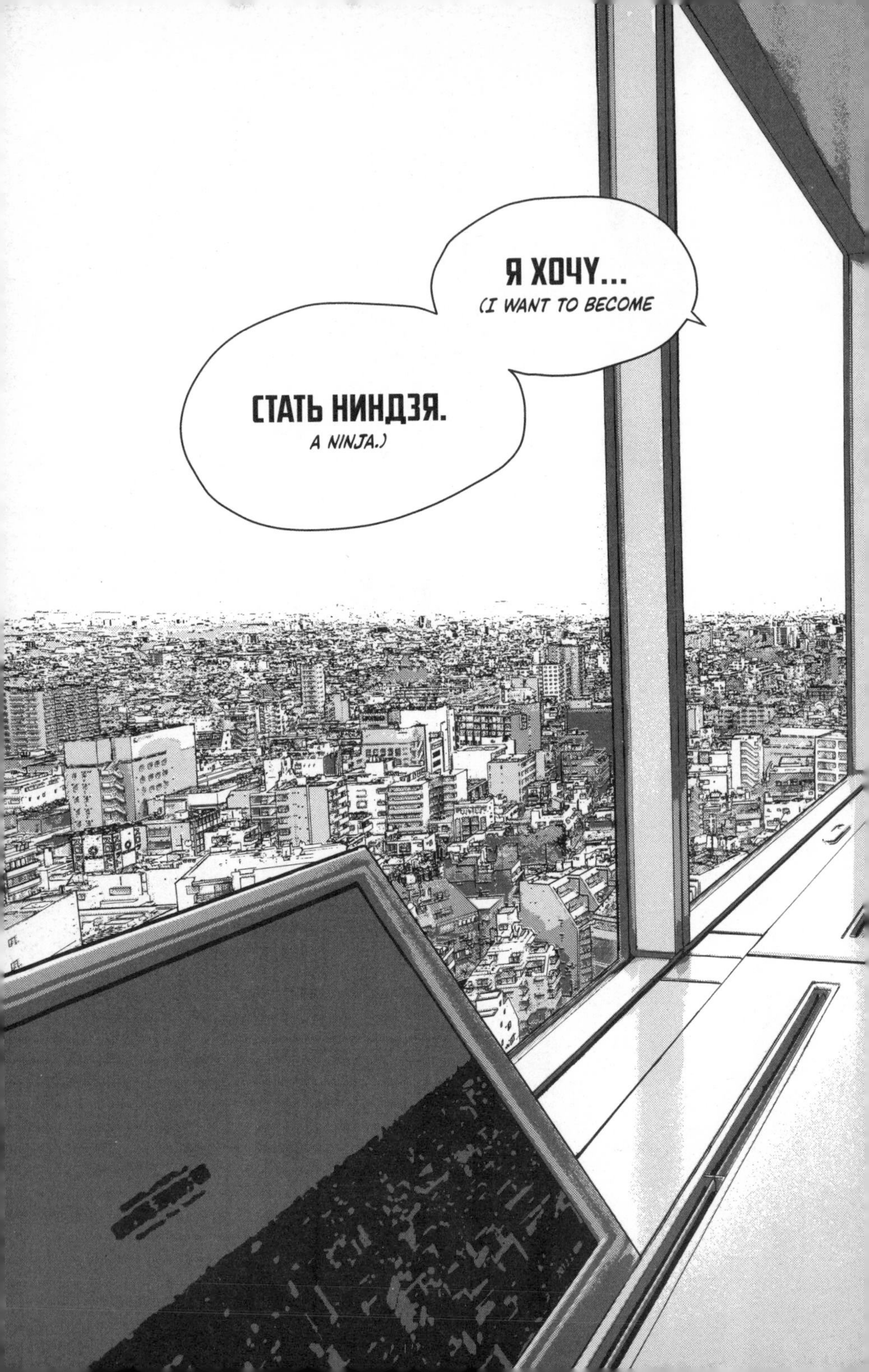
Я ХОЧУ...
(I WANT TO BECOME
СТАТЬ НИНДЗЯ.
A NINJA.)

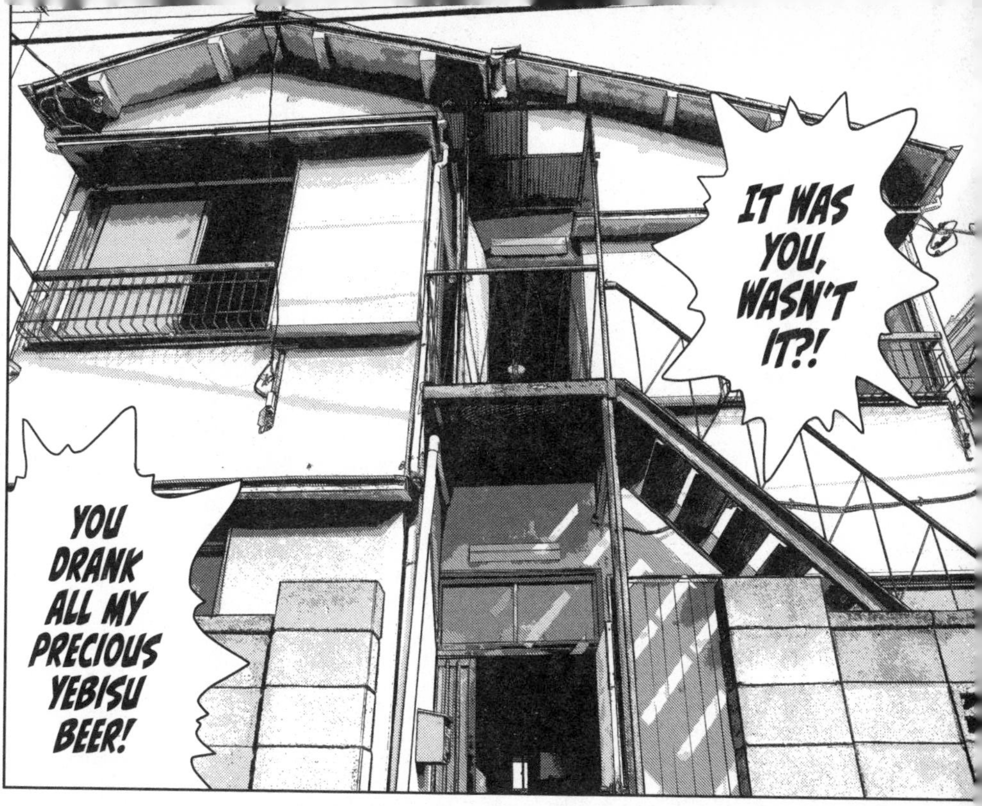
IT WAS YOU, WASN'T IT?!
YOU DRANK ALL MY PRECIOUS YEBISU BEER!
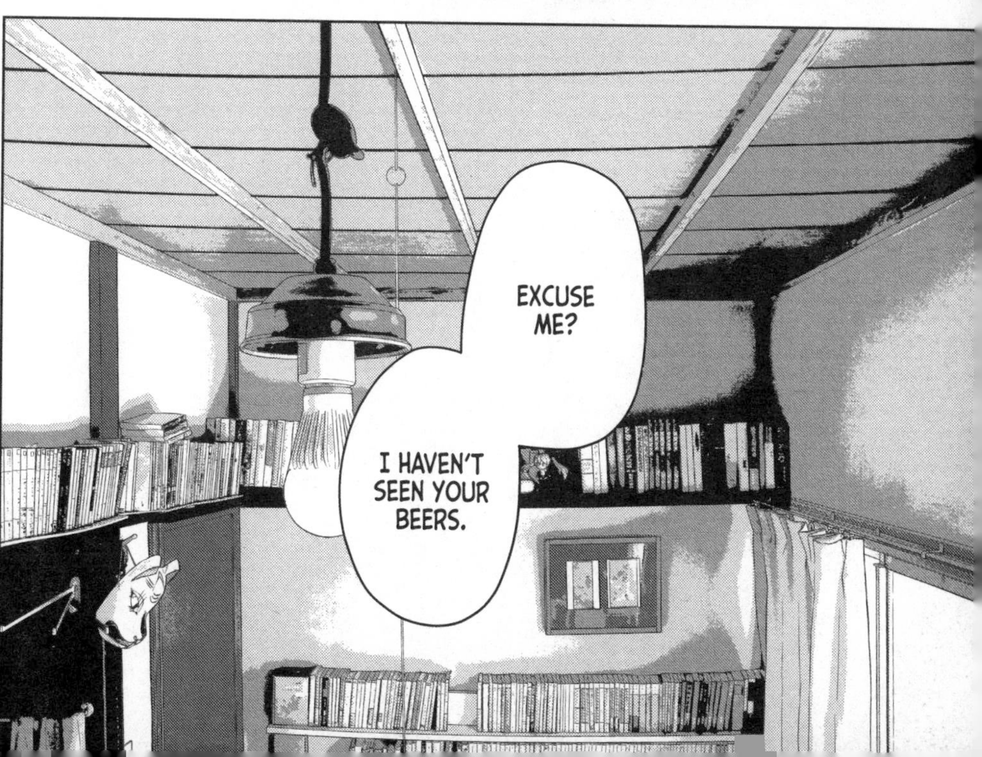
EXCUSE ME?
I HAVEN'T SEEN YOUR BEERS.

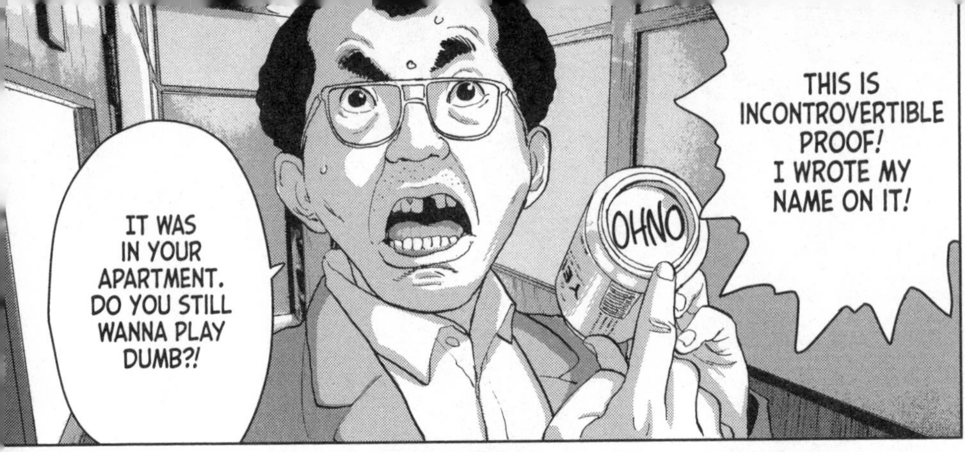
THIS IS INCONTROVERTIBLE PROOF! I WROTE MY NAME ON IT!
OHNO
IT WAS IN YOUR APARTMENT. DO YOU STILL WANNA PLAY DUMB?!

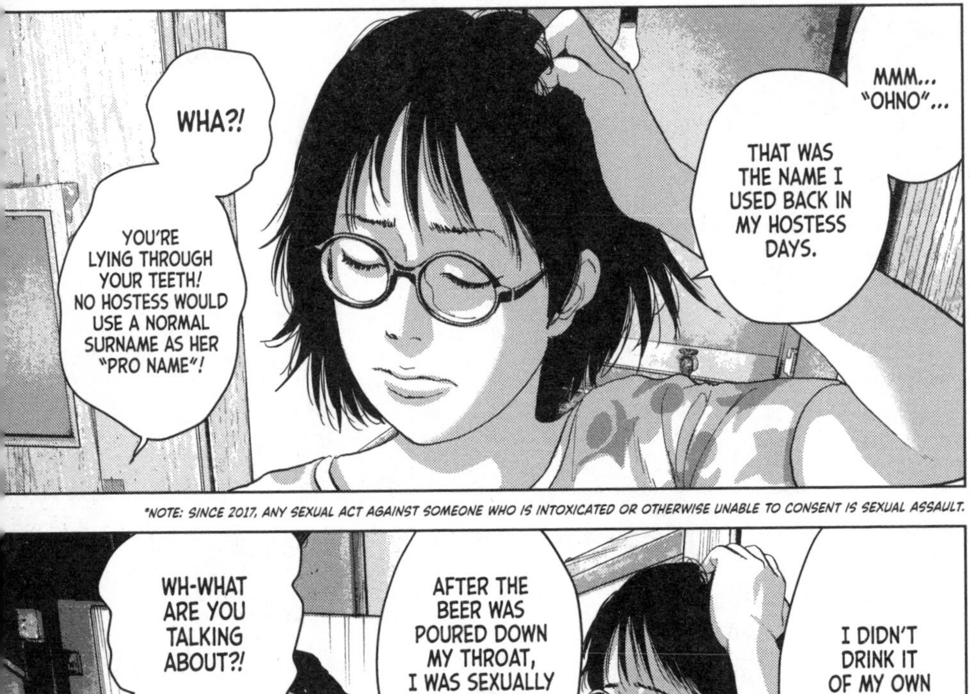
MMM... "OHNO"...
THAT WAS THE NAME I USED BACK IN MY HOSTESS DAYS.
WHA?!
YOU'RE LYING THROUGH YOUR TEETH! NO HOSTESS WOULD USE A NORMAL SURNAME AS HER "PRO NAME"!

*NOTE: SINCE 2017, ANY SEXUAL ACT AGAINST SOMEONE WHO IS INTOXICATED OR OTHERWISE UNABLE TO CONSENT IS SEXUAL ASSAULT.

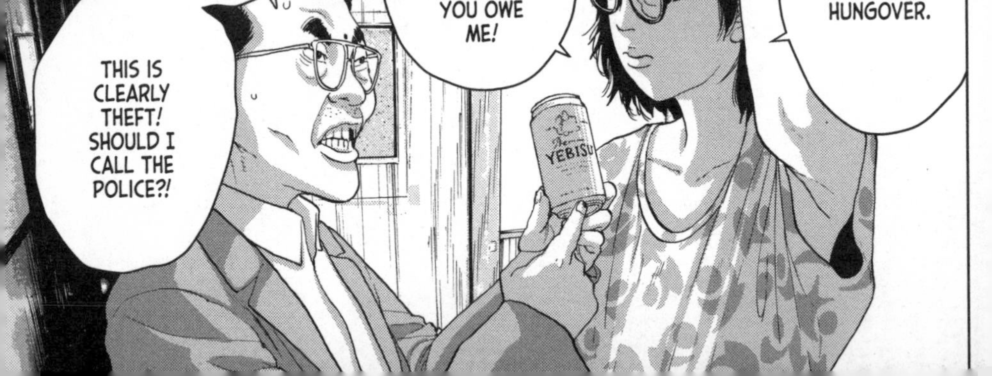
I DIDN'T DRINK IT OF MY OWN WILL. I'M HUNGOVER.
AFTER THE BEER WAS POURED DOWN MY THROAT, I WAS SEXUALLY ASSAULTED. YOU OWE ME!
WH-WHAT ARE YOU TALKING ABOUT?!
THIS IS CLEARLY THEFT! SHOULD I CALL THE POLICE?!
YEBISU

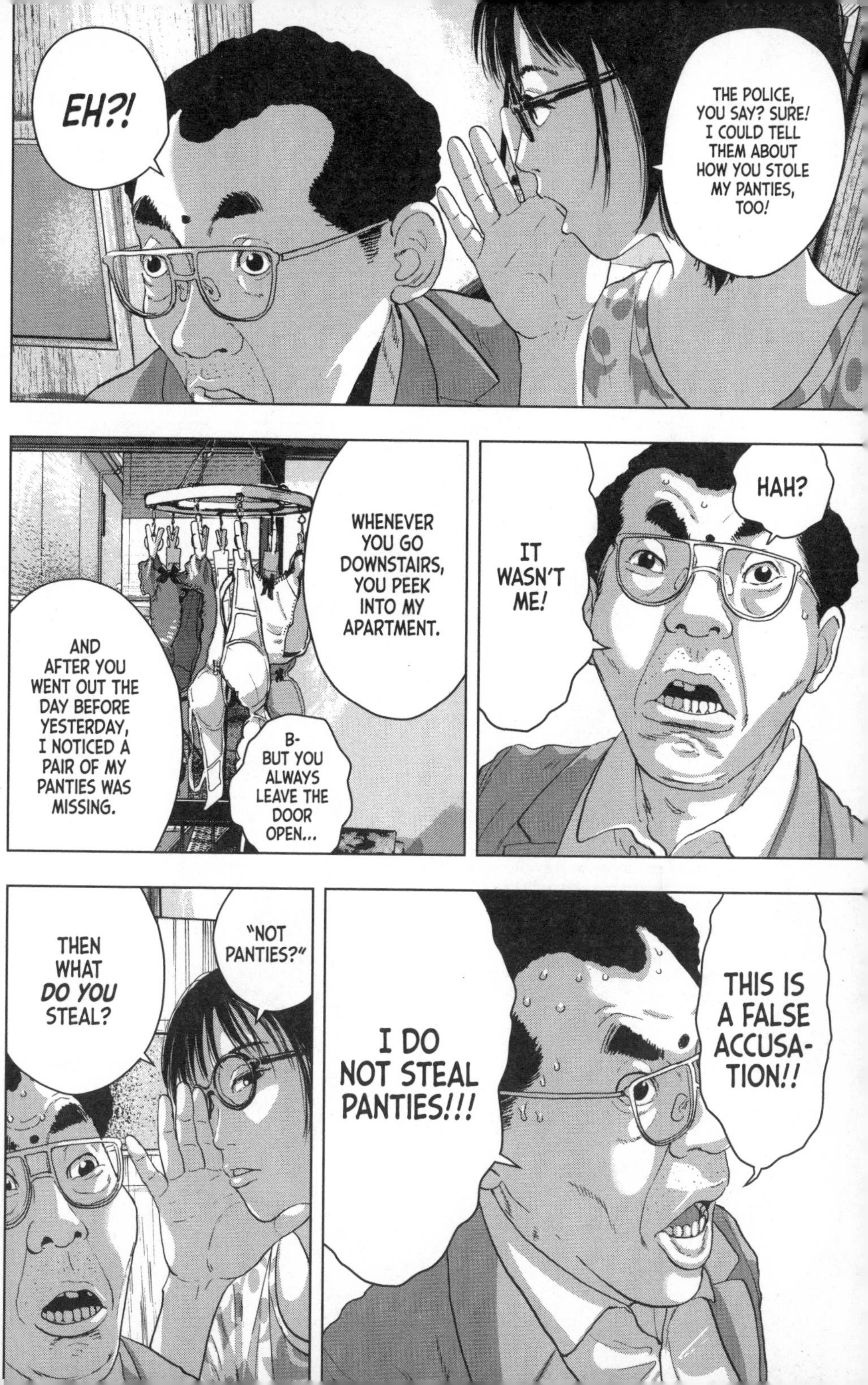
THE POLICE, YOU SAY? SURE! I COULD TELL THEM ABOUT HOW YOU STOLE MY PANTIES, TOO!
EH?!
HAH?
IT WASN'T ME!
WHENEVER YOU GO DOWNSTAIRS, YOU PEEK INTO MY APARTMENT.
AND AFTER YOU WENT OUT THE DAY BEFORE YESTERDAY, I NOTICED A PAIR OF MY PANTIES WAS MISSING.
B- BUT YOU ALWAYS LEAVE THE DOOR OPEN...
THIS IS A FALSE ACCUSA-TION!!
I DO NOT STEAL PANTIES!!!
"NOT PANTIES?"
THEN WHAT *DO YOU* STEAL?

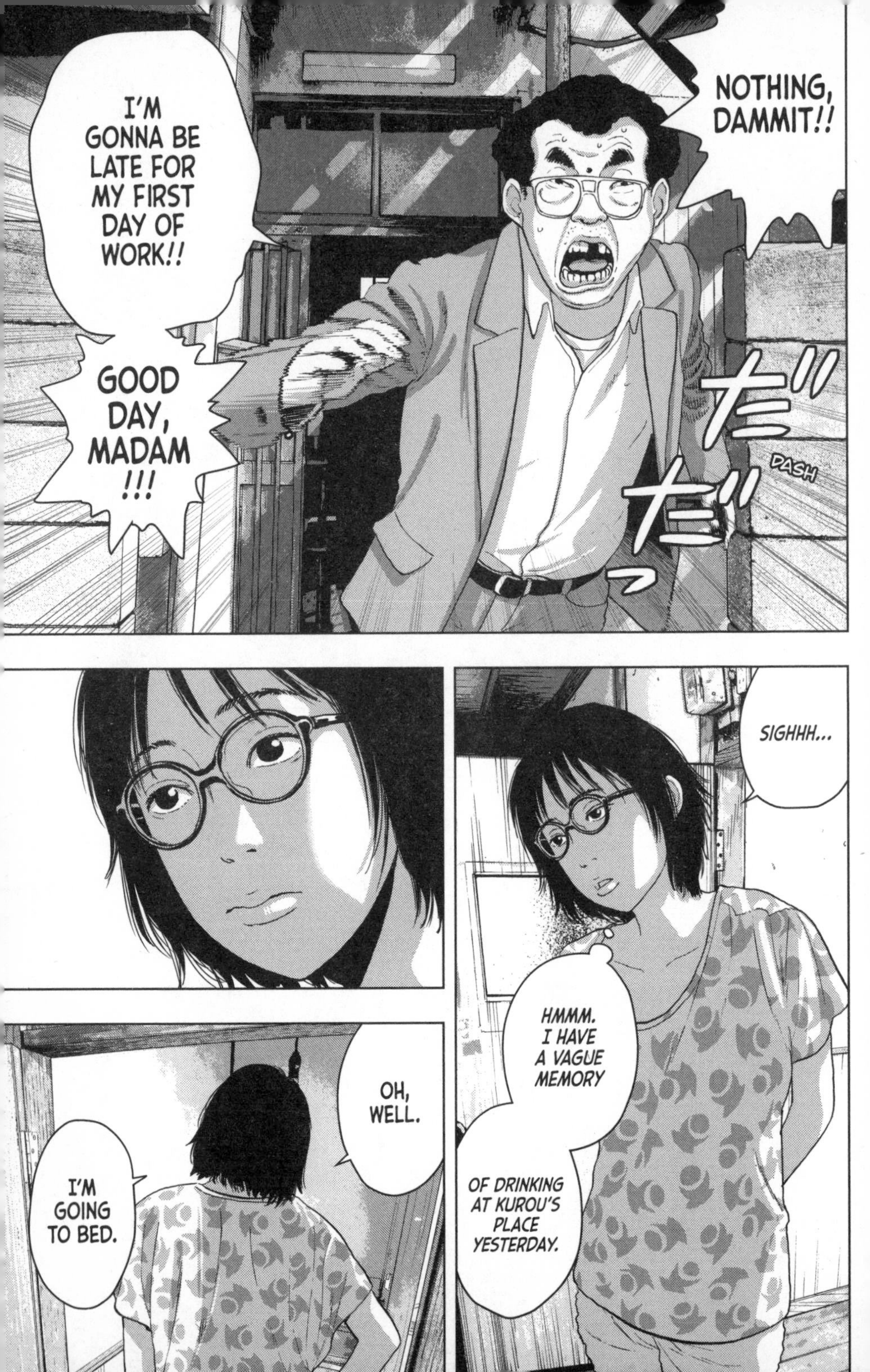
NOTHING, DAMMIT!!
I'M GONNA BE LATE FOR MY FIRST DAY OF WORK!!
GOOD DAY, MADAM!!!
DASH
SIGHHH...
HMMM. I HAVE A VAGUE MEMORY
OF DRINKING AT KUROU'S PLACE YESTERDAY.
OH, WELL.
I'M GOING TO BED.

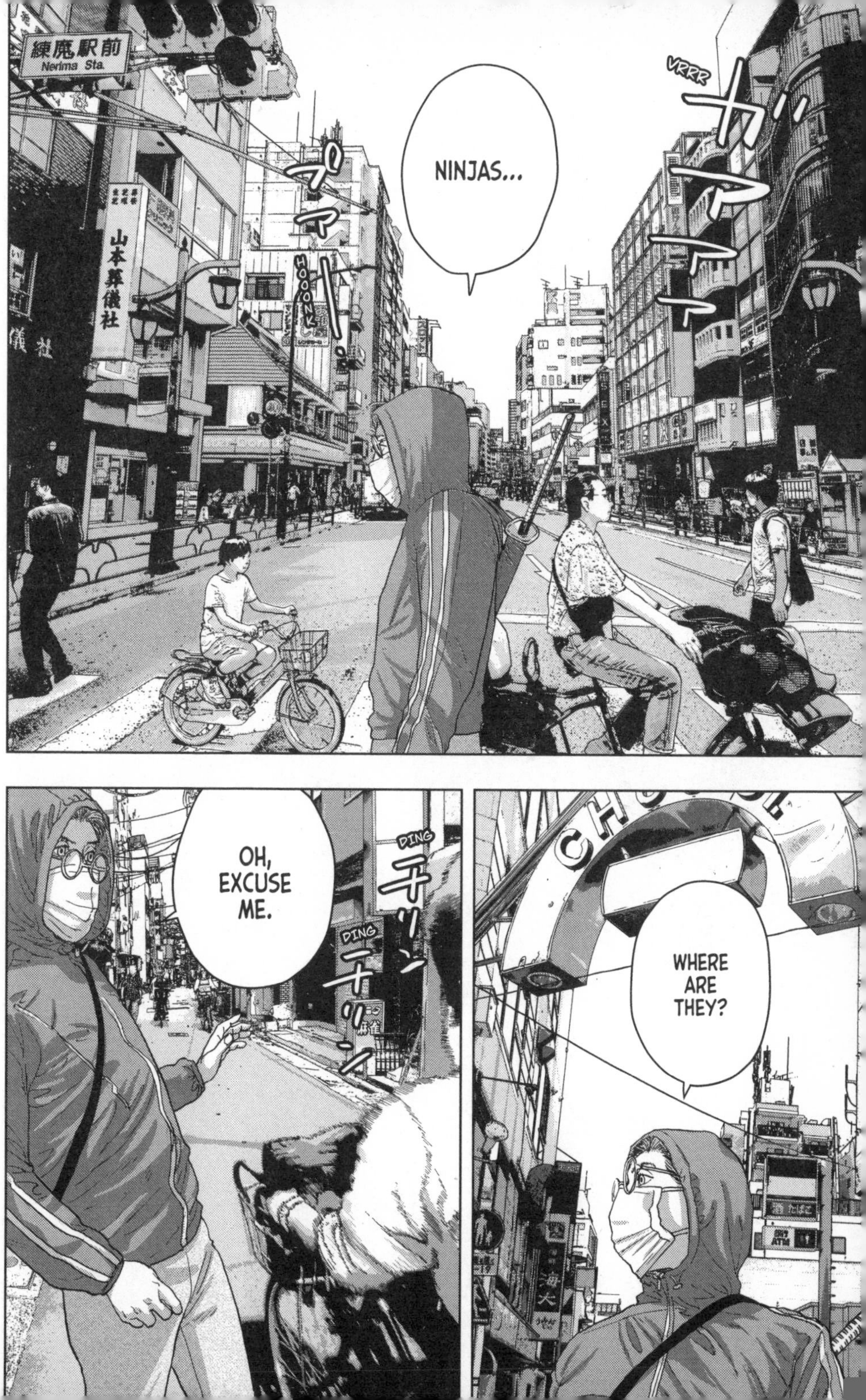
練魔駅前
Nerima Sta.
VRRR
NINJAS...
HOOONK
山本葬儀社
WHERE ARE THEY?
DING
DING
OH, EXCUSE ME.

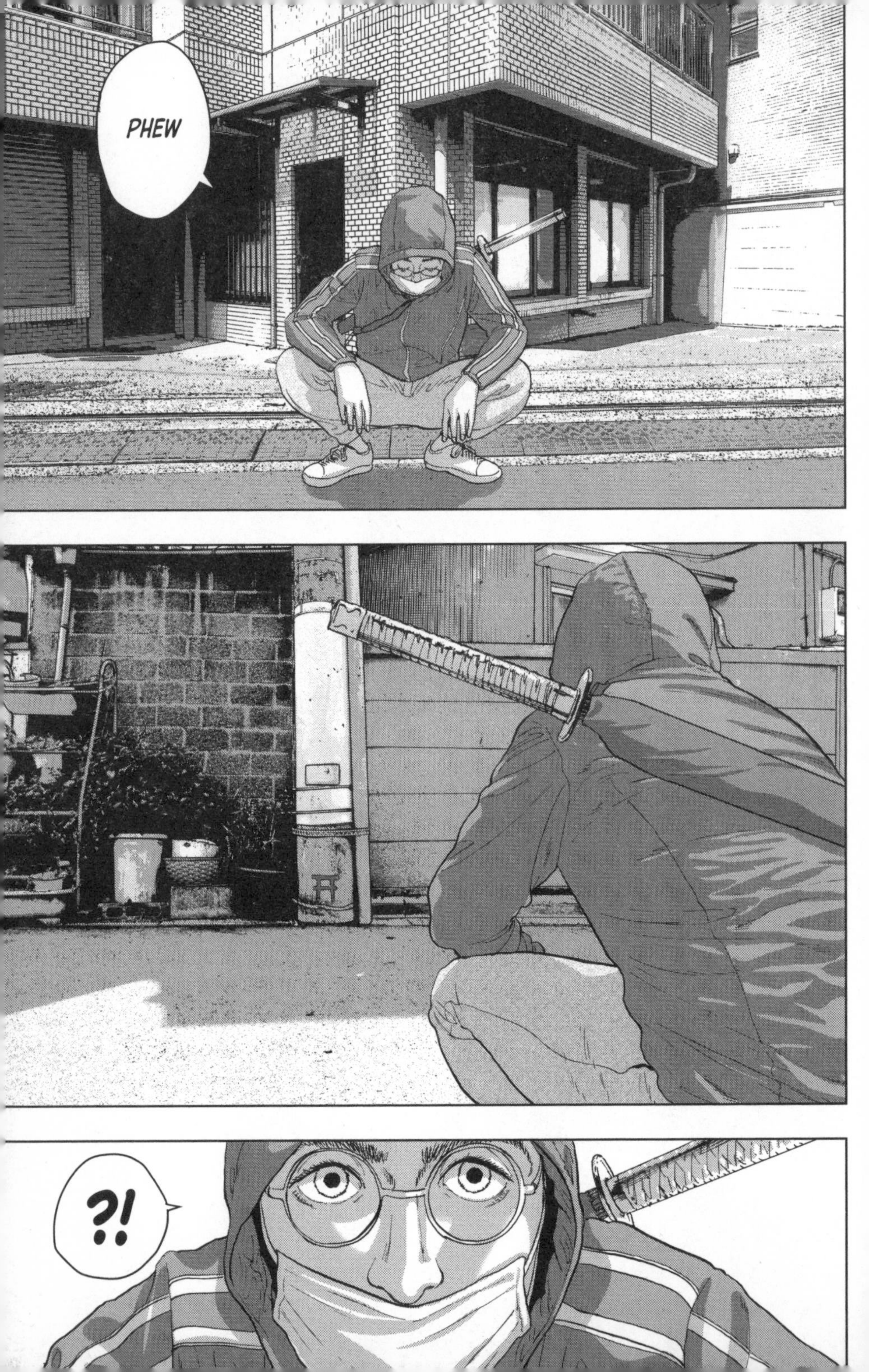
PHEW
?!

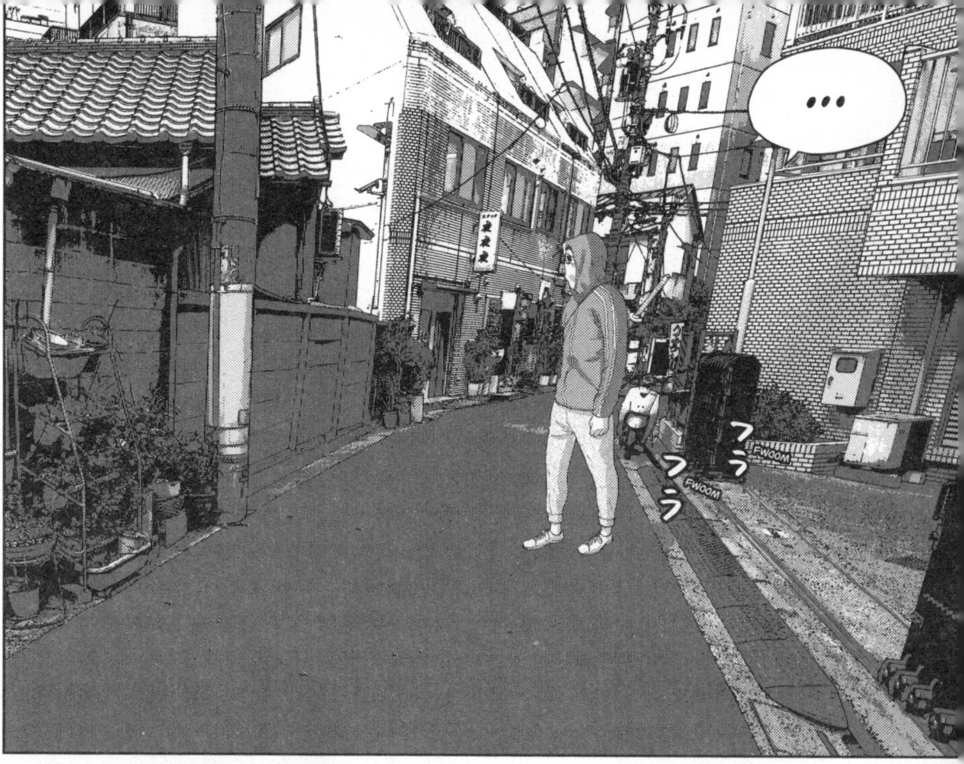
...
フラ
FWOOM
フラ
FWOOM
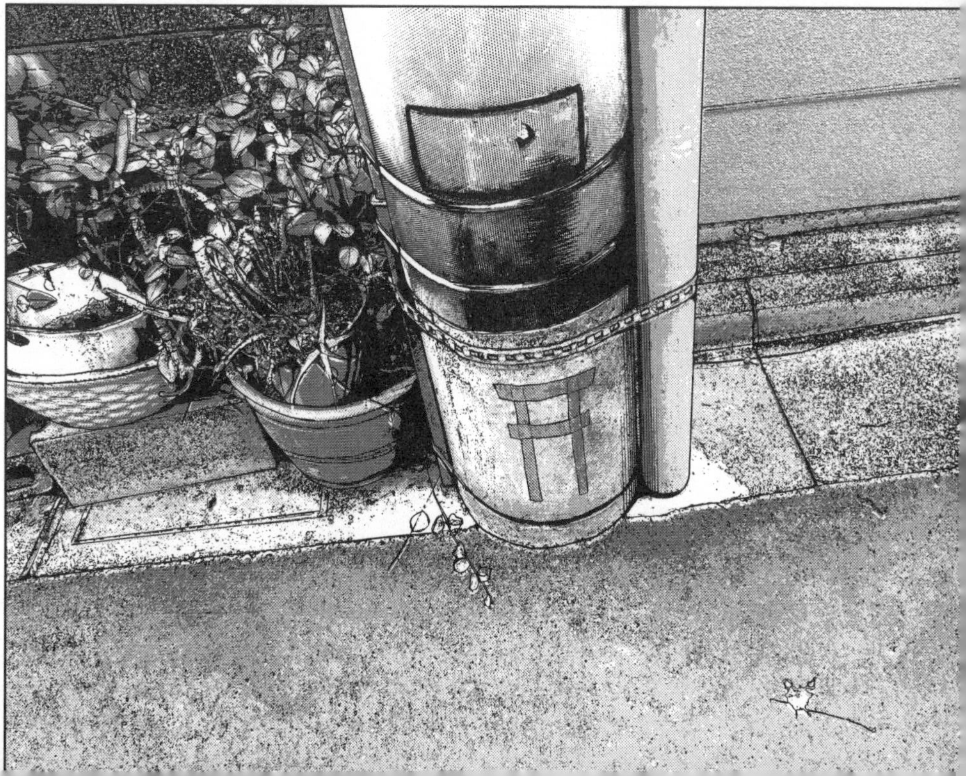

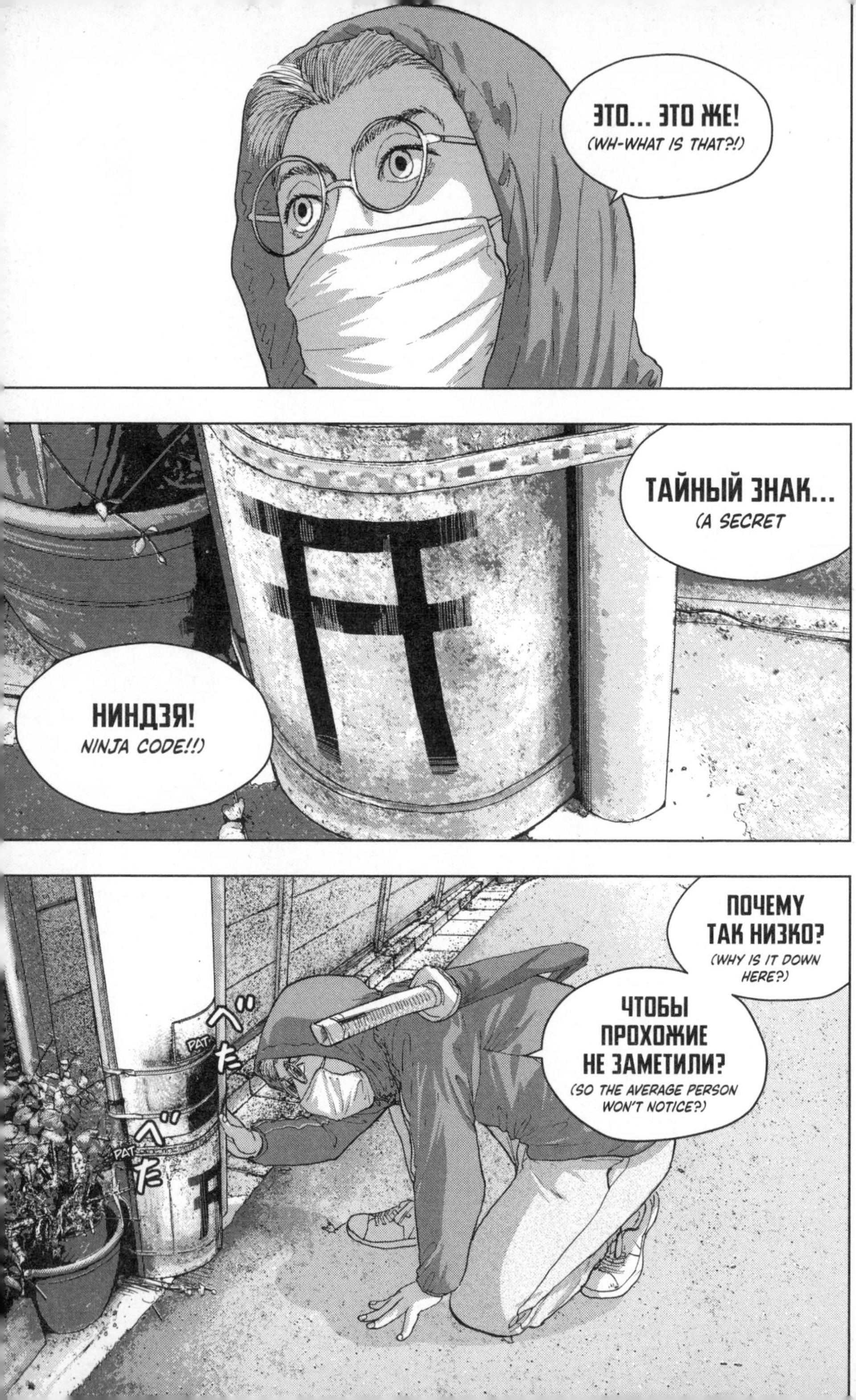
ЭТО... ЭТО ЖЕ!
(WH-WHAT IS THAT?!)
ТАЙНЫЙ ЗНАК...
(A SECRET
НИНДЗЯ!
NINJA CODE!!)
ПОЧЕМУ ТАК НИЗКО?
(WHY IS IT DOWN HERE?)
ЧТОБЫ ПРОХОЖИЕ НЕ ЗАМЕТИЛИ?
(SO THE AVERAGE PERSON WON'T NOTICE?)
PAT
PAT

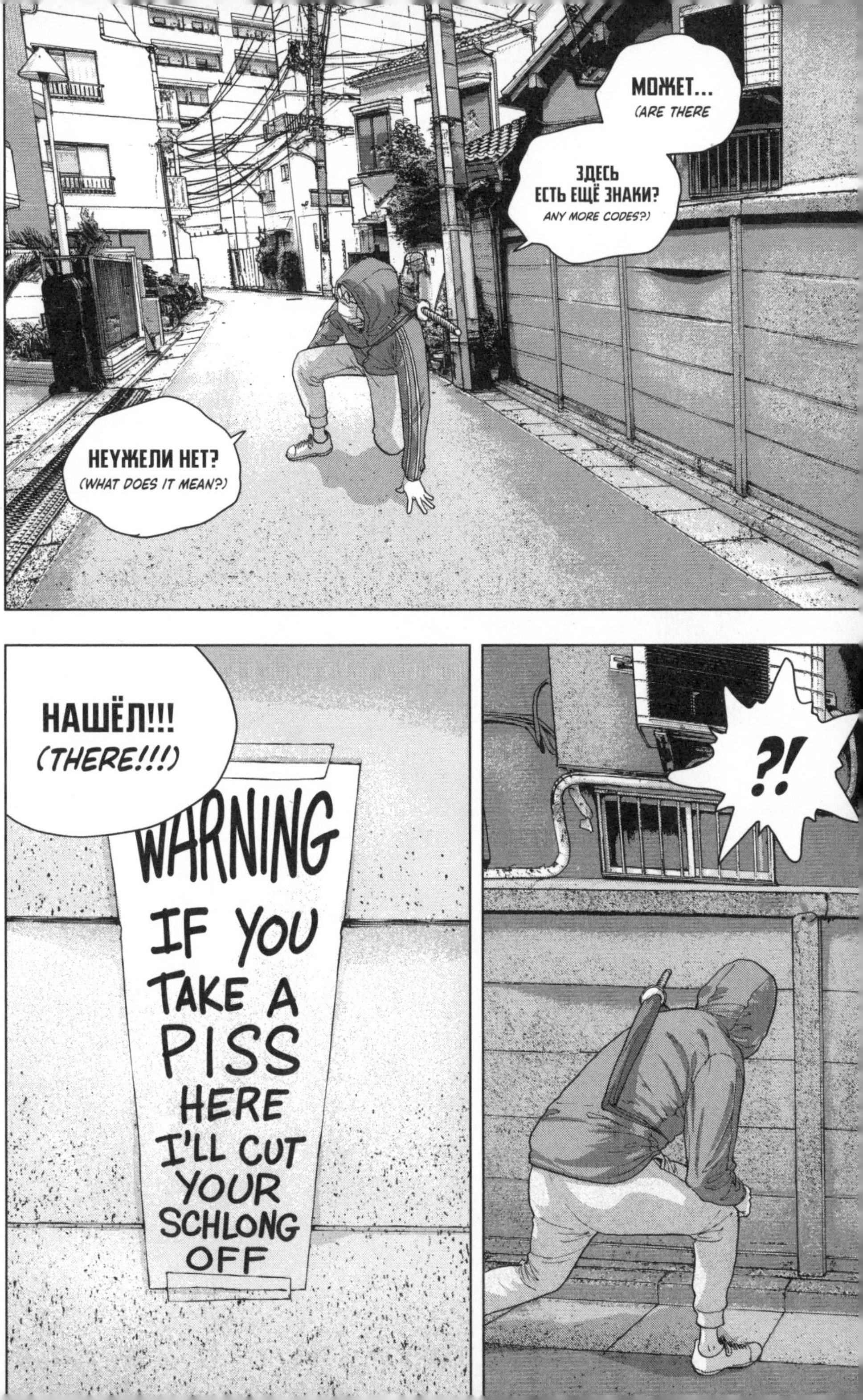
Может...
(ARE THERE
Здесь
есть ещё знаки?
ANY MORE CODES?)
Неужели нет?
(WHAT DOES IT MEAN?)
?!
Нашёл!!!
(THERE!!!)
WARNING
IF YOU
TAKE A
PISS
HERE
I'LL CUT
YOUR
SCHLONG
OFF

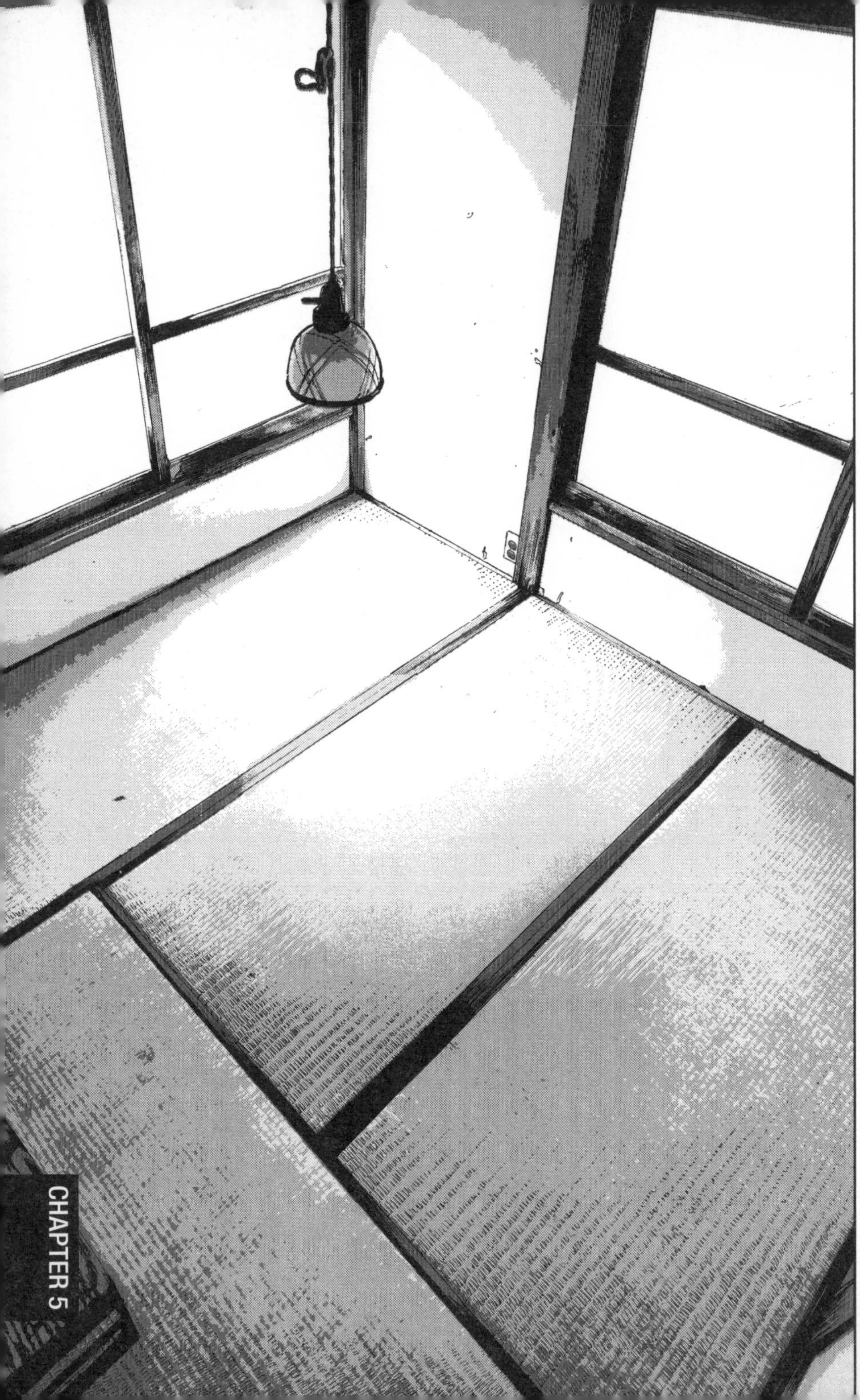

CHAPTER 5

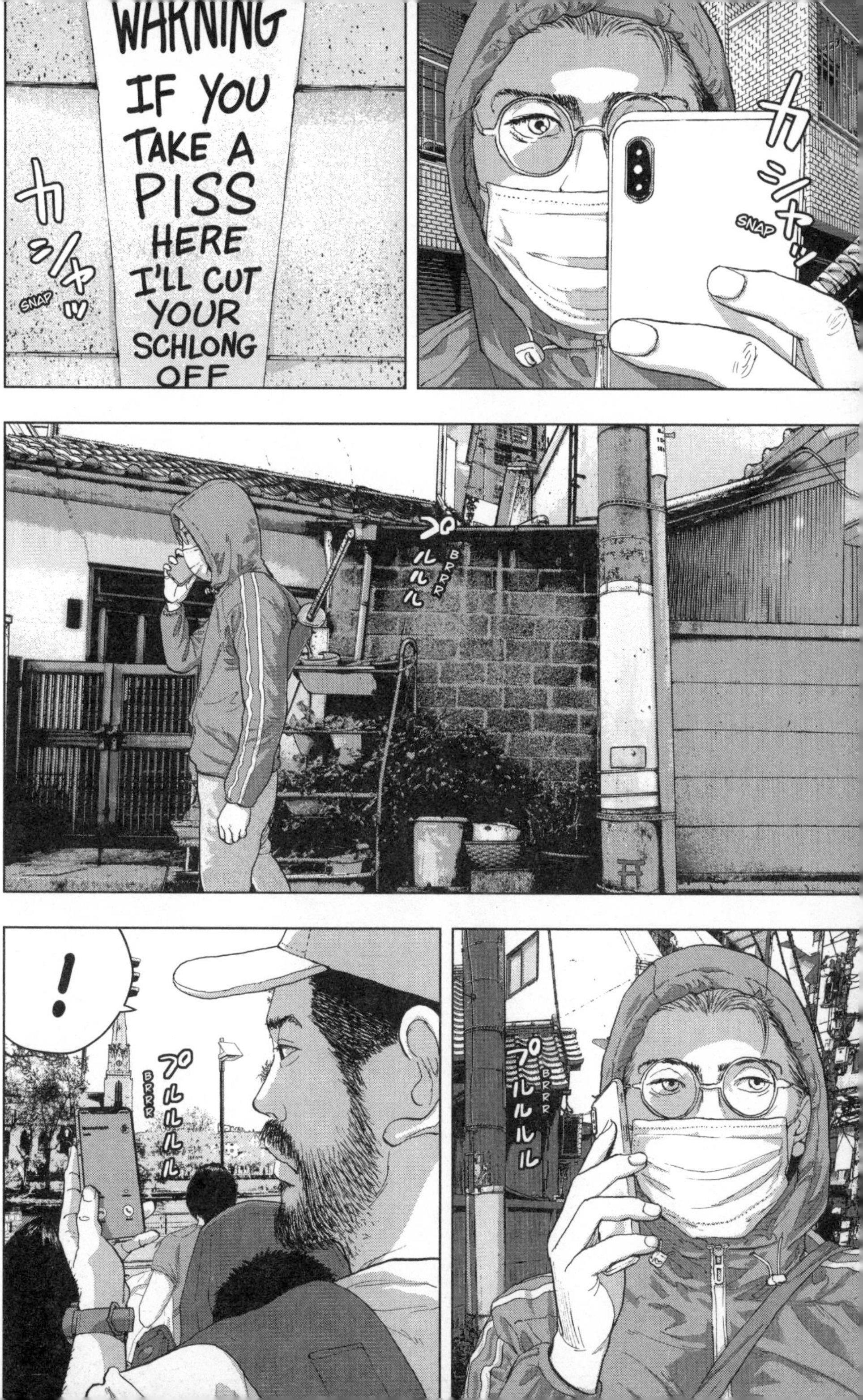
カシャッ
SNAP
WARNING
IF YOU TAKE A PISS HERE I'LL CUT YOUR SCHLONG OFF
カシャッ
SNAP
プルルル
BRRR
プルルルル
BRRR
!
プルルルル
BRRR

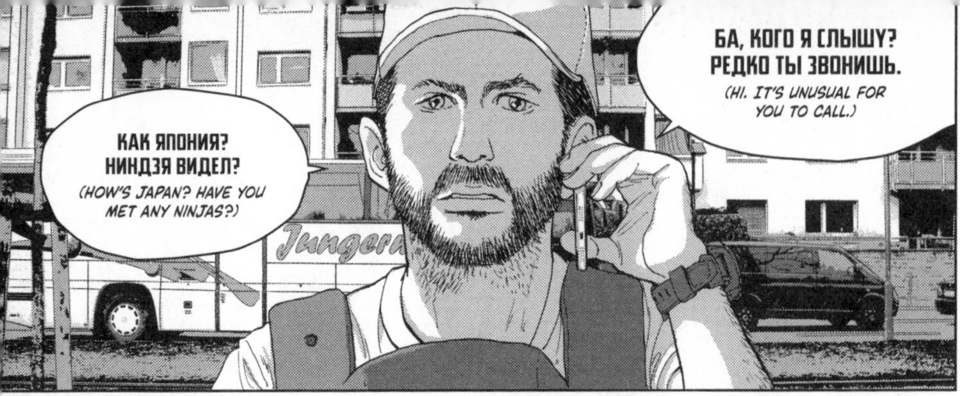
БА, КОГО Я СЛЫШУ? РЕДКО ТЫ ЗВОНИШЬ.
(HI. IT'S UNUSUAL FOR YOU TO CALL.)
КАК ЯПОНИЯ? НИНДЗЯ ВИДЕЛ?
(HOW'S JAPAN? HAVE YOU MET ANY NINJAS?)
Jungern

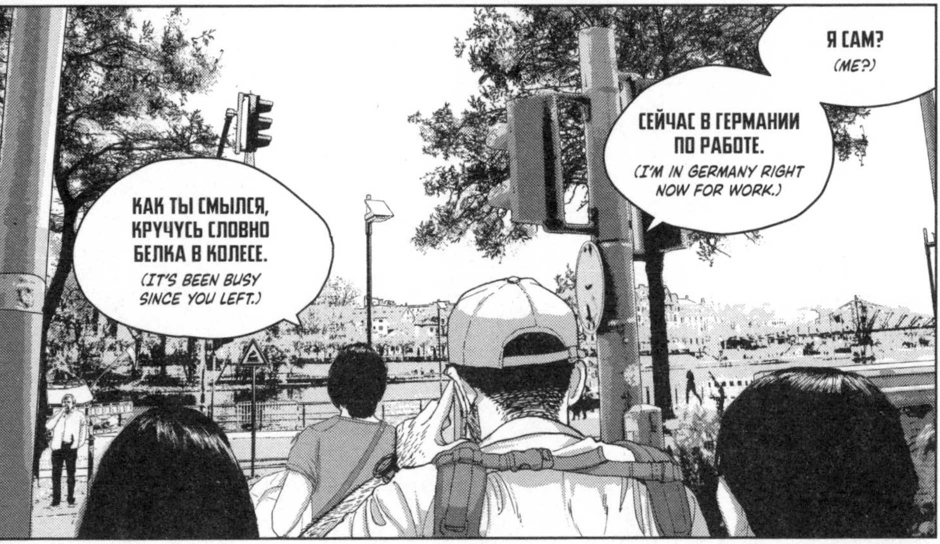
Я САМ?
(ME?)
СЕЙЧАС В ГЕРМАНИИ ПО РАБОТЕ.
(I'M IN GERMANY RIGHT NOW FOR WORK.)
КАК ТЫ СМЫЛСЯ, КРУЧУСЬ СЛОВНО БЕЛКА В КОЛЕСЕ.
(IT'S BEEN BUSY SINCE YOU LEFT.)

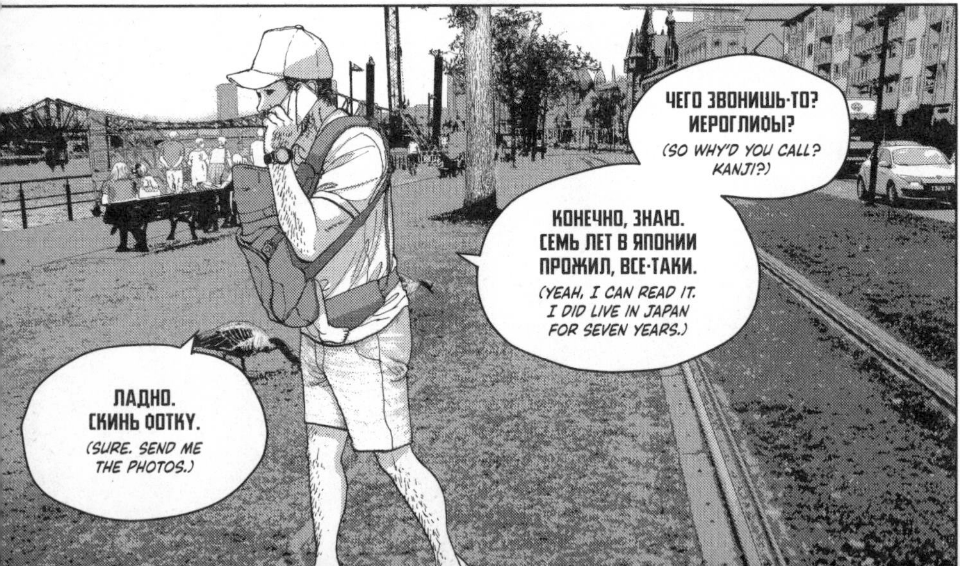
ЧЕГО ЗВОНИШЬ-ТО? ИЕРОГЛИФЫ?
(SO WHY'D YOU CALL? KANJI?)
КОНЕЧНО, ЗНАЮ. СЕМЬ ЛЕТ В ЯПОНИИ ПРОЖИЛ, ВСЕ-ТАКИ.
(YEAH, I CAN READ IT. I DID LIVE IN JAPAN FOR SEVEN YEARS.)
ЛАДНО. СКИНЬ ФОТКУ.
(SURE. SEND ME THE PHOTOS.)

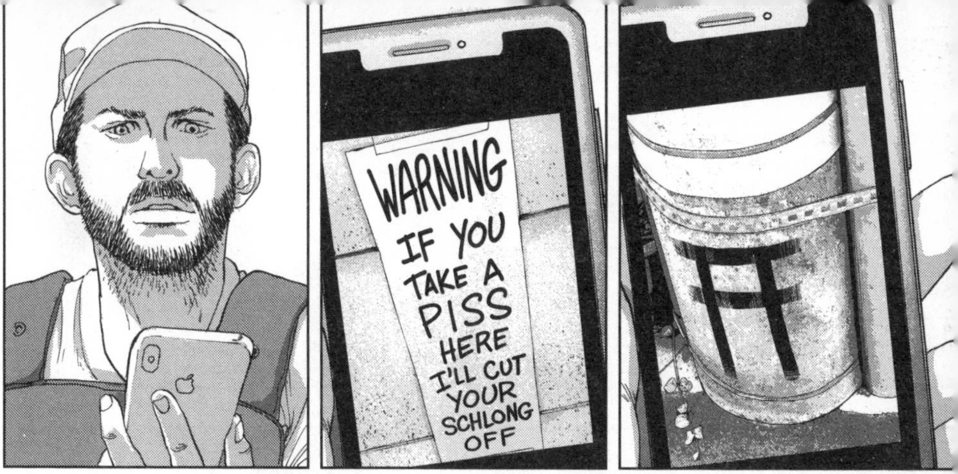
WARNING
IF YOU TAKE A PISS HERE I'LL CUT YOUR SCHLONG OFF

*PHOTO ON THE RIGHT: THE KANJI FOR "TORII," PROBABLY INDICATING THAT A SHRINE IS NEARBY.

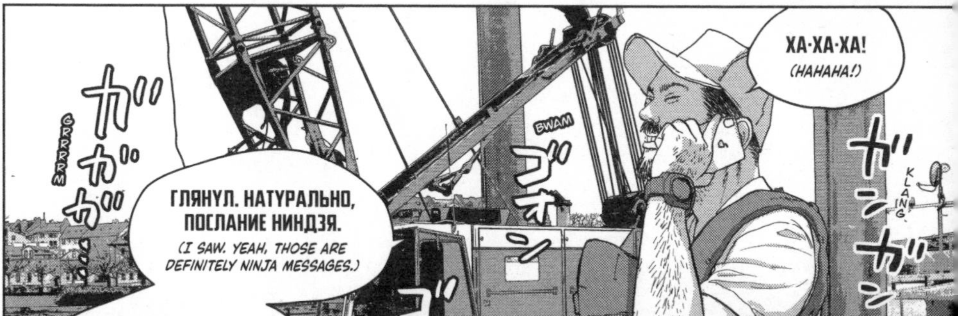
ХА-ХА-ХА! (HAHAHA!)
KLANG
KLANG
BWAM
BWAM
ГЛЯНУЛ. НАТУРАЛЬНО, ПОСЛАНИЕ НИНДЗЯ. (I SAW. YEAH, THOSE ARE DEFINITELY NINJA MESSAGES.)
МОЛОДЕЦ Я САМ ТАКОЕ ВПЕРВЫЕ ВИЖУ. (I'M IMPRESSED. THIS IS THE FIRST TIME I'VE SEEN THEM.)
GRRRRM

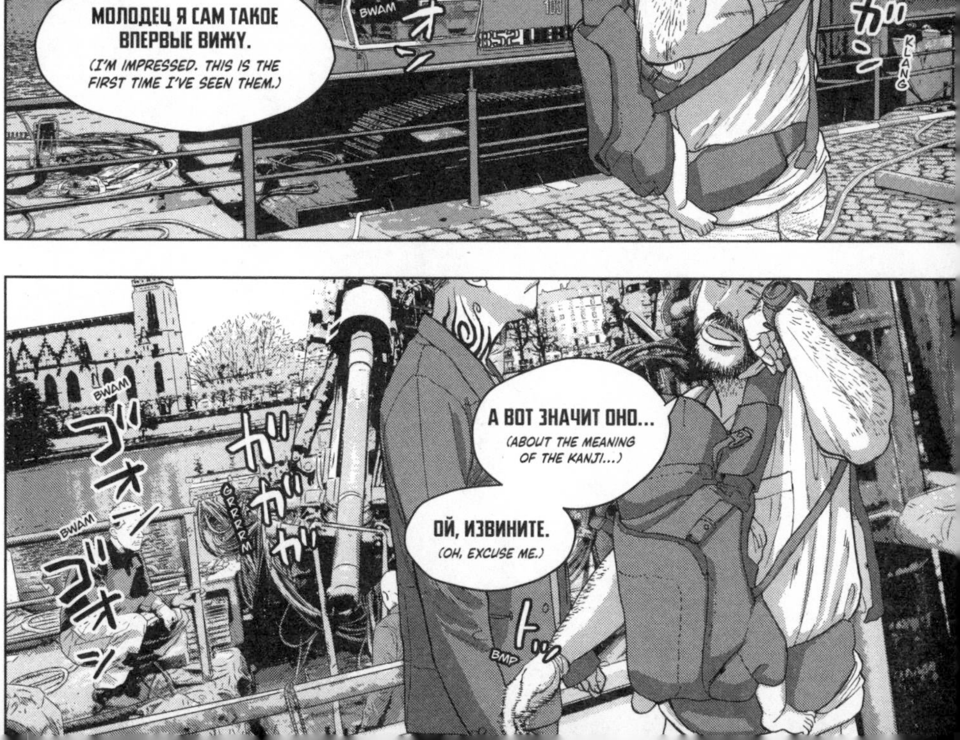
А ВОТ ЗНАЧИТ ОНО... (ABOUT THE MEANING OF THE KANJI...)
ОЙ, ИЗВИНИТЕ. (OH, EXCUSE ME.)
BMP
GRRRRM
BWAM
BWAM

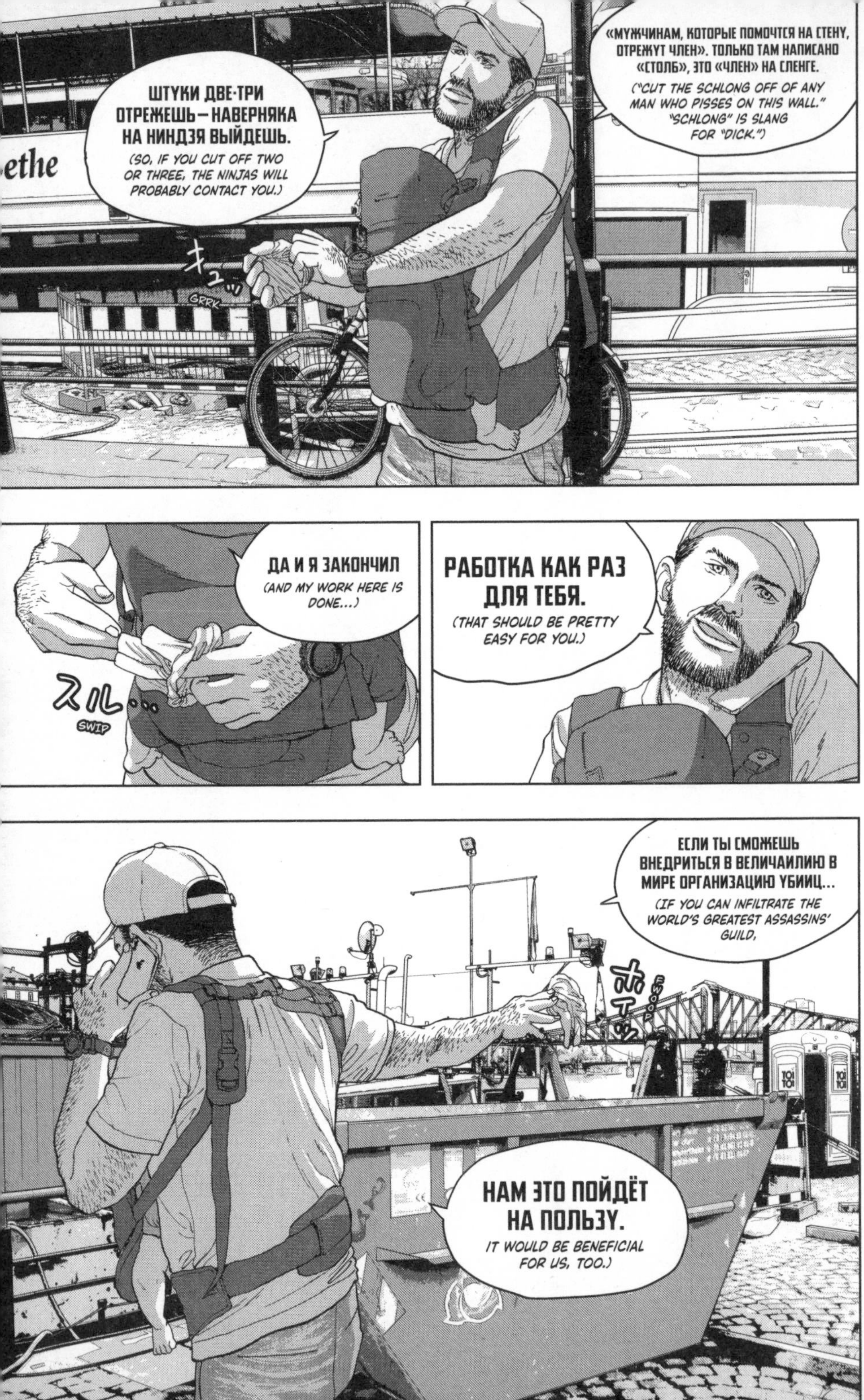
«МУЖЧИНАМ, КОТОРЫЕ ПОМОЧАТСЯ НА СТЕНУ, ОТРЕЖУТ ЧЛЕН». ТОЛЬКО ТАМ НАПИСАНО «СТОЛБ», ЭТО «ЧЛЕН» НА СЛЕНГЕ. ("CUT THE SCHLONG OFF OF ANY MAN WHO PISSES ON THIS WALL." "SCHLONG" IS SLANG FOR "DICK.")
ШТУКИ ДВЕ-ТРИ ОТРЕЖЕШЬ — НАВЕРНЯКА НА НИНДЗЯ ВЫЙДЕШЬ. (SO, IF YOU CUT OFF TWO OR THREE, THE NINJAS WILL PROBABLY CONTACT YOU.)
キュッ GRRK
РАБОТКА КАК РАЗ ДЛЯ ТЕБЯ. (THAT SHOULD BE PRETTY EASY FOR YOU.)
ДА И Я ЗАКОНЧИЛ (AND MY WORK HERE IS DONE...)
スル… SWIP
ЕСЛИ ТЫ СМОЖЕШЬ ВНЕДРИТЬСЯ В ВЕЛИЧАЙШУЮ В МИРЕ ОРГАНИЗАЦИЮ УБИЙЦ... (IF YOU CAN INFILTRATE THE WORLD'S GREATEST ASSASSINS' GUILD,
ホイッ FWOOP
НАМ ЭТО ПОЙДЁТ НА ПОЛЬЗУ. IT WOULD BE BENEFICIAL FOR US, TOO.)

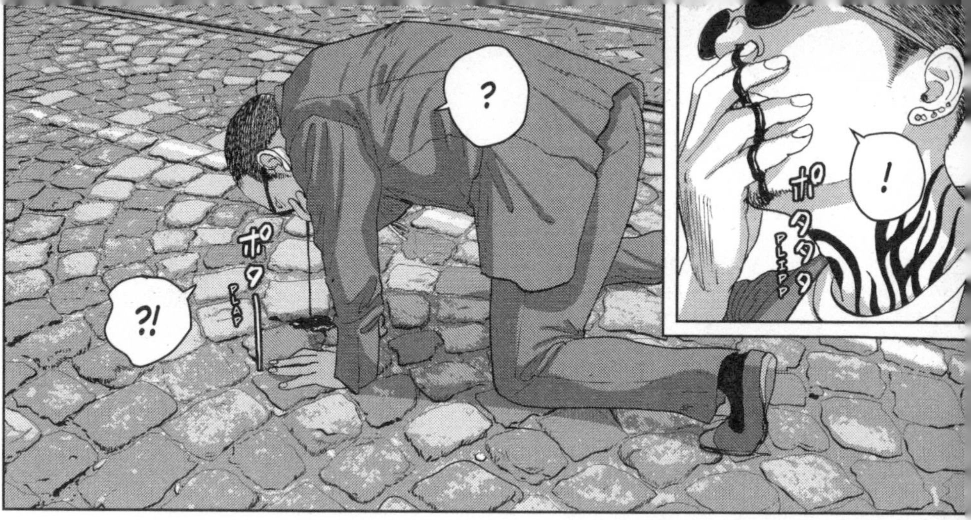
!
ポタタタ
PLIPP
?
ポタ
PLAP
?!

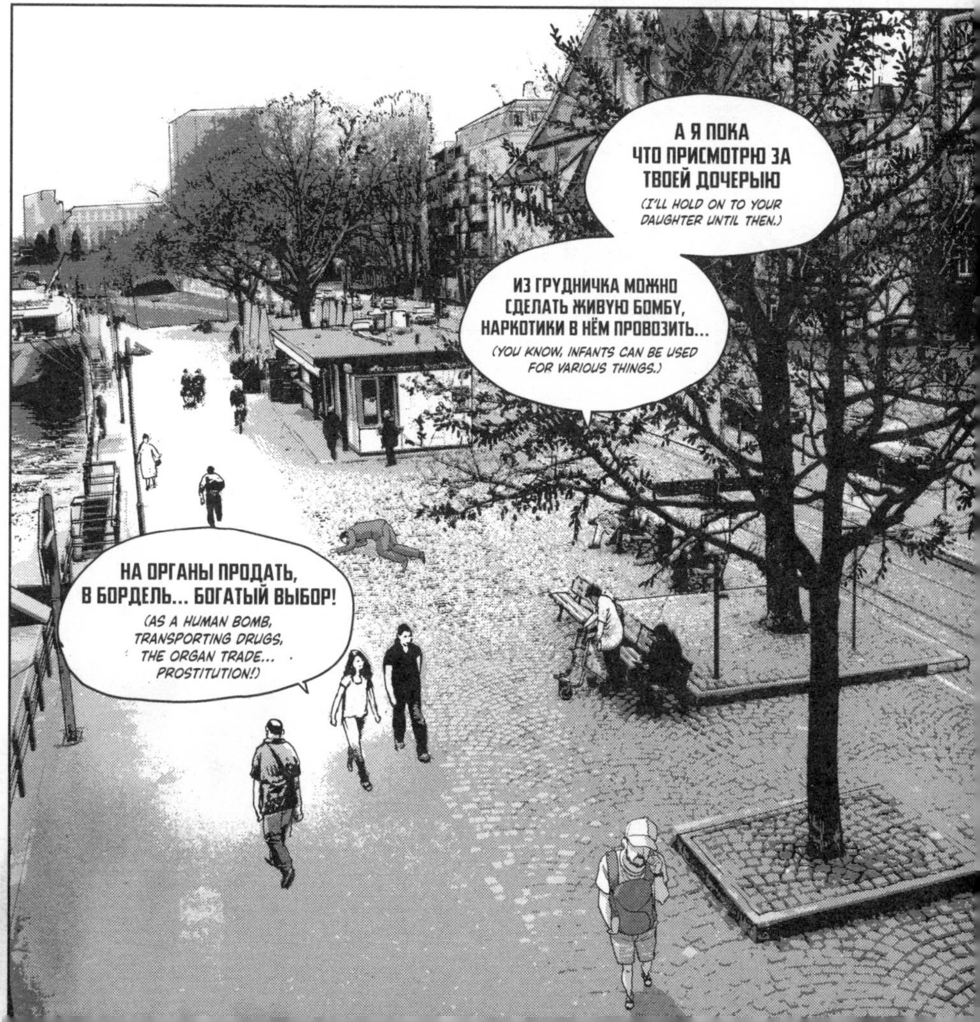
А Я ПОКА ЧТО ПРИСМОТРЮ ЗА ТВОЕЙ ДОЧЕРЬЮ
(I'LL HOLD ON TO YOUR DAUGHTER UNTIL THEN.)
ИЗ ГРУДНИЧКА МОЖНО СДЕЛАТЬ ЖИВУЮ БОМБУ, НАРКОТИКИ В НЁМ ПРОВОЗИТЬ...
(YOU KNOW, INFANTS CAN BE USED FOR VARIOUS THINGS.)
НА ОРГАНЫ ПРОДАТЬ, В БОРДЕЛЬ... БОГАТЫЙ ВЫБОР!
(AS A HUMAN BOMB, TRANSPORTING DRUGS, THE ORGAN TRADE... PROSTITUTION!)

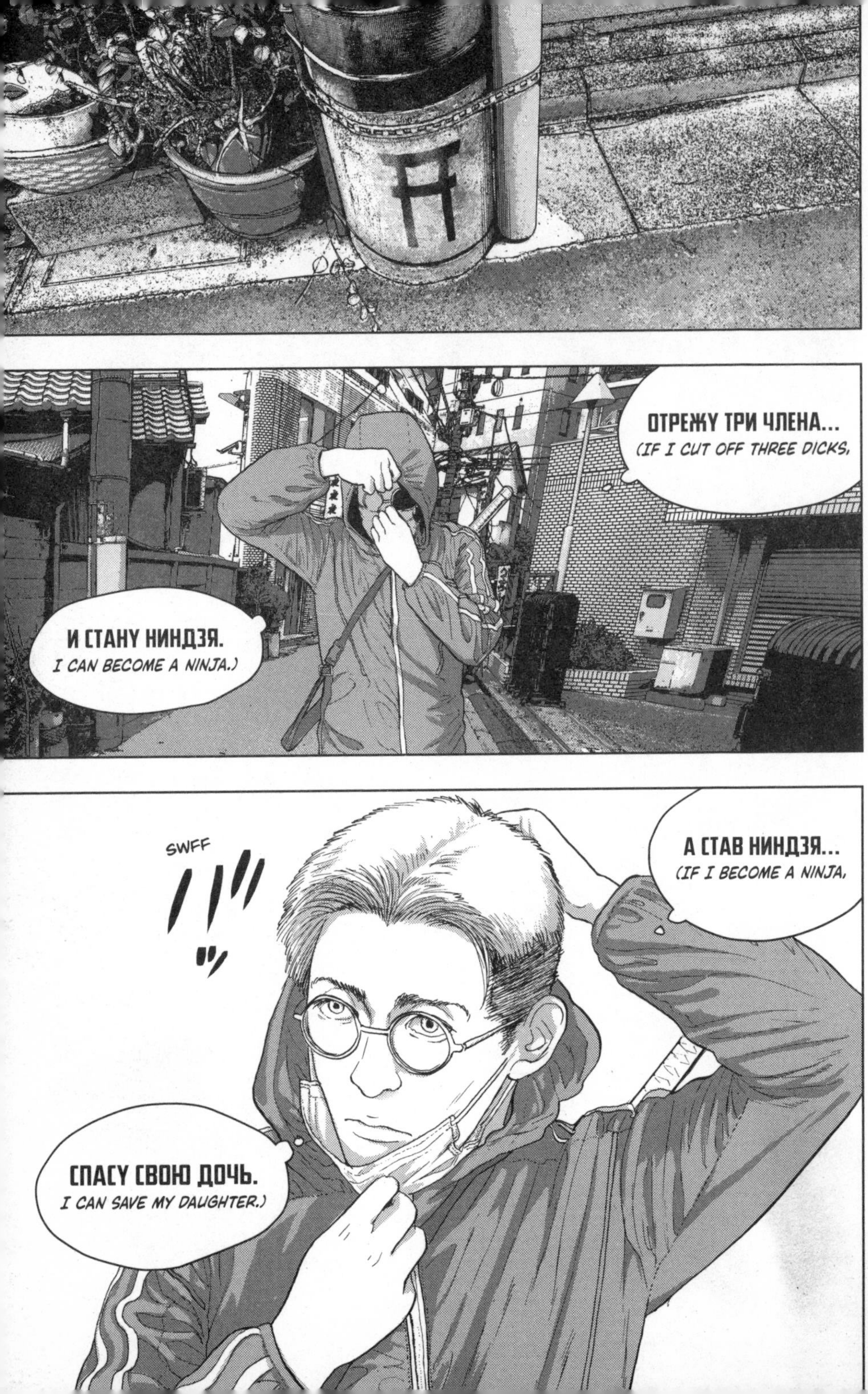
ОТРЕЖУ ТРИ ЧЛЕНА... (IF I CUT OFF THREE DICKS,
И СТАНУ НИНДЗЯ. I CAN BECOME A NINJA.)
SWFF
А СТАВ НИНДЗЯ... (IF I BECOME A NINJA,
СПАСУ СВОЮ ДОЧЬ. I CAN SAVE MY DAUGHTER.)

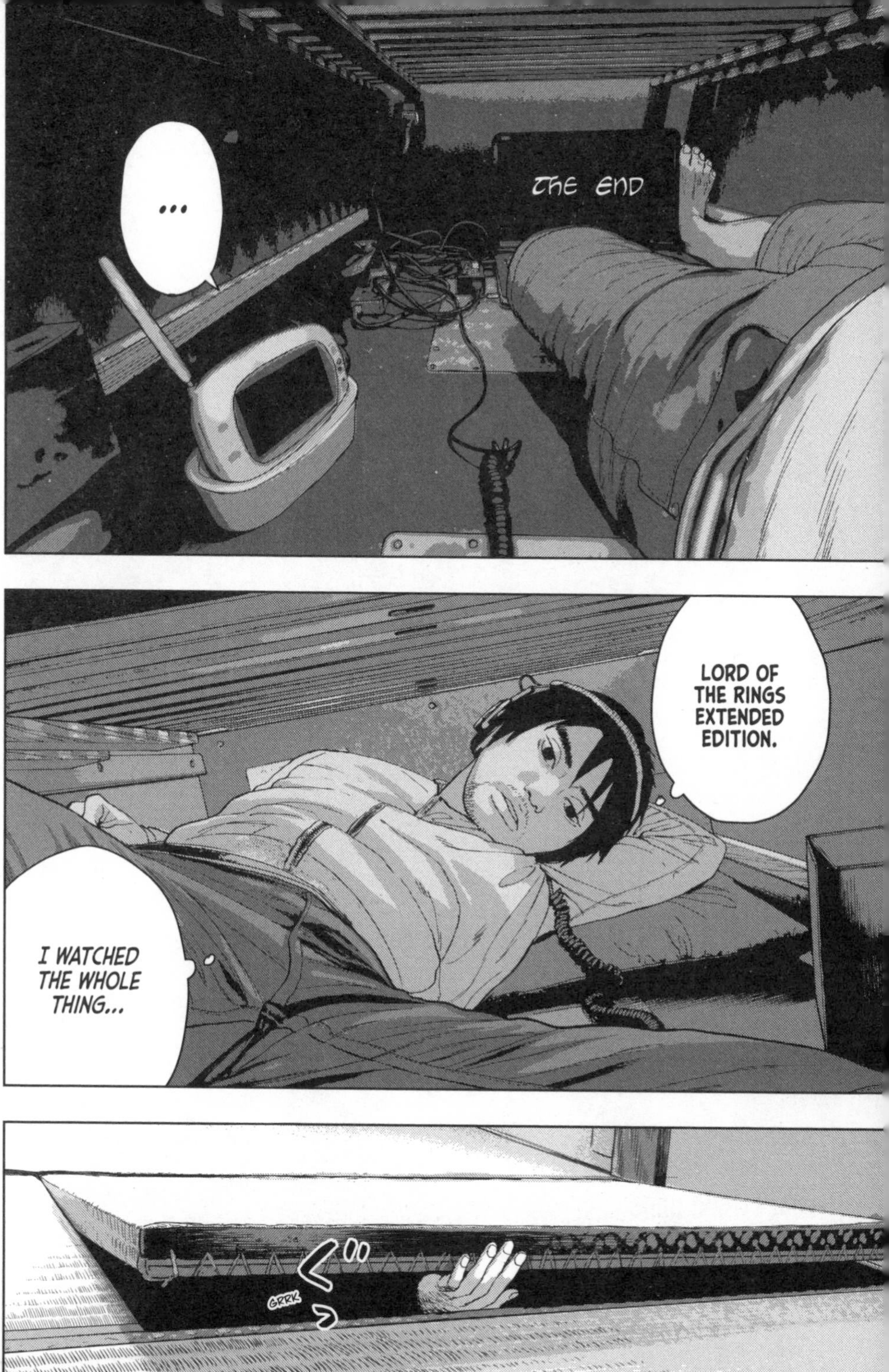

THE END
...
LORD OF THE RINGS EXTENDED EDITION.
I WATCHED THE WHOLE THING...
GRRK

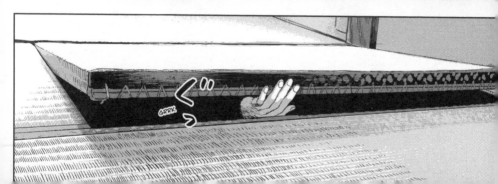

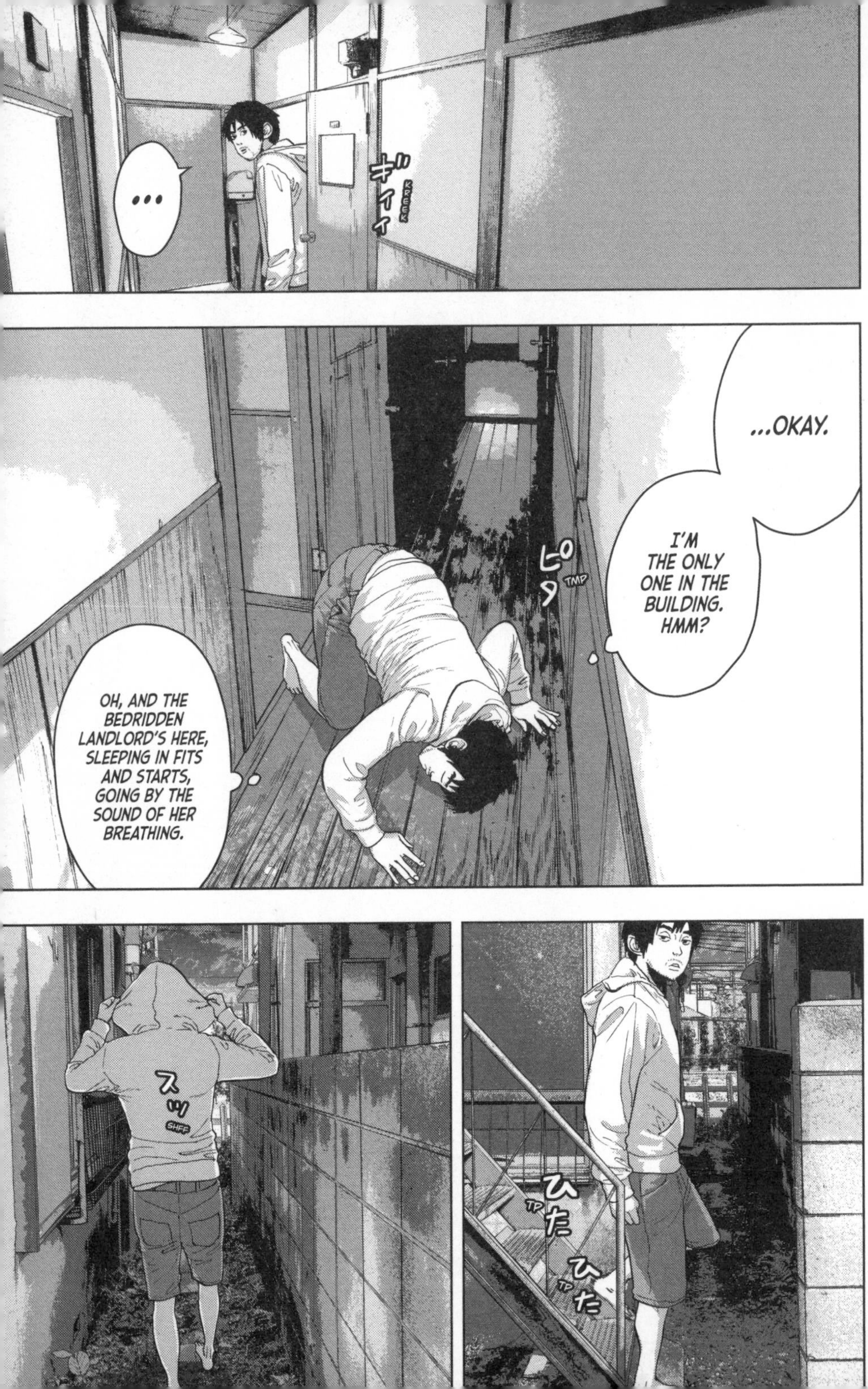
...
ギイイ
KREEK
...OKAY.
I'M THE ONLY ONE IN THE BUILDING. HMM?
ピタ
TMP
OH, AND THE BEDRIDDEN LANDLORD'S HERE, SLEEPING IN FITS AND STARTS, GOING BY THE SOUND OF HER BREATHING.
ひた
TP
ひた
TP
スッ
SHFF

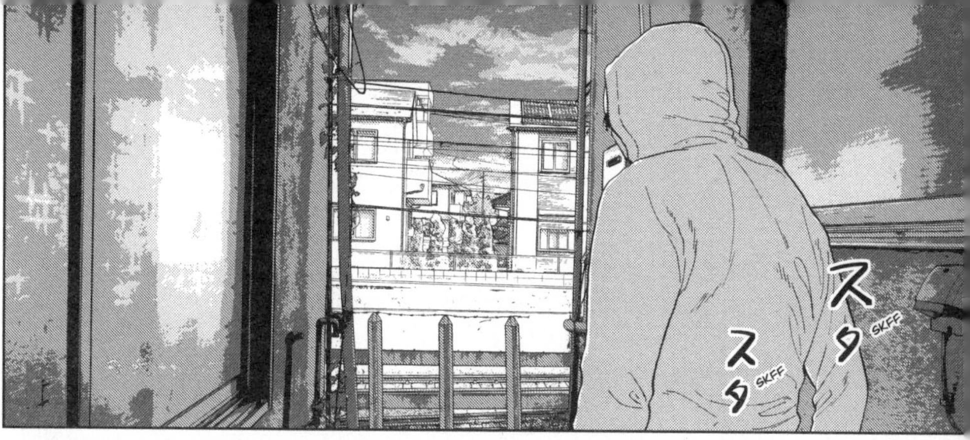
スタ SKFF
スタ SKFF
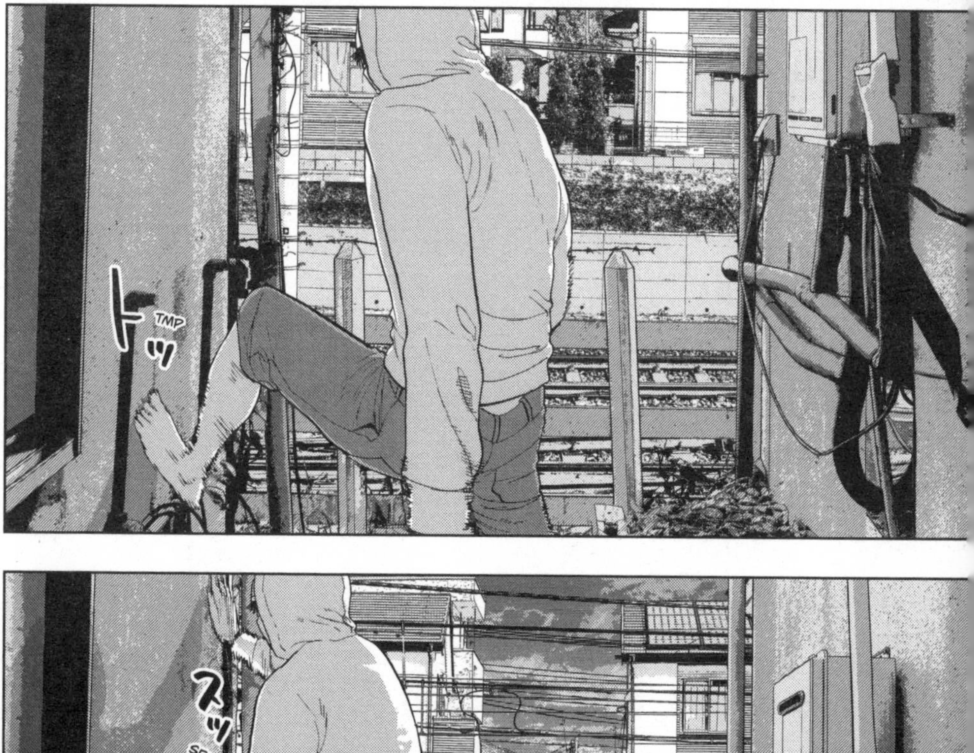
トッ TMP
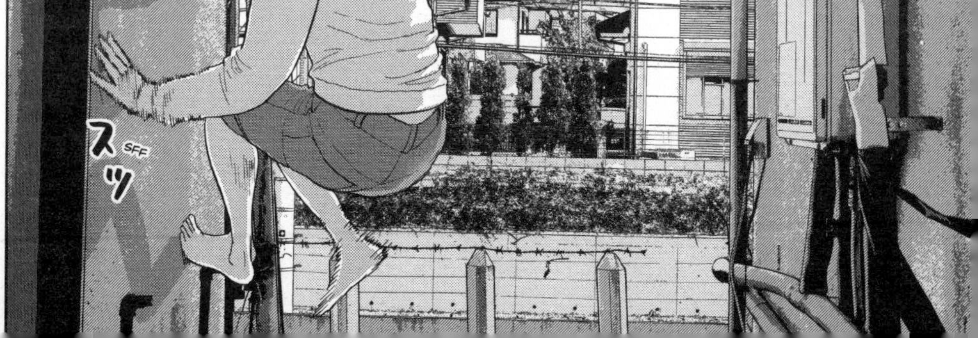
スッ SFF
スッ SFF

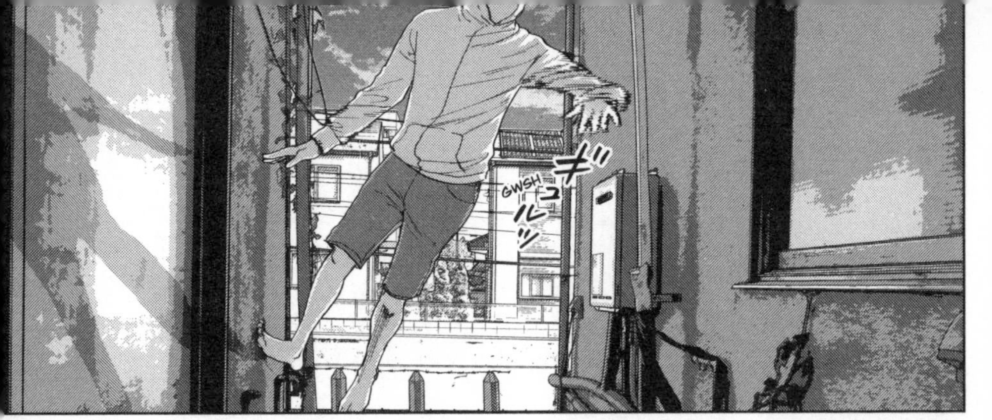
ギュルッ
GWSH

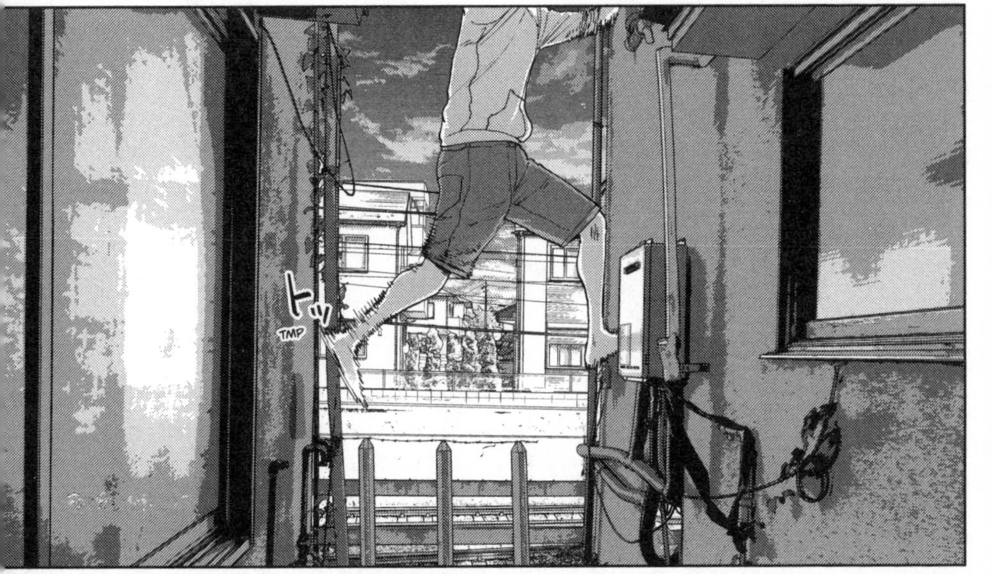
トッ
TMP

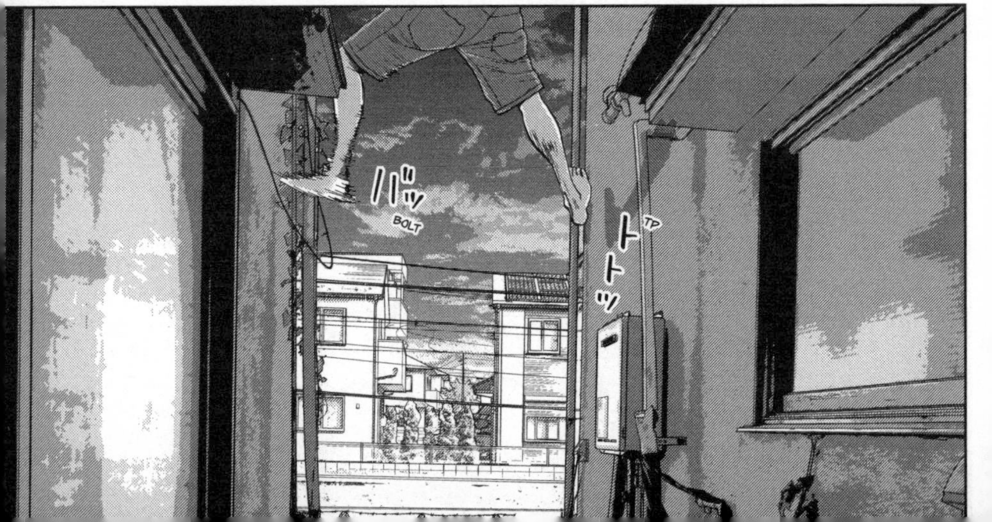
バッ
BOLT
トトッ
TP

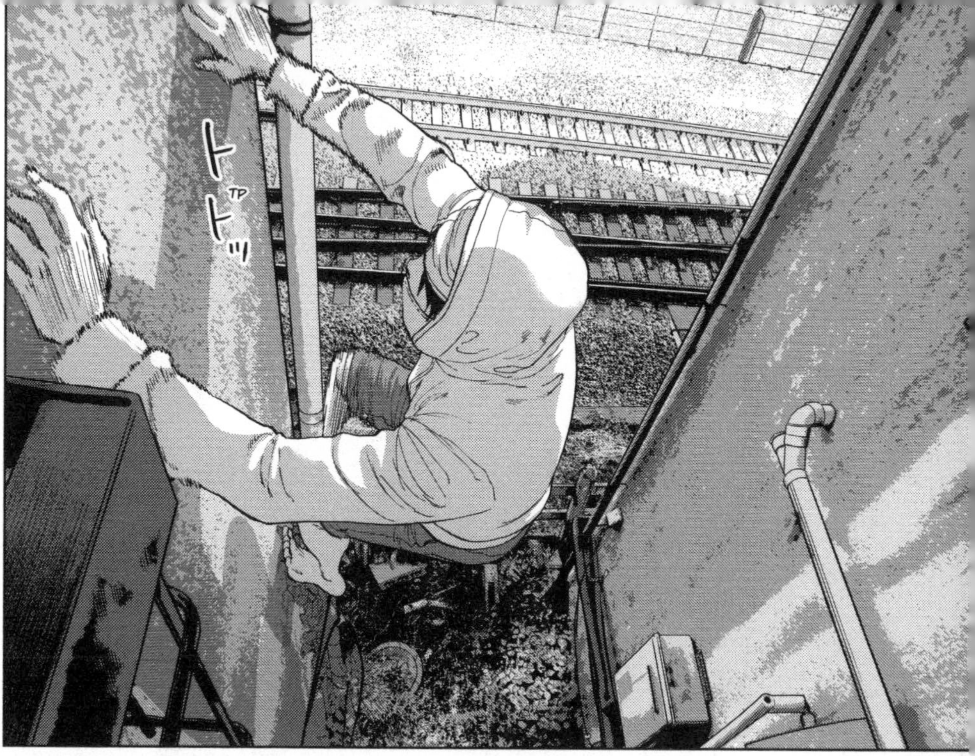
トトッ
TP
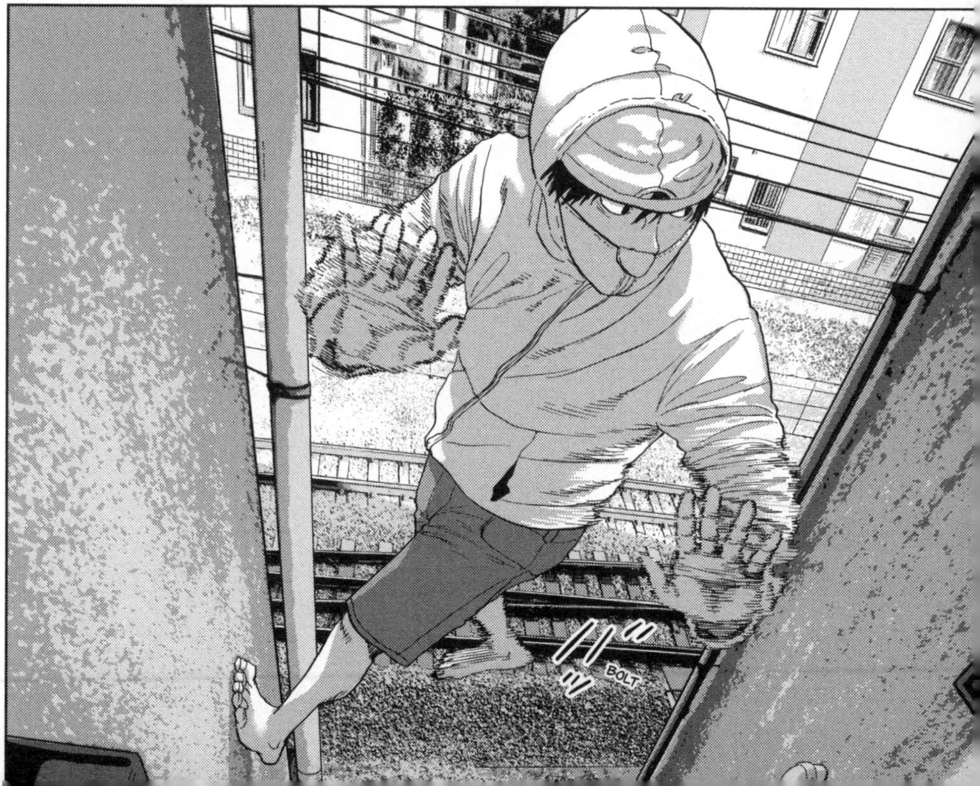
バッ
BOLT

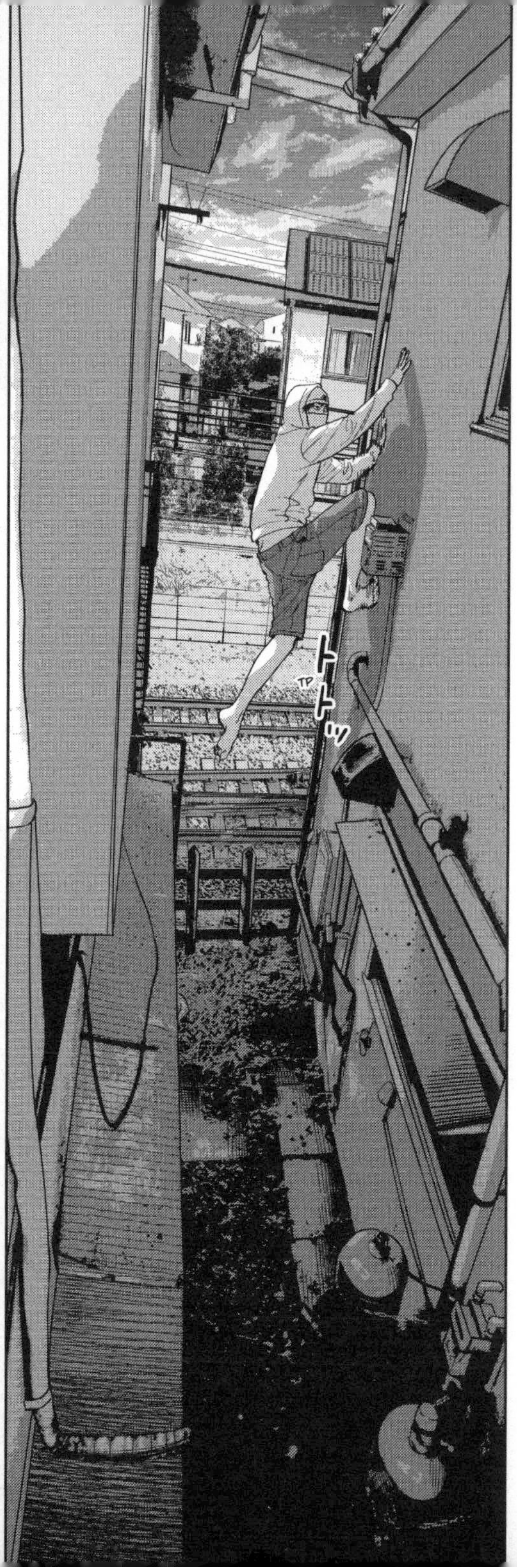
トトッ
TP
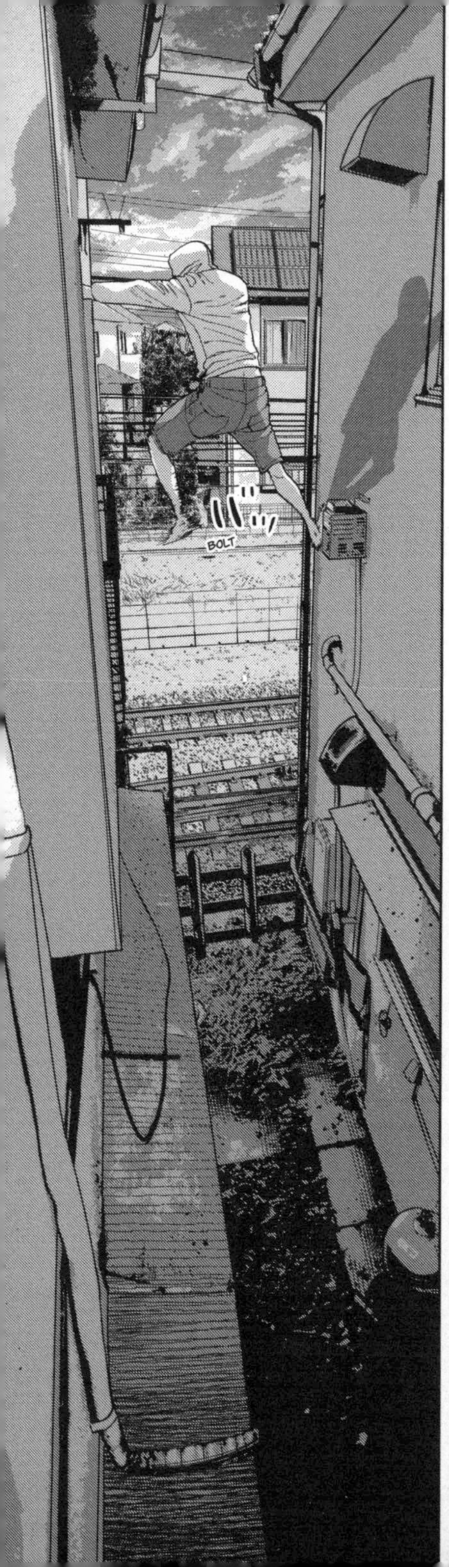
バッ
BOLT

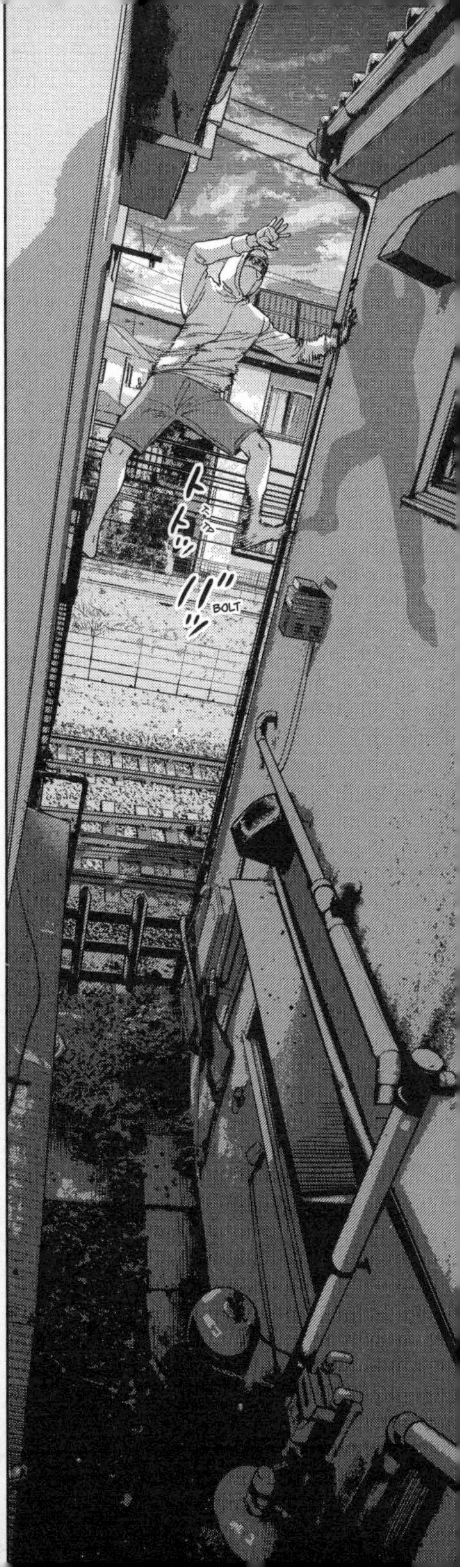
トトッ
TA-TP
バッ
BOLT
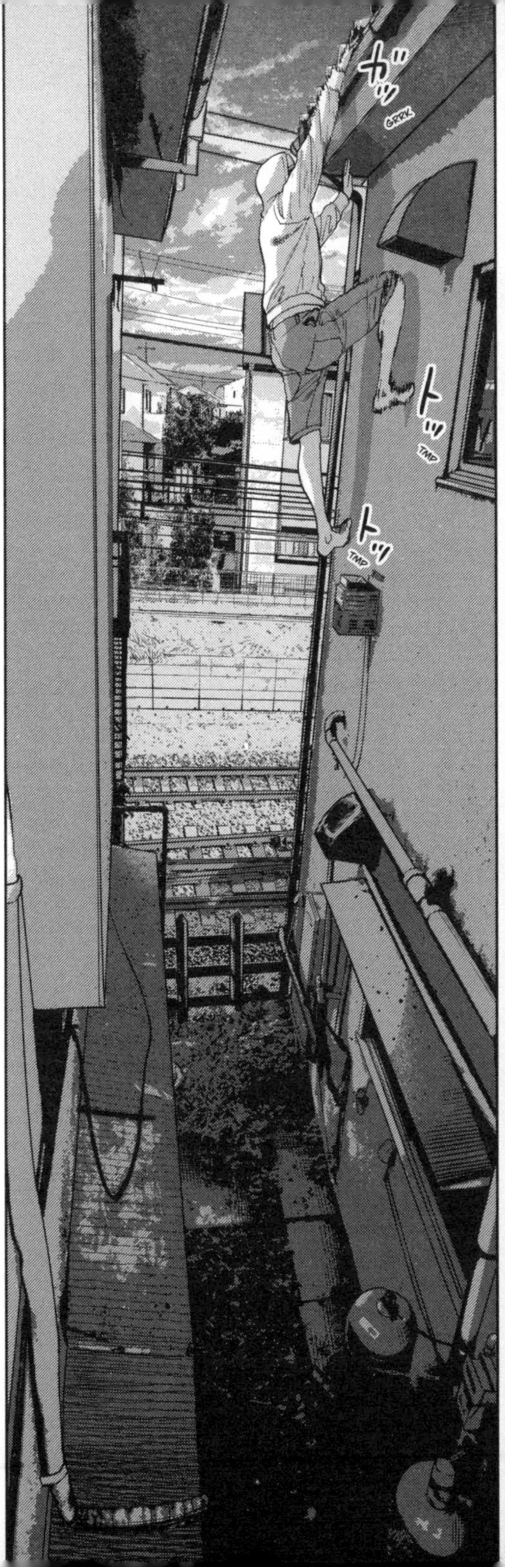
ガッ
GRRK
トッ
TMP
トッ
TMP

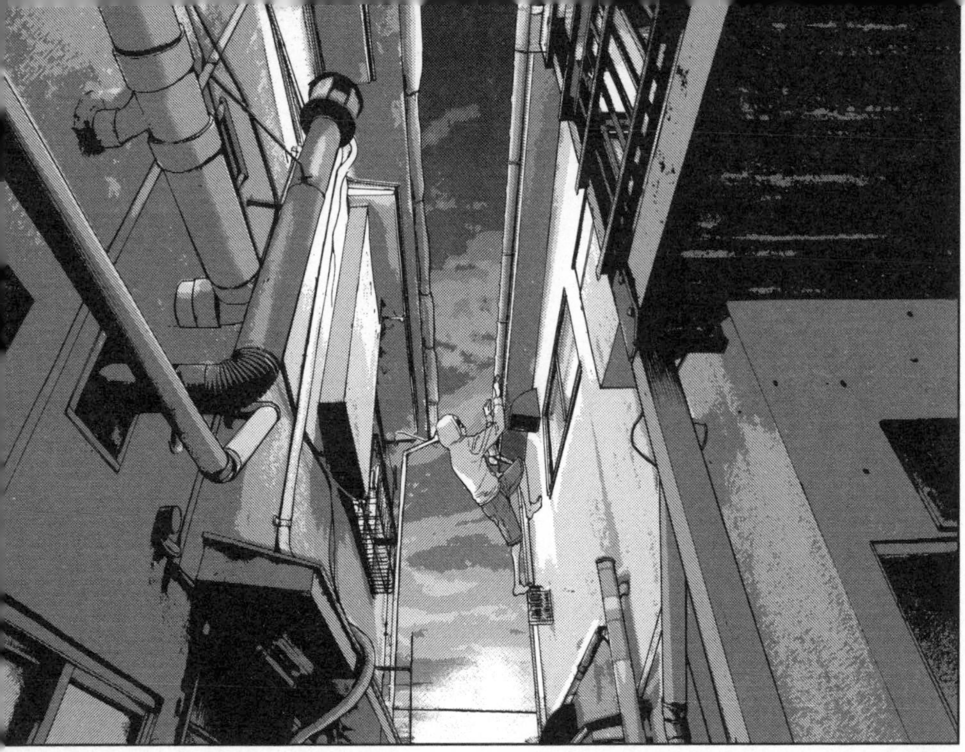

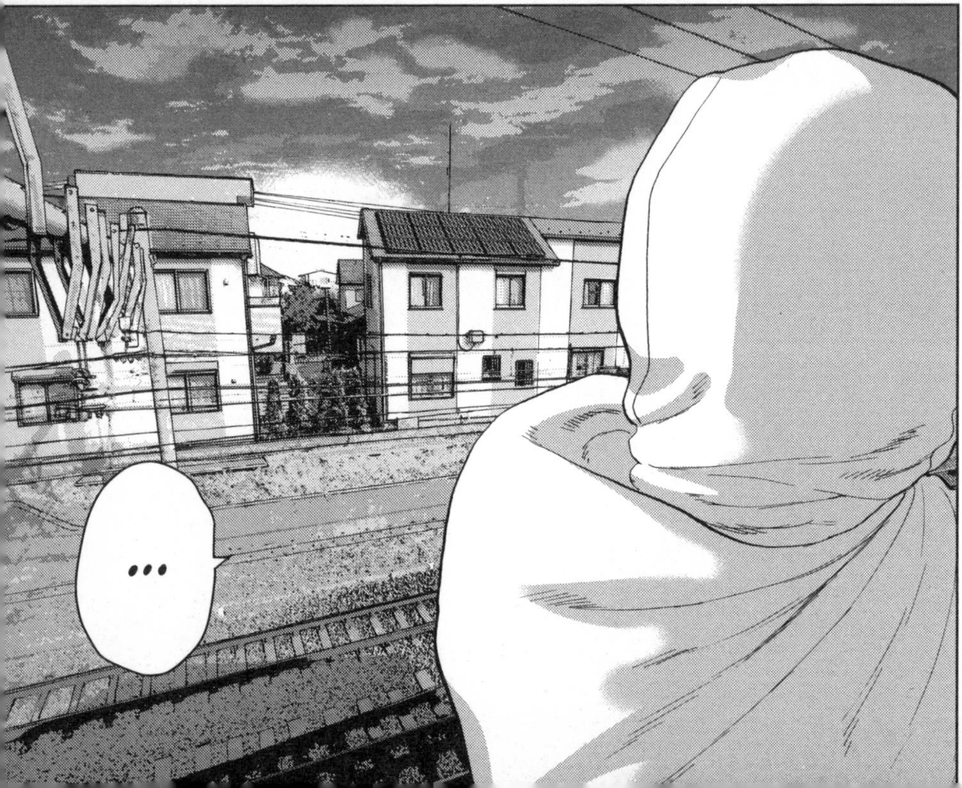
...

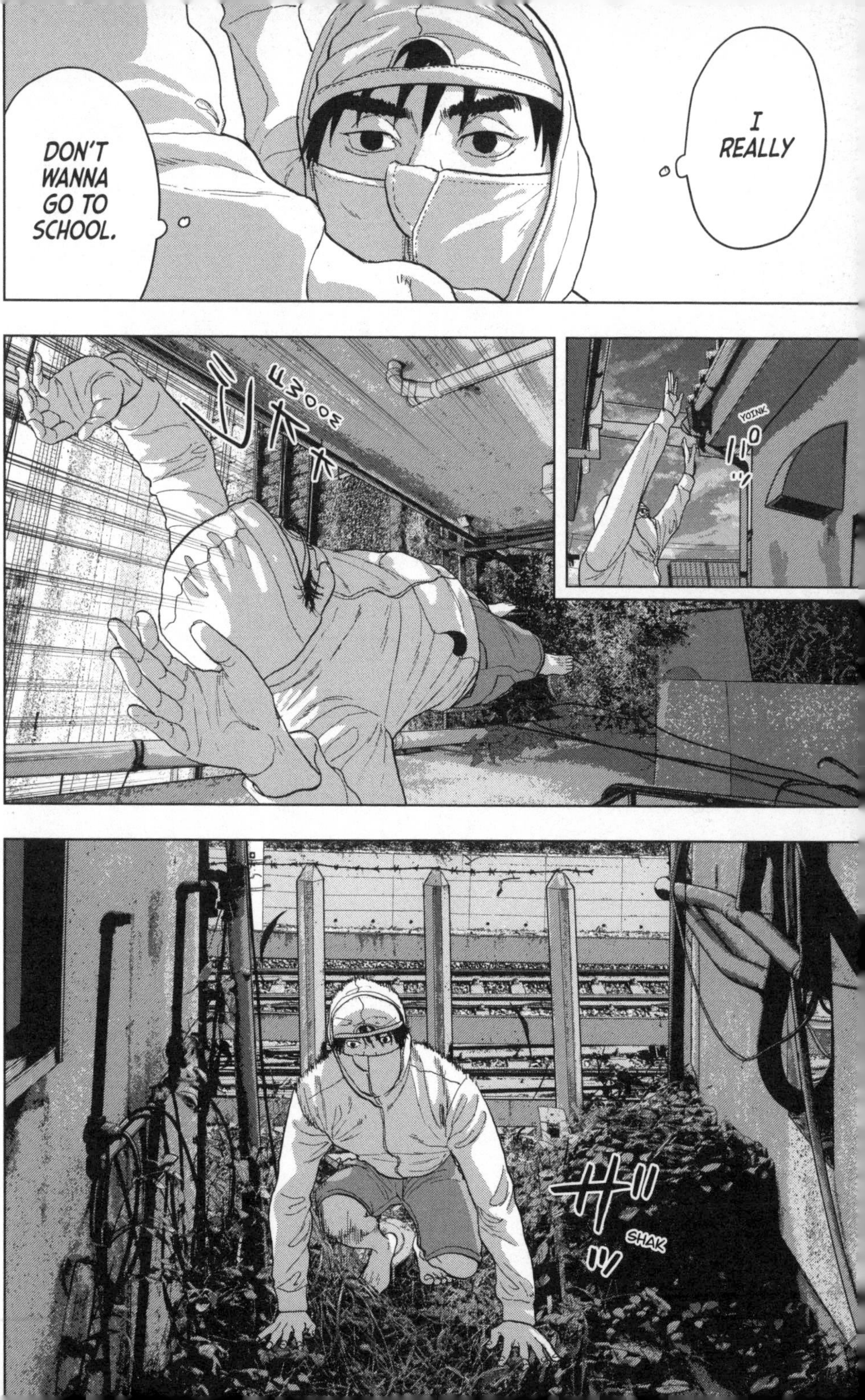

I REALLY
DON'T WANNA GO TO SCHOOL.
YOINK
SHAK

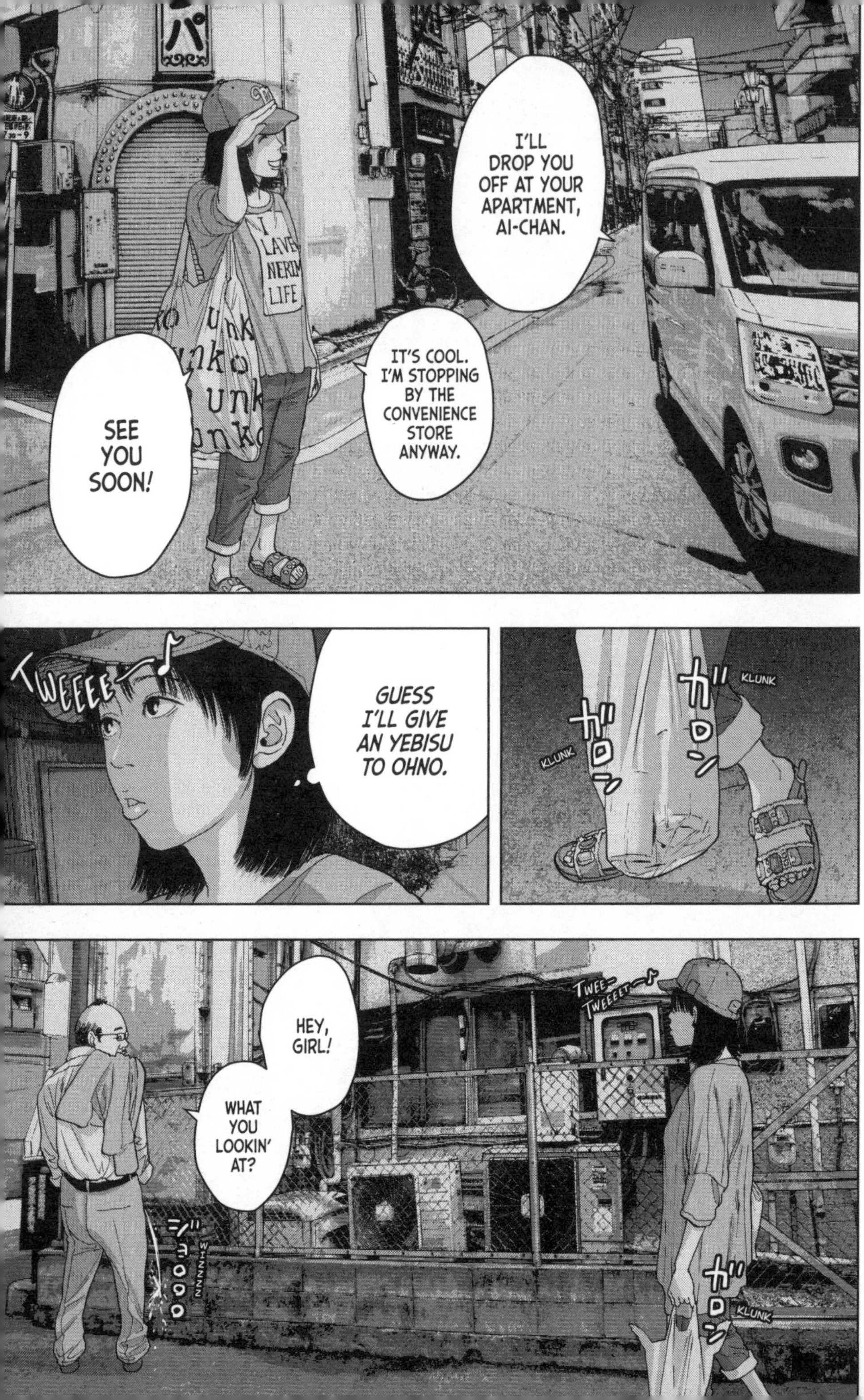
I'LL DROP YOU OFF AT YOUR APARTMENT, AI-CHAN.
IT'S COOL. I'M STOPPING BY THE CONVENIENCE STORE ANYWAY.
SEE YOU SOON!
KLUNK
KLUNK
TWEEEE
GUESS I'LL GIVE AN YEBISU TO OHNO.
TWEE-TWEEEET
KLUNK
HEY, GIRL!
WHAT YOU LOOKIN' AT?
WIZZZZ

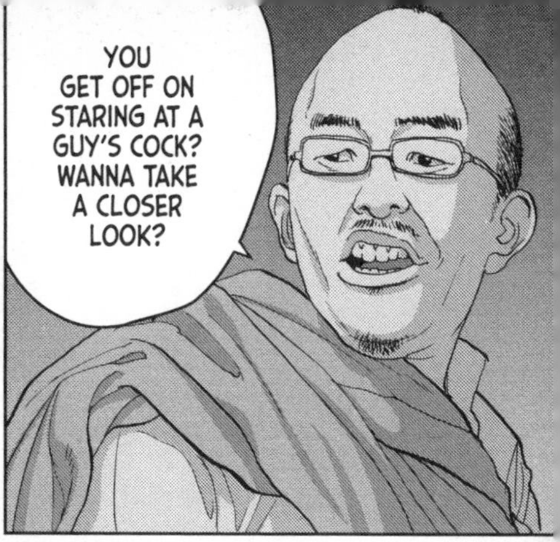
YOU GET OFF ON STARING AT A GUY'S COCK? WANNA TAKE A CLOSER LOOK?

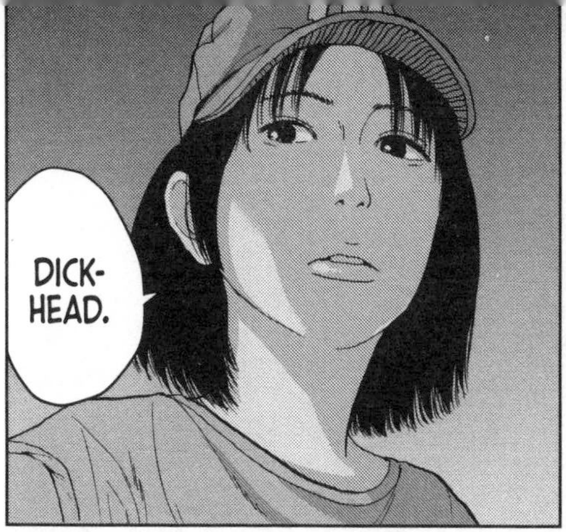
DICK-HEAD.

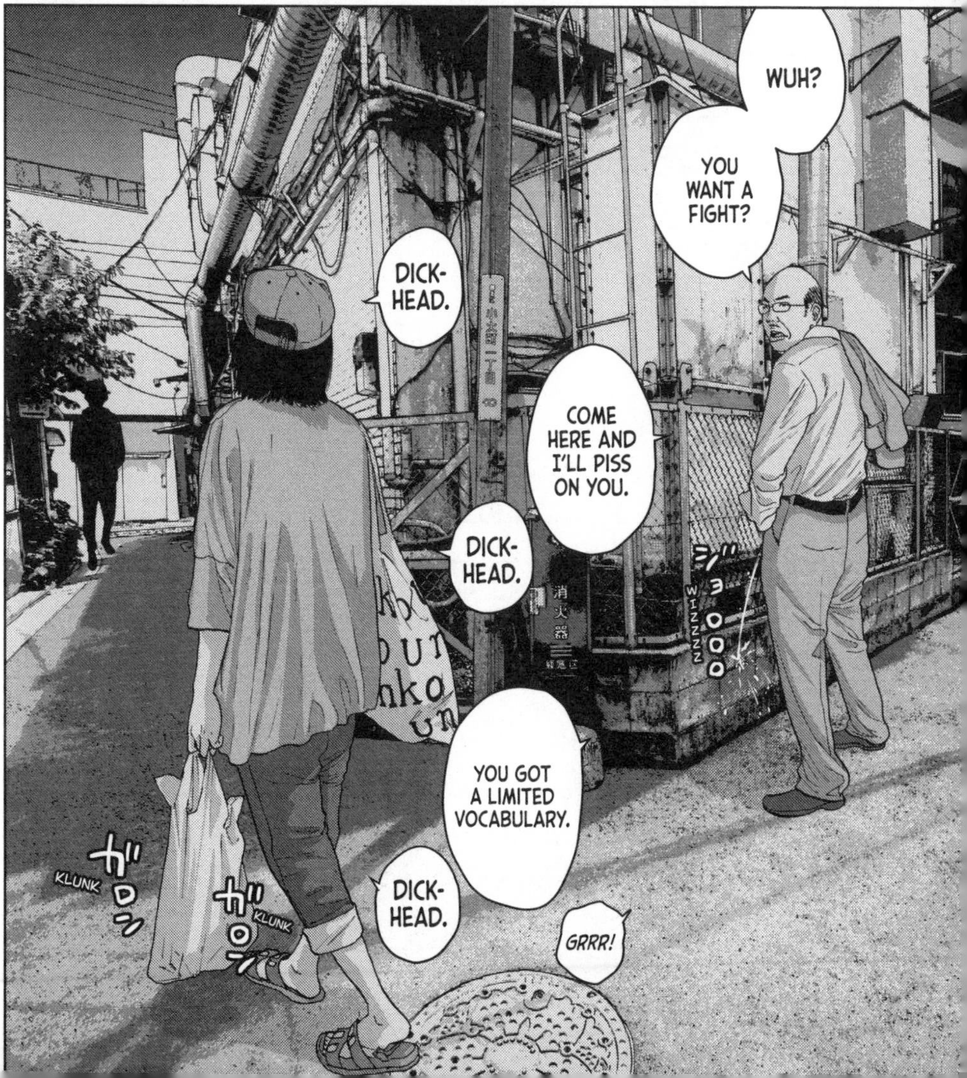
WUH?
YOU WANT A FIGHT?
DICK-HEAD.
COME HERE AND I'LL PISS ON YOU.
DICK-HEAD.
WIZZZZ
YOU GOT A LIMITED VOCABULARY.
GRRR!
DICK-HEAD.
KLUNK
KLUNK

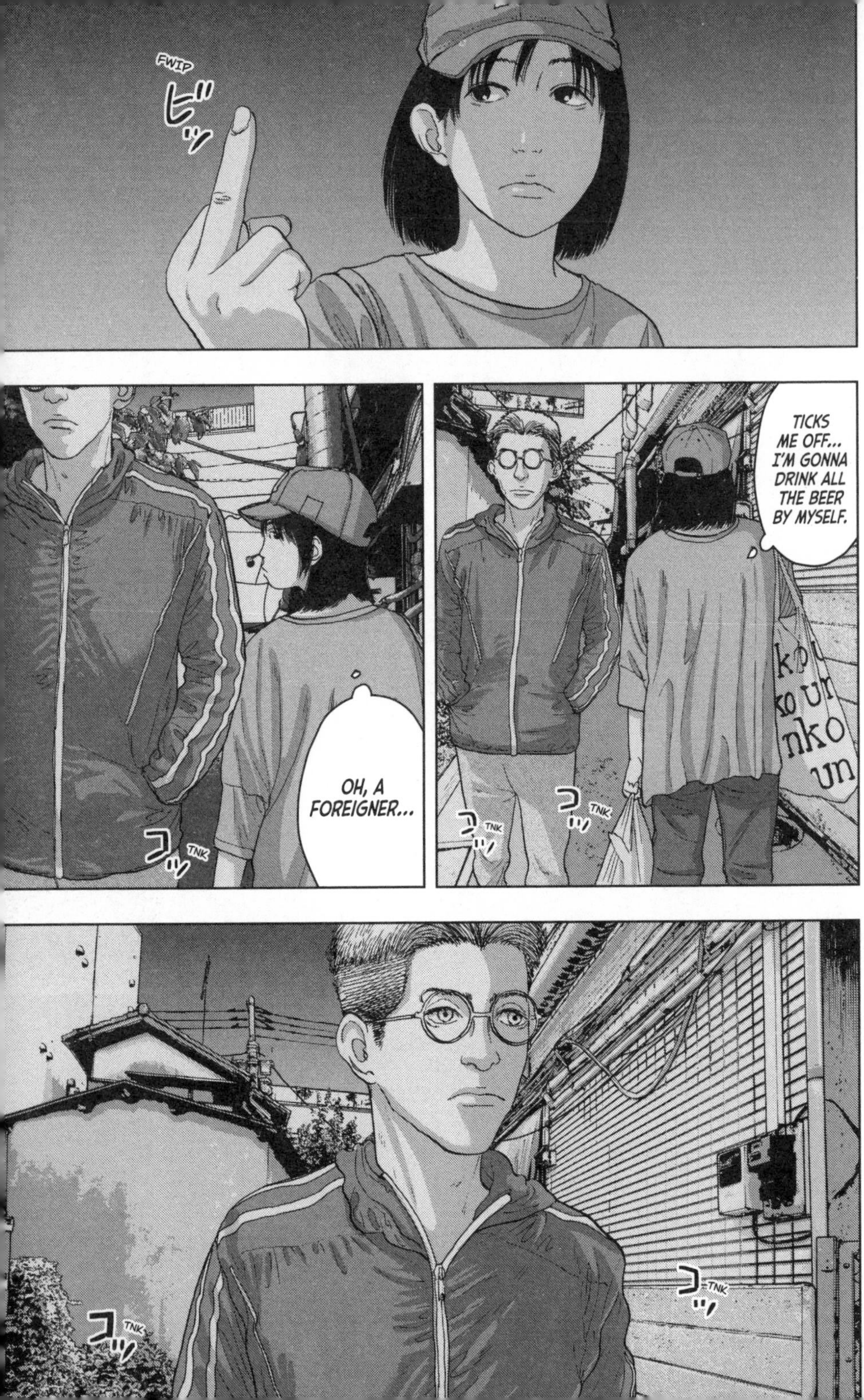
FWIP
ビッ
TICKS ME OFF... I'M GONNA DRINK ALL THE BEER BY MYSELF.
コッ TNK
コッ TNK
OH, A FOREIGNER...
コッ TNK
コッ TNK
コッ TNK

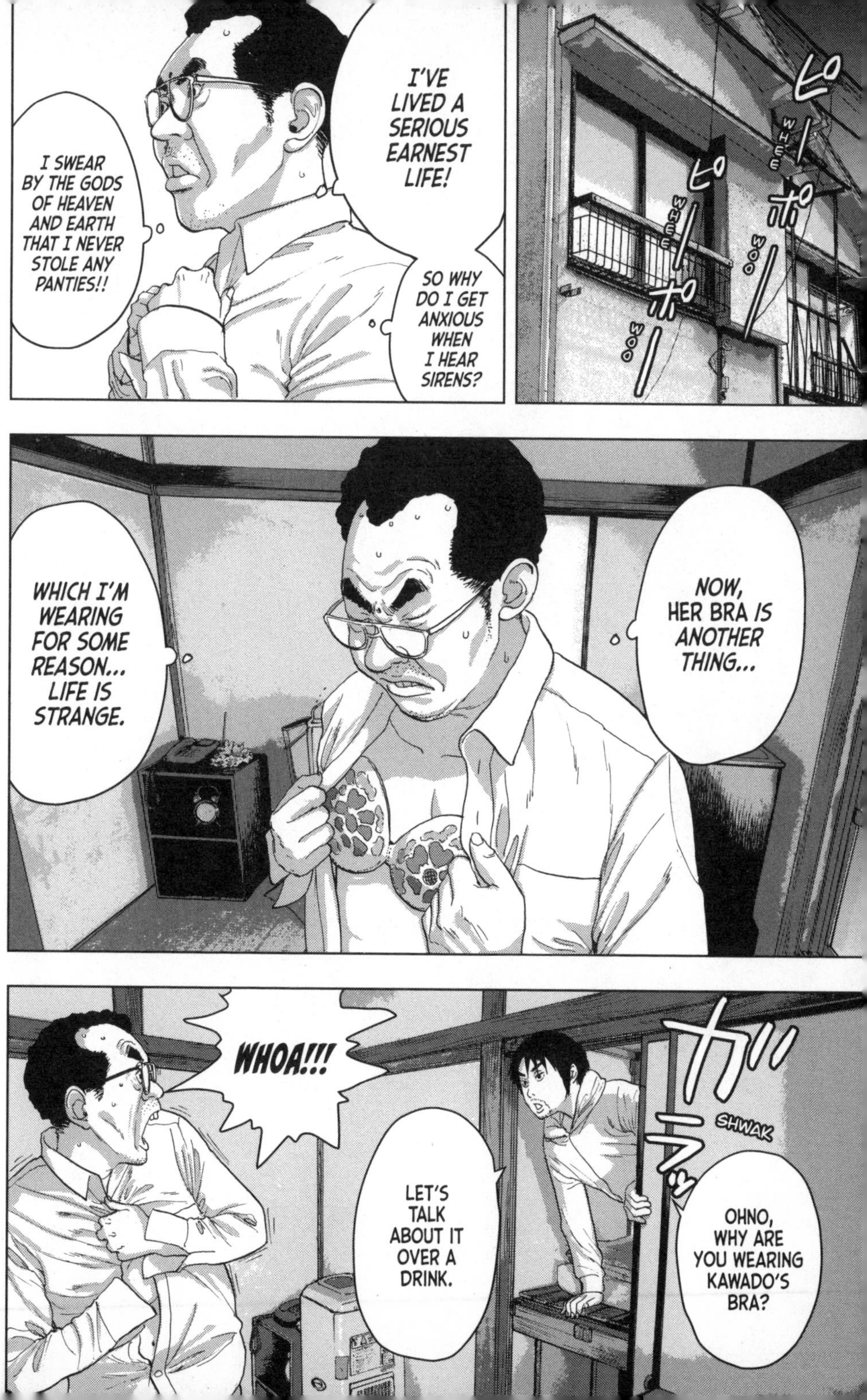
ピーポーピーポー
WHEE WOO WHEE WOO
I'VE LIVED A SERIOUS EARNEST LIFE!
I SWEAR BY THE GODS OF HEAVEN AND EARTH THAT I NEVER STOLE ANY PANTIES!!
SO WHY DO I GET ANXIOUS WHEN I HEAR SIRENS?
NOW, HER BRA IS ANOTHER THING...
WHICH I'M WEARING FOR SOME REASON... LIFE IS STRANGE.
ガラッ
SHWAK
OHNO, WHY ARE YOU WEARING KAWADO'S BRA?
WHOA!!!
LET'S TALK ABOUT IT OVER A DRINK.

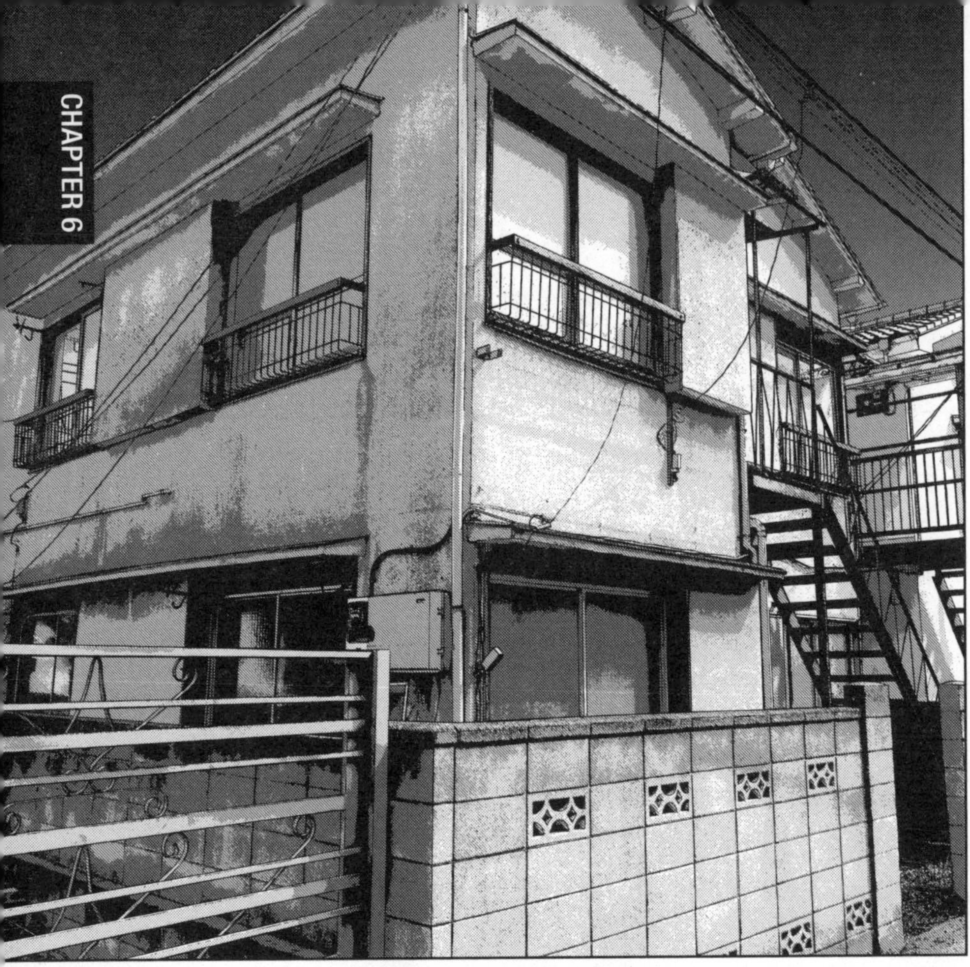
CHAPTER 6

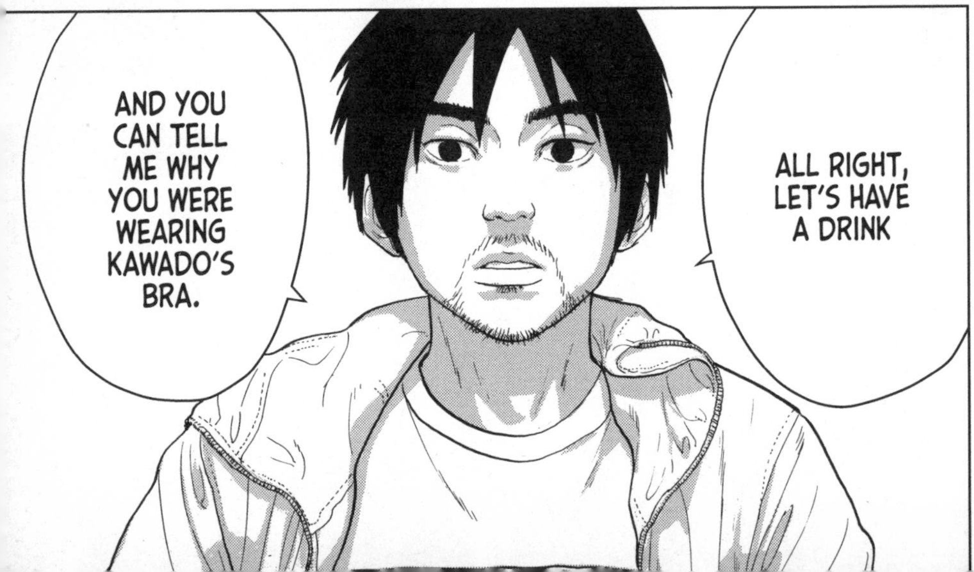
ALL RIGHT, LET'S HAVE A DRINK
AND YOU CAN TELL ME WHY YOU WERE WEARING KAWADO'S BRA.

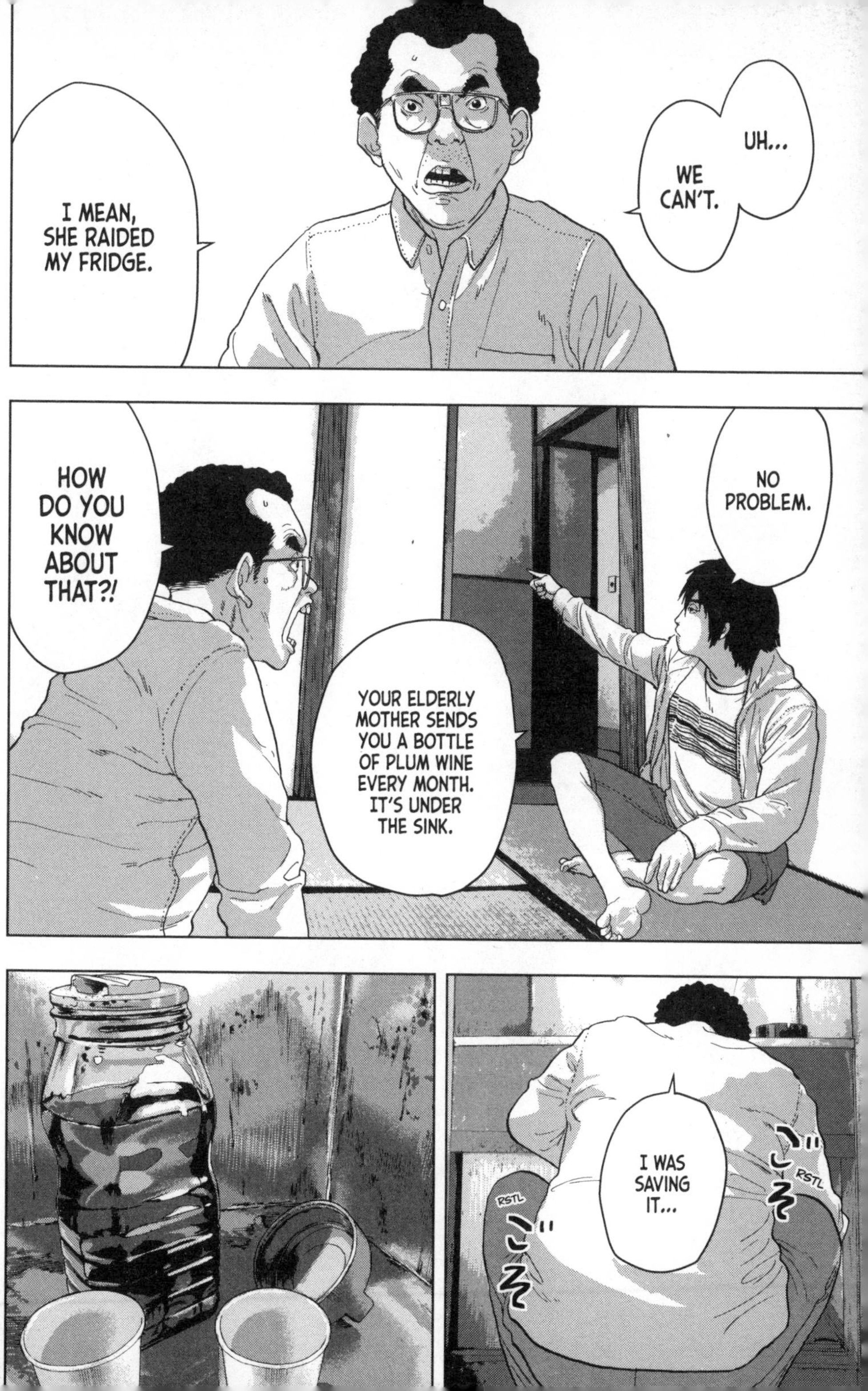
UH... WE CAN'T.
I MEAN, SHE RAIDED MY FRIDGE.
NO PROBLEM.
YOUR ELDERLY MOTHER SENDS YOU A BOTTLE OF PLUM WINE EVERY MONTH. IT'S UNDER THE SINK.
HOW DO YOU KNOW ABOUT THAT?!
RSTL
I WAS SAVING IT...
RSTL

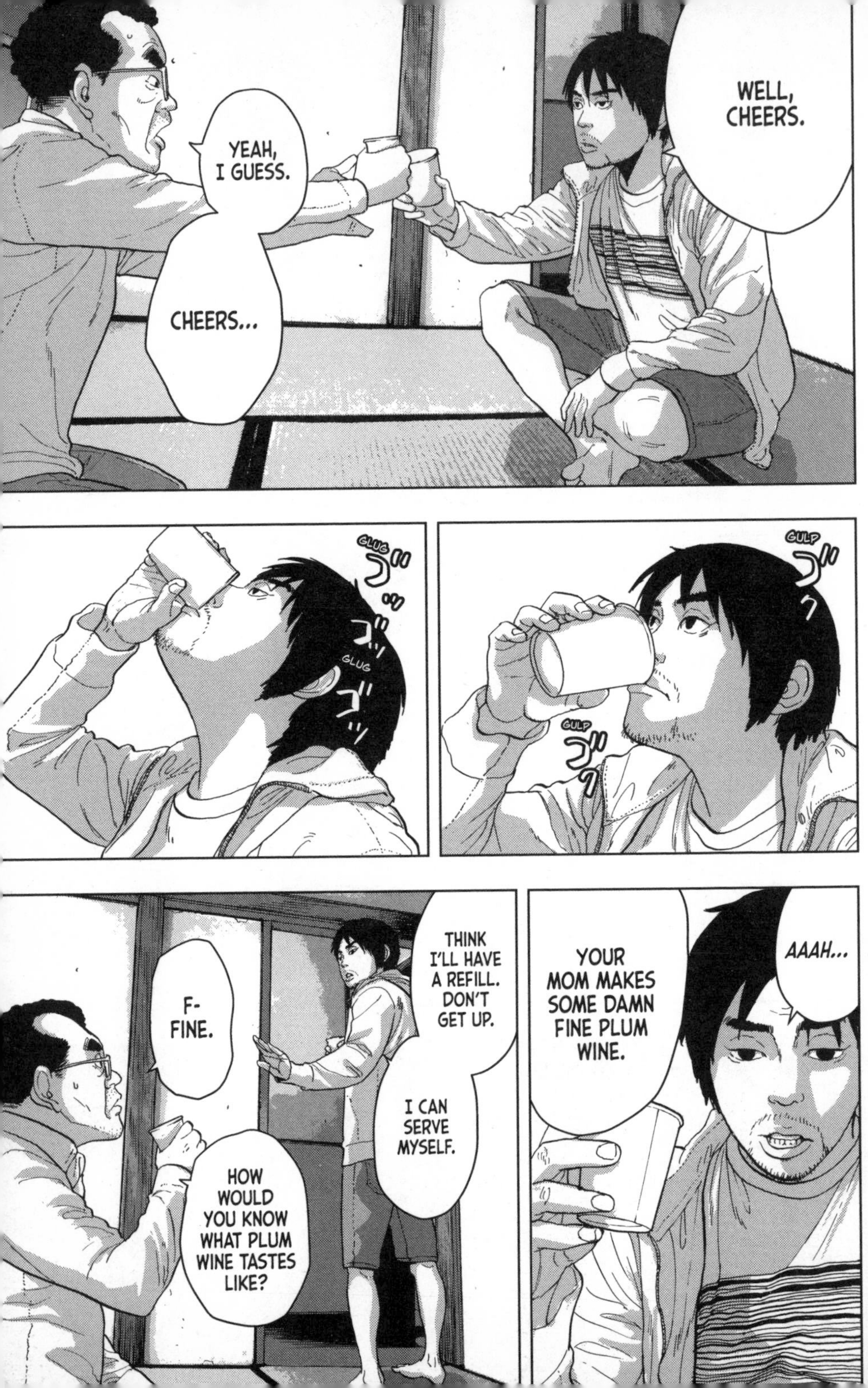
WELL, CHEERS.
YEAH, I GUESS.
CHEERS...
GULP
ゴク
GULP
ゴク
GLUG
ゴッ
GLUG
ゴッ
ゴッ
AAAH...
YOUR MOM MAKES SOME DAMN FINE PLUM WINE.
THINK I'LL HAVE A REFILL. DON'T GET UP.
I CAN SERVE MYSELF.
F-FINE.
HOW WOULD YOU KNOW WHAT PLUM WINE TASTES LIKE?

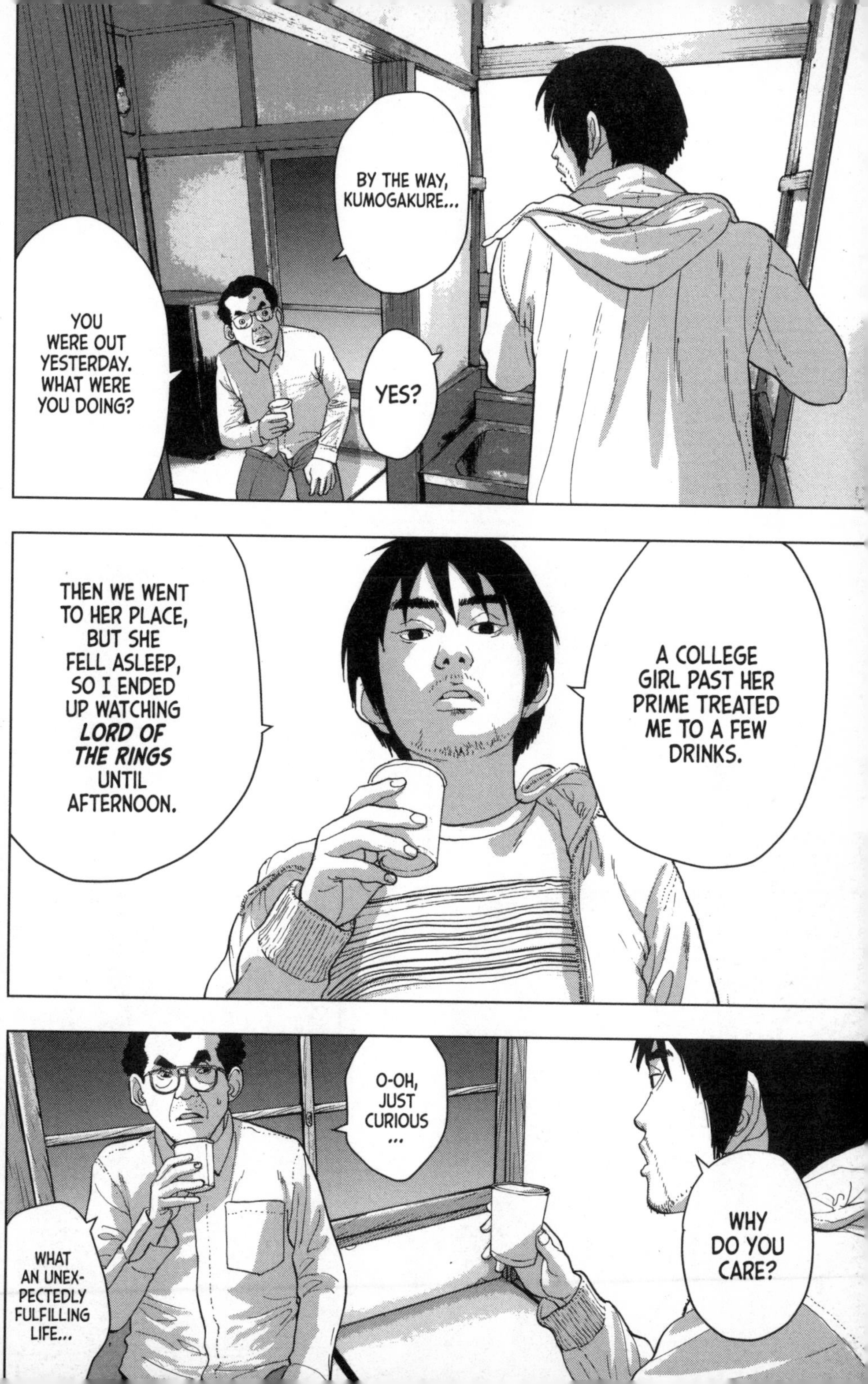
BY THE WAY, KUMOGAKURE...
YES?
YOU WERE OUT YESTERDAY. WHAT WERE YOU DOING?
A COLLEGE GIRL PAST HER PRIME TREATED ME TO A FEW DRINKS.
THEN WE WENT TO HER PLACE, BUT SHE FELL ASLEEP, SO I ENDED UP WATCHING *LORD OF THE RINGS* UNTIL AFTERNOON.
WHY DO YOU CARE?
O-OH, JUST CURIOUS...
WHAT AN UNEXPECTEDLY FULFILLING LIFE...

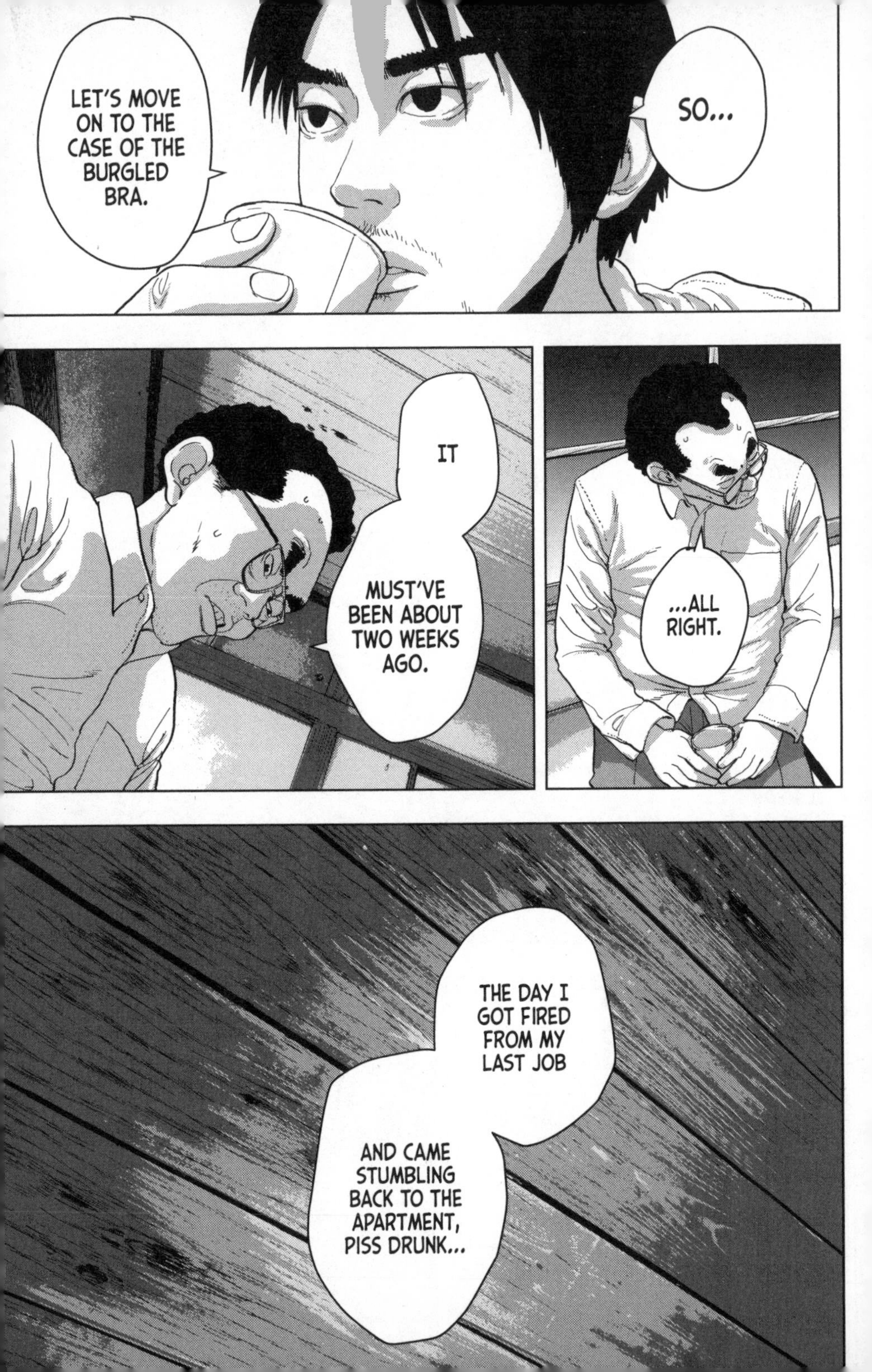
SO...
LET'S MOVE ON TO THE CASE OF THE BURGLED BRA.
...ALL RIGHT.
IT MUST'VE BEEN ABOUT TWO WEEKS AGO.
THE DAY I GOT FIRED FROM MY LAST JOB
AND CAME STUMBLING BACK TO THE APARTMENT, PISS DRUNK...

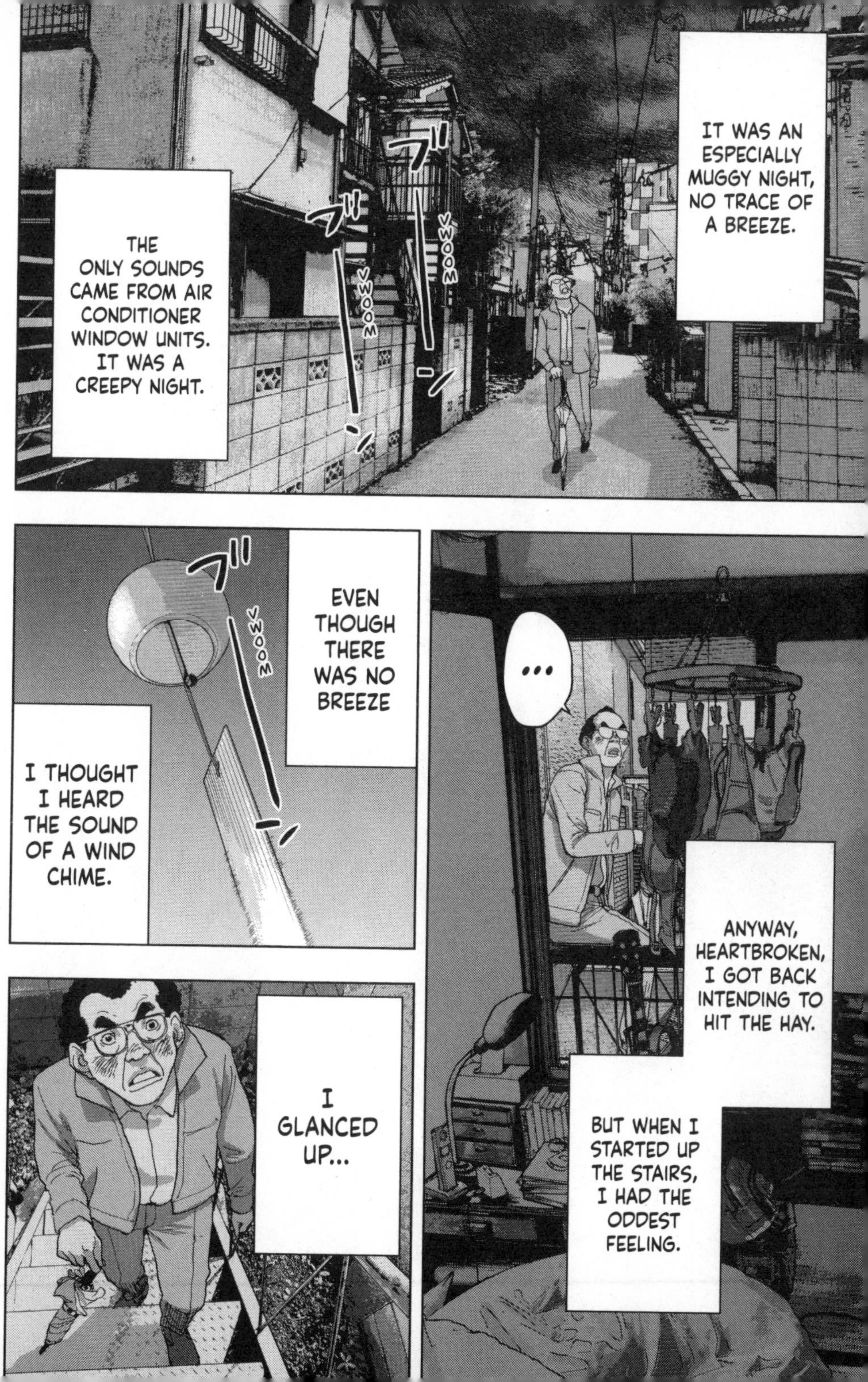
IT WAS AN ESPECIALLY MUGGY NIGHT, NO TRACE OF A BREEZE.
VWOOM
VWOOM
THE ONLY SOUNDS CAME FROM AIR CONDITIONER WINDOW UNITS. IT WAS A CREEPY NIGHT.
...
ANYWAY, HEARTBROKEN, I GOT BACK INTENDING TO HIT THE HAY.
BUT WHEN I STARTED UP THE STAIRS, I HAD THE ODDEST FEELING.
EVEN THOUGH THERE WAS NO BREEZE
VWOOM
I THOUGHT I HEARD THE SOUND OF A WIND CHIME.
I GLANCED UP...

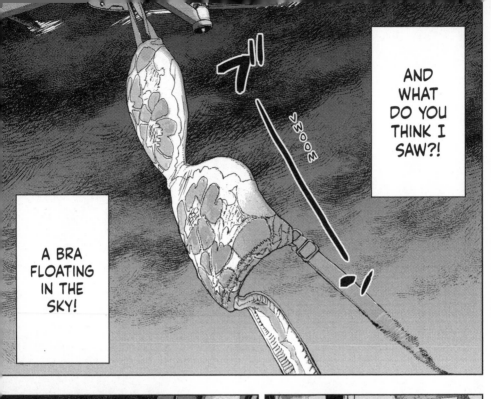

AND WHAT DO YOU THINK I SAW?!

A BRA FLOATING IN THE SKY!

MY MIND TOLD ME NOT TO GET INVOLVED.

BUT MY BODY CLAMBERED UP THE STAIRS...

I WAS STUNNED.

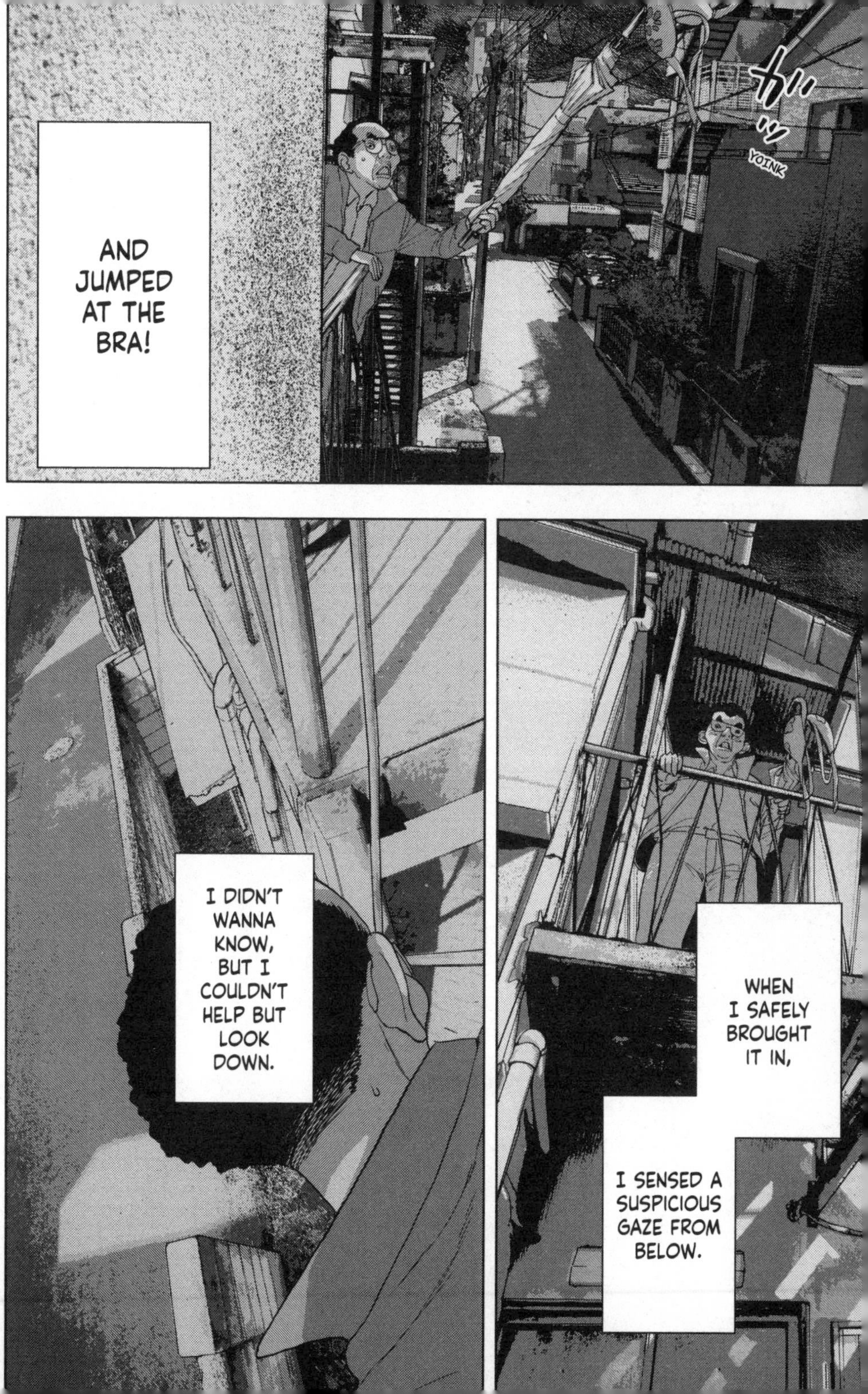
AND JUMPED AT THE BRA!
YOINK
WHEN I SAFELY BROUGHT IT IN,
I SENSED A SUSPICIOUS GAZE FROM BELOW.
I DIDN'T WANNA KNOW, BUT I COULDN'T HELP BUT LOOK DOWN.

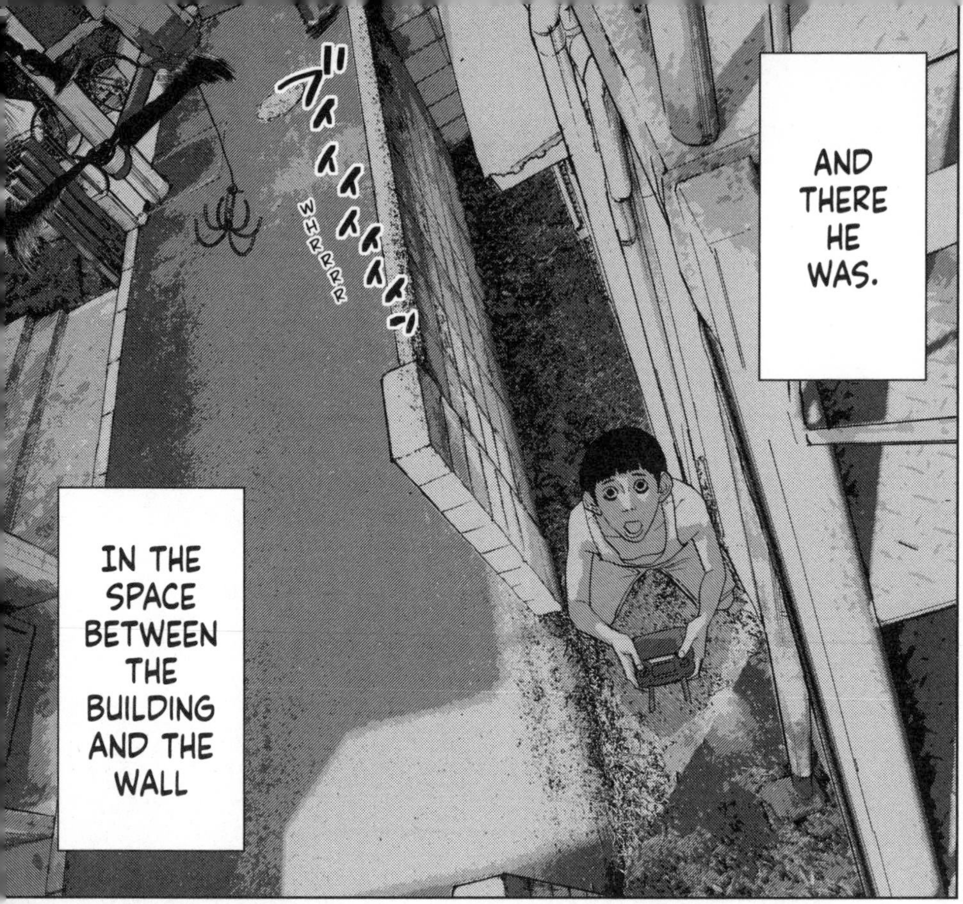
AND THERE HE WAS.
WHRRRR
IN THE SPACE BETWEEN THE BUILDING AND THE WALL

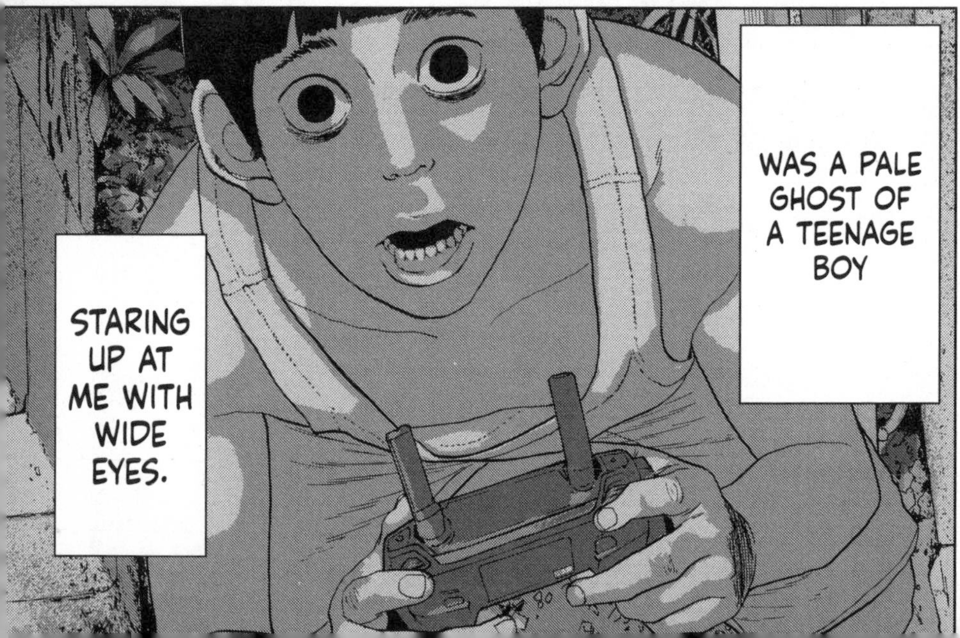
WAS A PALE GHOST OF A TEENAGE BOY
STARING UP AT ME WITH WIDE EYES.

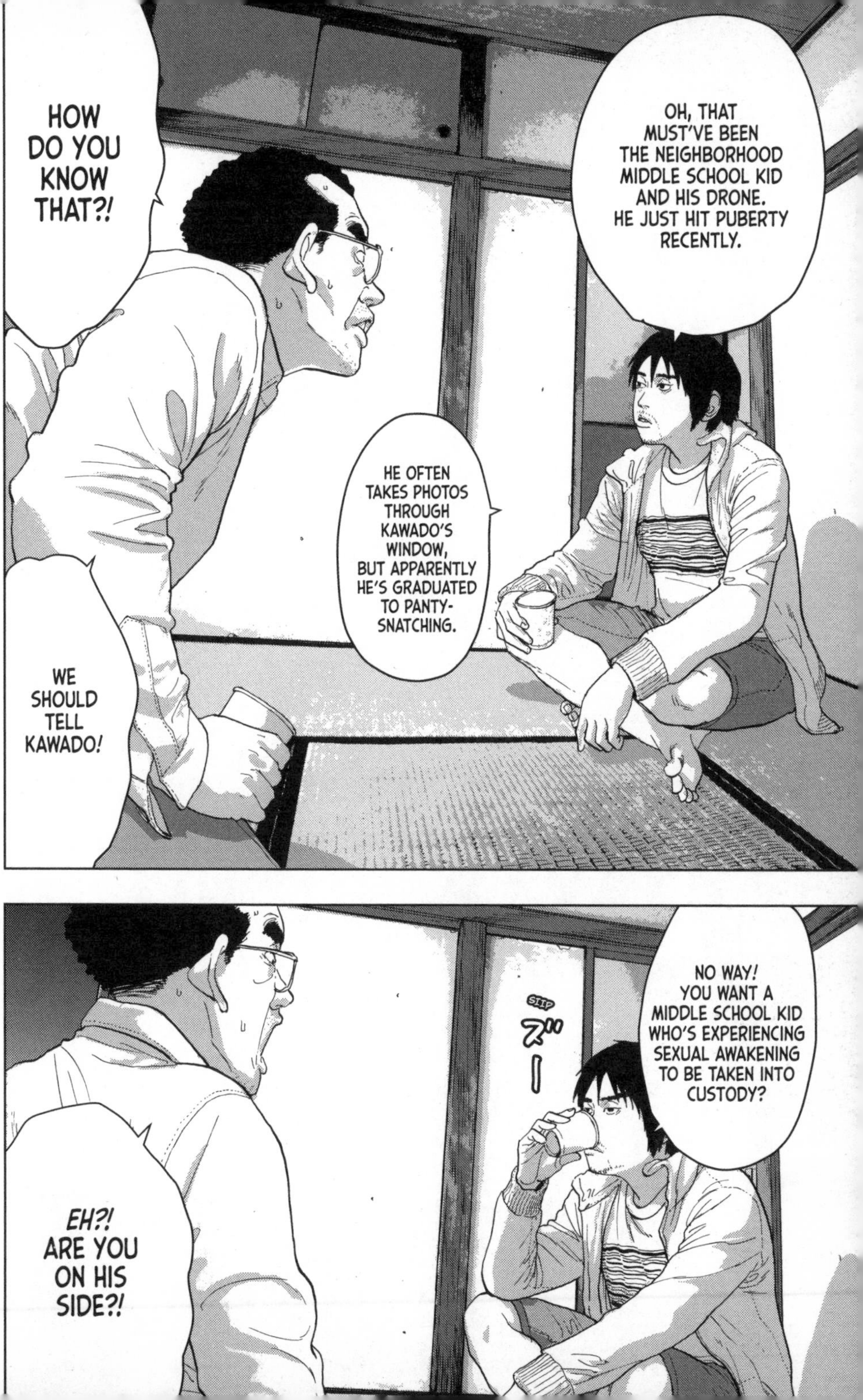
OH, THAT MUST'VE BEEN THE NEIGHBORHOOD MIDDLE SCHOOL KID AND HIS DRONE. HE JUST HIT PUBERTY RECENTLY.
HOW DO YOU KNOW THAT?!
HE OFTEN TAKES PHOTOS THROUGH KAWADO'S WINDOW, BUT APPARENTLY HE'S GRADUATED TO PANTY-SNATCHING.
WE SHOULD TELL KAWADO!
NO WAY! YOU WANT A MIDDLE SCHOOL KID WHO'S EXPERIENCING SEXUAL AWAKENING TO BE TAKEN INTO CUSTODY?
SIIP
ズー
EH?! ARE YOU ON HIS SIDE?!

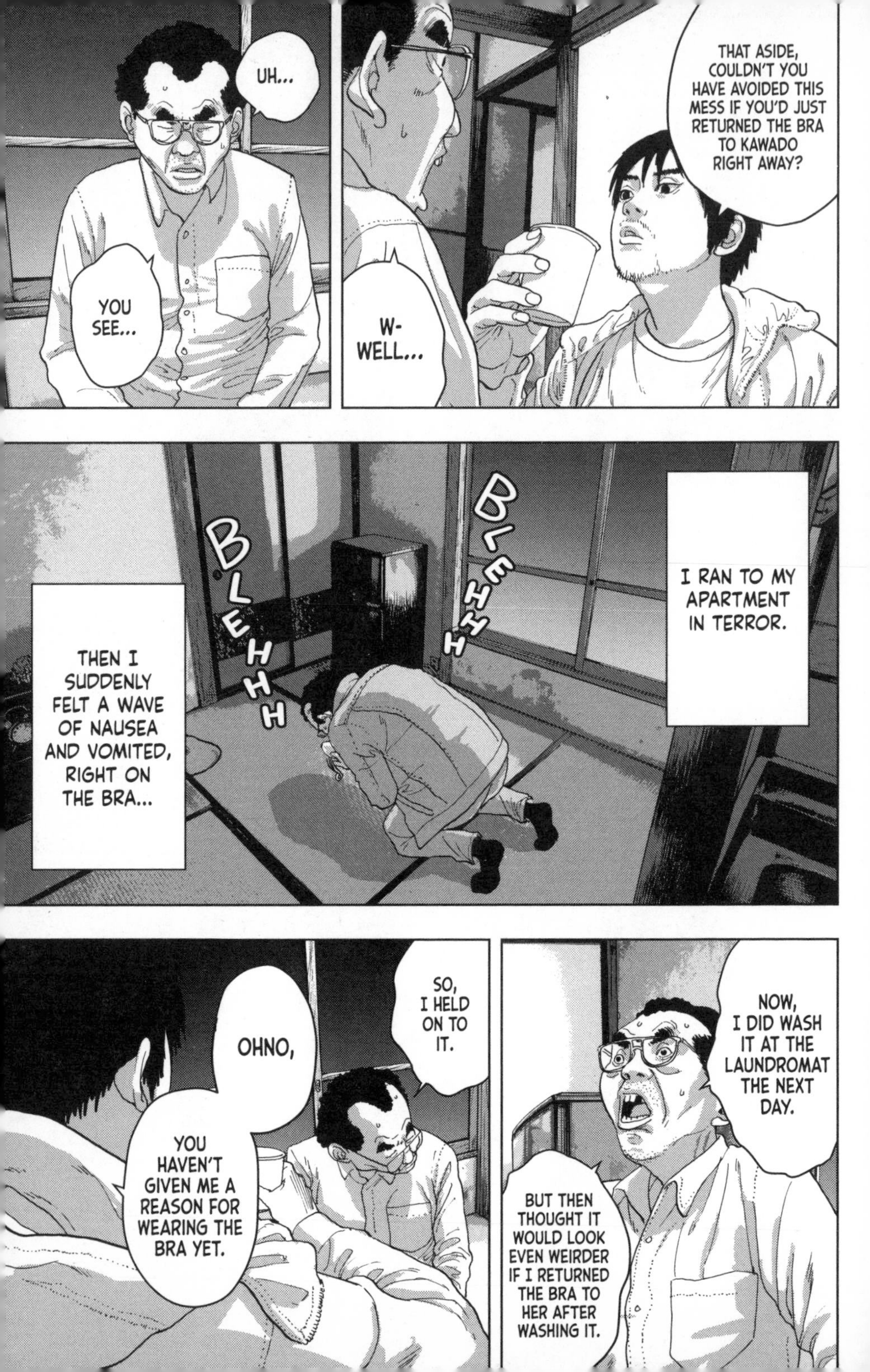
THAT ASIDE, COULDN'T YOU HAVE AVOIDED THIS MESS IF YOU'D JUST RETURNED THE BRA TO KAWADO RIGHT AWAY?
W-WELL...
UH...
YOU SEE...
I RAN TO MY APARTMENT IN TERROR.
BLEHHH
BLEHHH
THEN I SUDDENLY FELT A WAVE OF NAUSEA AND VOMITED, RIGHT ON THE BRA...
NOW, I DID WASH IT AT THE LAUNDROMAT THE NEXT DAY.
BUT THEN THOUGHT IT WOULD LOOK EVEN WEIRDER IF I RETURNED THE BRA TO HER AFTER WASHING IT.
SO, I HELD ON TO IT.
OHNO,
YOU HAVEN'T GIVEN ME A REASON FOR WEARING THE BRA YET.

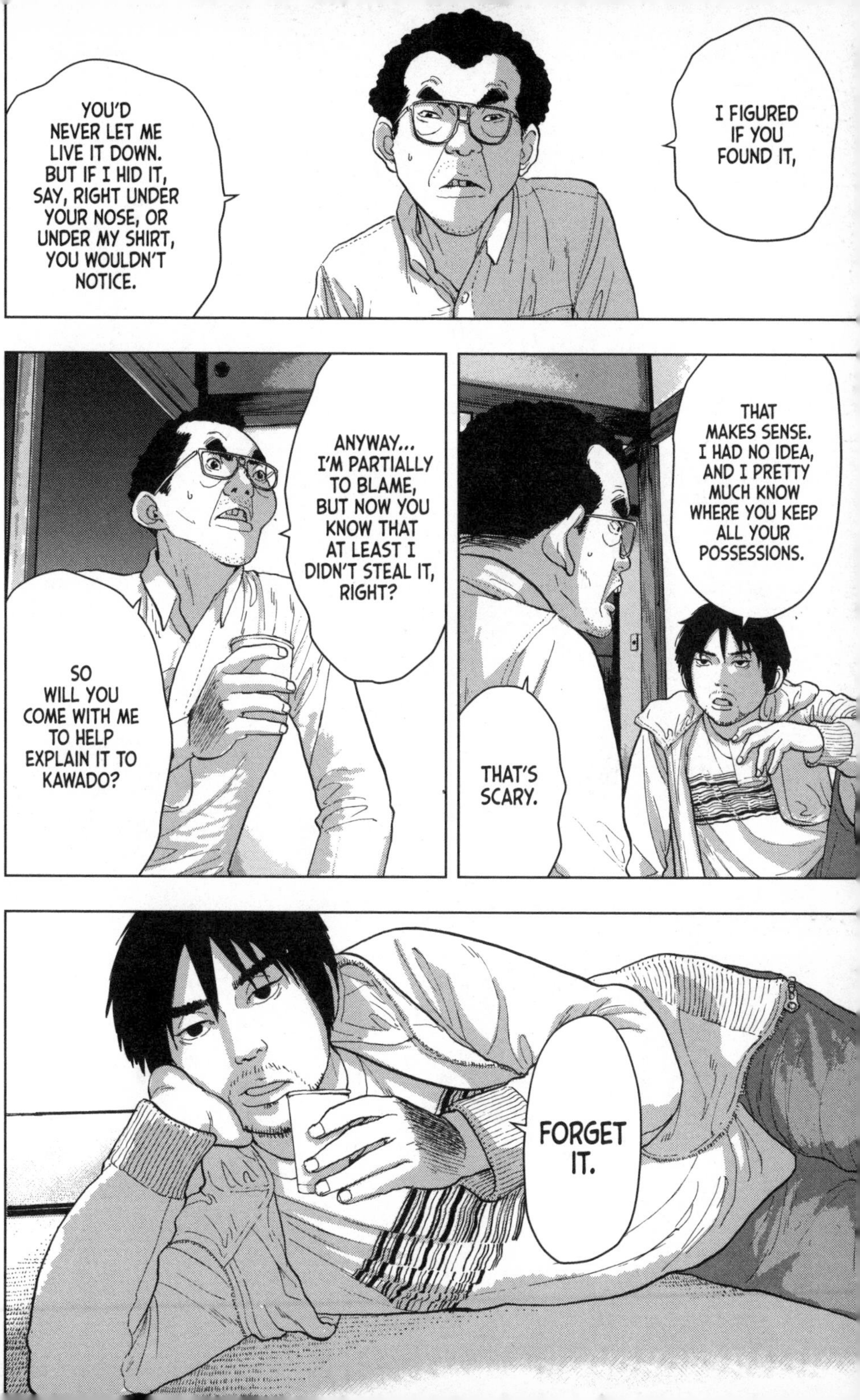
I FIGURED IF YOU FOUND IT,
YOU'D NEVER LET ME LIVE IT DOWN. BUT IF I HID IT, SAY, RIGHT UNDER YOUR NOSE, OR UNDER MY SHIRT, YOU WOULDN'T NOTICE.
THAT MAKES SENSE. I HAD NO IDEA, AND I PRETTY MUCH KNOW WHERE YOU KEEP ALL YOUR POSSESSIONS.
THAT'S SCARY.
ANYWAY... I'M PARTIALLY TO BLAME, BUT NOW YOU KNOW THAT AT LEAST I DIDN'T STEAL IT, RIGHT?
SO WILL YOU COME WITH ME TO HELP EXPLAIN IT TO KAWADO?
FORGET IT.

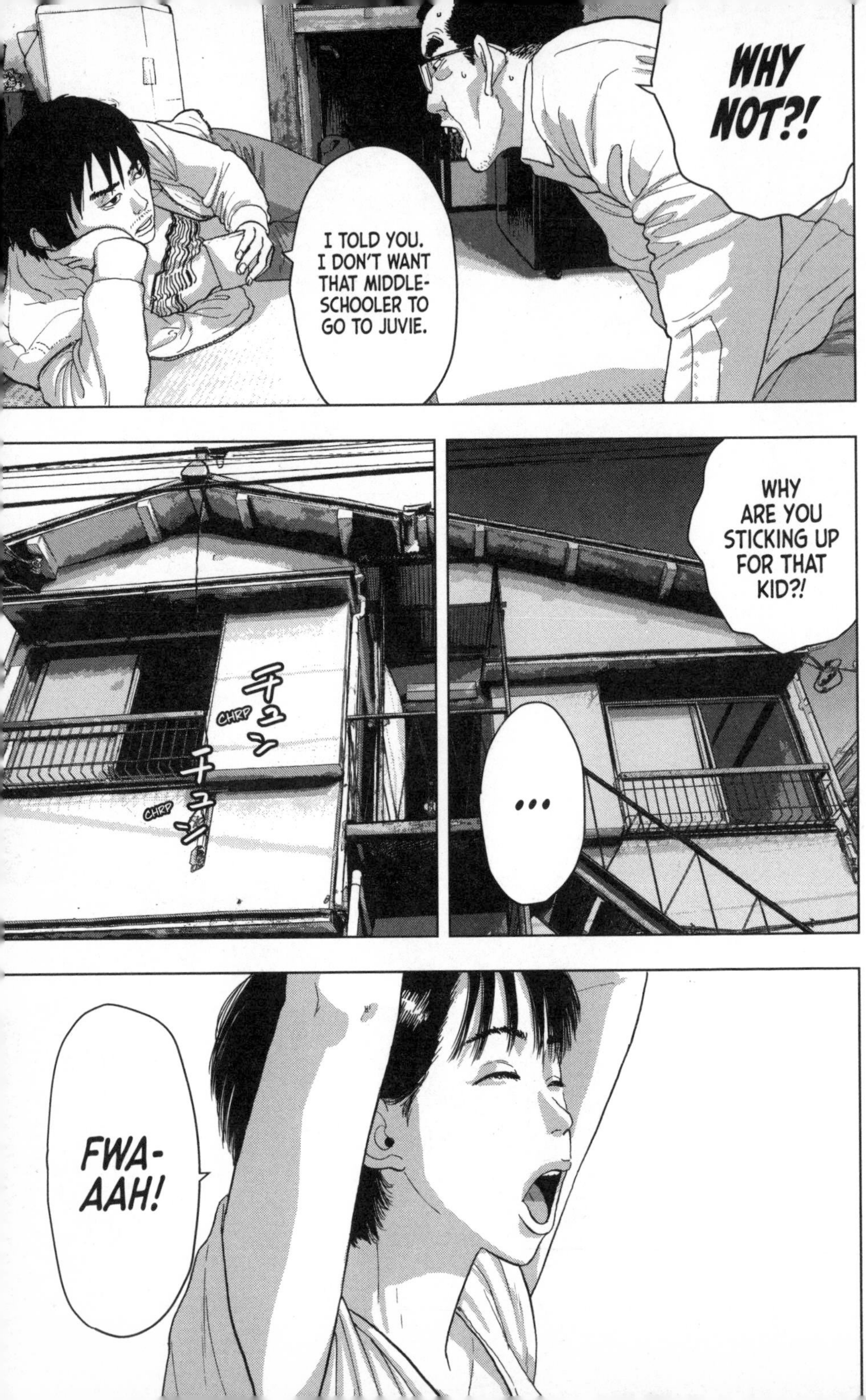
WHY NOT?!
I TOLD YOU. I DON'T WANT THAT MIDDLE-SCHOOLER TO GO TO JUVIE.
WHY ARE YOU STICKING UP FOR THAT KID?!
...
チュン CHRP
チュン CHRP
FWA-AAH!

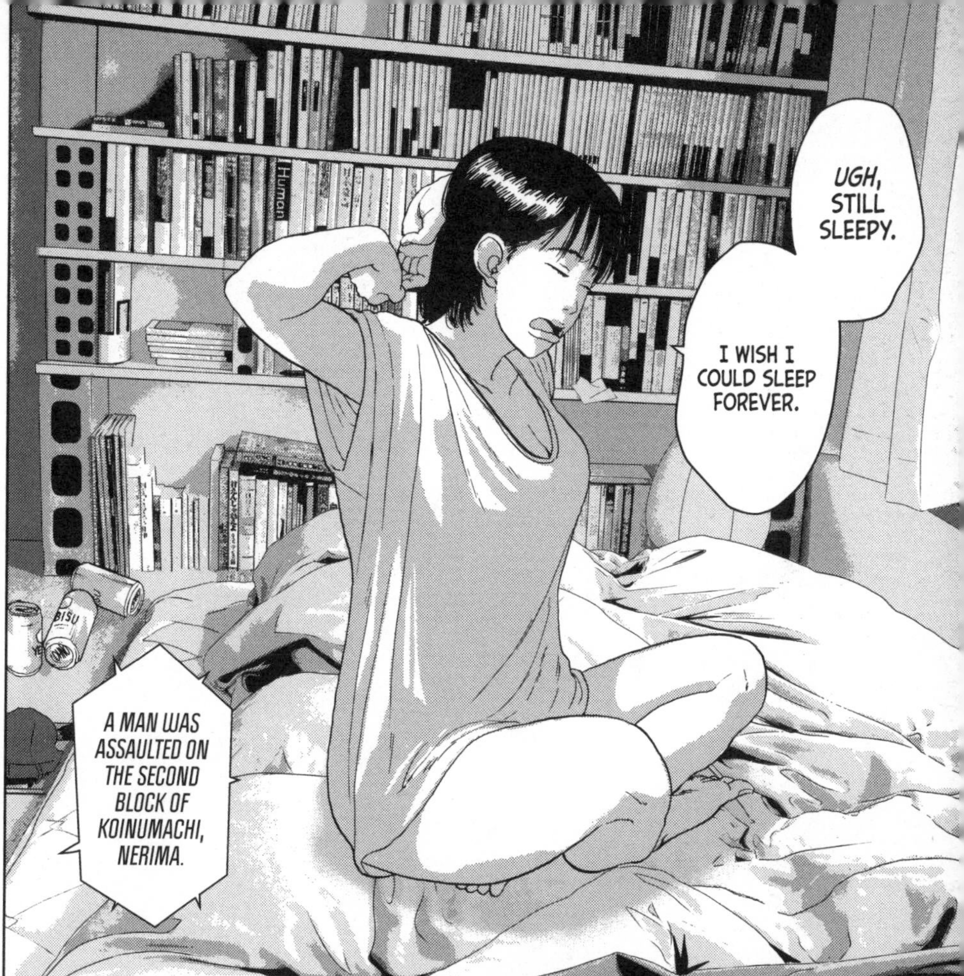
UGH, STILL SLEEPY.
I WISH I COULD SLEEP FOREVER.
A MAN WAS ASSAULTED ON THE SECOND BLOCK OF KOINUMACHI, NERIMA.
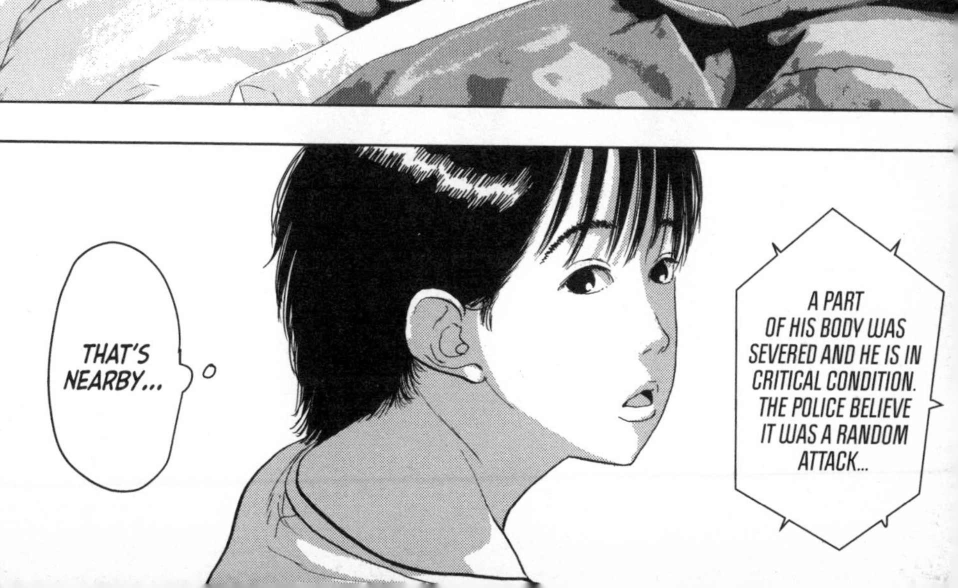
A PART OF HIS BODY WAS SEVERED AND HE IS IN CRITICAL CONDITION. THE POLICE BELIEVE IT WAS A RANDOM ATTACK...
THAT'S NEARBY...

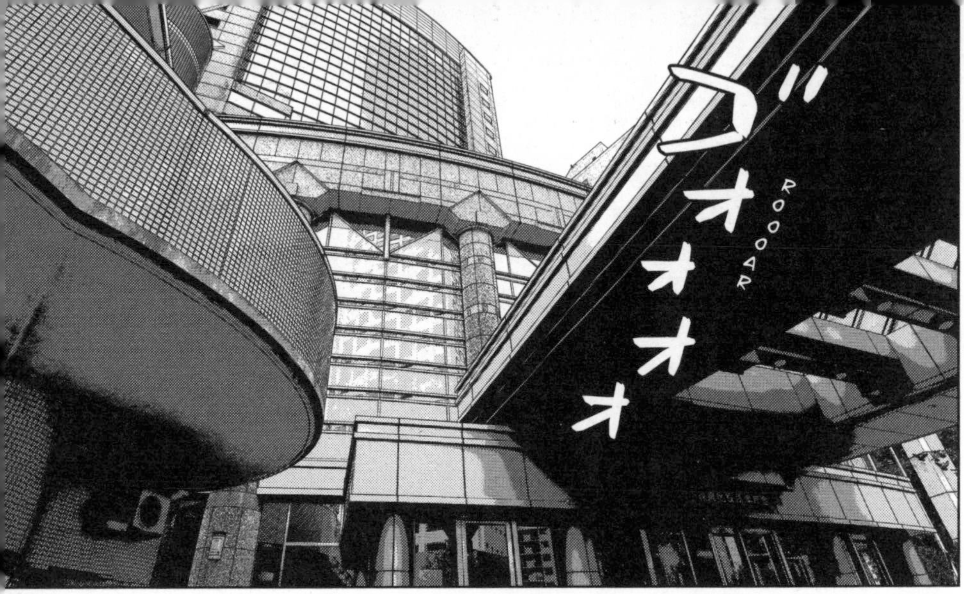
ゴォォォォ
ROOOAR
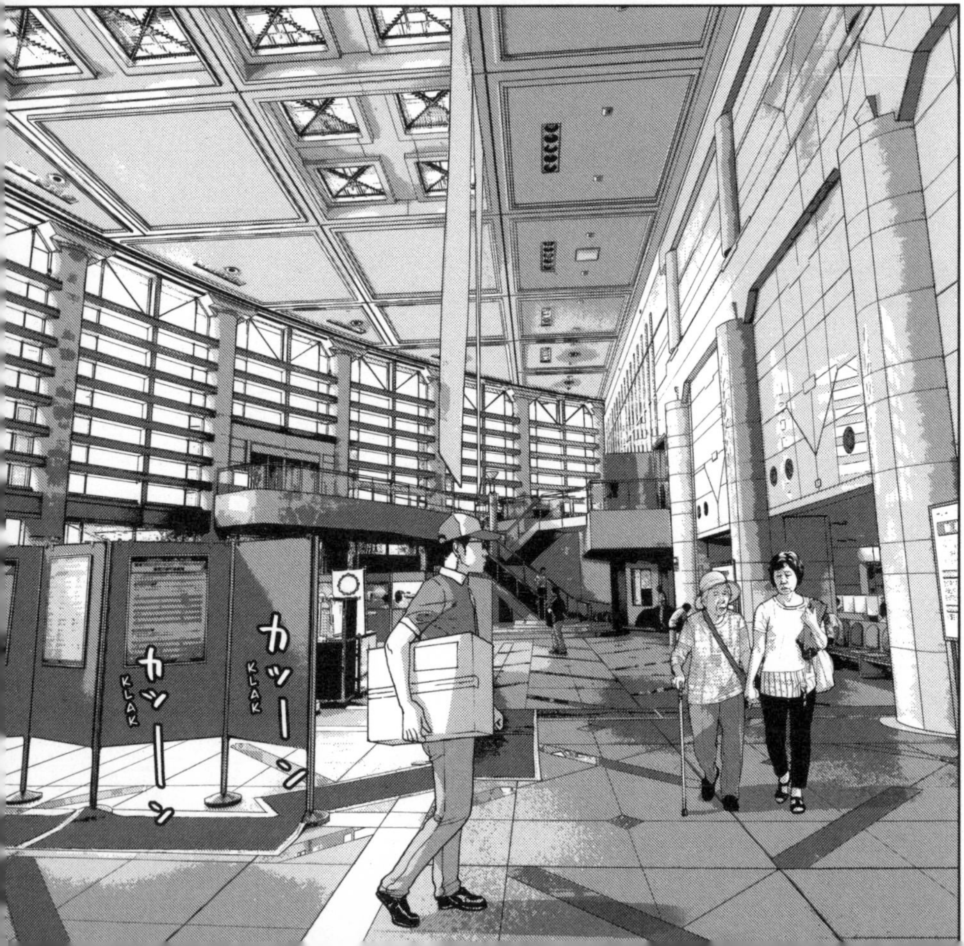
カツーン
KLAK
カツーン
KLAK

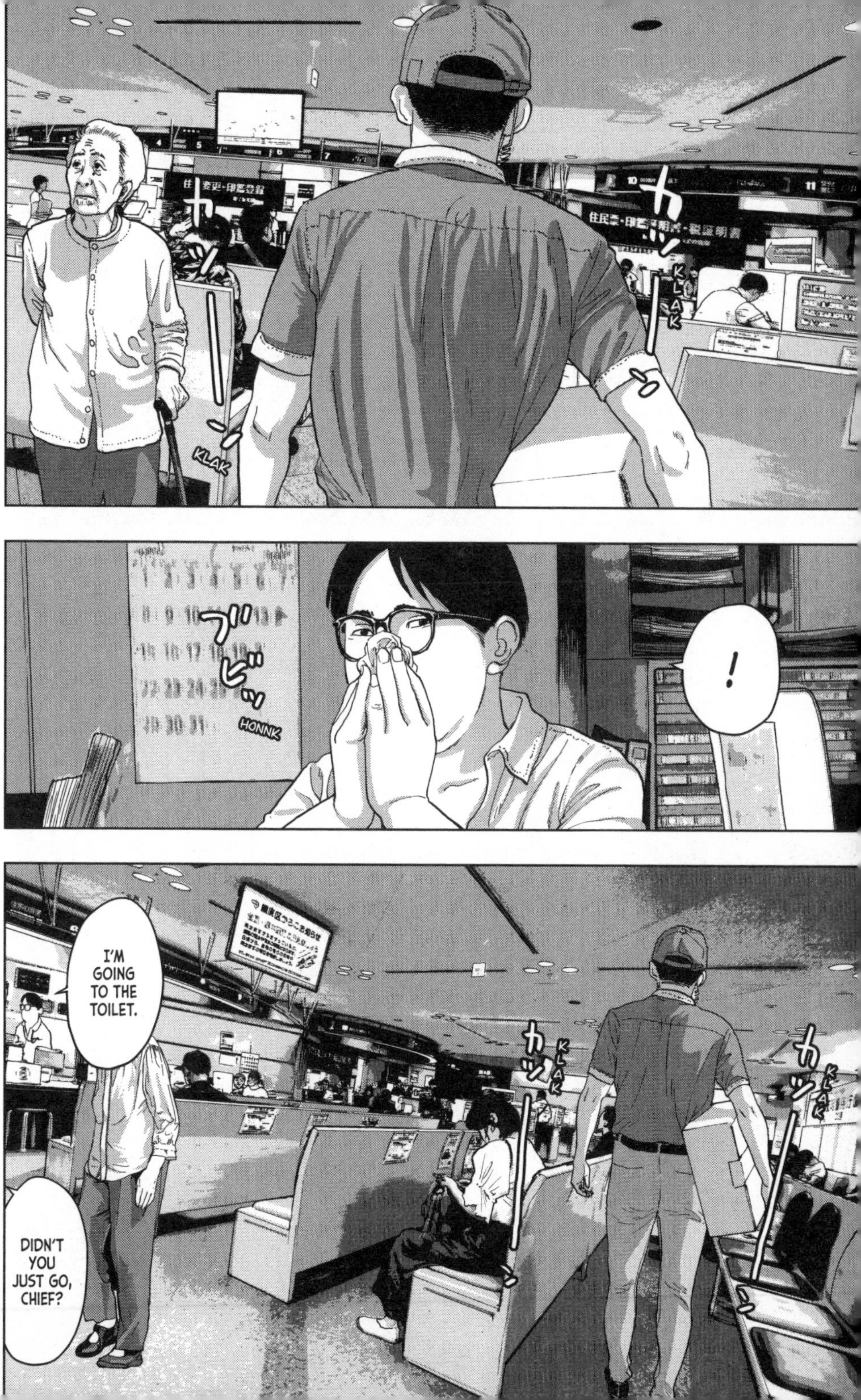

カッ
KLAK
カッ
KLAK
!
ブビッ
HONNK
カッ
KLAK
カッ
KLAK
I'M GOING TO THE TOILET.
DIDN'T YOU JUST GO, CHIEF?

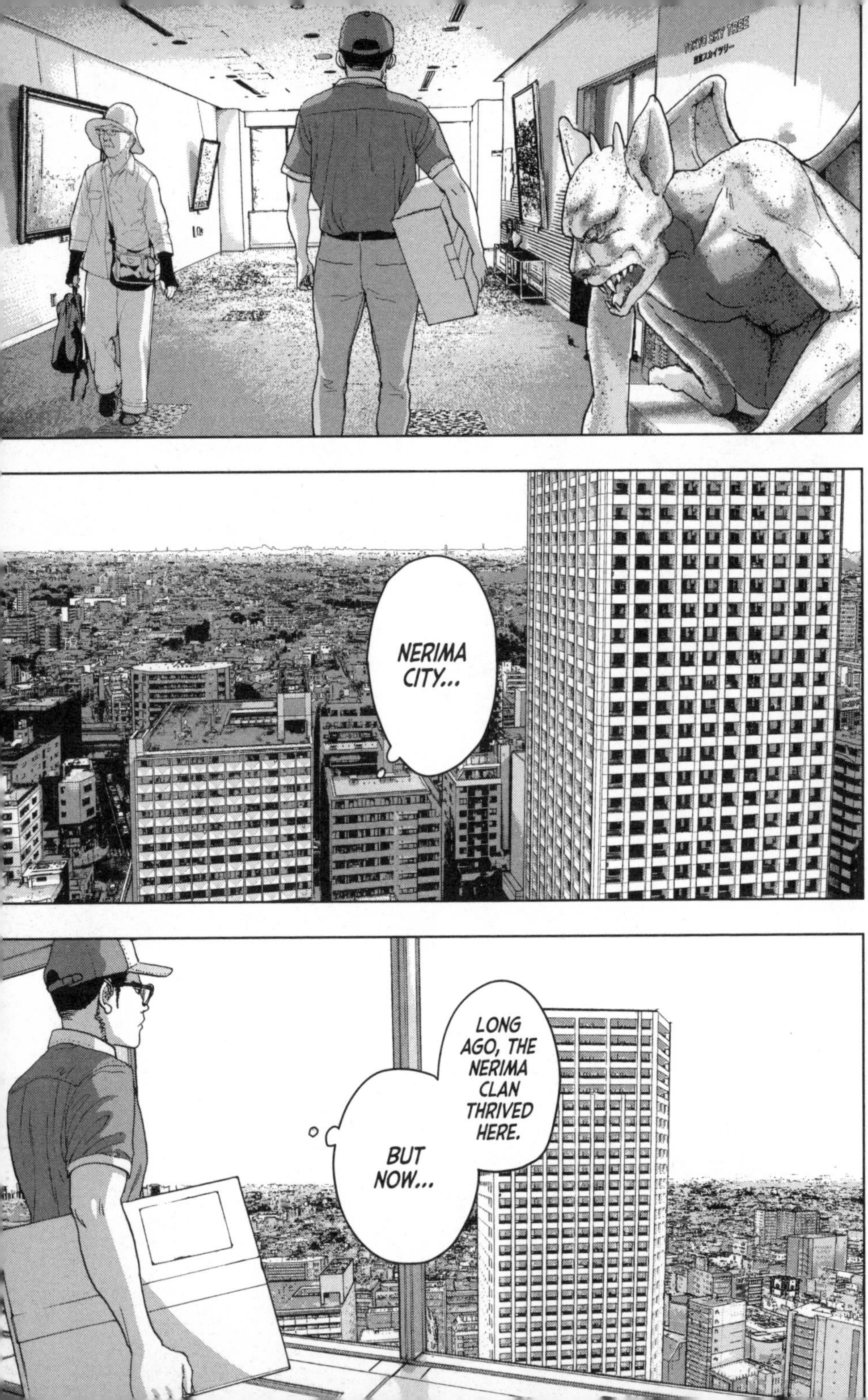
TOKYO SKY TREE
東京スカイツリー
NERIMA CITY...
LONG AGO, THE NERIMA CLAN THRIVED HERE.
BUT NOW...

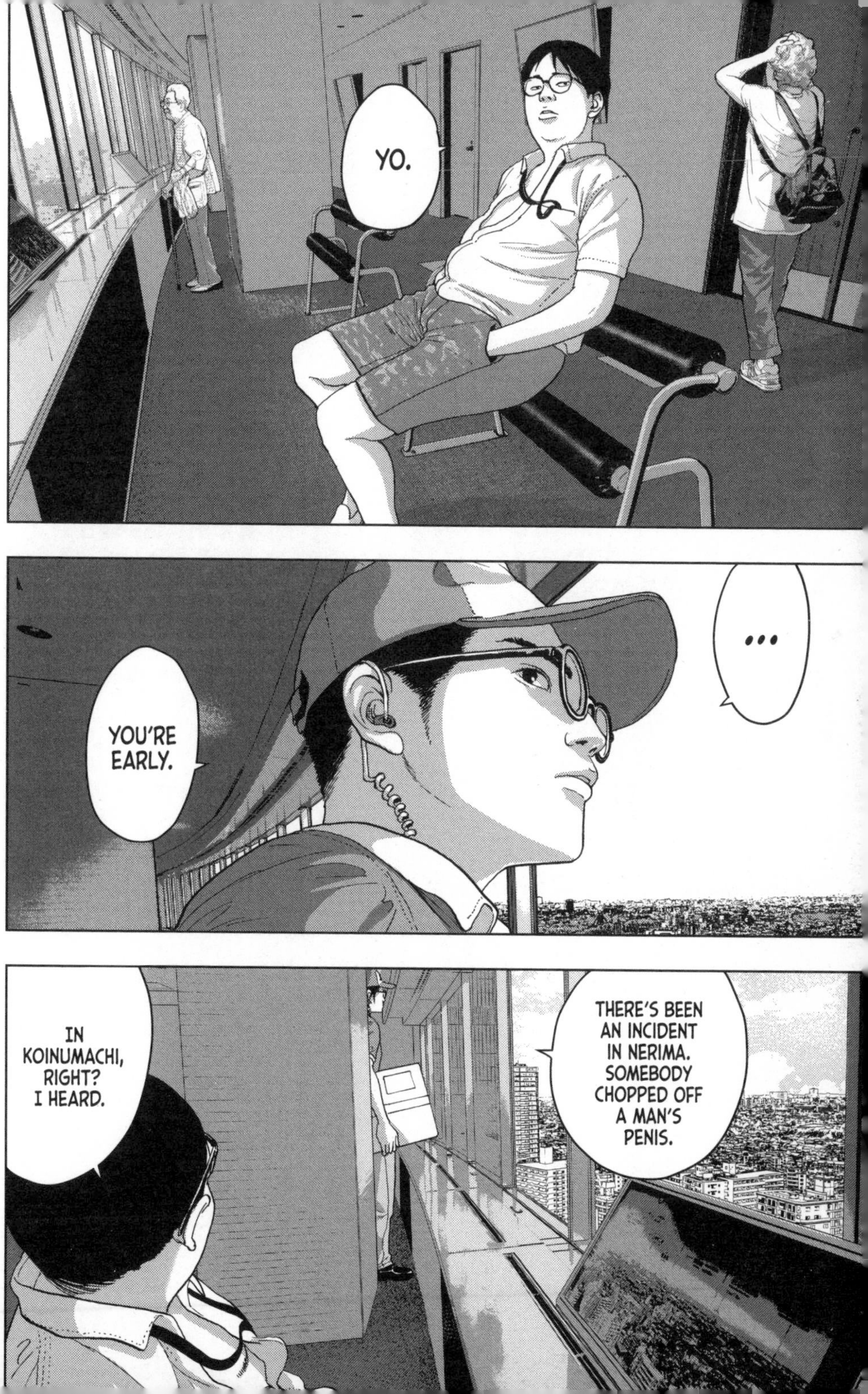
YO.
...
YOU'RE EARLY.
THERE'S BEEN AN INCIDENT IN NERIMA. SOMEBODY CHOPPED OFF A MAN'S PENIS.
IN KOINUMACHI, RIGHT? I HEARD.

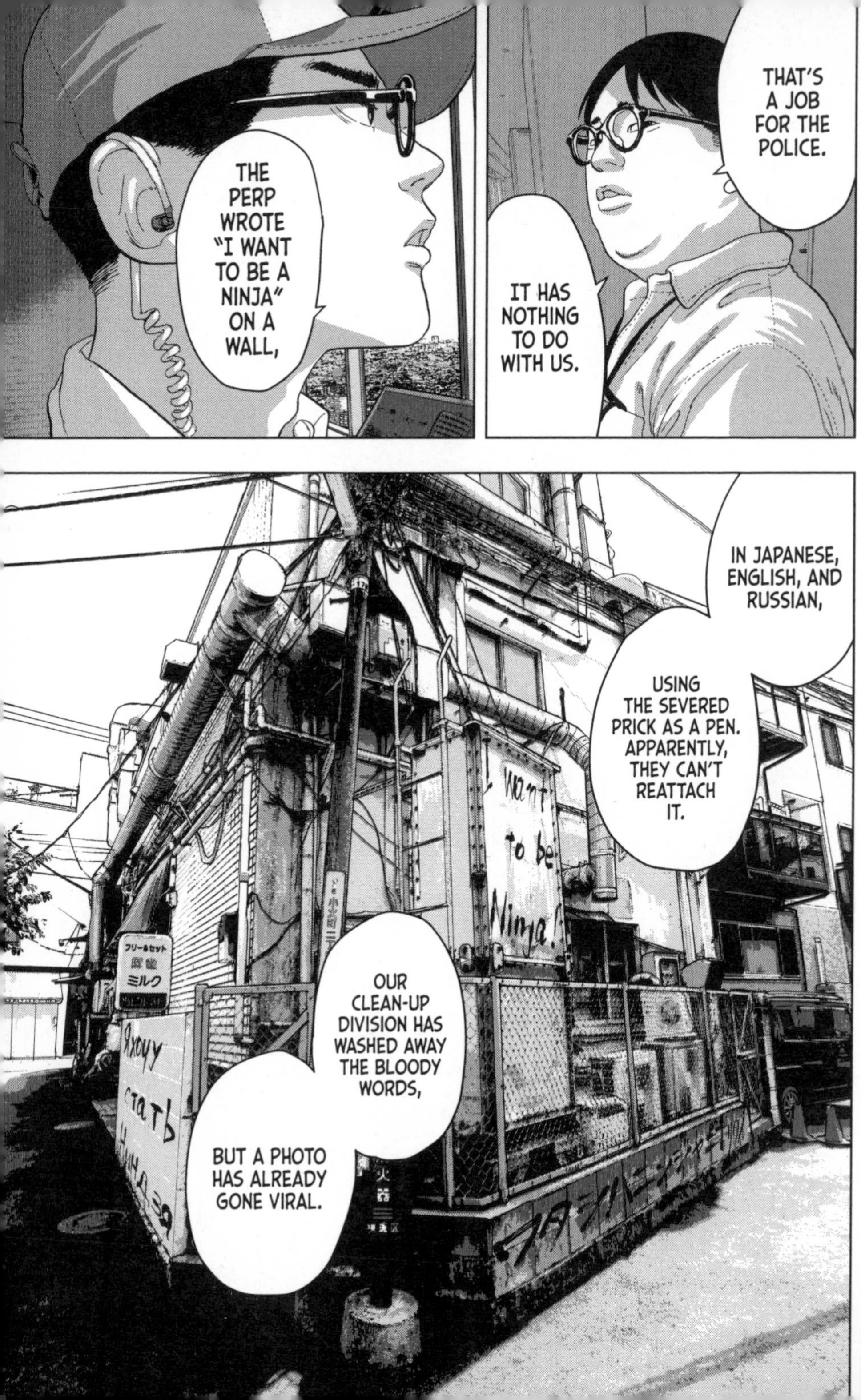
THAT'S A JOB FOR THE POLICE.
IT HAS NOTHING TO DO WITH US.
THE PERP WROTE "I WANT TO BE A NINJA" ON A WALL,
IN JAPANESE, ENGLISH, AND RUSSIAN,
USING THE SEVERED PRICK AS A PEN. APPARENTLY, THEY CAN'T REATTACH IT.
OUR CLEAN-UP DIVISION HAS WASHED AWAY THE BLOODY WORDS,
BUT A PHOTO HAS ALREADY GONE VIRAL.

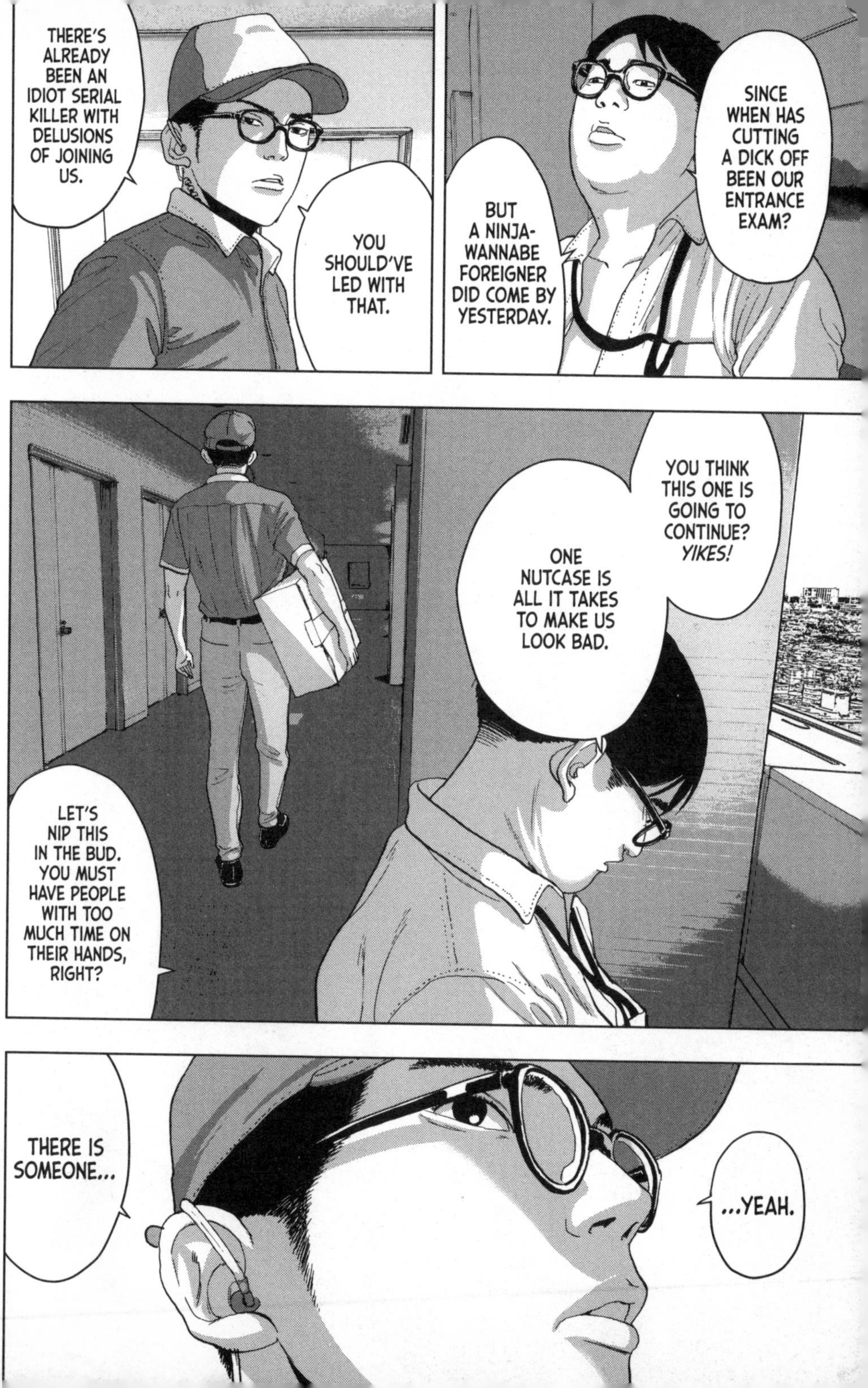
SINCE WHEN HAS CUTTING A DICK OFF BEEN OUR ENTRANCE EXAM?
BUT A NINJA-WANNABE FOREIGNER DID COME BY YESTERDAY.
YOU SHOULD'VE LED WITH THAT.
THERE'S ALREADY BEEN AN IDIOT SERIAL KILLER WITH DELUSIONS OF JOINING US.
YOU THINK THIS ONE IS GOING TO CONTINUE? *YIKES!*
ONE NUTCASE IS ALL IT TAKES TO MAKE US LOOK BAD.
LET'S NIP THIS IN THE BUD. YOU MUST HAVE PEOPLE WITH TOO MUCH TIME ON THEIR HANDS, RIGHT?
...YEAH.
THERE IS SOMEONE...

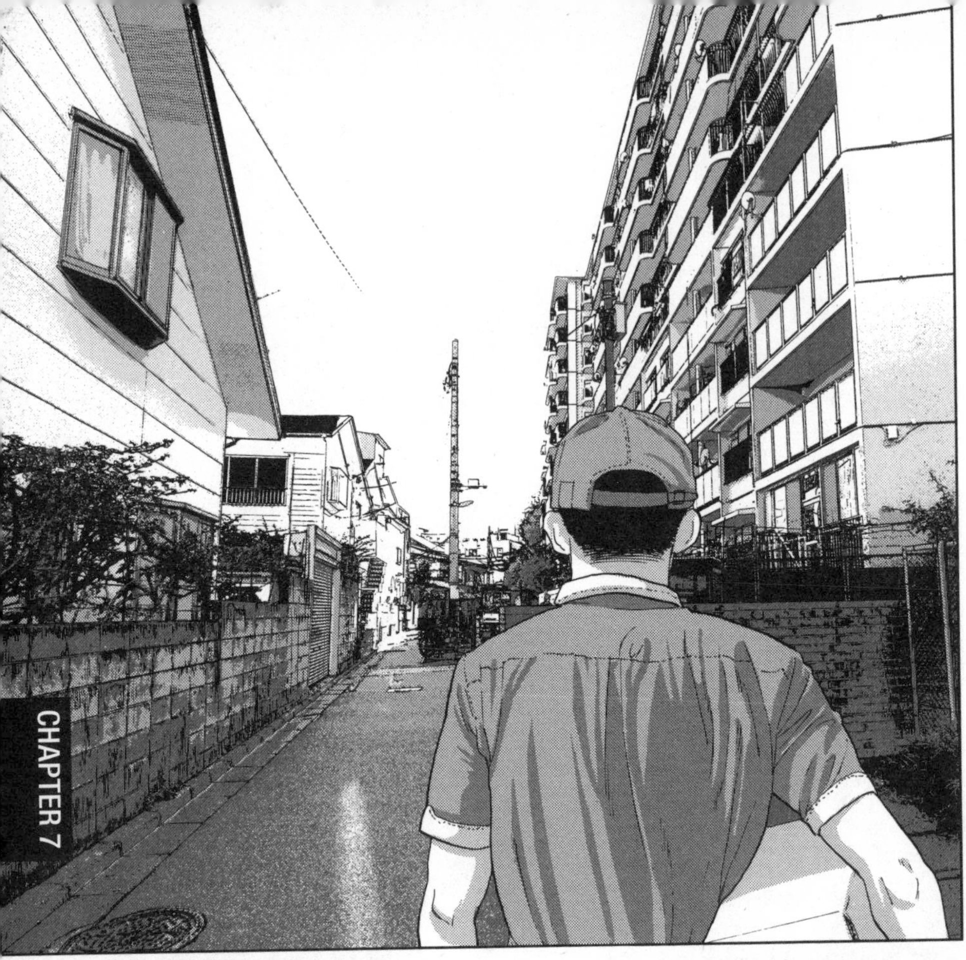
CHAPTER 7

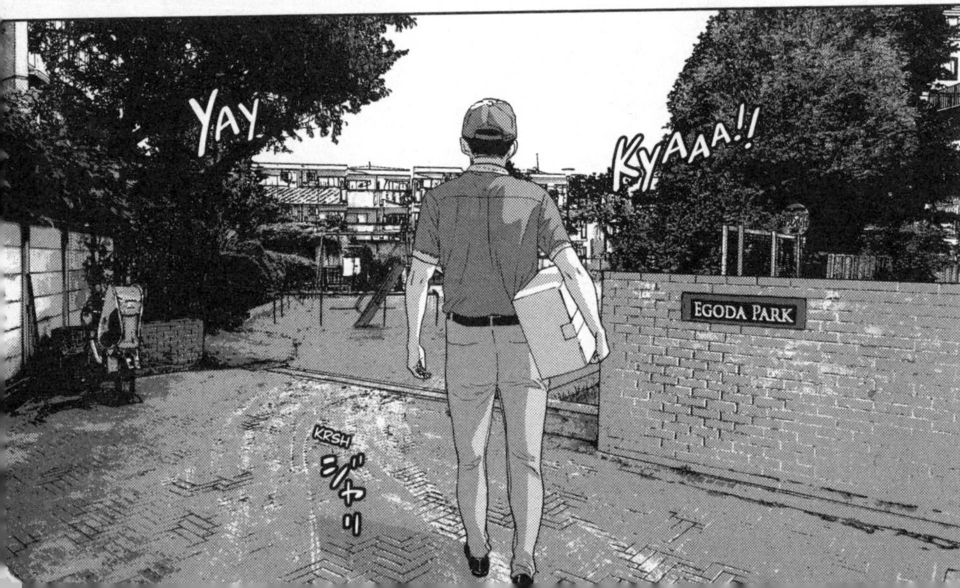
KYAAA!!
YAY
EGODA PARK
KRSH
ジャリ

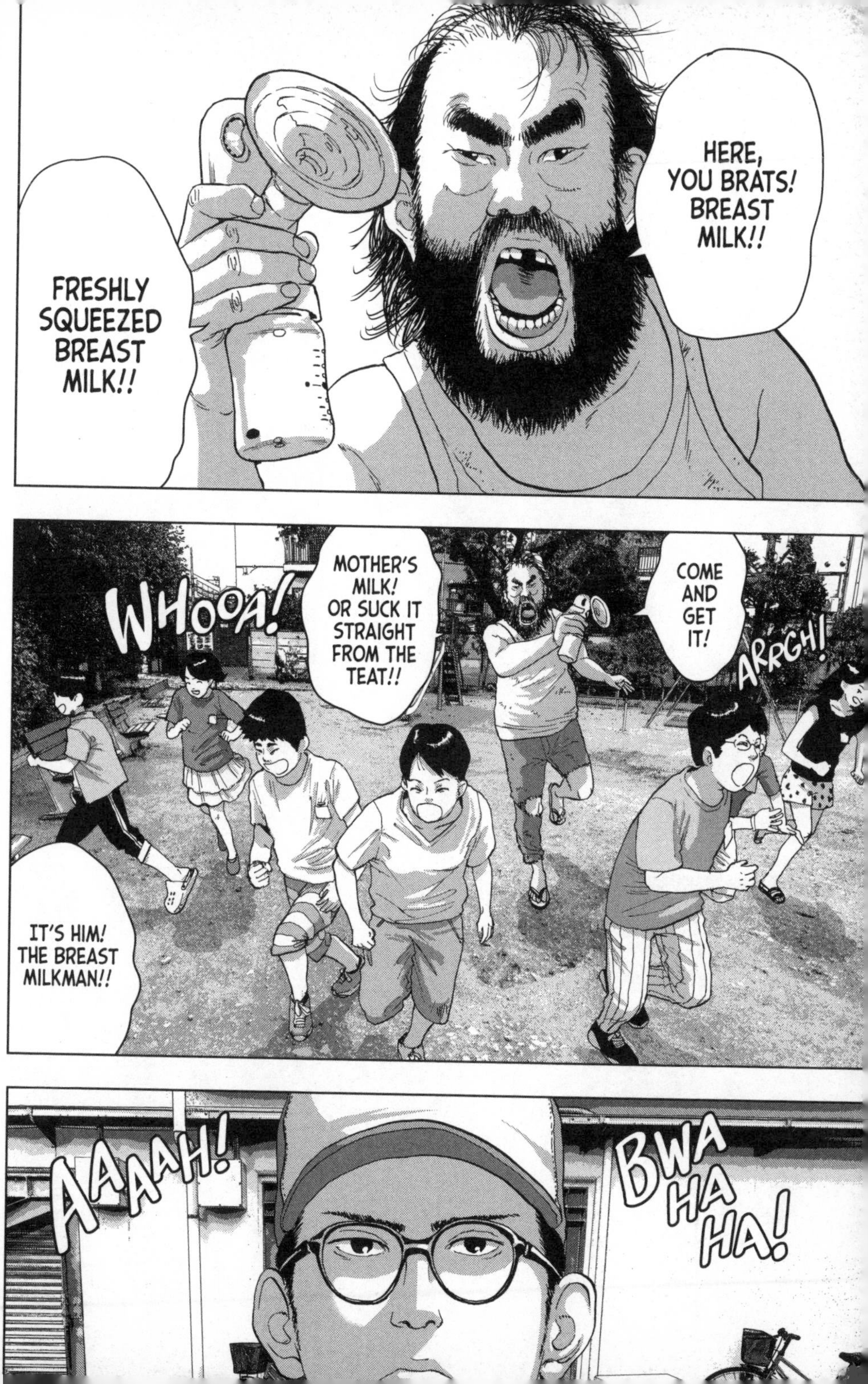
HERE, YOU BRATS! BREAST MILK!!
FRESHLY SQUEEZED BREAST MILK!!
ARRGH!
COME AND GET IT!
MOTHER'S MILK! OR SUCK IT STRAIGHT FROM THE TEAT!!
WHOOA!
IT'S HIM! THE BREAST MILKMAN!!
BWA HA HA!
AAAAH!

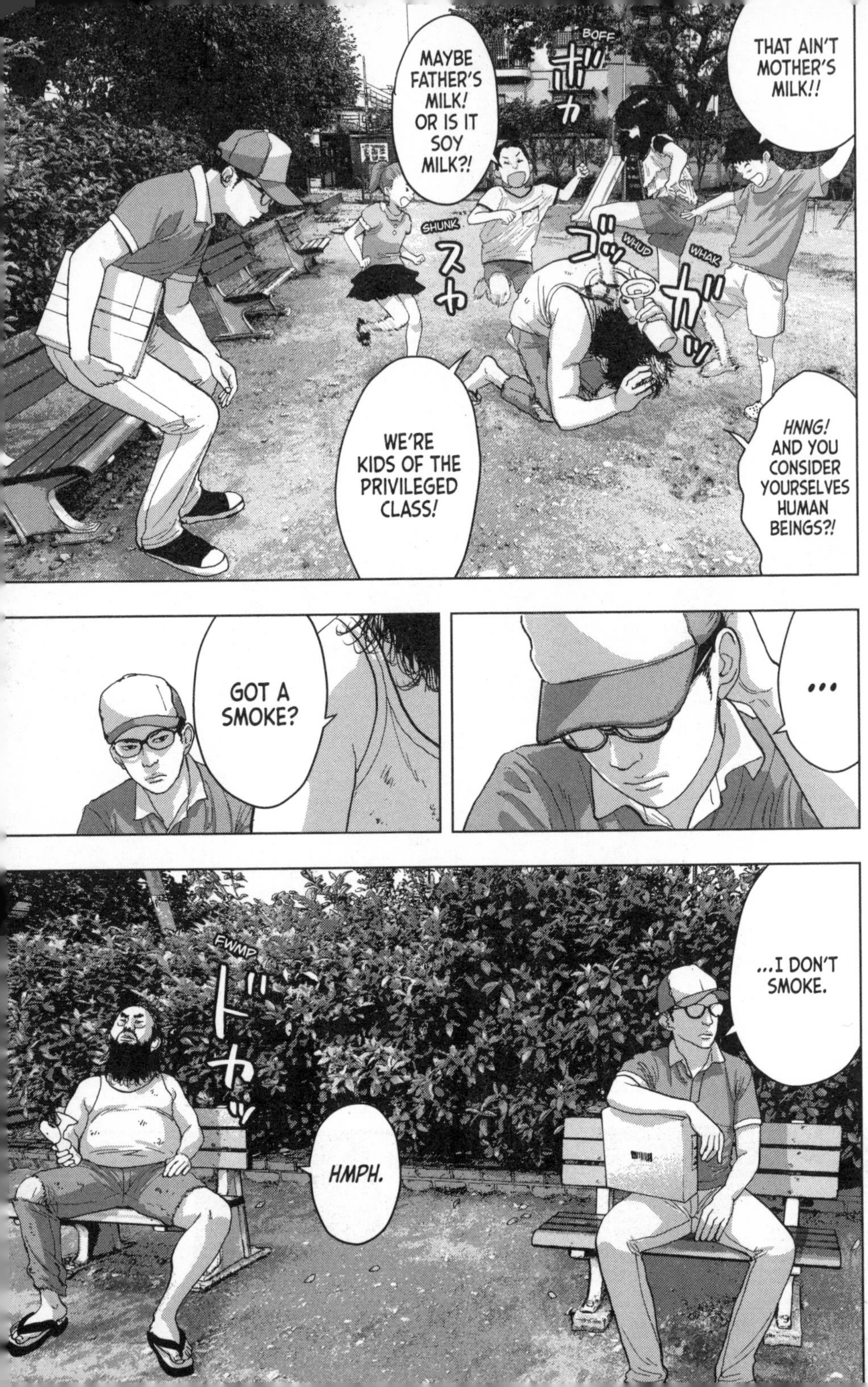
THAT AIN'T MOTHER'S MILK!!
BOFF
MAYBE FATHER'S MILK! OR IS IT SOY MILK?!
WHAK
WHUD
SHUNK
HNNG! AND YOU CONSIDER YOURSELVES HUMAN BEINGS?!
WE'RE KIDS OF THE PRIVILEGED CLASS!
...
GOT A SMOKE?
...I DON'T SMOKE.
FWMP
HMPH.

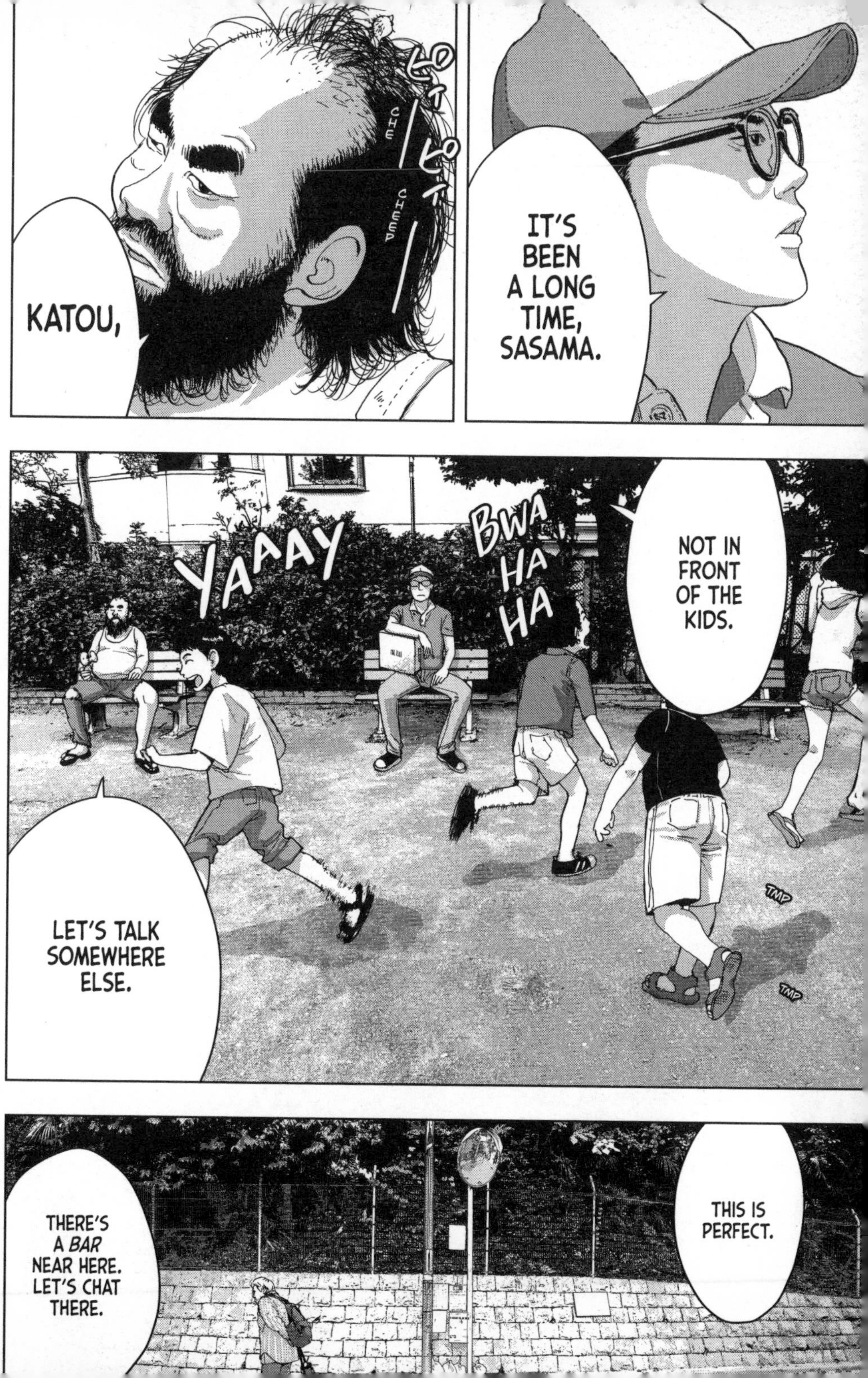

KATOU,
CHE
CHEEP
IT'S BEEN A LONG TIME, SASAMA.
YAAAY
LET'S TALK SOMEWHERE ELSE.
BWA HA HA
NOT IN FRONT OF THE KIDS.
TMP
TMP
THERE'S A BAR NEAR HERE. LET'S CHAT THERE.
THIS IS PERFECT.

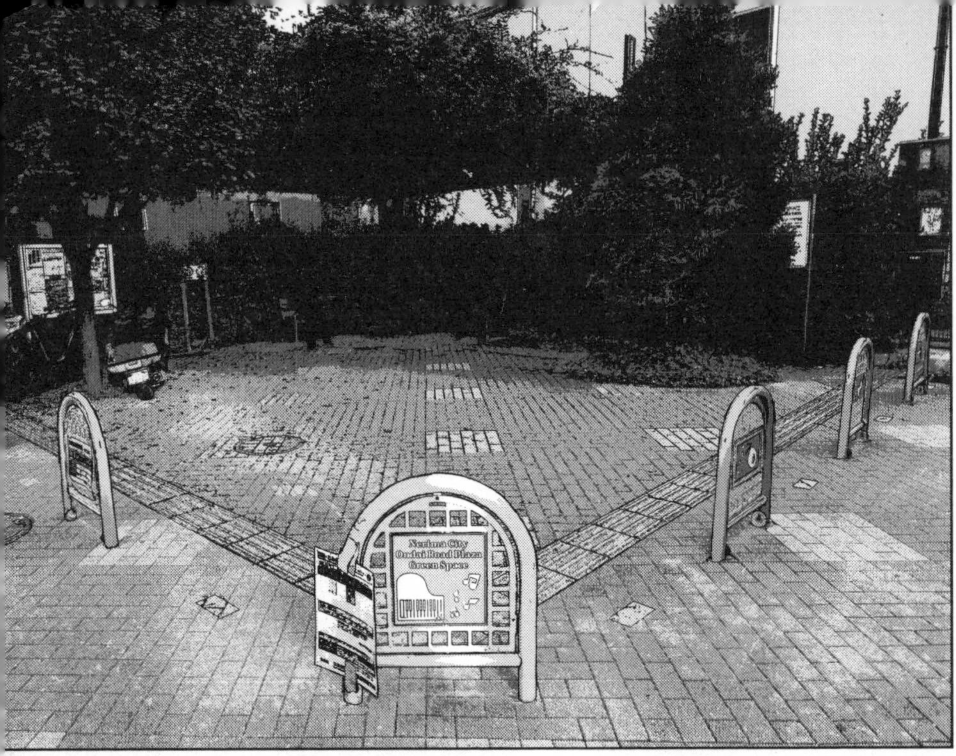
Nerima City
Oudai Road Plaza
Green Space

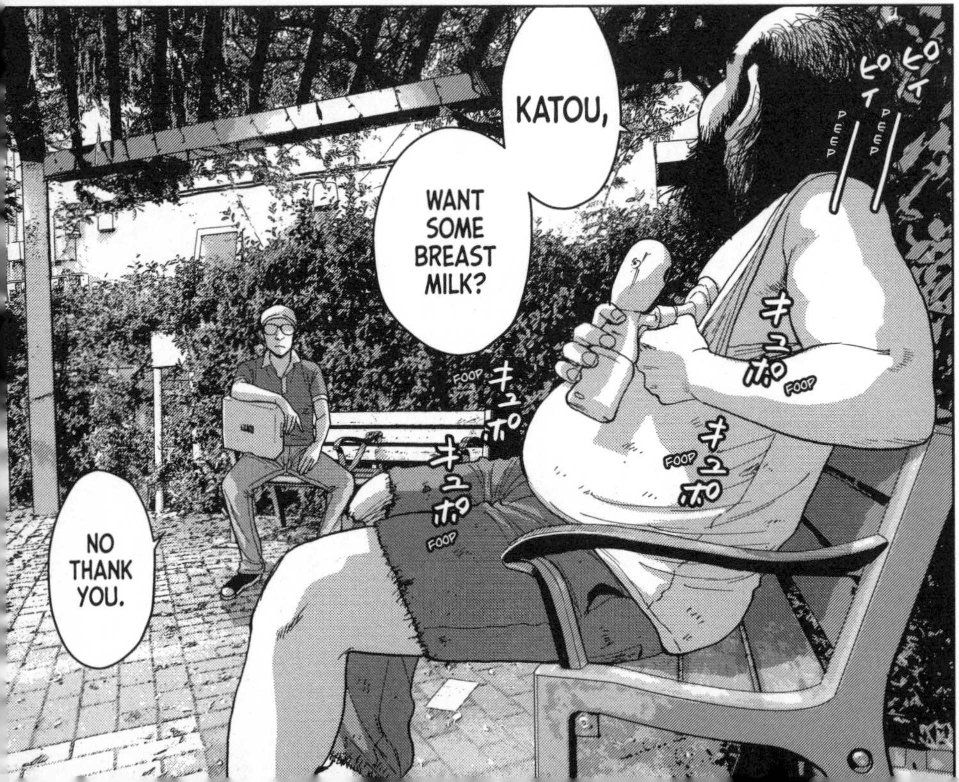
ピイ ピイ
PEEP PEEP
KATOU,
WANT SOME BREAST MILK?
キュポ FOOP
キュポ FOOP
キュポ FOOP
キュポ FOOP
NO THANK YOU.

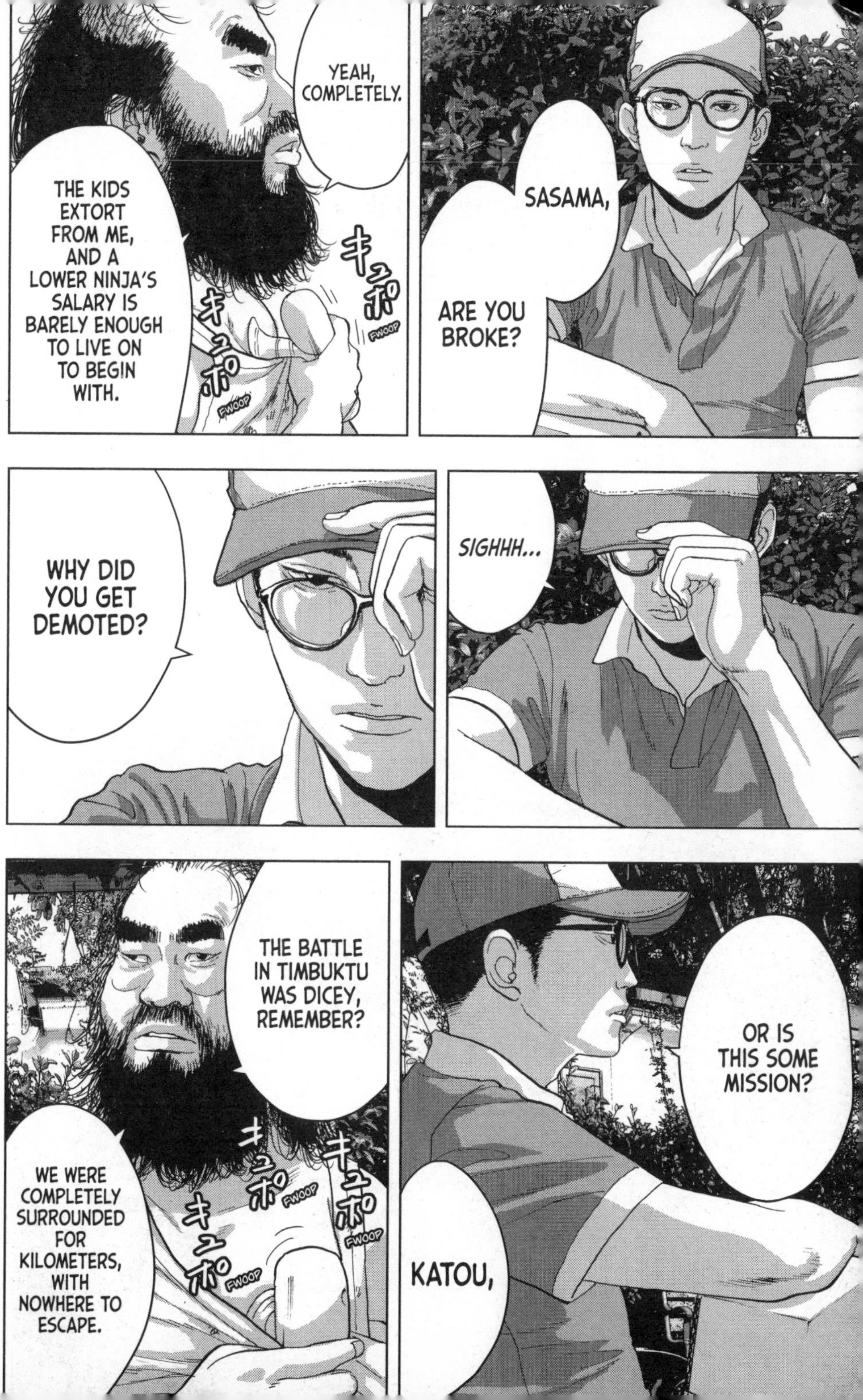
SASAMA,
ARE YOU BROKE?
YEAH, COMPLETELY.
THE KIDS EXTORT FROM ME, AND A LOWER NINJA'S SALARY IS BARELY ENOUGH TO LIVE ON TO BEGIN WITH.
キュポ
FWOOP
キュポ
FWOOP
SIGHHH...
WHY DID YOU GET DEMOTED?
KATOU,
OR IS THIS SOME MISSION?
THE BATTLE IN TIMBUKTU WAS DICEY, REMEMBER?
WE WERE COMPLETELY SURROUNDED FOR KILOMETERS, WITH NOWHERE TO ESCAPE.
キュポ
FWOOP
キュポ
FWOOP
キュポ
FWOOP

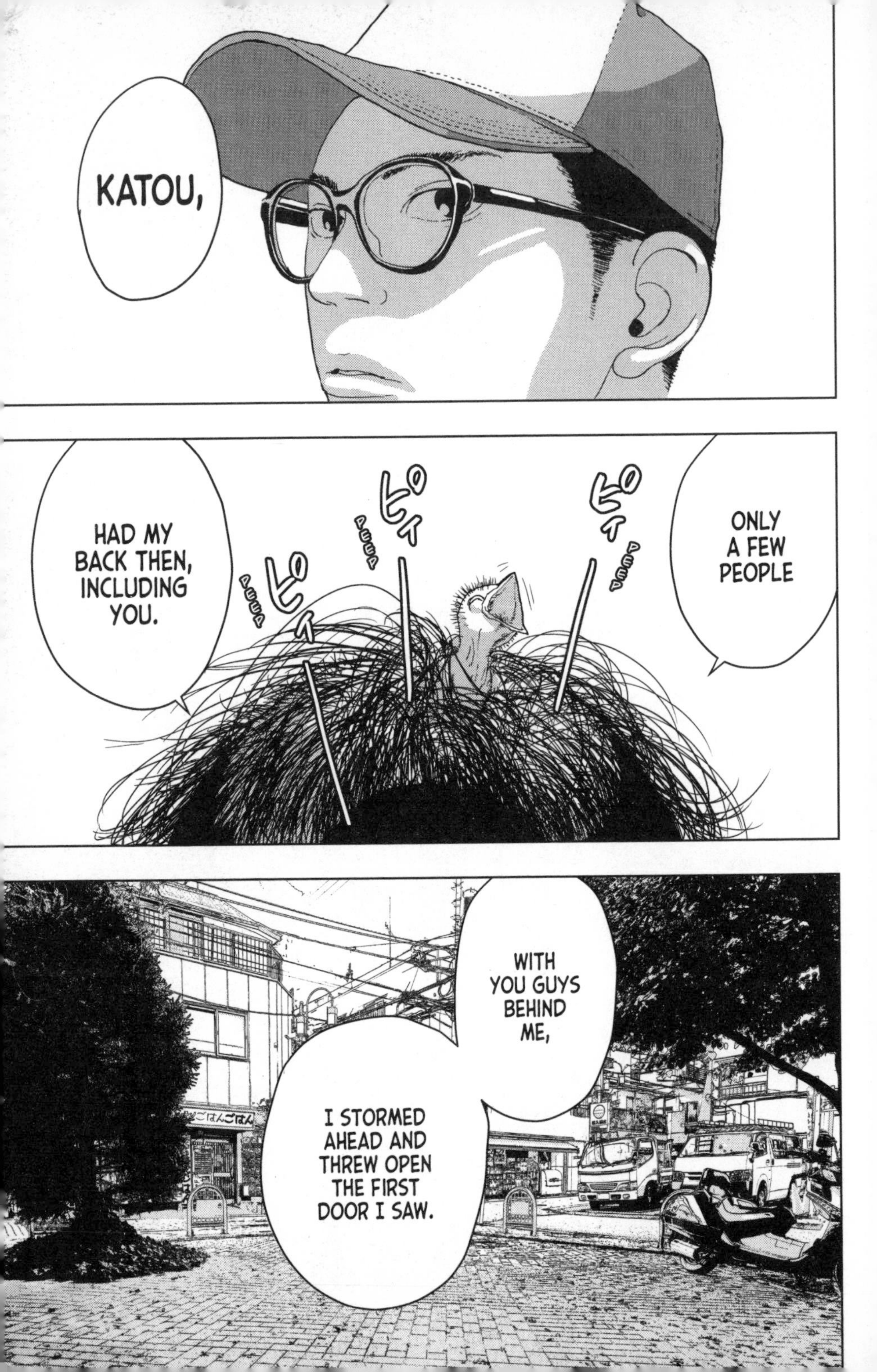
KATOU,
ONLY A FEW PEOPLE
ピィ PEEP
ピィ PEEP
ピィ PEEP
HAD MY BACK THEN, INCLUDING YOU.
WITH YOU GUYS BEHIND ME,
I STORMED AHEAD AND THREW OPEN THE FIRST DOOR I SAW.
ごはんごはん

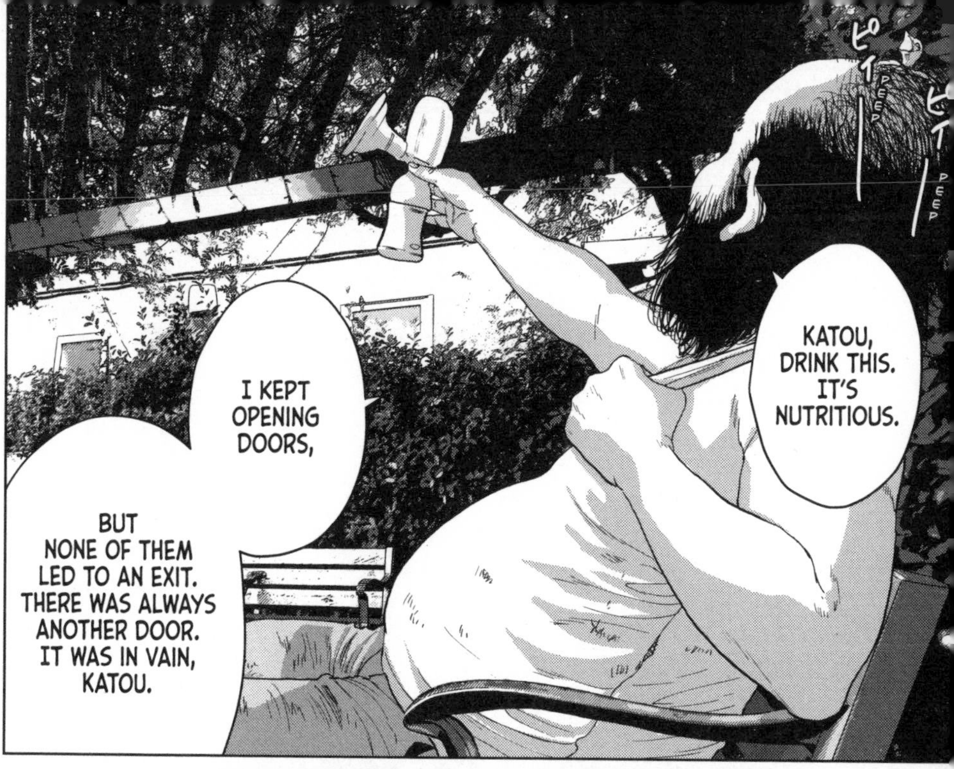
ピイー PEEP
ピイー PEEP
KATOU, DRINK THIS. IT'S NUTRITIOUS.
I KEPT OPENING DOORS,
BUT NONE OF THEM LED TO AN EXIT. THERE WAS ALWAYS ANOTHER DOOR. IT WAS IN VAIN, KATOU.

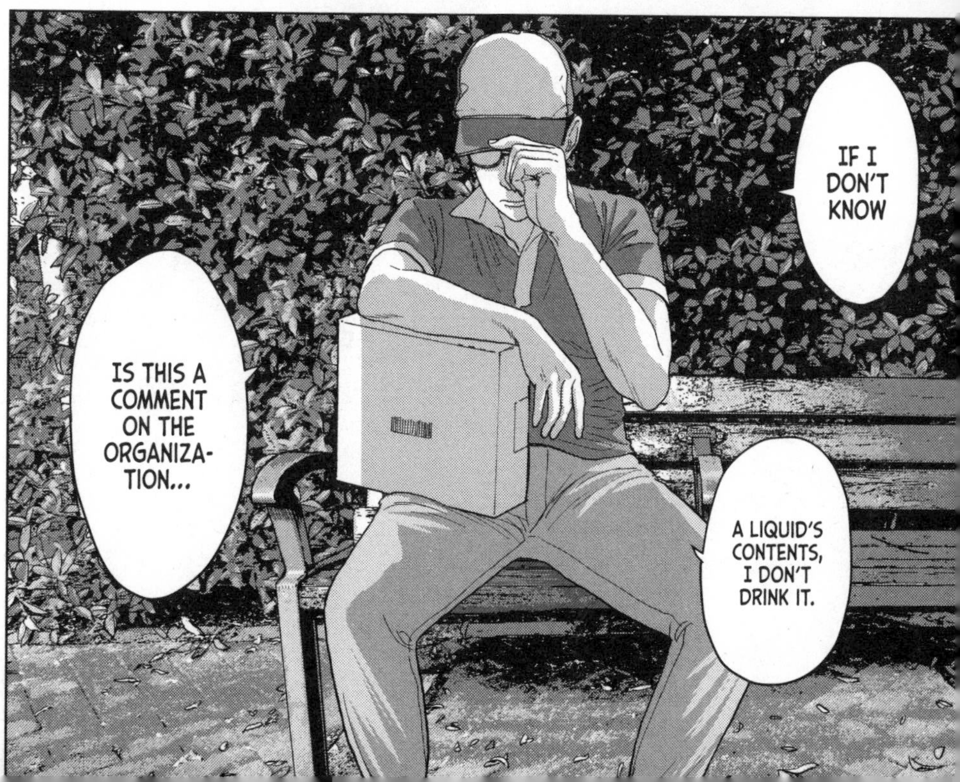
IF I DON'T KNOW
A LIQUID'S CONTENTS, I DON'T DRINK IT.
IS THIS A COMMENT ON THE ORGANIZA-TION...

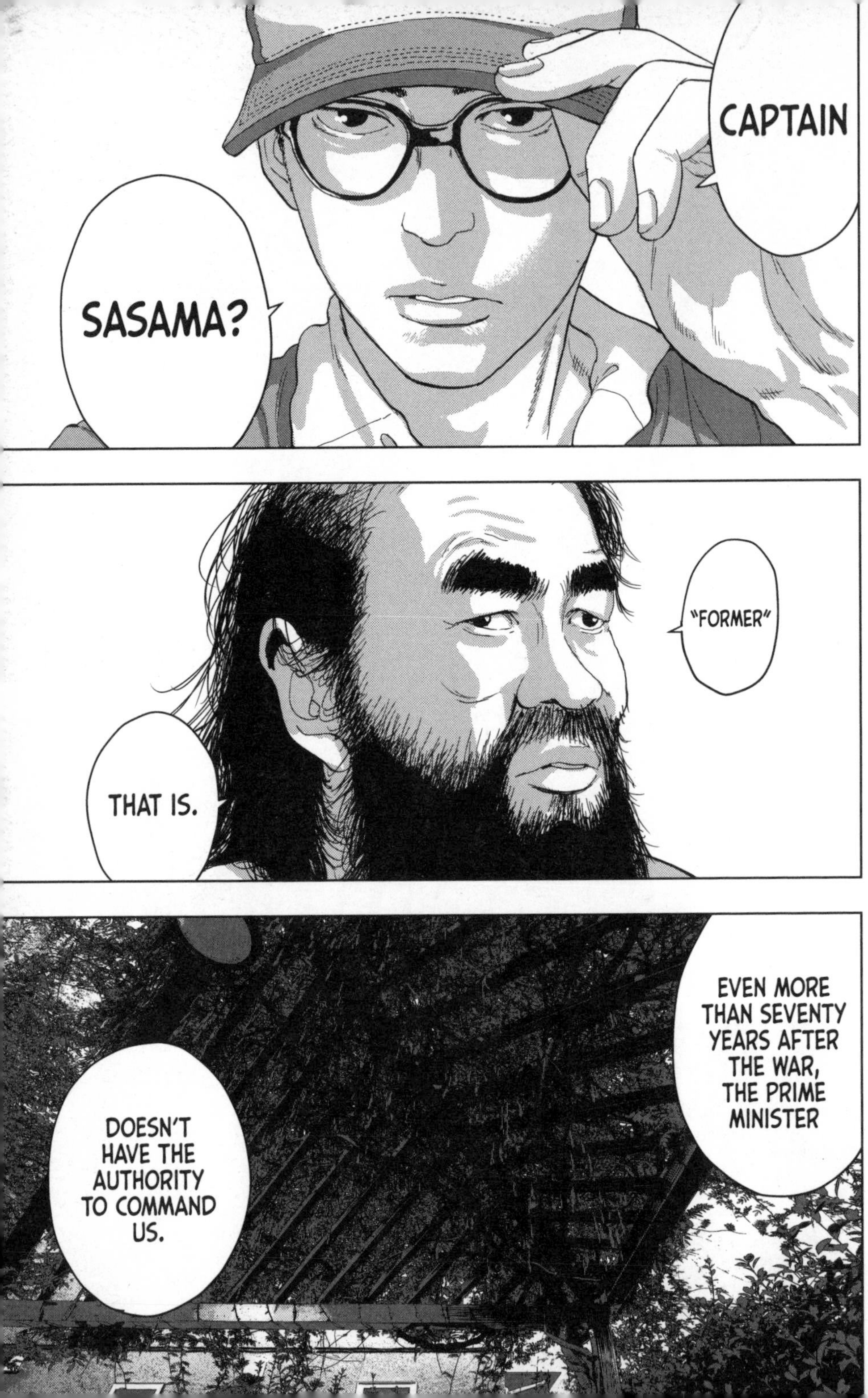
CAPTAIN
SASAMA?
"FORMER"
THAT IS.
EVEN MORE THAN SEVENTY YEARS AFTER THE WAR, THE PRIME MINISTER
DOESN'T HAVE THE AUTHORITY TO COMMAND US.

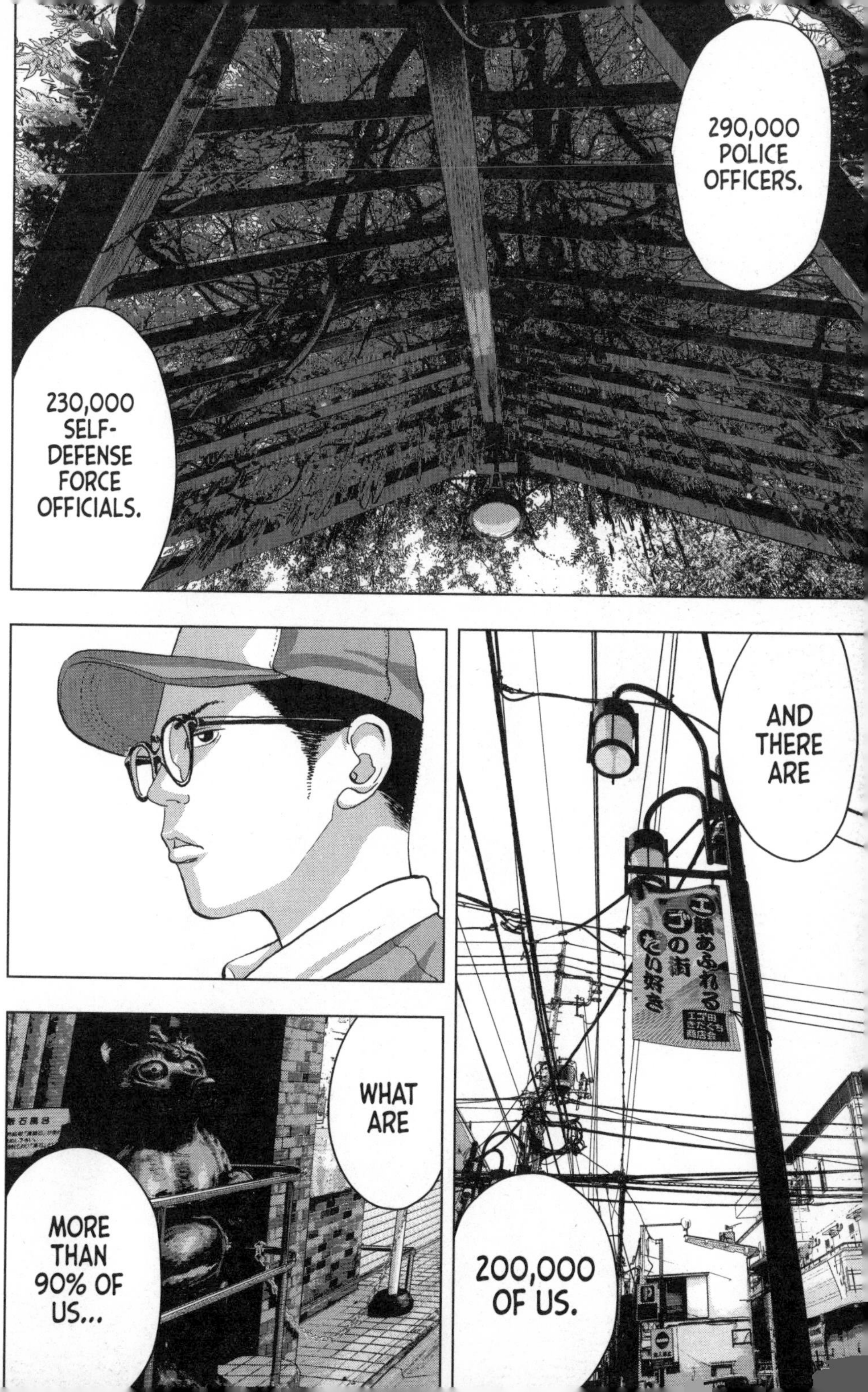
290,000 POLICE OFFICERS.
230,000 SELF-DEFENSE FORCE OFFICIALS.
AND THERE ARE
200,000 OF US.
WHAT ARE
MORE THAN 90% OF US...

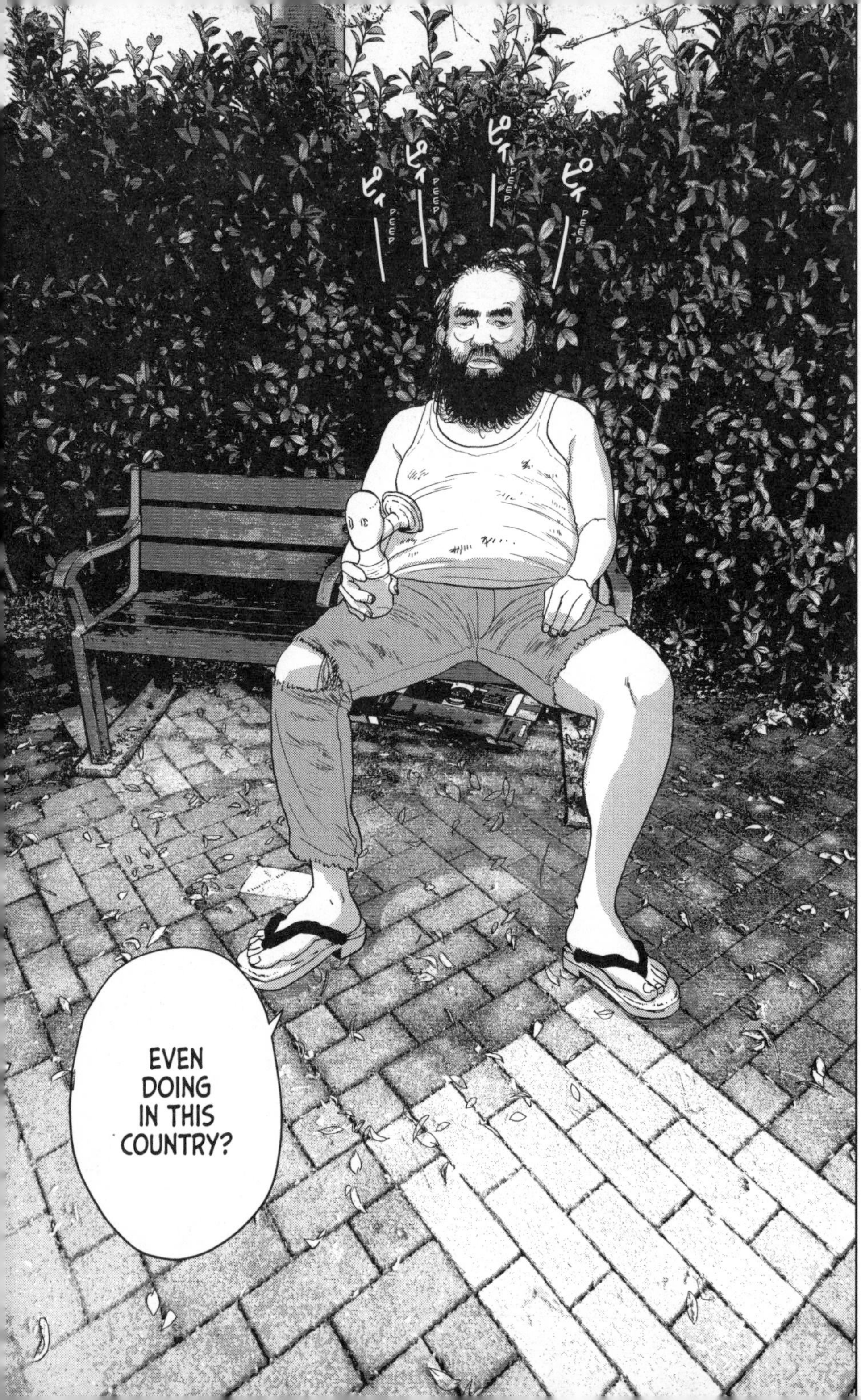
ピィー PEEP
ピィー PEEP
ピィー PEEP
ピィー PEEP
EVEN DOING IN THIS COUNTRY?

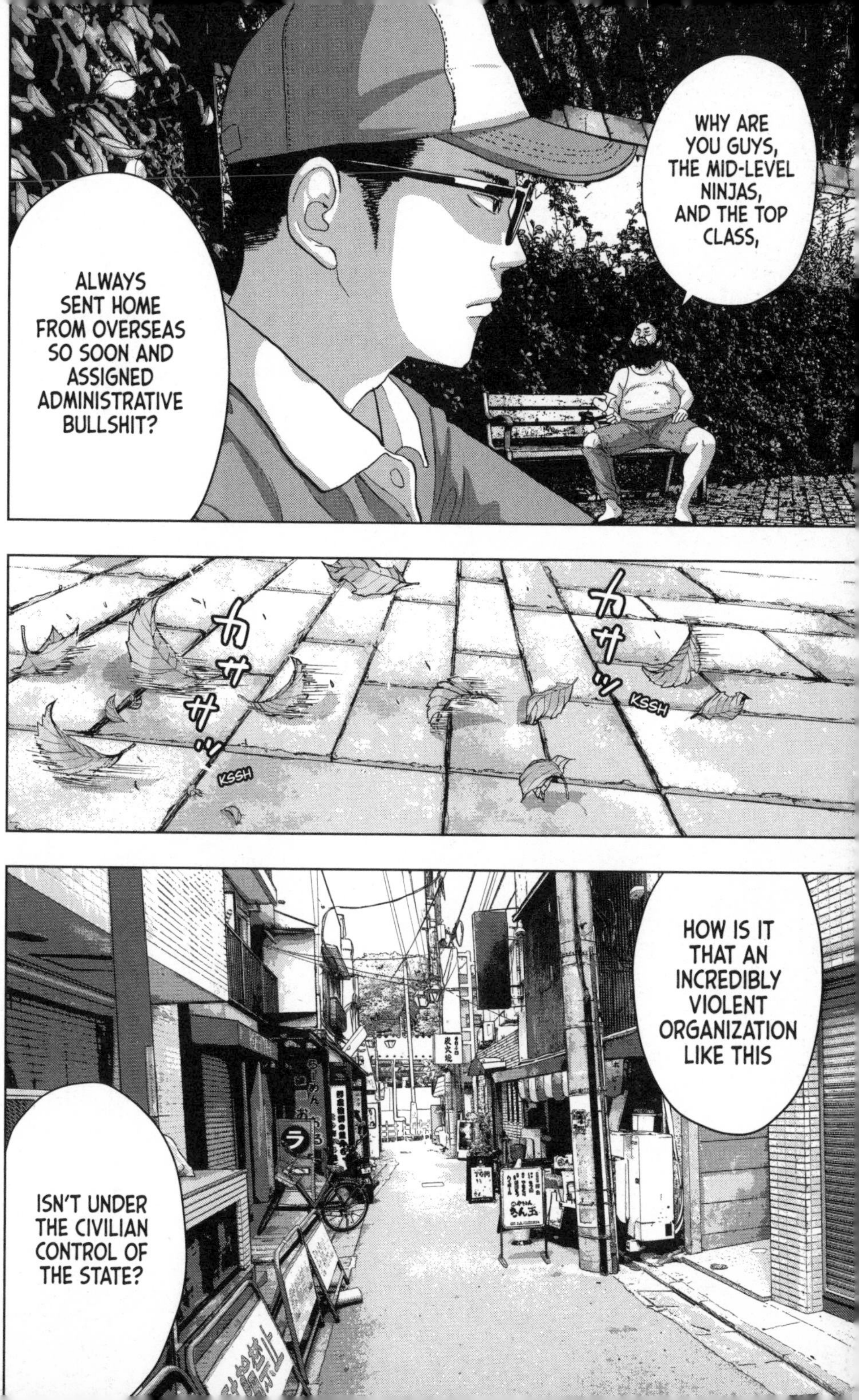
WHY ARE YOU GUYS, THE MID-LEVEL NINJAS, AND THE TOP CLASS,
ALWAYS SENT HOME FROM OVERSEAS SO SOON AND ASSIGNED ADMINISTRATIVE BULLSHIT?
カサッ
KSSH
カササッ
KSSH
HOW IS IT THAT AN INCREDIBLY VIOLENT ORGANIZATION LIKE THIS
ISN'T UNDER THE CIVILIAN CONTROL OF THE STATE?

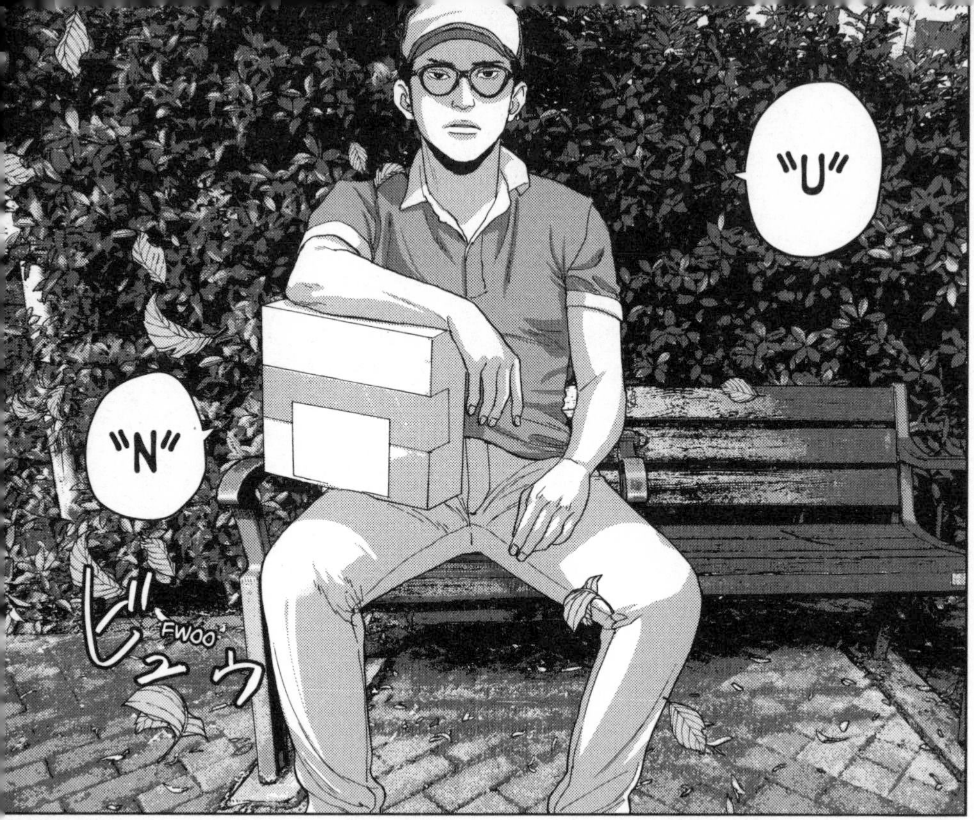
"U"
"N"
FWOO
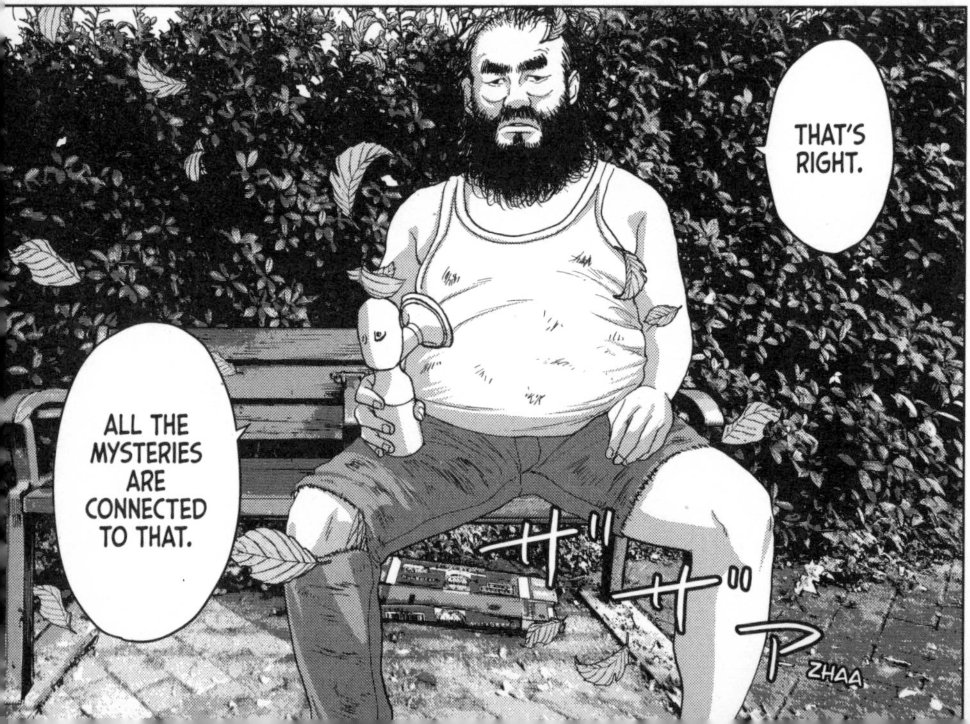
THAT'S RIGHT.
ALL THE MYSTERIES ARE CONNECTED TO THAT.
ZHAA

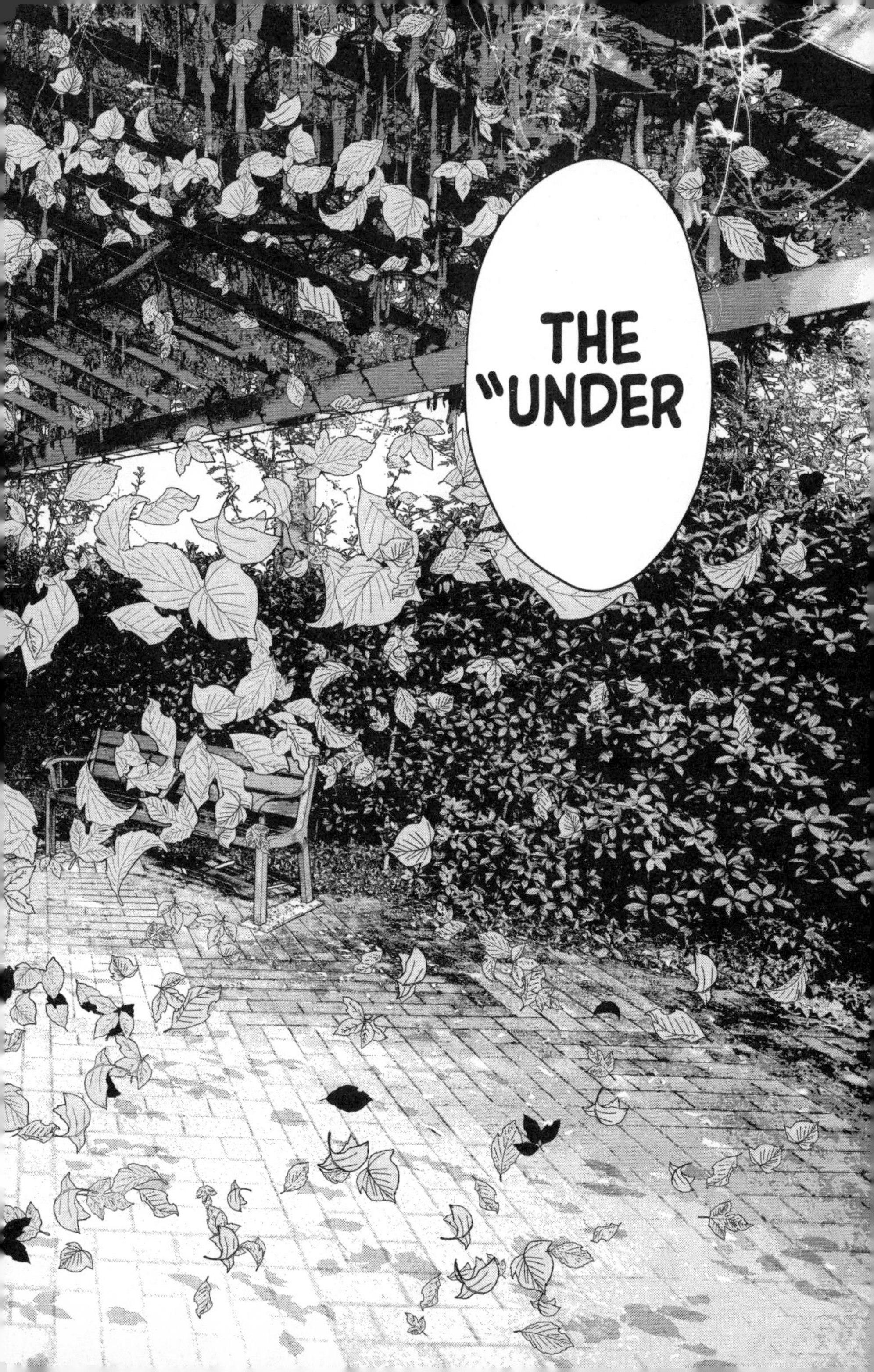
THE "UNDER

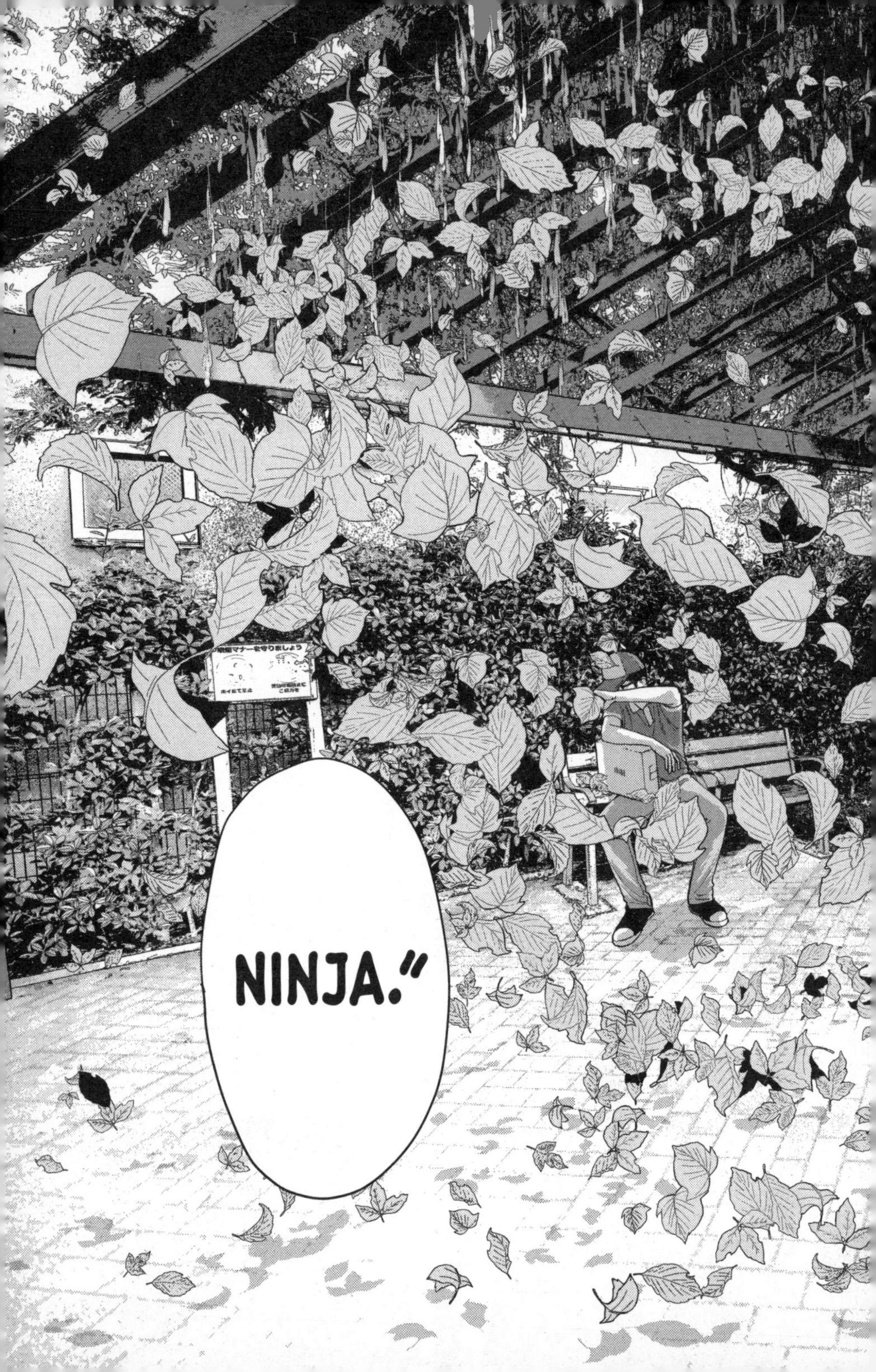
NINJA."

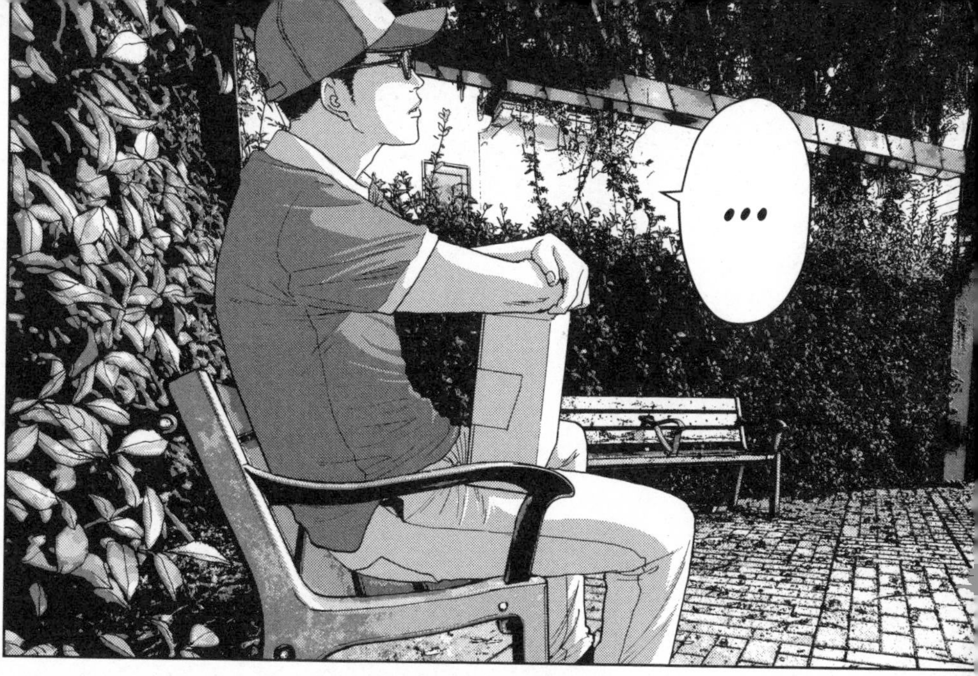
...
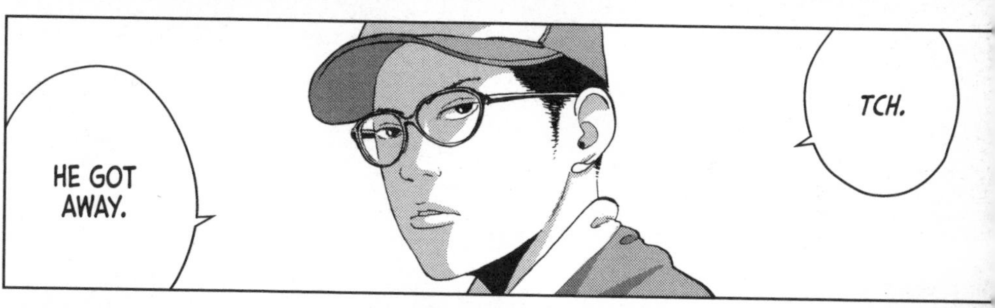
TCH.
HE GOT AWAY.
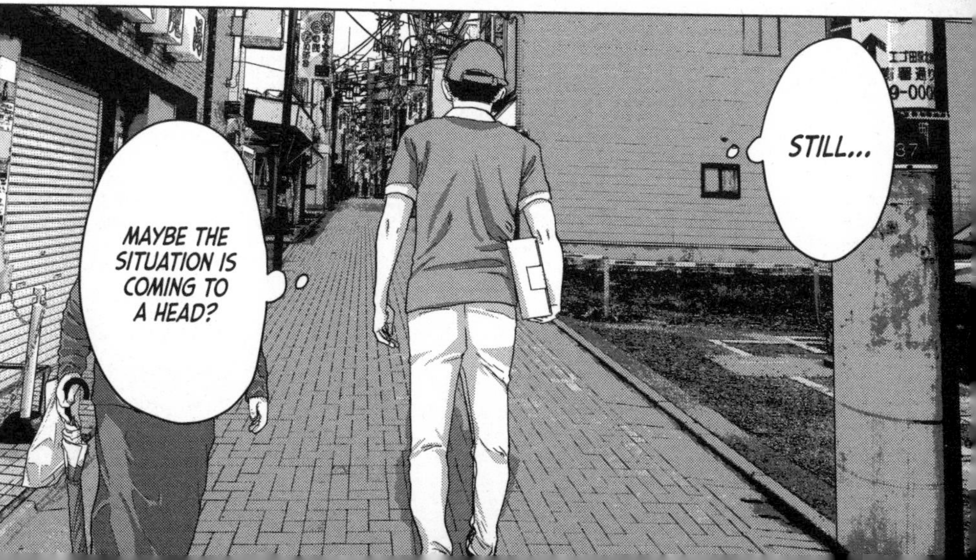
STILL...
MAYBE THE SITUATION IS COMING TO A HEAD?

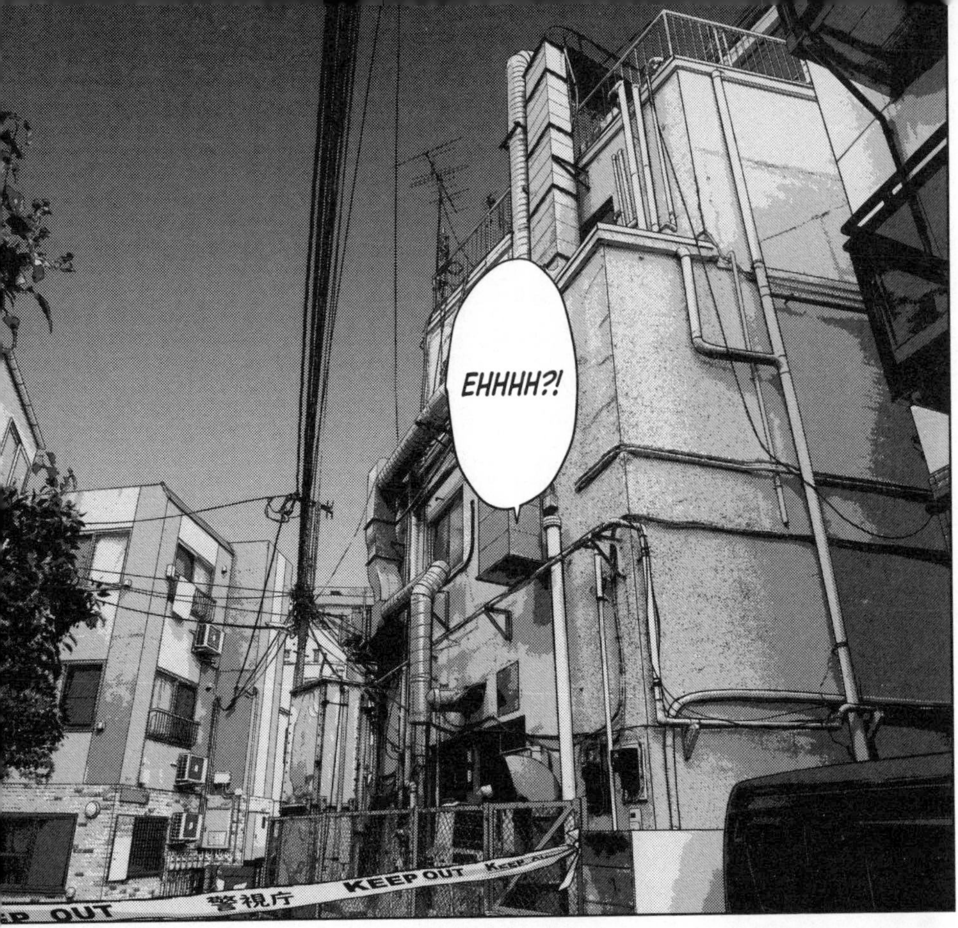
EHHHH?!
KEEP OUT
警視庁
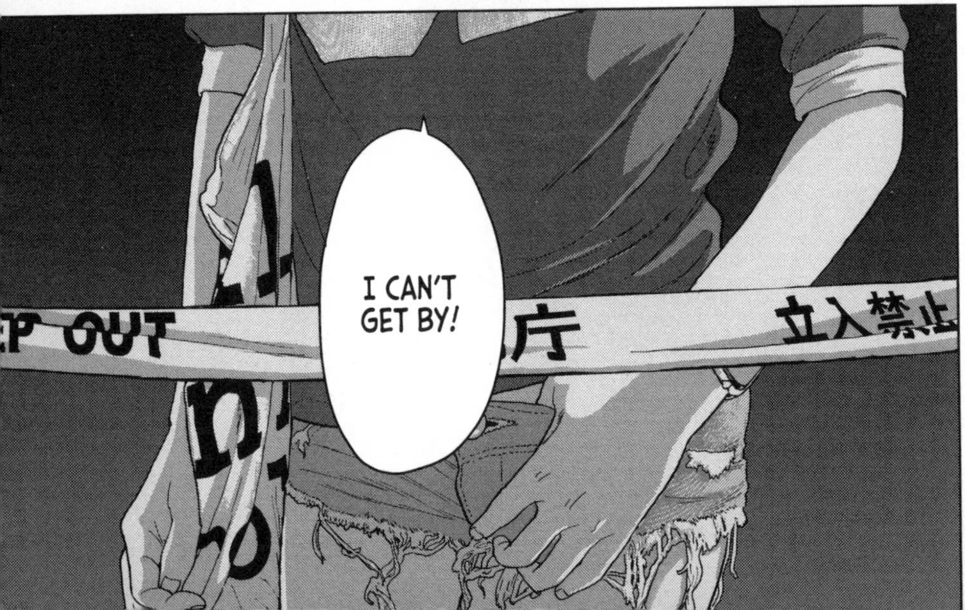
I CAN'T GET BY!
立入禁止

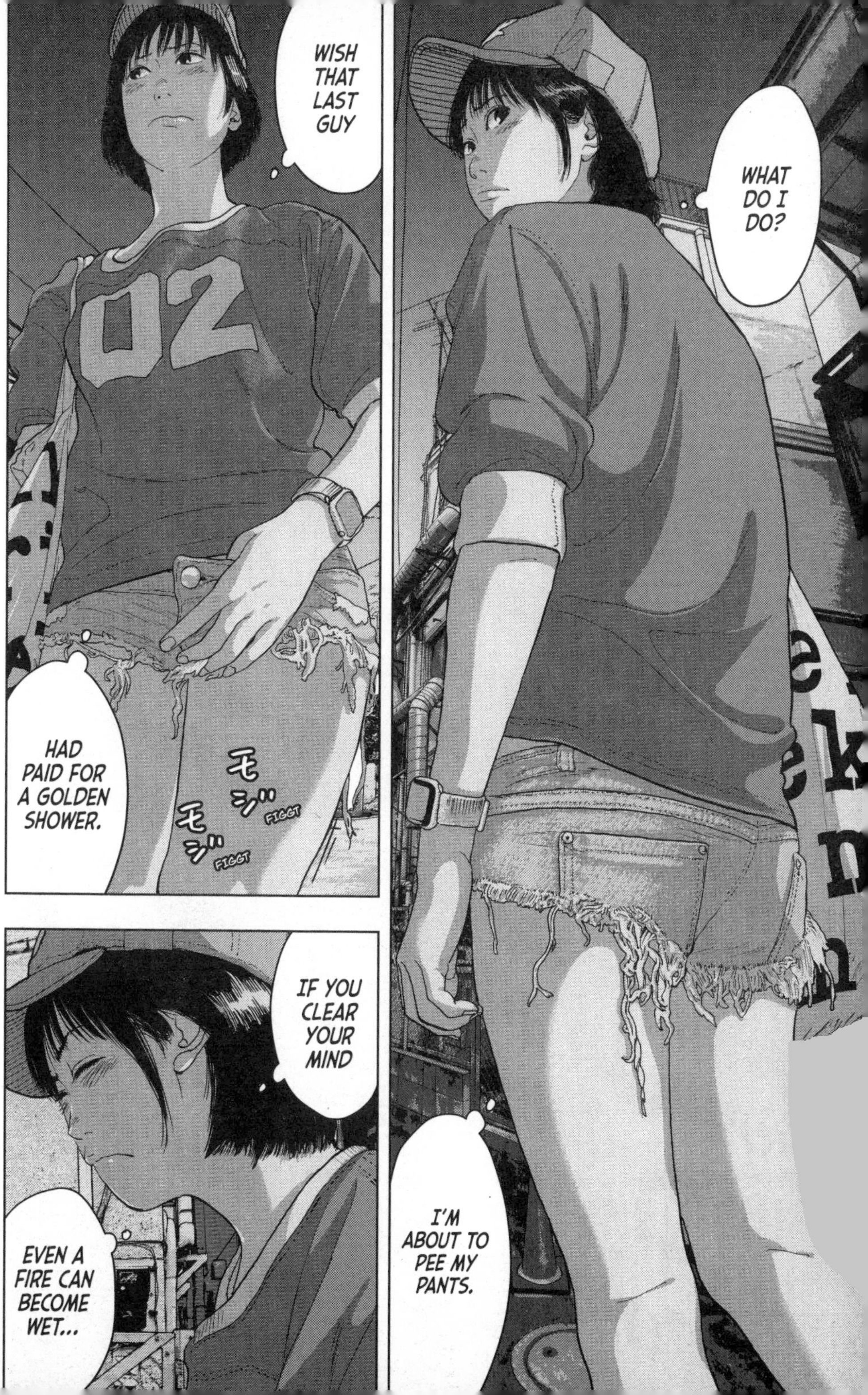
WHAT DO I DO?
I'M ABOUT TO PEE MY PANTS.
WISH THAT LAST GUY
HAD PAID FOR A GOLDEN SHOWER.
モジ
FIGGT
モジ
FIGGT
IF YOU CLEAR YOUR MIND
EVEN A FIRE CAN BECOME WET...

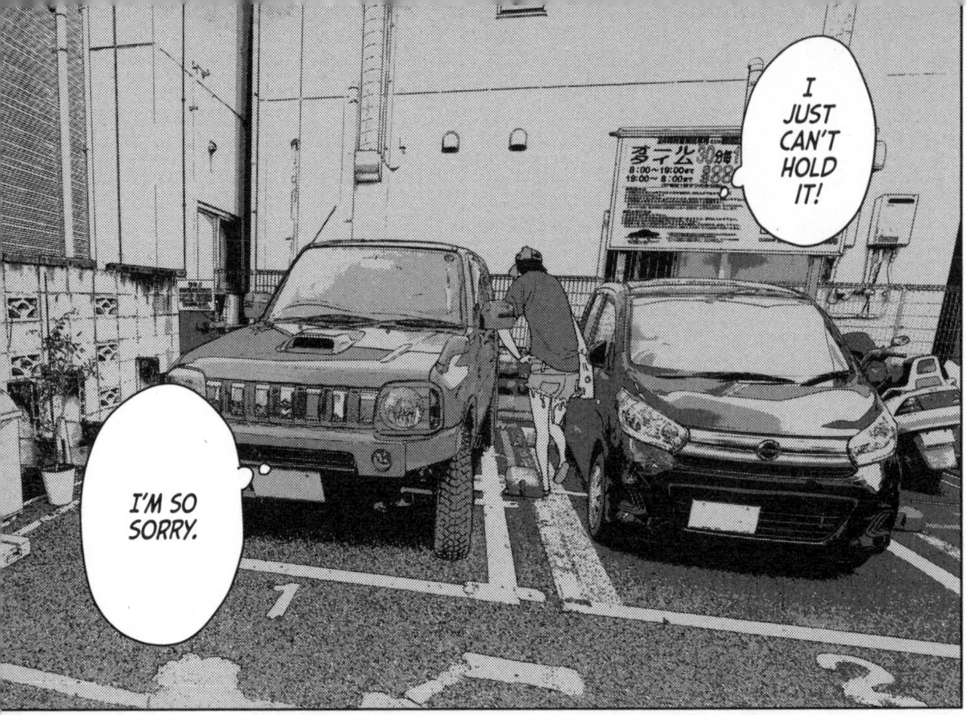
I JUST CAN'T HOLD IT!
I'M SO SORRY.

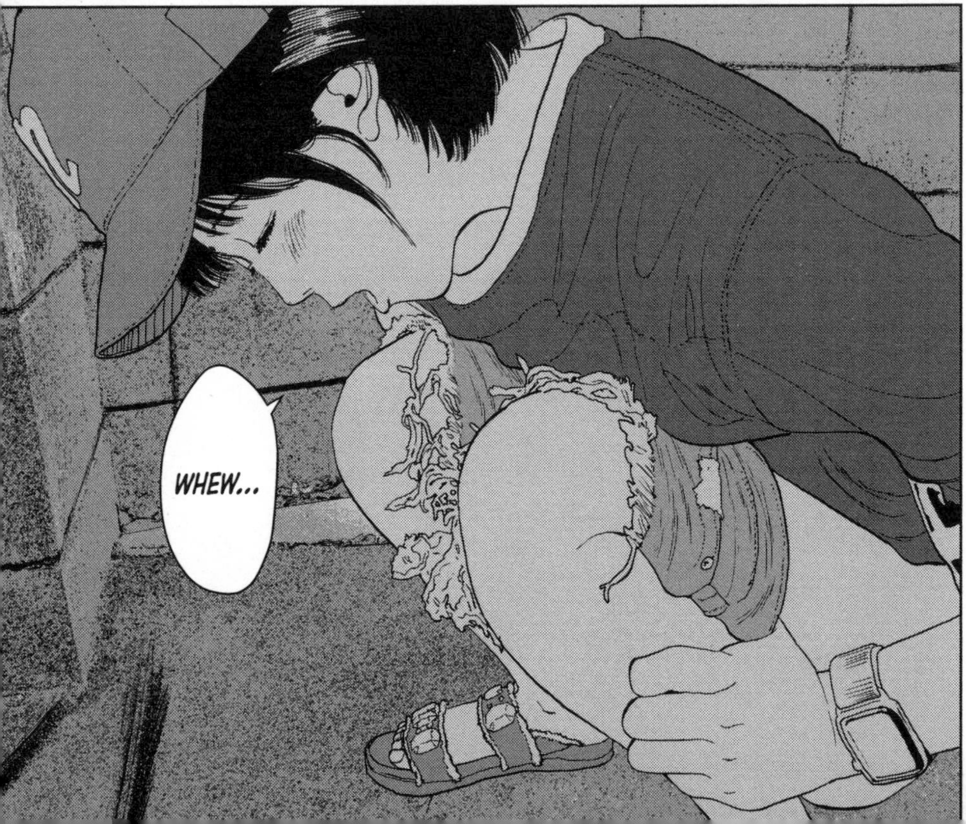
WHEW...

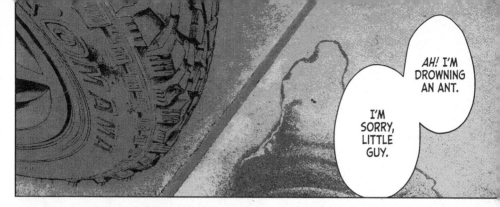

AH! I'M DROWNING AN ANT.

I'M SORRY, LITTLE GUY.

ヒョコ
PEEK

CHAPTER 8

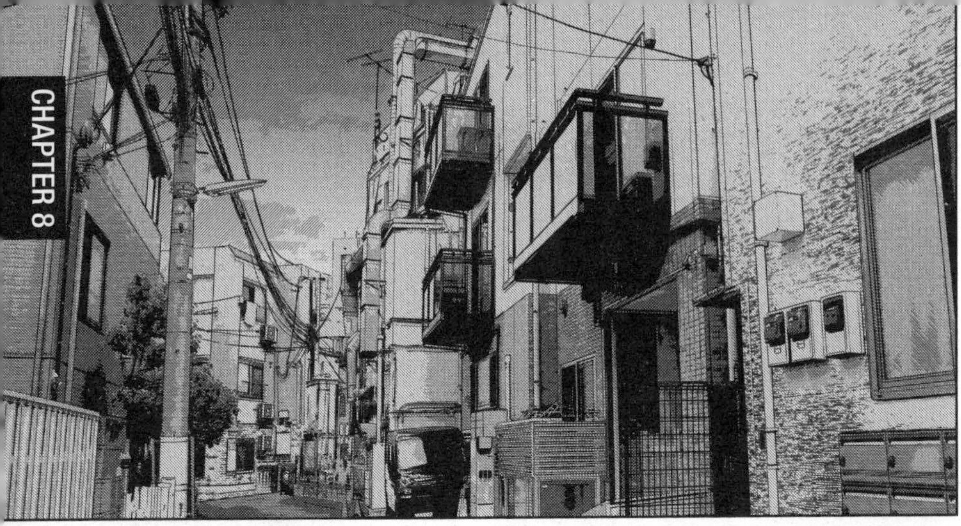

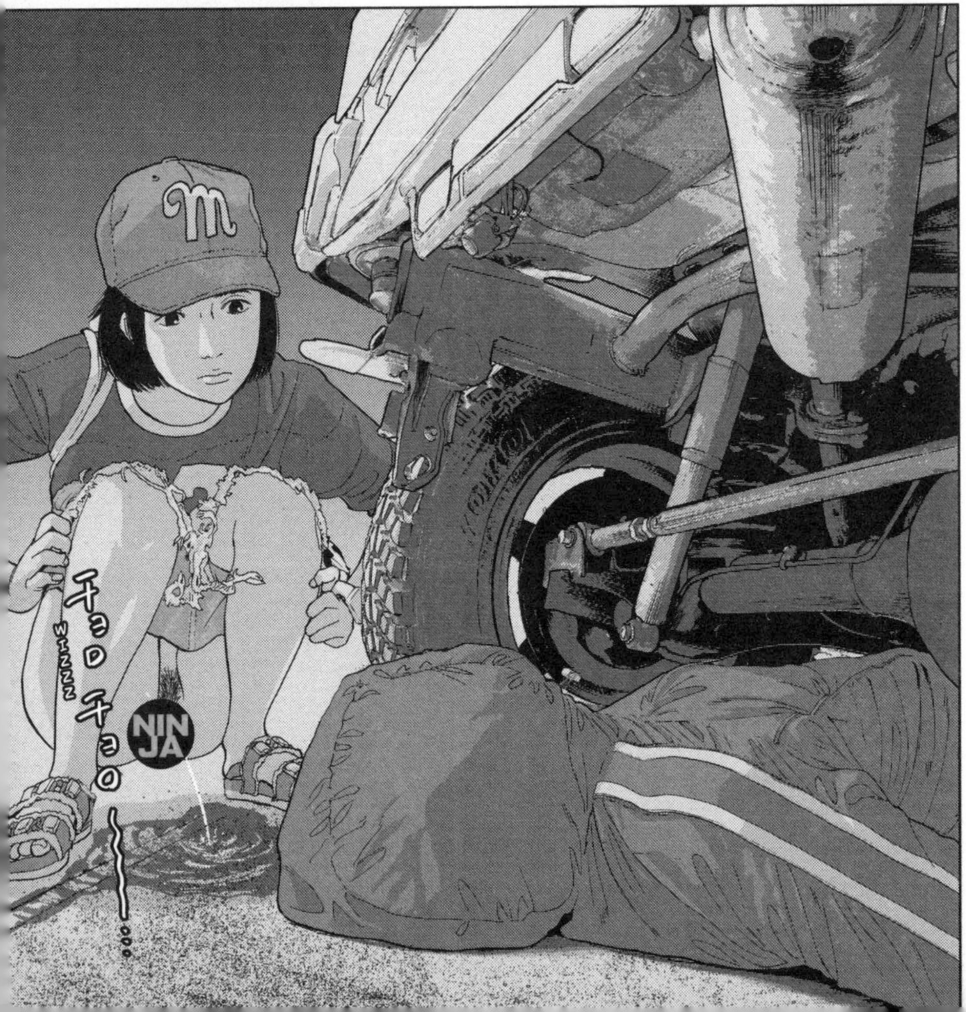
チョロ チョロ〜〜〜…
WIZZZ

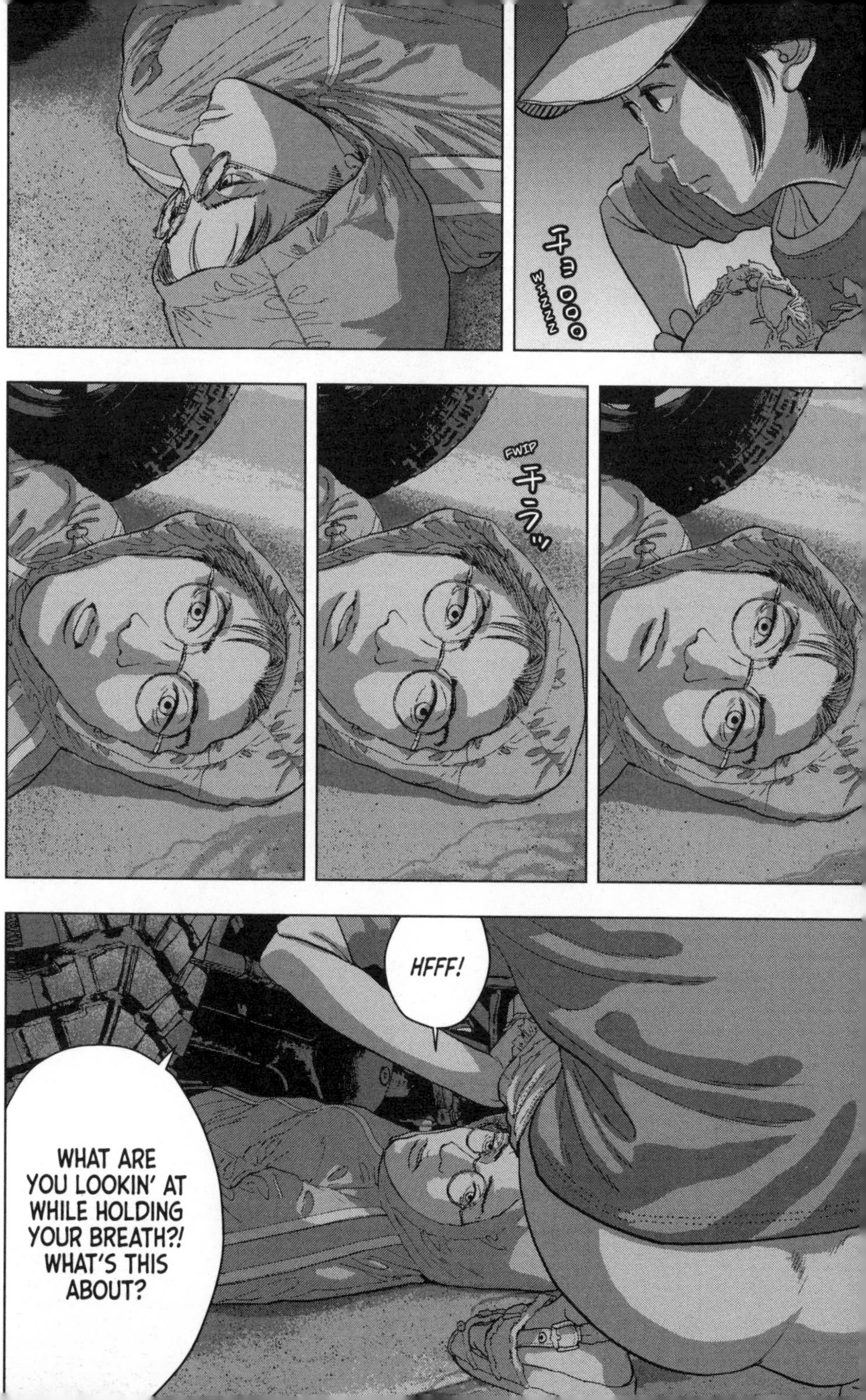
WINNN
FWIP
チラッ
HFFF!
WHAT ARE YOU LOOKIN' AT WHILE HOLDING YOUR BREATH?! WHAT'S THIS ABOUT?

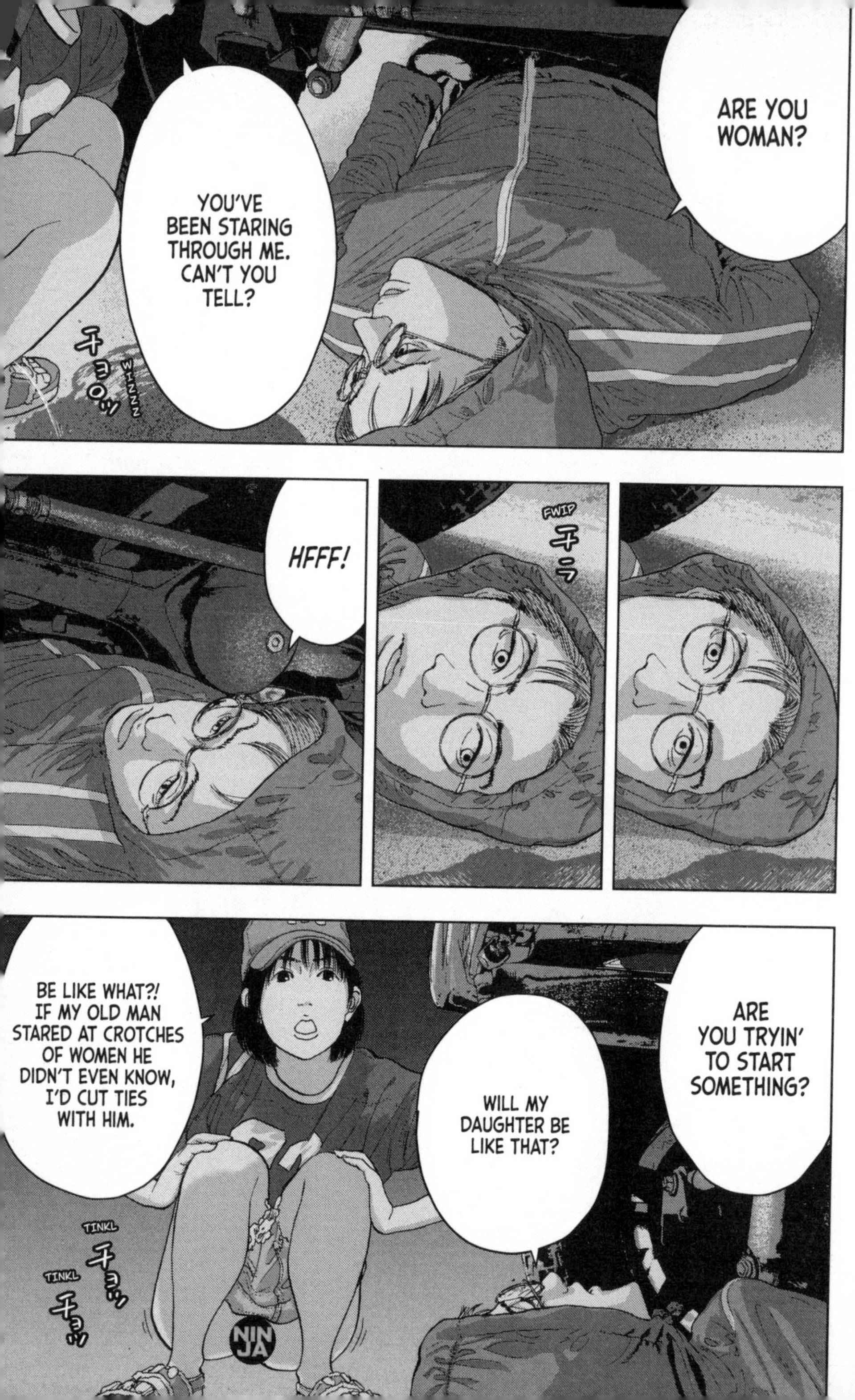
ARE YOU WOMAN?
YOU'VE BEEN STARING THROUGH ME. CAN'T YOU TELL?
WIZZZ
チョロッ
FWIP
チラ
HFFF!
ARE YOU TRYIN' TO START SOMETHING?
WILL MY DAUGHTER BE LIKE THAT?
BE LIKE WHAT?! IF MY OLD MAN STARED AT CROTCHES OF WOMEN HE DIDN'T EVEN KNOW, I'D CUT TIES WITH HIM.
TINKL
チョロッ
TINKL
チョロッ

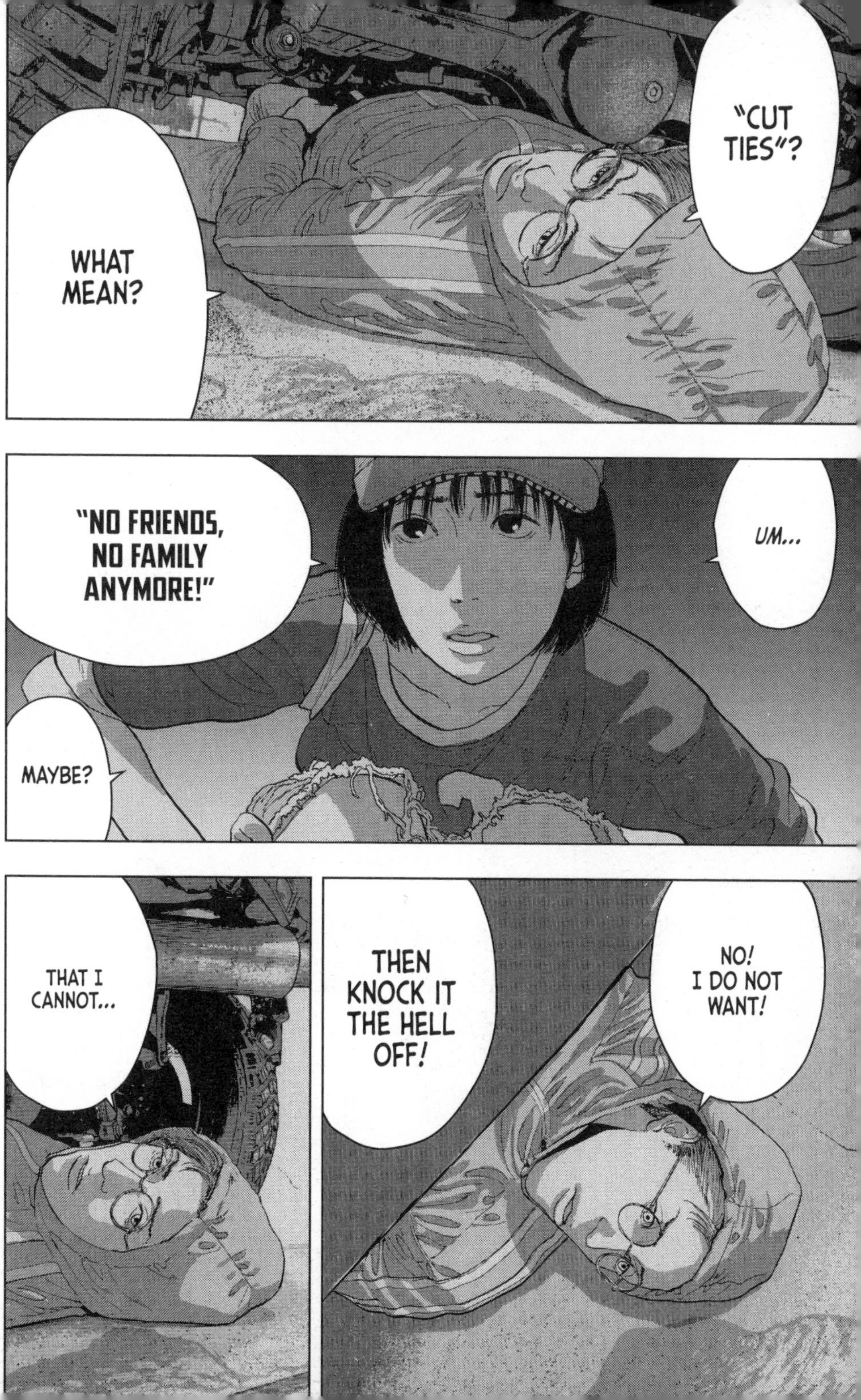
"CUT TIES"?
WHAT MEAN?
UM...
"NO FRIENDS, NO FAMILY ANYMORE!"
MAYBE?
NO! I DO NOT WANT!
THEN KNOCK IT THE HELL OFF!
THAT I CANNOT...

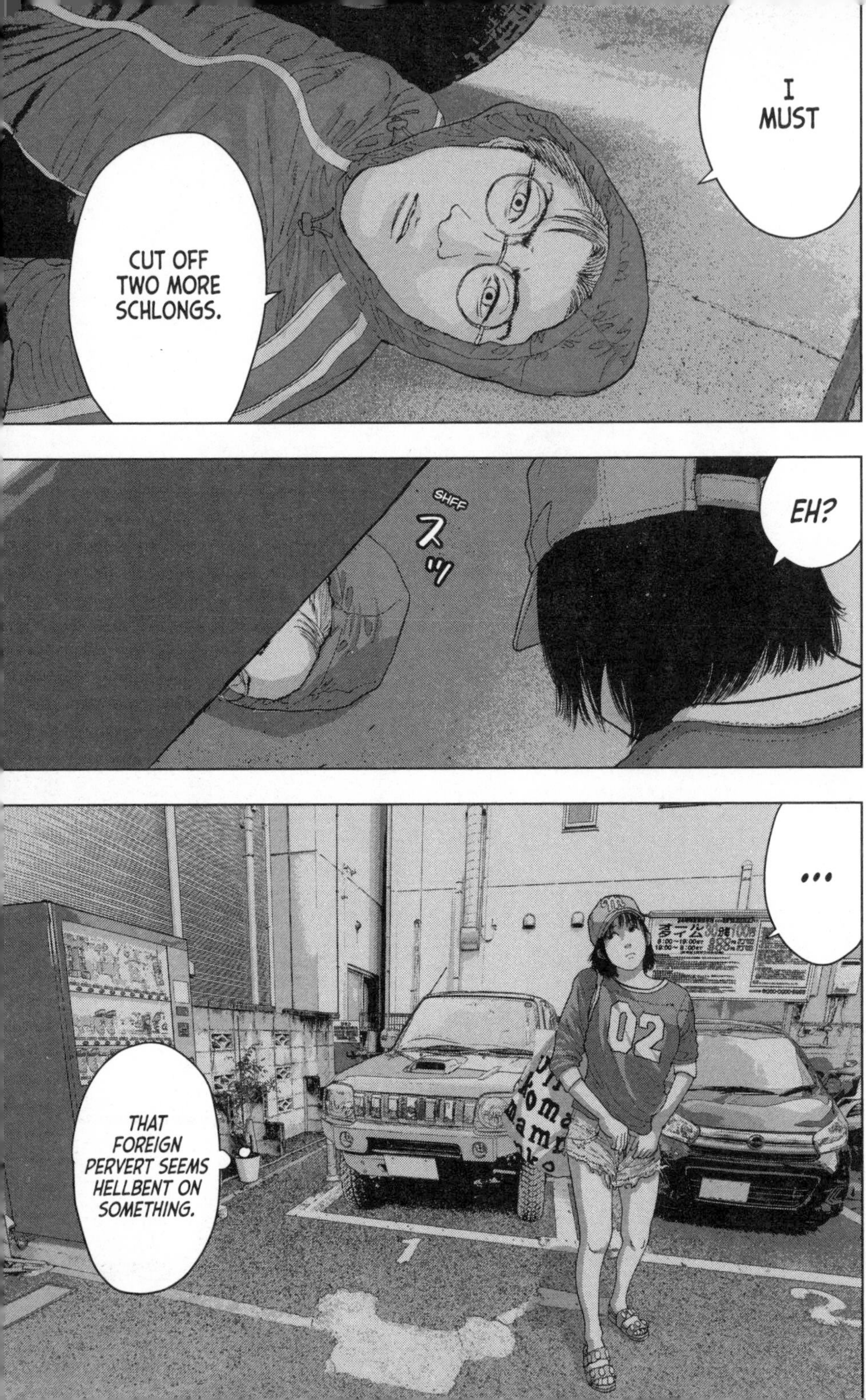
I MUST
CUT OFF TWO MORE SCHLONGS.
EH?
SHFF
スッ
...
THAT FOREIGN PERVERT SEEMS HELLBENT ON SOMETHING.

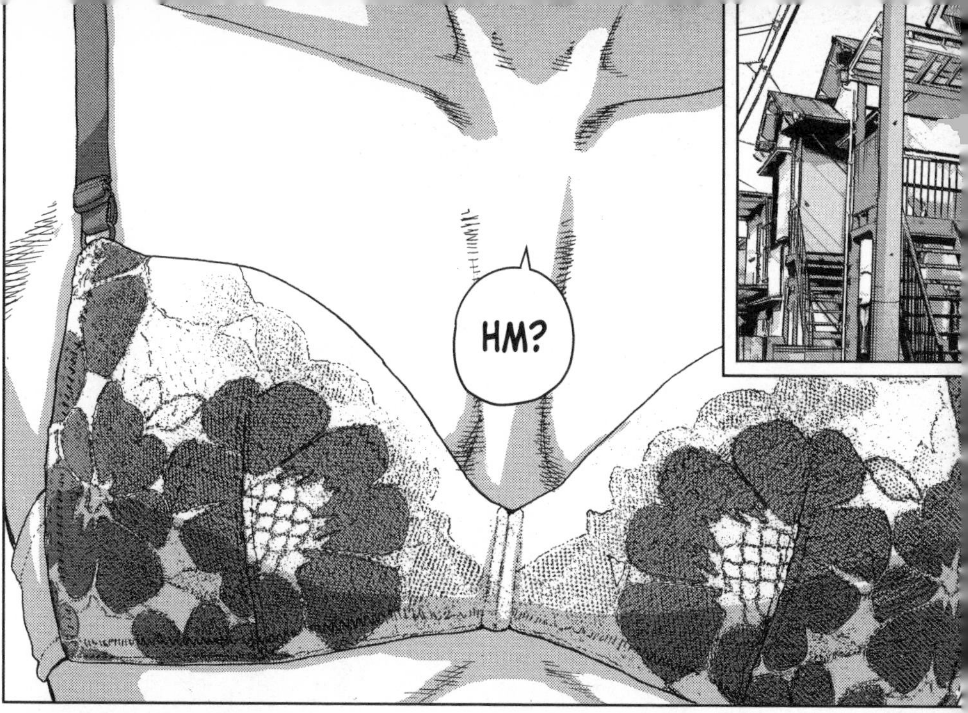
HM?
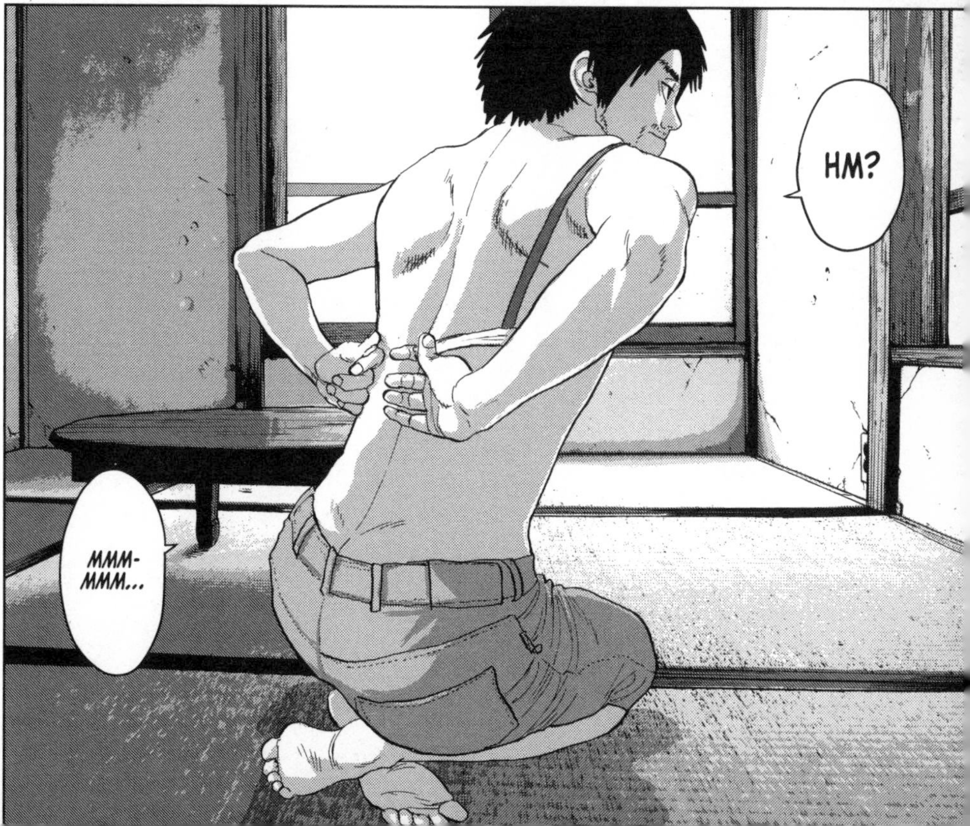
HM?
MMM-MMM...

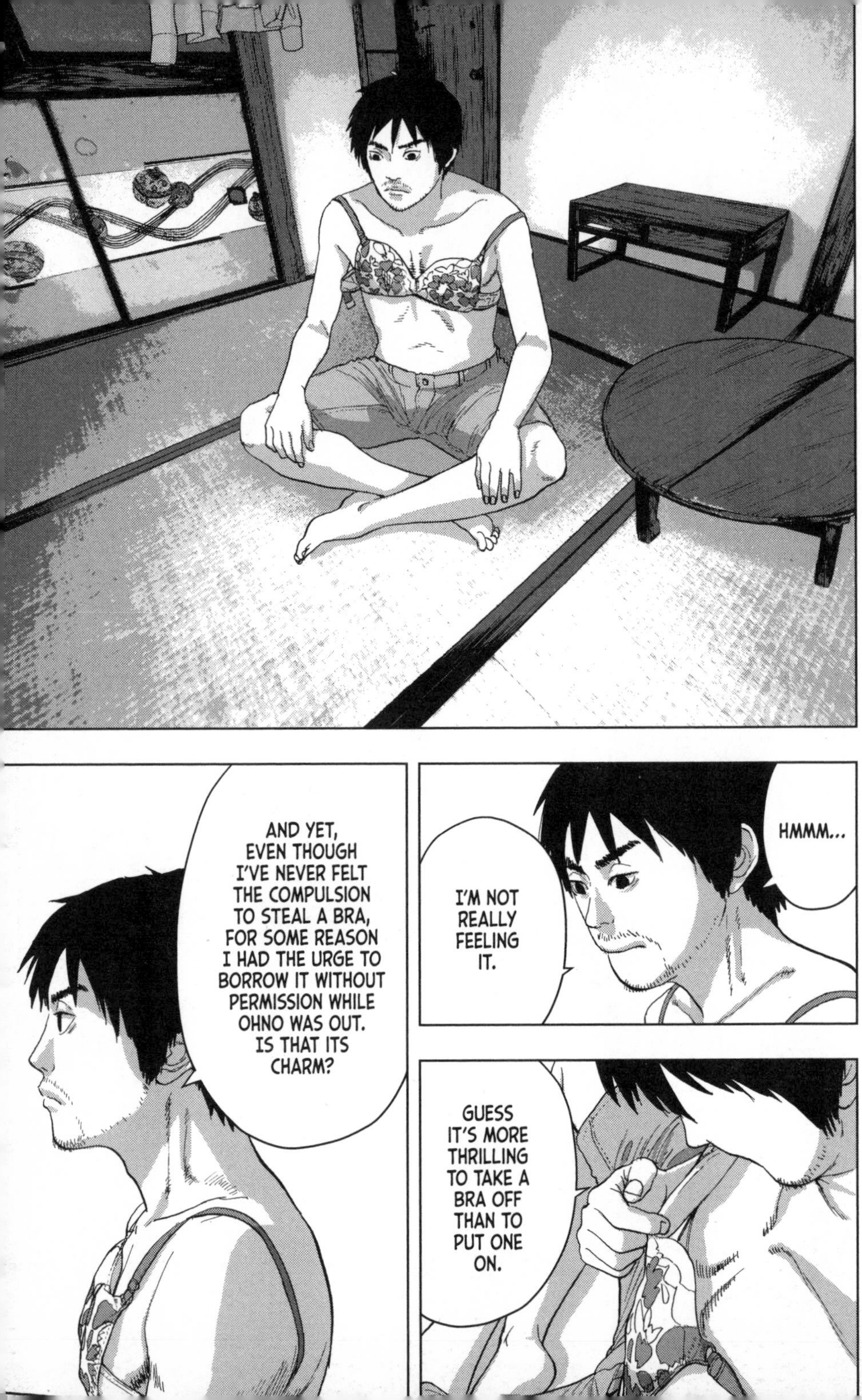
AND YET, EVEN THOUGH I'VE NEVER FELT THE COMPULSION TO STEAL A BRA, FOR SOME REASON I HAD THE URGE TO BORROW IT WITHOUT PERMISSION WHILE OHNO WAS OUT. IS THAT ITS CHARM?
HMMM...
I'M NOT REALLY FEELING IT.
GUESS IT'S MORE THRILLING TO TAKE A BRA OFF THAN TO PUT ONE ON.

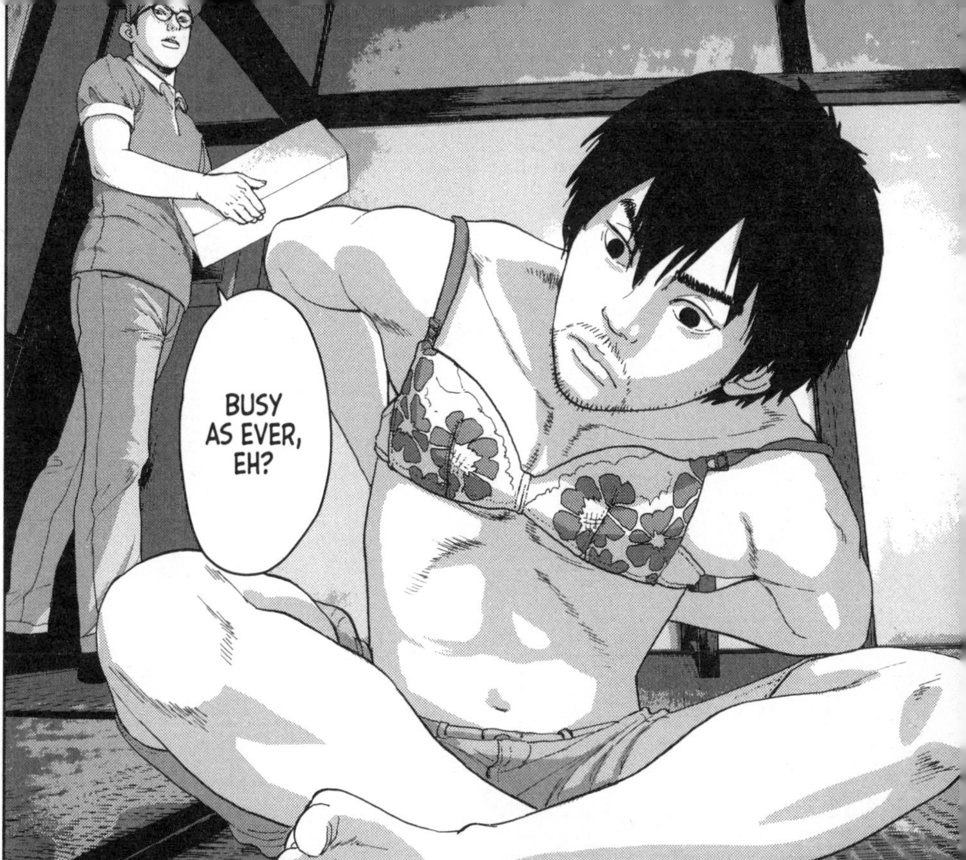
BUSY AS EVER, EH?

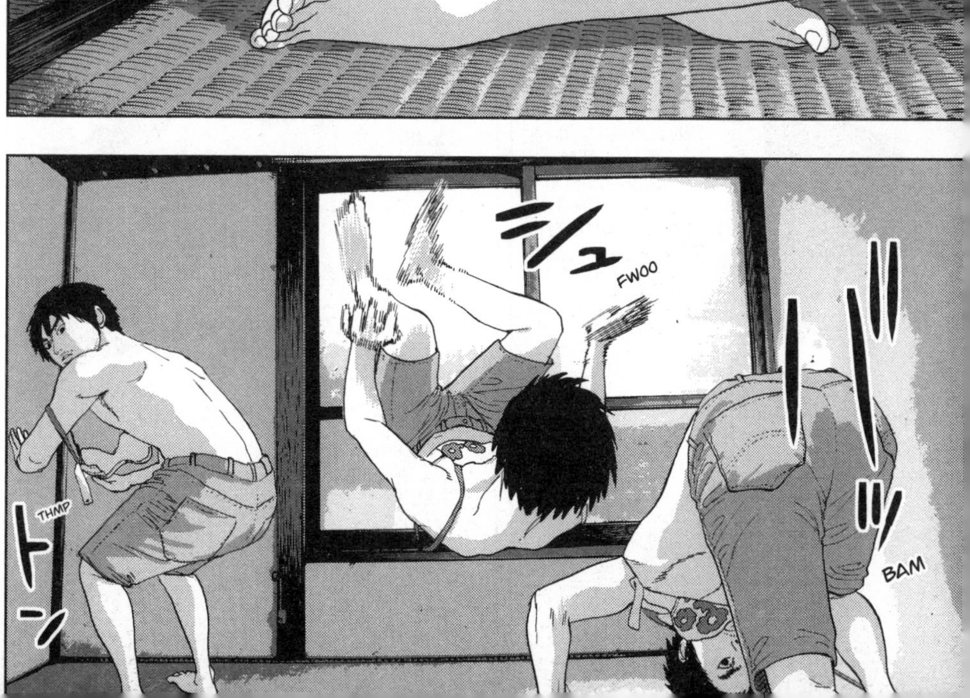
BAM
シュ
FWOO
THMP

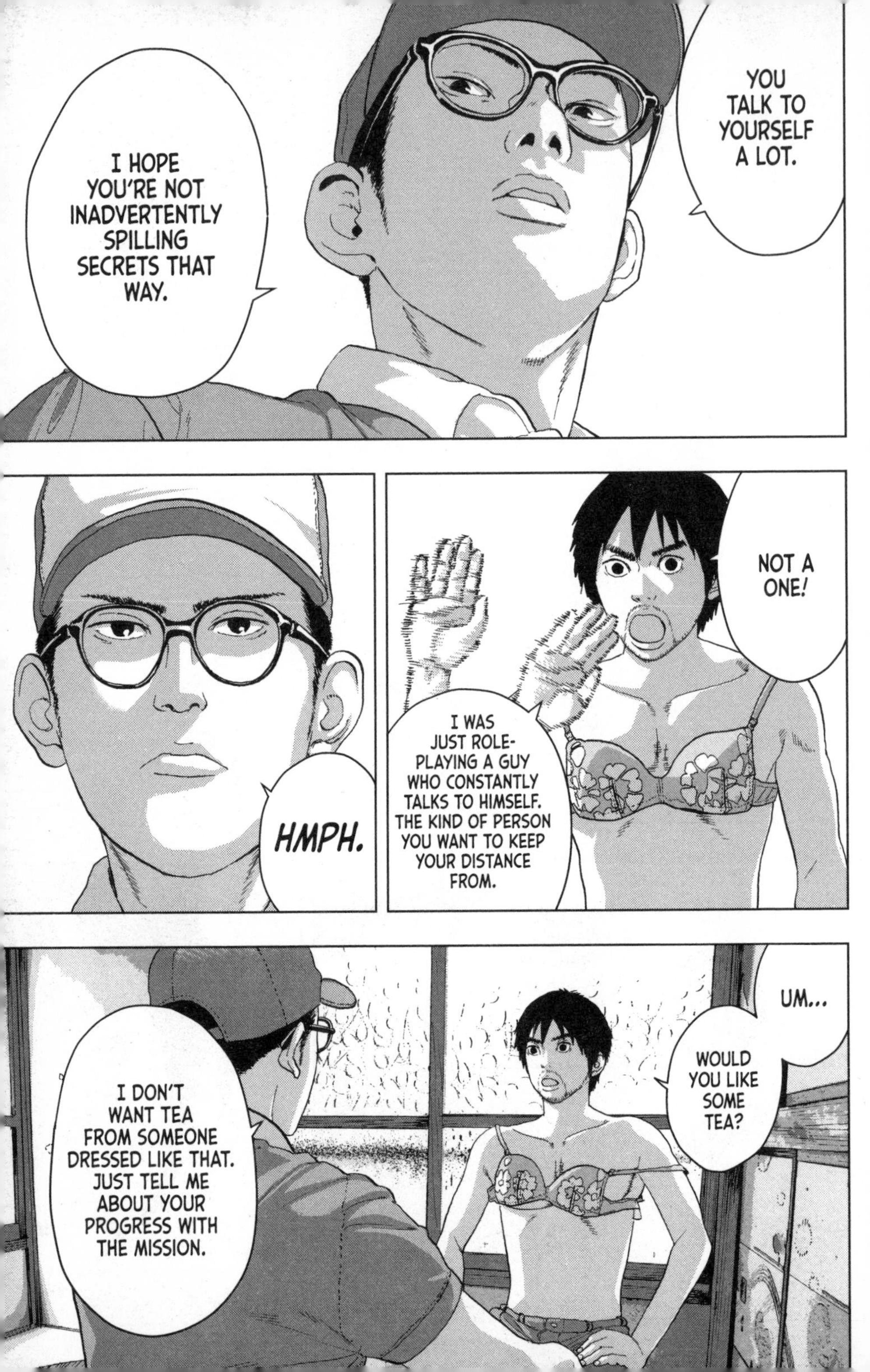
YOU TALK TO YOURSELF A LOT.
I HOPE YOU'RE NOT INADVERTENTLY SPILLING SECRETS THAT WAY.
NOT A ONE!
I WAS JUST ROLE-PLAYING A GUY WHO CONSTANTLY TALKS TO HIMSELF. THE KIND OF PERSON YOU WANT TO KEEP YOUR DISTANCE FROM.
HMPH.
UM...
WOULD YOU LIKE SOME TEA?
I DON'T WANT TEA FROM SOMEONE DRESSED LIKE THAT. JUST TELL ME ABOUT YOUR PROGRESS WITH THE MISSION.

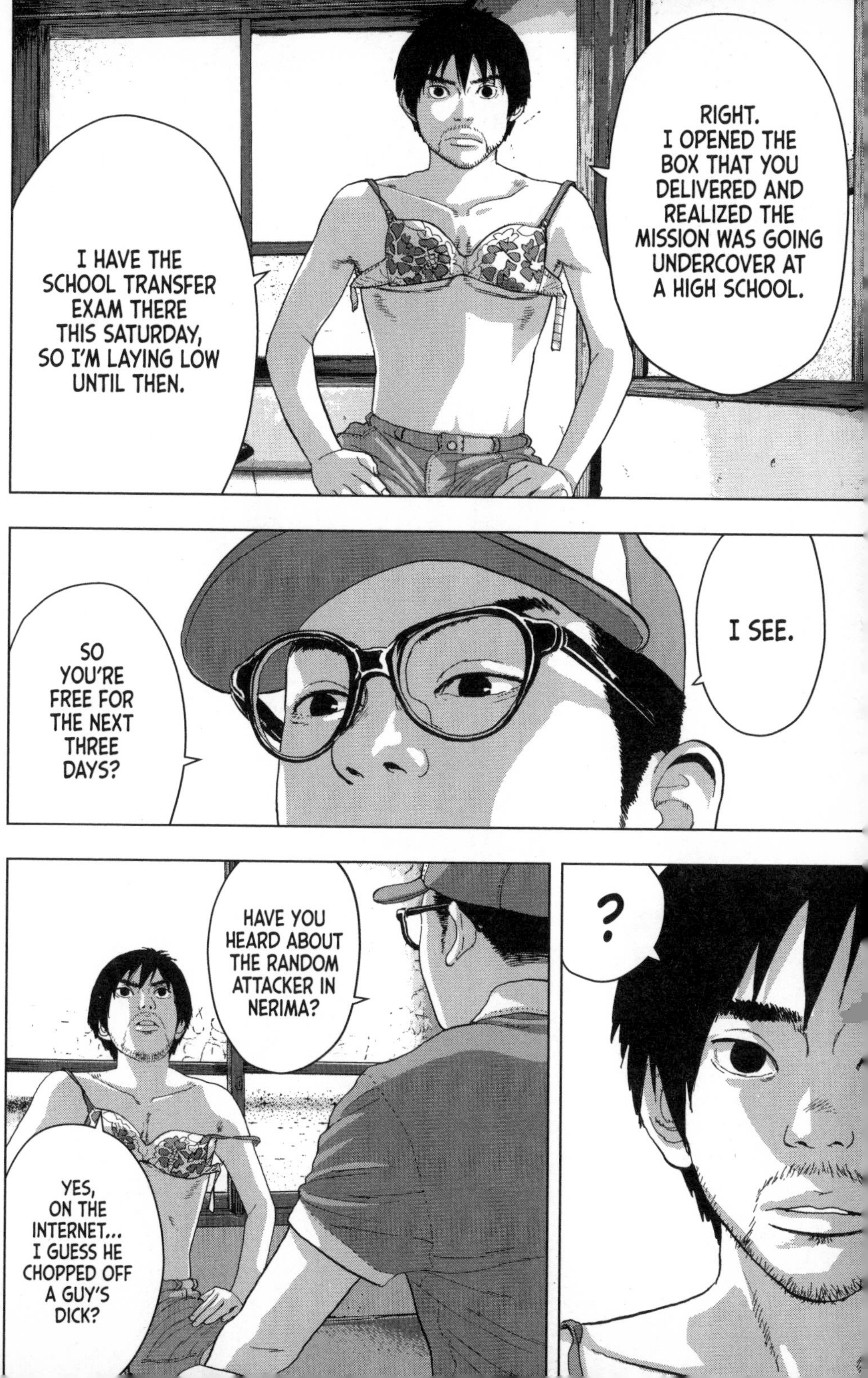
RIGHT. I OPENED THE BOX THAT YOU DELIVERED AND REALIZED THE MISSION WAS GOING UNDERCOVER AT A HIGH SCHOOL.
I HAVE THE SCHOOL TRANSFER EXAM THERE THIS SATURDAY, SO I'M LAYING LOW UNTIL THEN.
I SEE.
SO YOU'RE FREE FOR THE NEXT THREE DAYS?
?
HAVE YOU HEARD ABOUT THE RANDOM ATTACKER IN NERIMA?
YES, ON THE INTERNET... I GUESS HE CHOPPED OFF A GUY'S DICK?

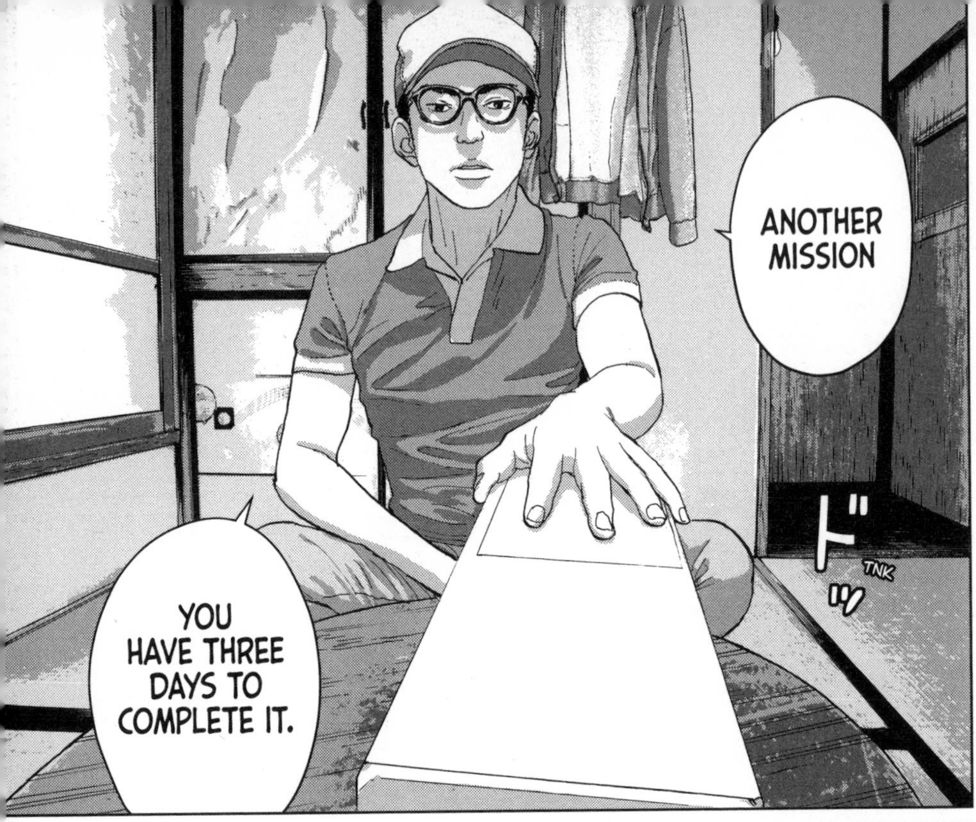
ANOTHER MISSION
YOU HAVE THREE DAYS TO COMPLETE IT.
ド
ツ
TNK

*NOTE: APPROXIMATELY 6'3".

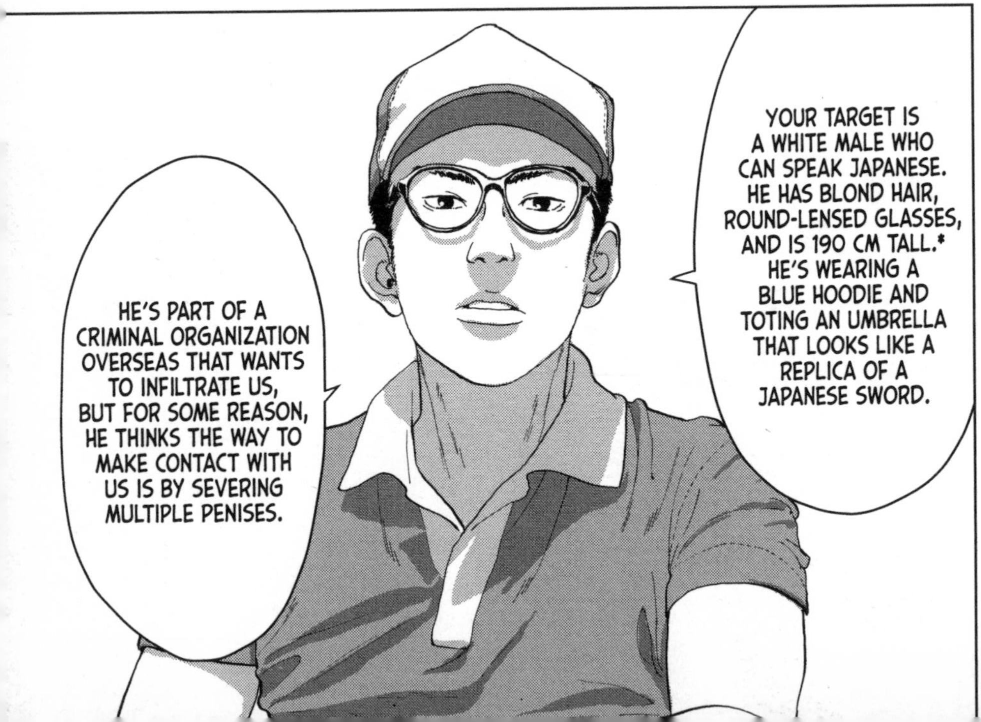
YOUR TARGET IS A WHITE MALE WHO CAN SPEAK JAPANESE. HE HAS BLOND HAIR, ROUND-LENSED GLASSES, AND IS 190 CM TALL.* HE'S WEARING A BLUE HOODIE AND TOTING AN UMBRELLA THAT LOOKS LIKE A REPLICA OF A JAPANESE SWORD.
HE'S PART OF A CRIMINAL ORGANIZATION OVERSEAS THAT WANTS TO INFILTRATE US, BUT FOR SOME REASON, HE THINKS THE WAY TO MAKE CONTACT WITH US IS BY SEVERING MULTIPLE PENISES.

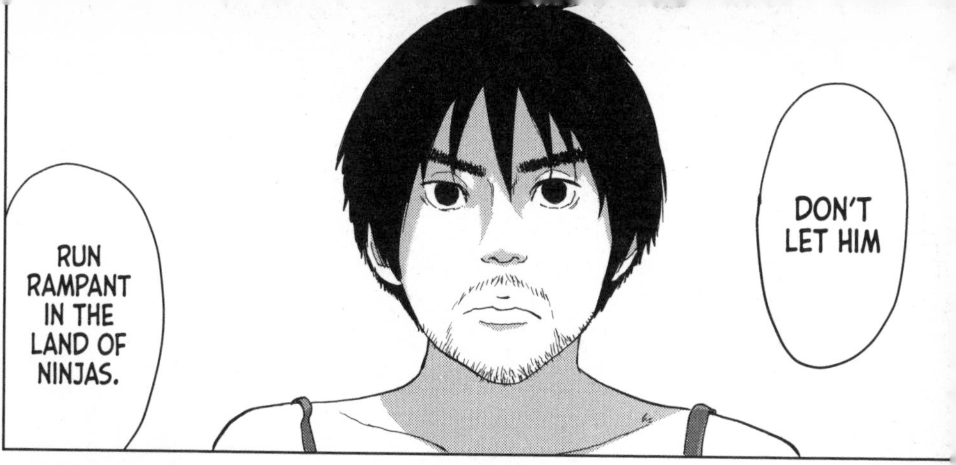
DON'T LET HIM
RUN RAMPANT IN THE LAND OF NINJAS.

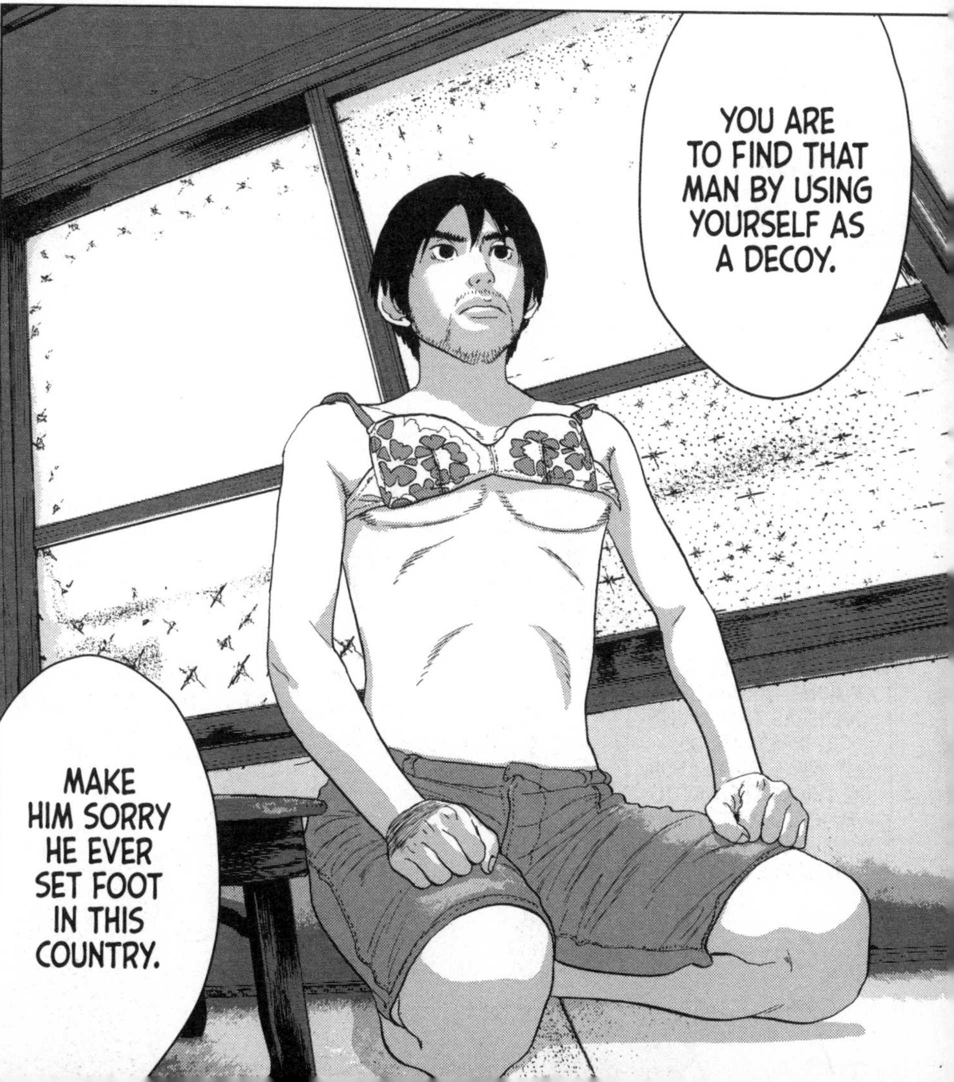
YOU ARE TO FIND THAT MAN BY USING YOURSELF AS A DECOY.
MAKE HIM SORRY HE EVER SET FOOT IN THIS COUNTRY.

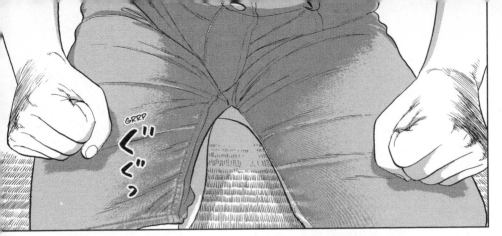

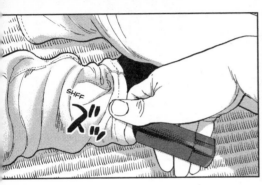

YOU'LL FIND A DUPLICATE OF THIS IN THE BOX.

A BILLY CLUB WITH A BUILT-IN TASER.

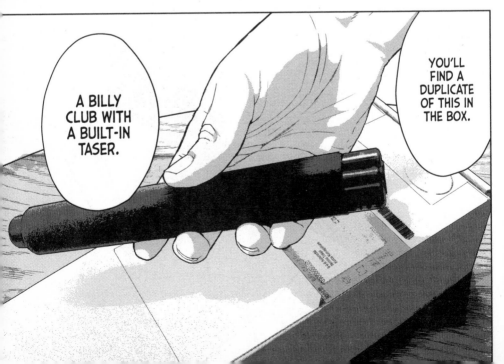

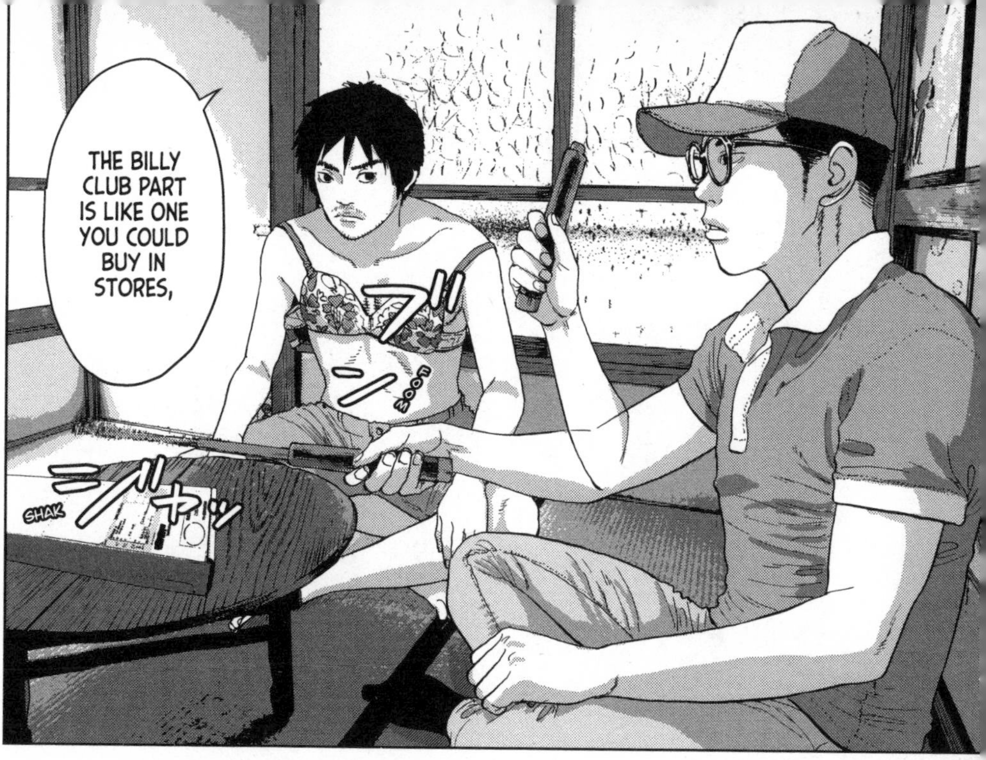
THE BILLY CLUB PART IS LIKE ONE YOU COULD BUY IN STORES,
FOOM
SHAK
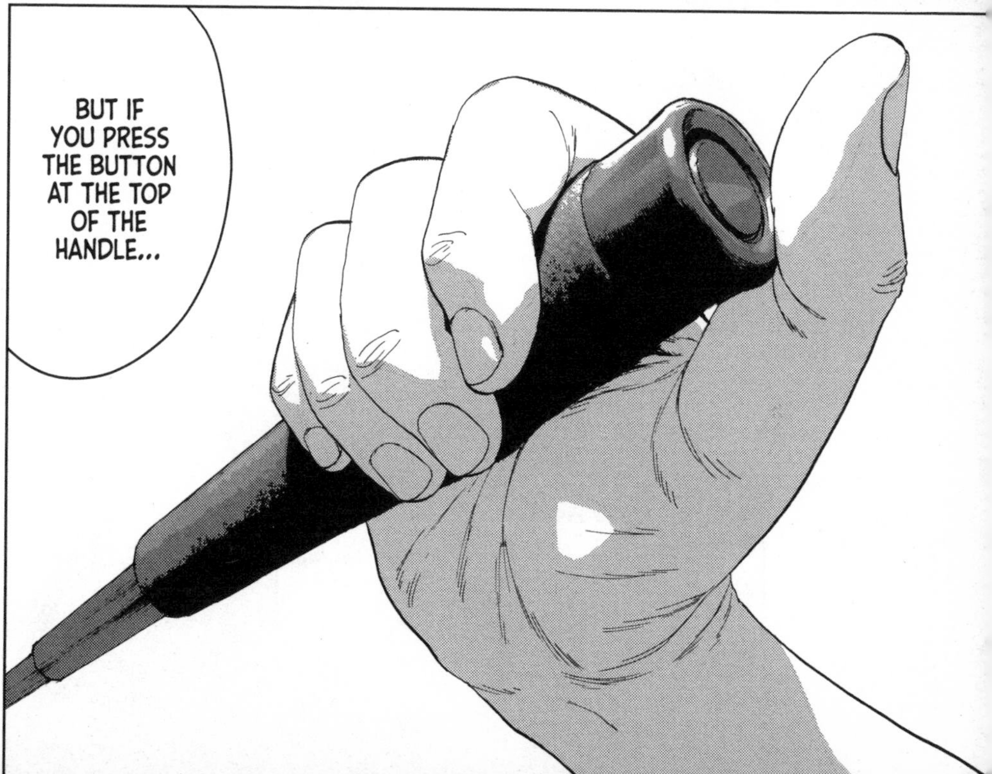
BUT IF YOU PRESS THE BUTTON AT THE TOP OF THE HANDLE...

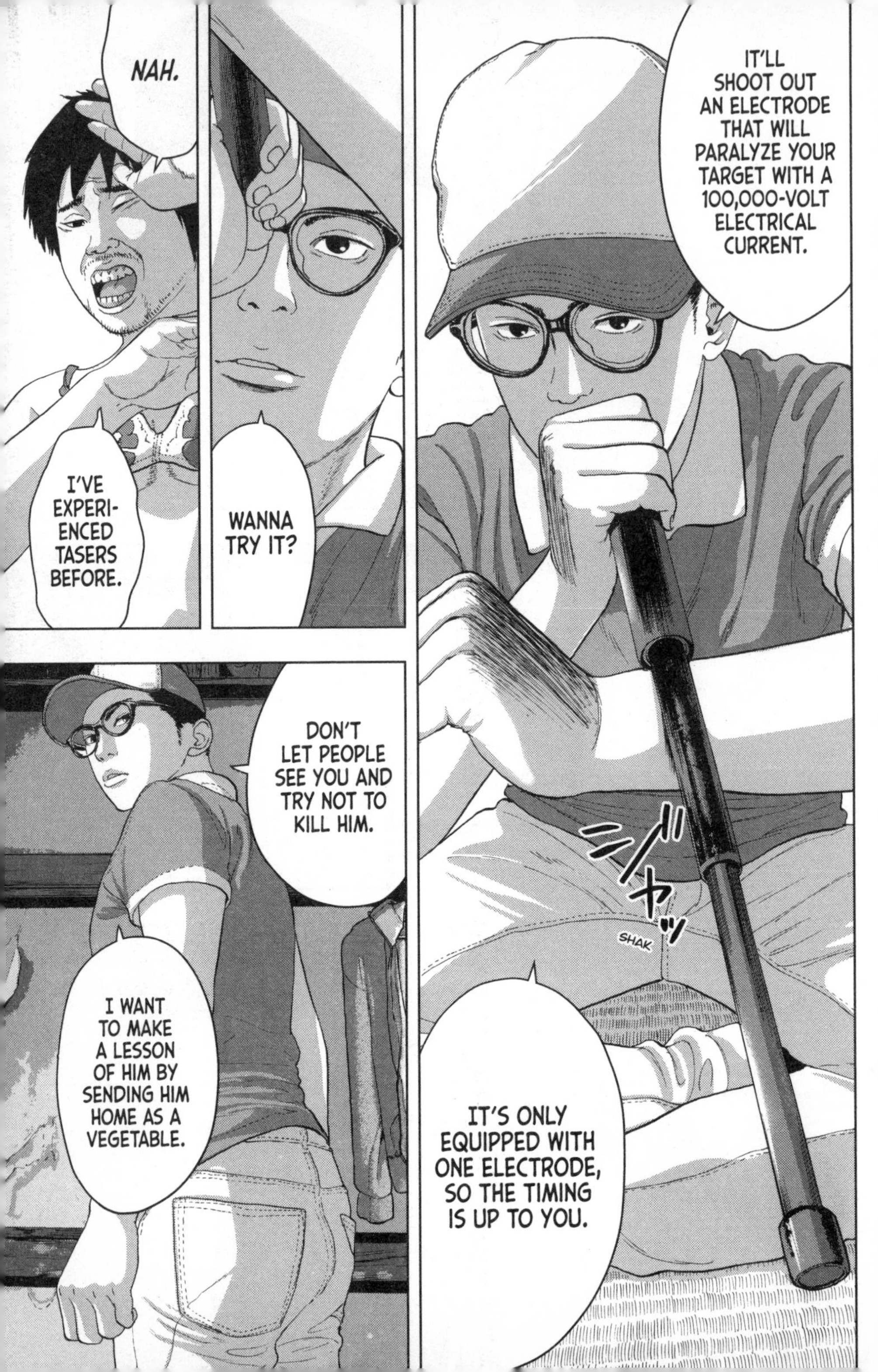
IT'LL SHOOT OUT AN ELECTRODE THAT WILL PARALYZE YOUR TARGET WITH A 100,000-VOLT ELECTRICAL CURRENT.
ジャッ
SHAK
IT'S ONLY EQUIPPED WITH ONE ELECTRODE, SO THE TIMING IS UP TO YOU.
WANNA TRY IT?
NAH.
I'VE EXPERI-ENCED TASERS BEFORE.
DON'T LET PEOPLE SEE YOU AND TRY NOT TO KILL HIM.
I WANT TO MAKE A LESSON OF HIM BY SENDING HIM HOME AS A VEGETABLE.

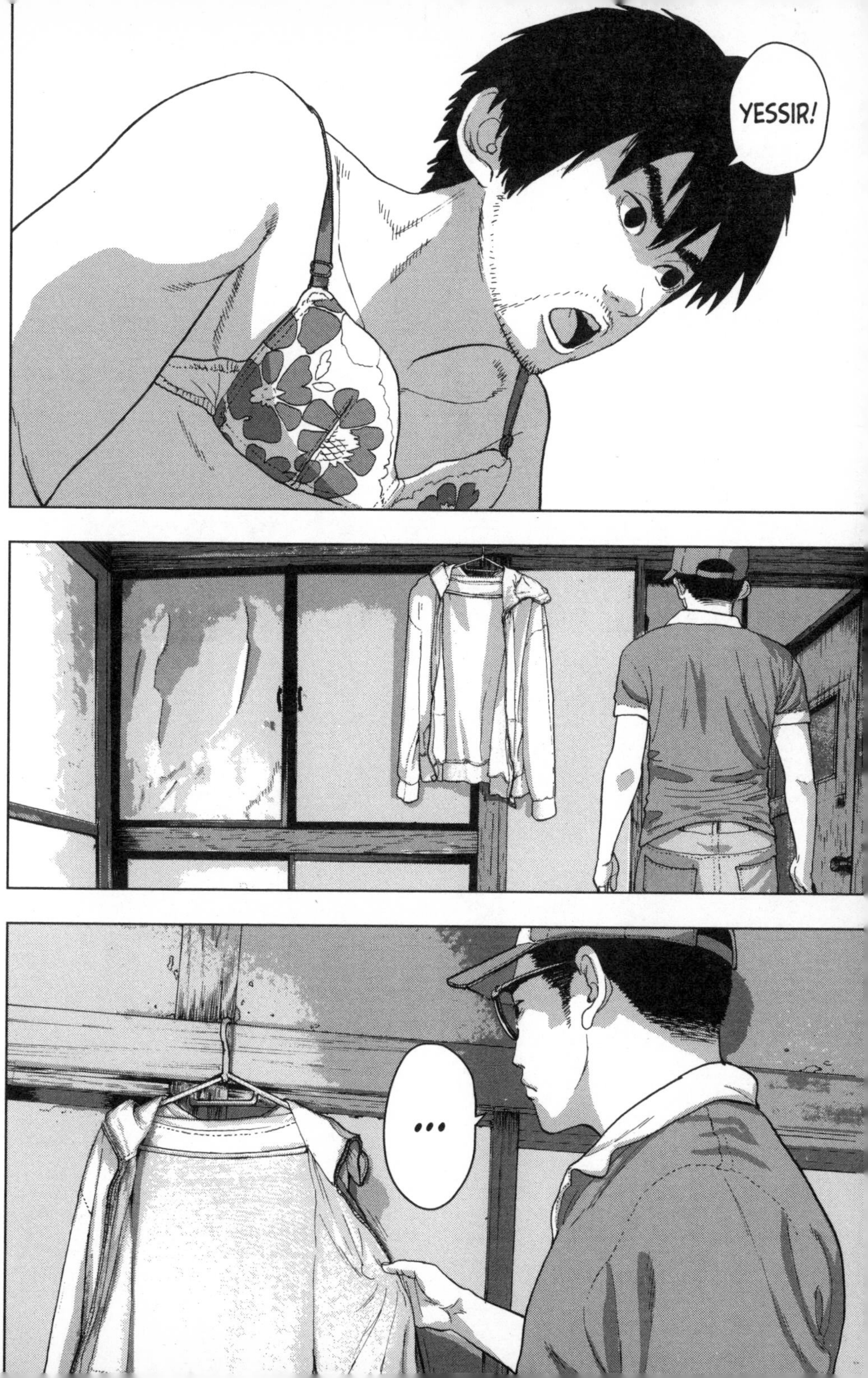
YESSIR!
...

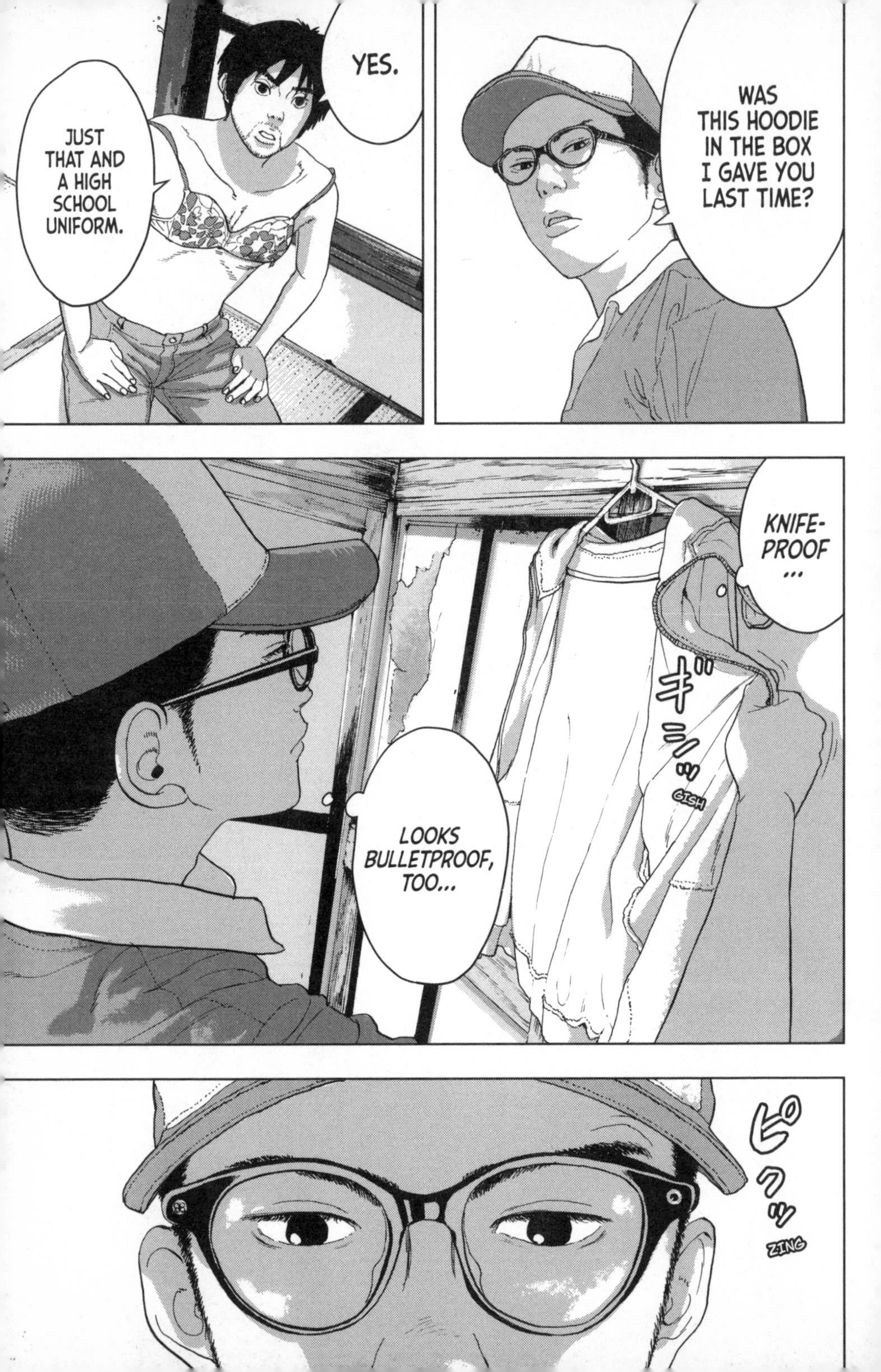
WAS THIS HOODIE IN THE BOX I GAVE YOU LAST TIME?
YES.
JUST THAT AND A HIGH SCHOOL UNIFORM.
KNIFE-PROOF...
ギシッ
GISH
LOOKS BULLETPROOF, TOO...
ピクッ
ZING

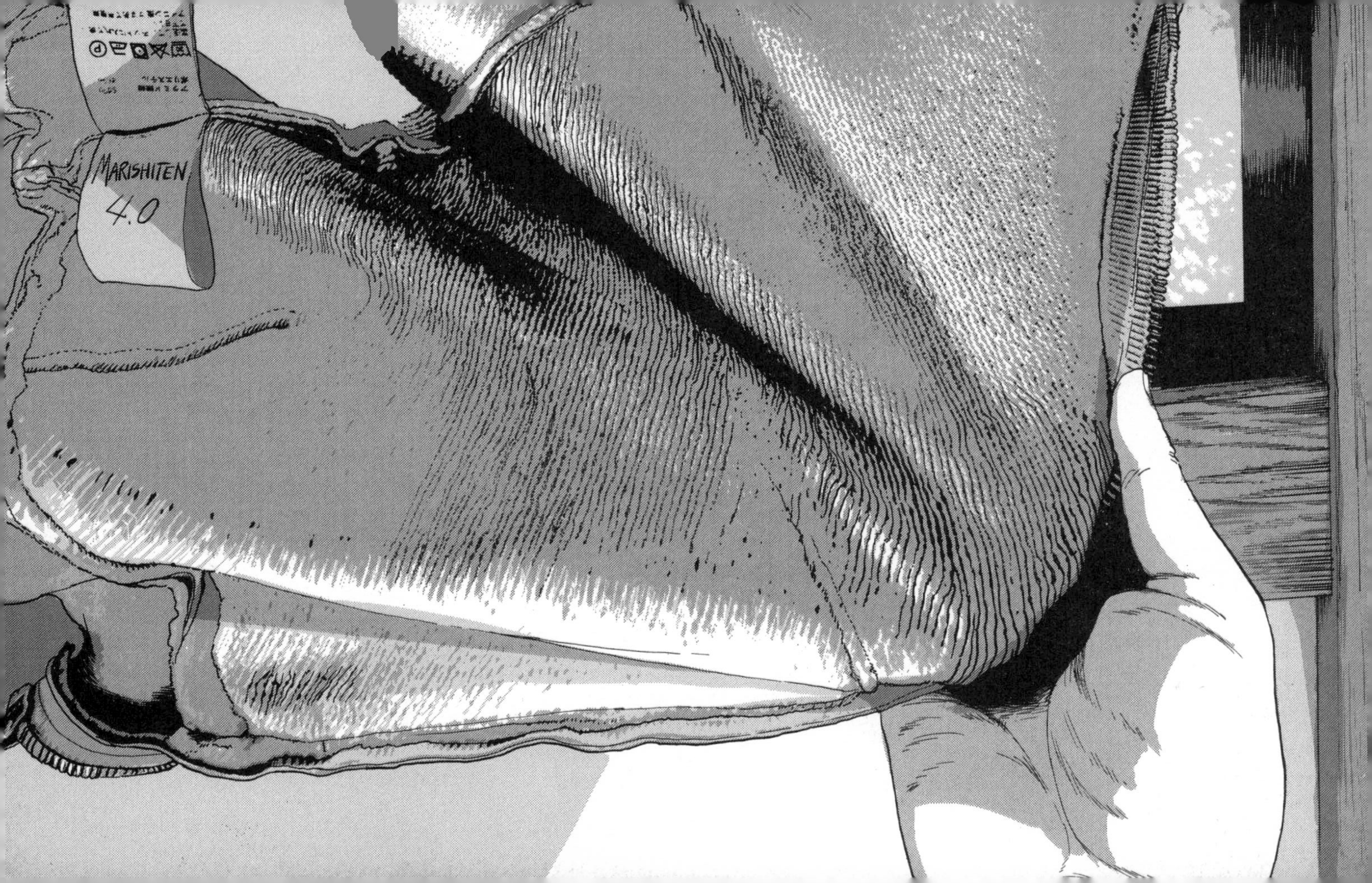
MARISHITEN
4.0

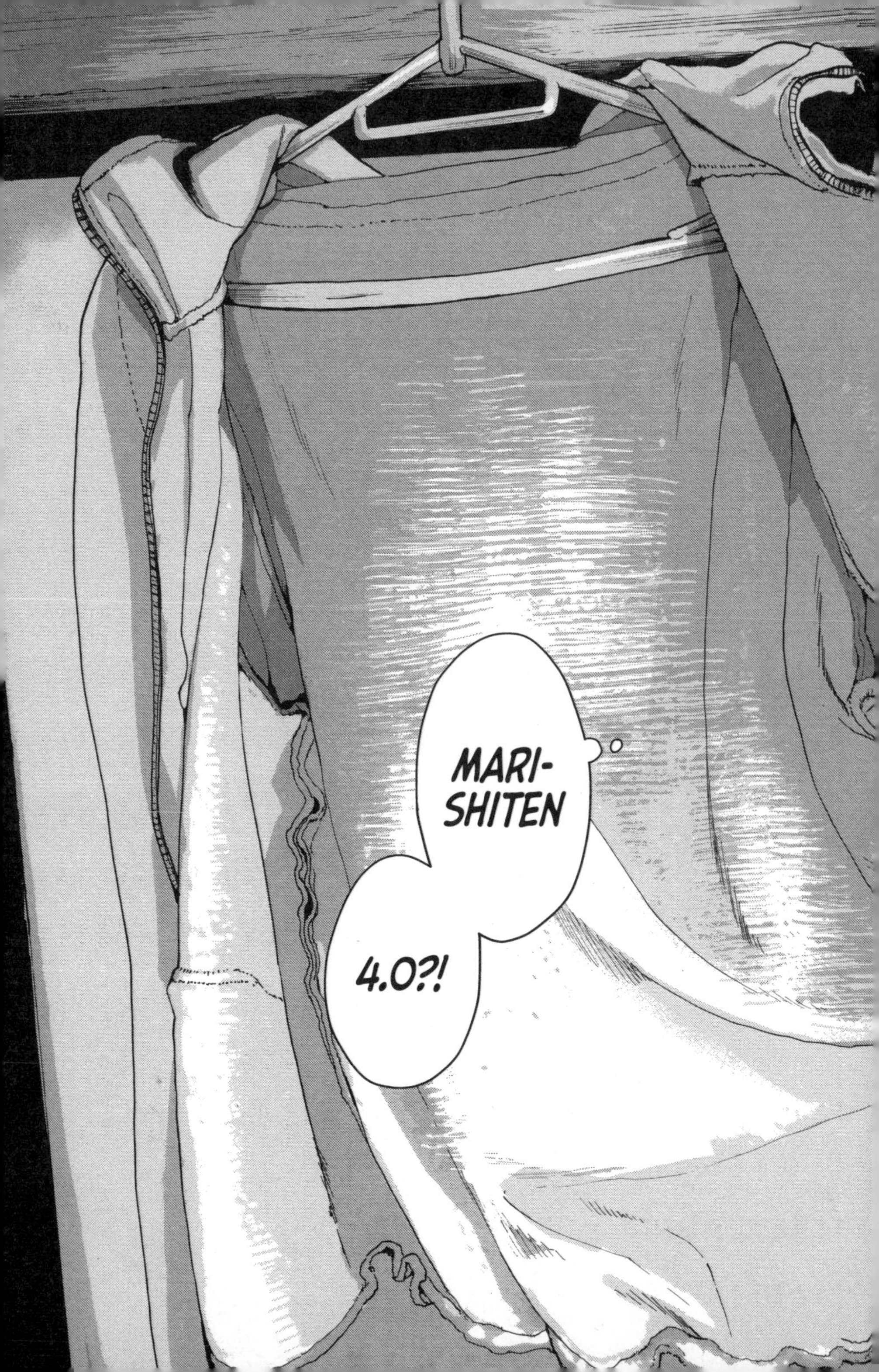
MARI-SHITEN
4.0?!

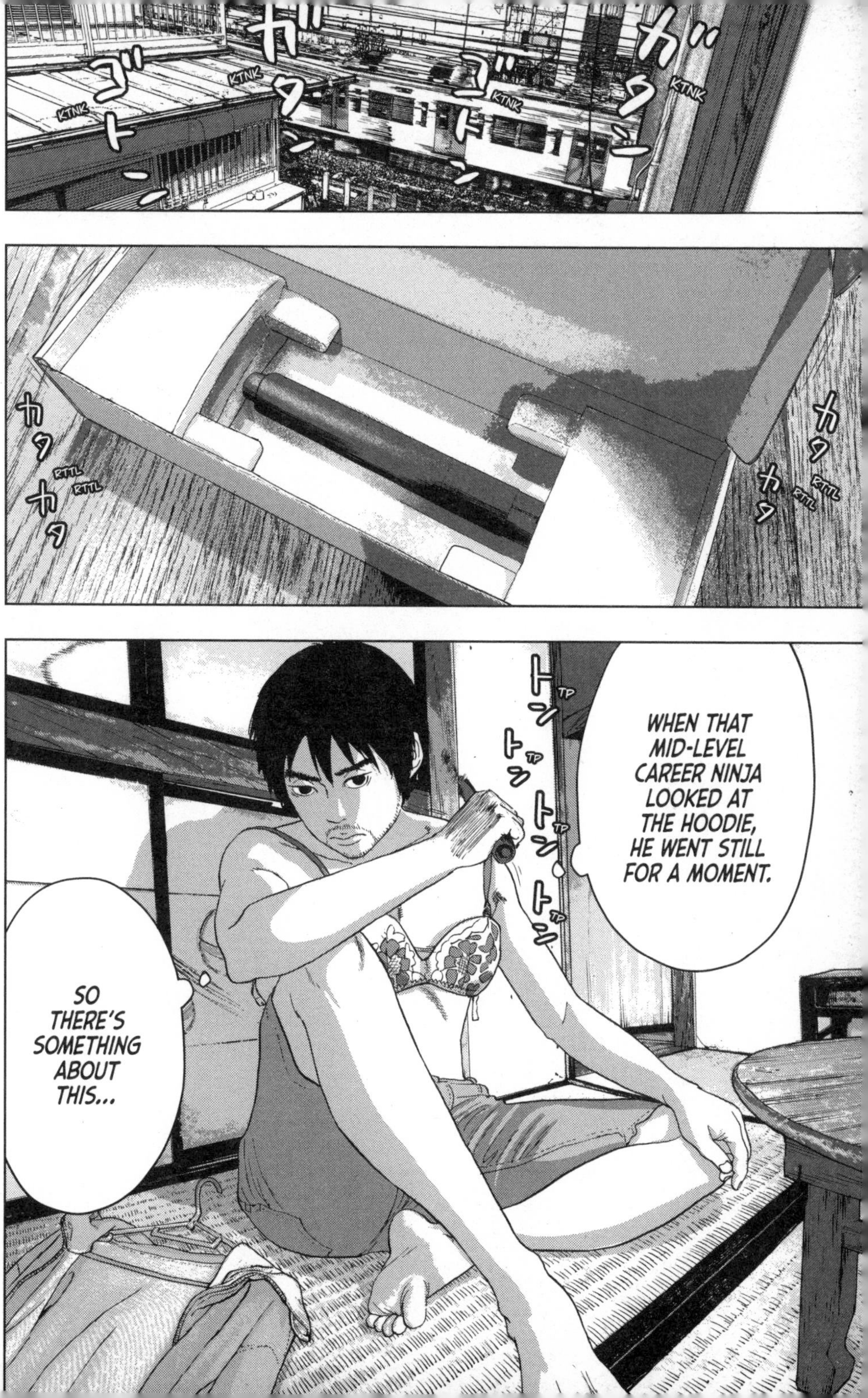
KTNK
KTNK
KTNK
カタカタ
RTTL RTTL
RTTL RTTL
TP TP TP TP
WHEN THAT MID-LEVEL CAREER NINJA LOOKED AT THE HOODIE, HE WENT STILL FOR A MOMENT.
SO THERE'S SOMETHING ABOUT THIS...

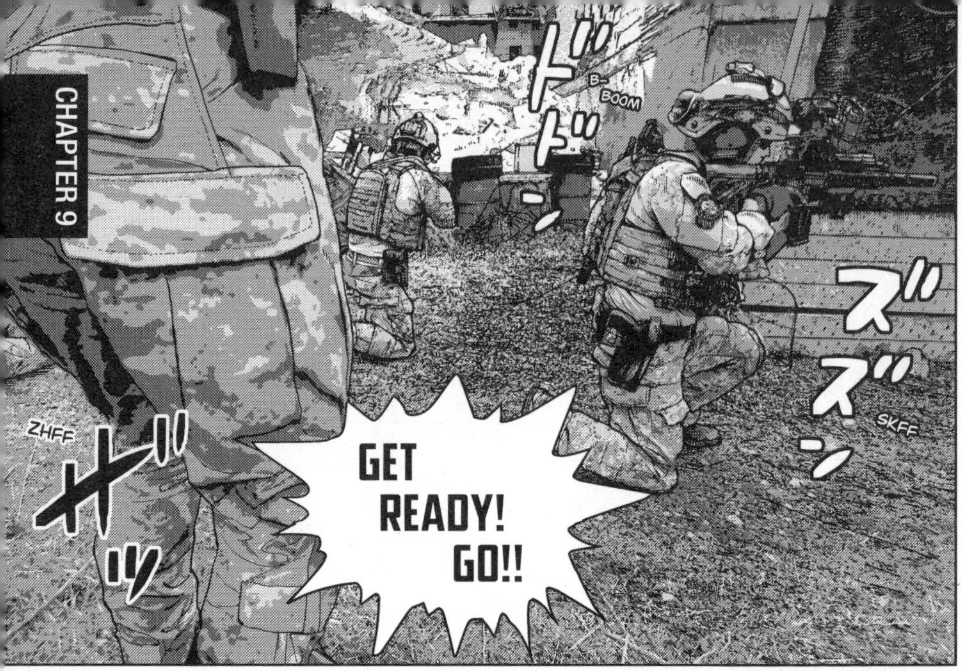
CHAPTER 9
B-BOOM
SKFF
GET READY! GO!!
ZHFF

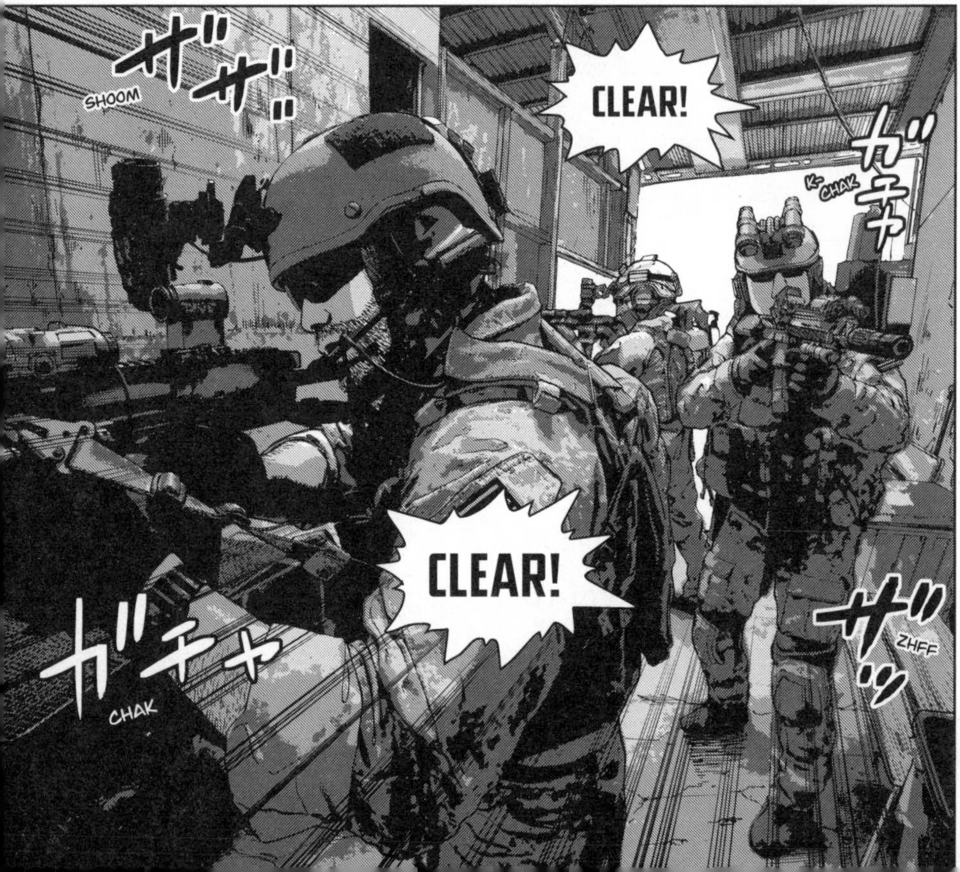
CLEAR!
K-CHAK
SHOOM
ZHFF
CLEAR!
CHAK

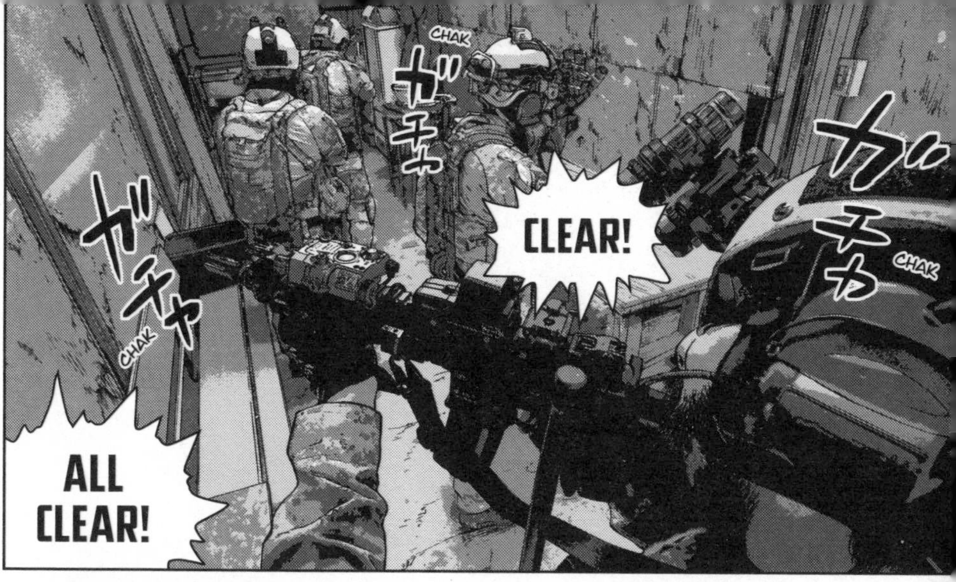
CHAK
CLEAR!
CHAK
CHAK
ALL CLEAR!

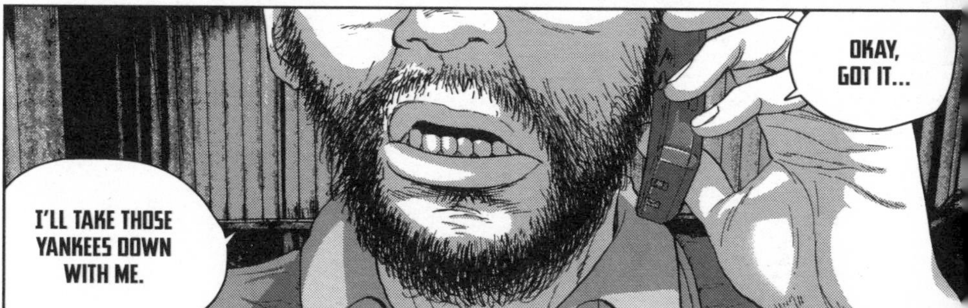
OKAY, GOT IT...
I'LL TAKE THOSE YANKEES DOWN WITH ME.

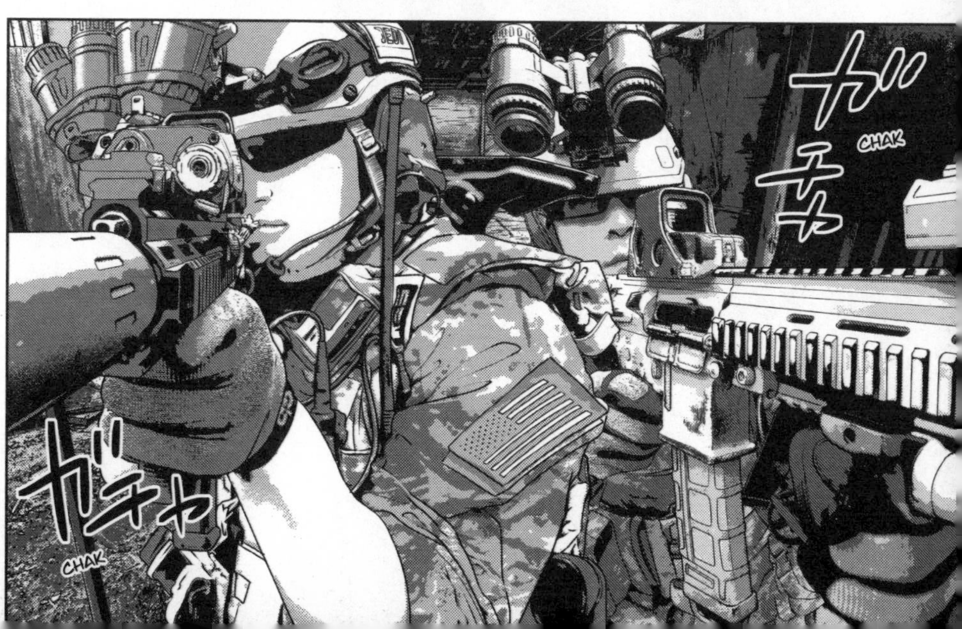
CHAK
JEDI
CHAK

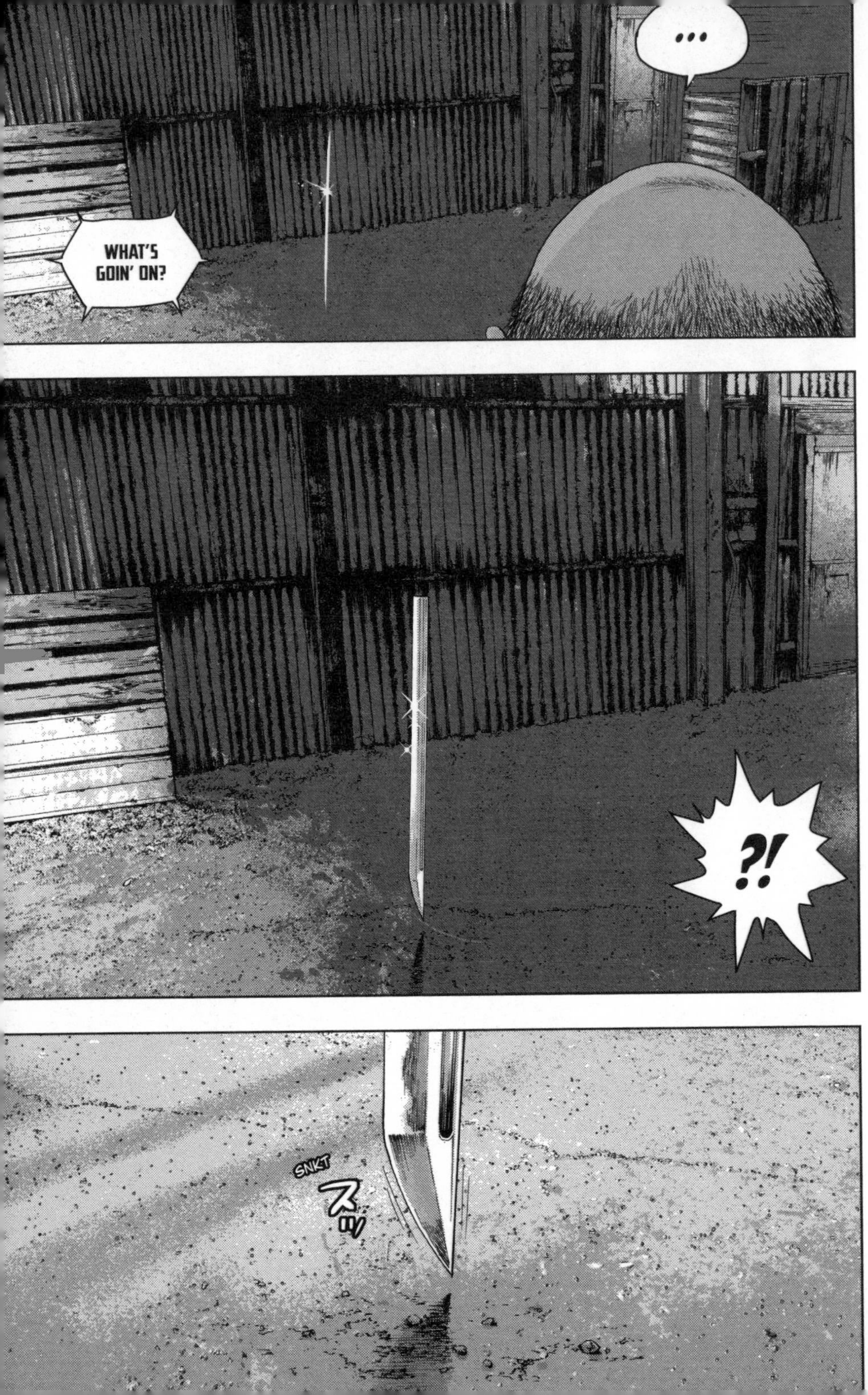
...
WHAT'S GOIN' ON?
?!
SNKT

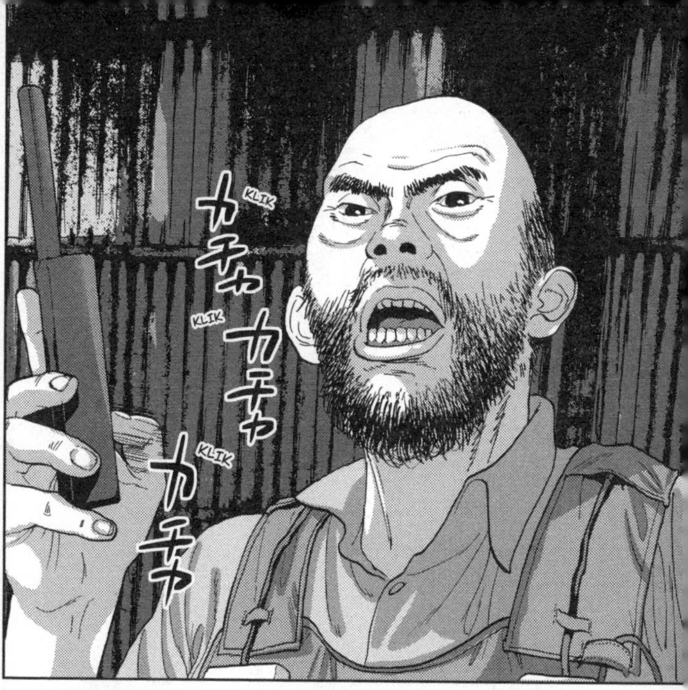
カチャ
KLIK
カチャ
KLIK
カチャ
KLIK
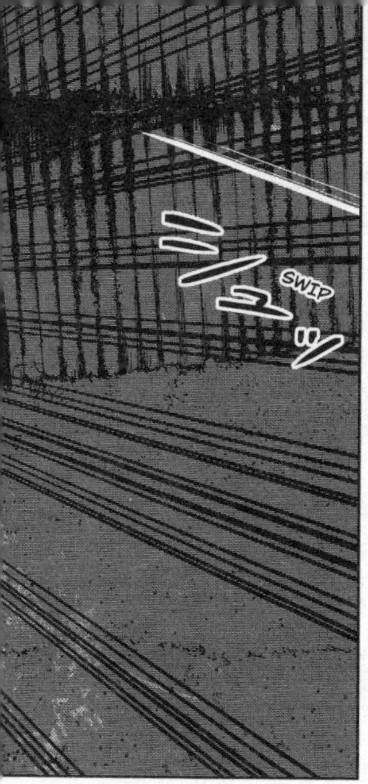
シュッ
SWIP
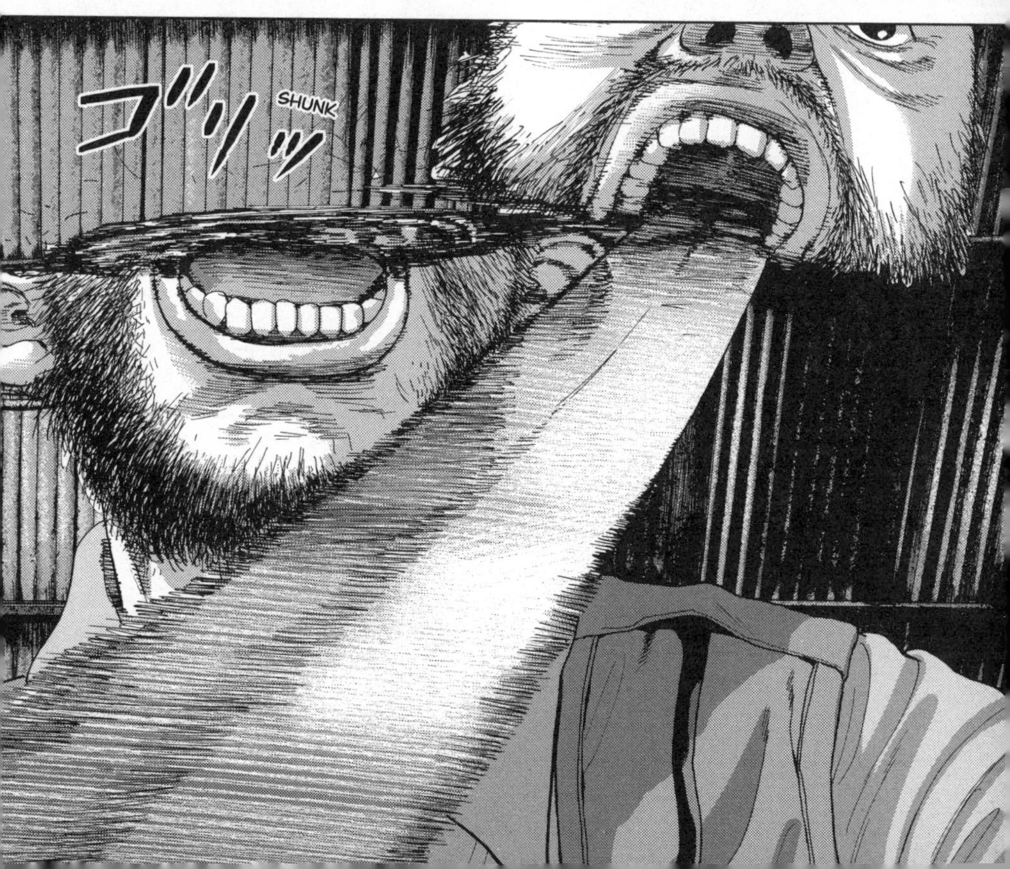
ゴリッ
SHUNK

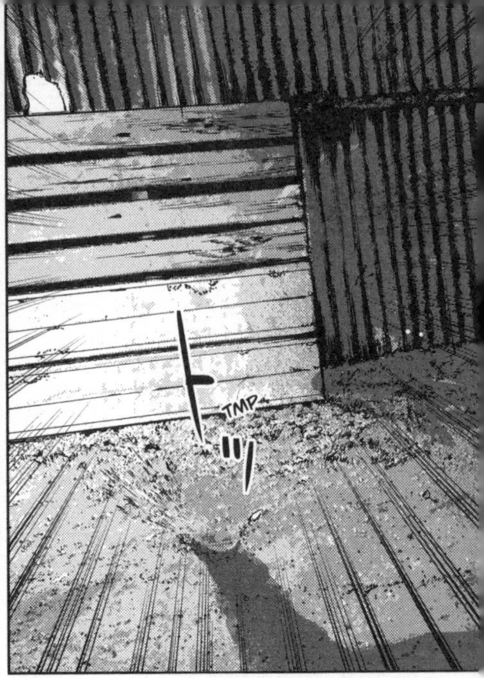
トッ
TMP
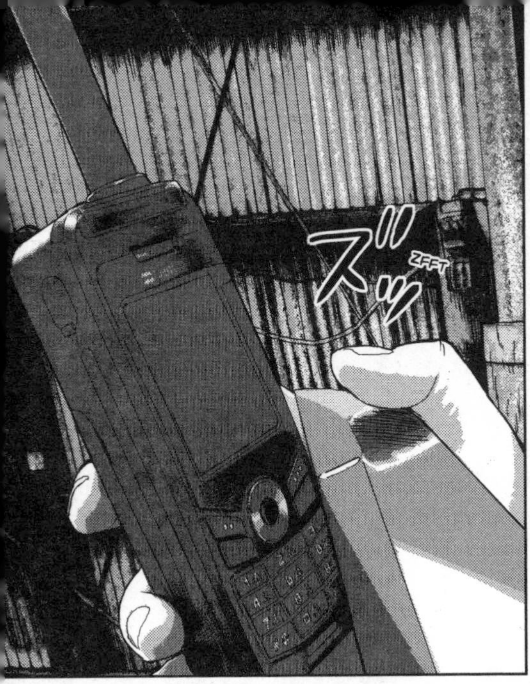
ズッ
ZFFT
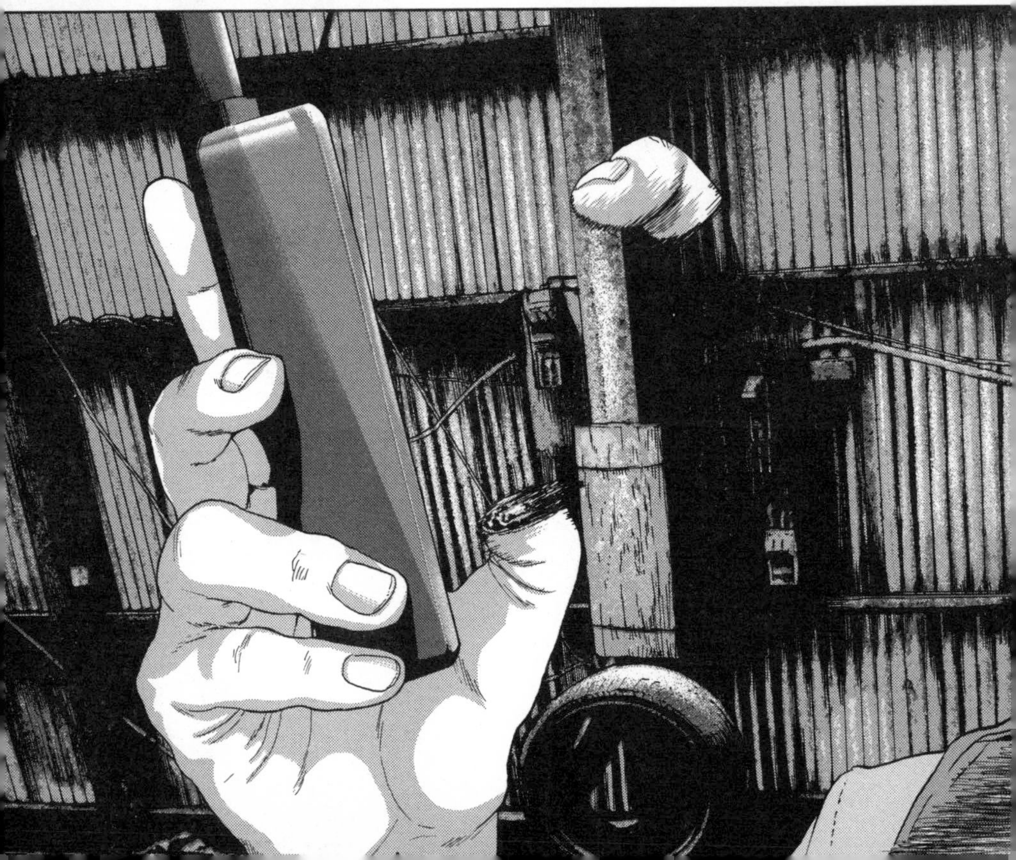

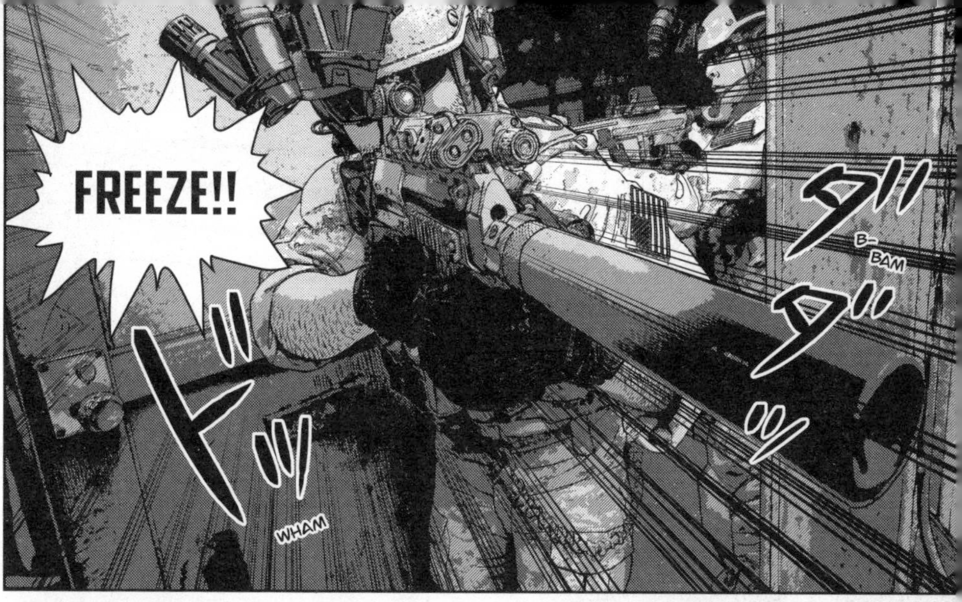
ダダッ
B-BAM
FREEZE!!
ドッ
WHAM

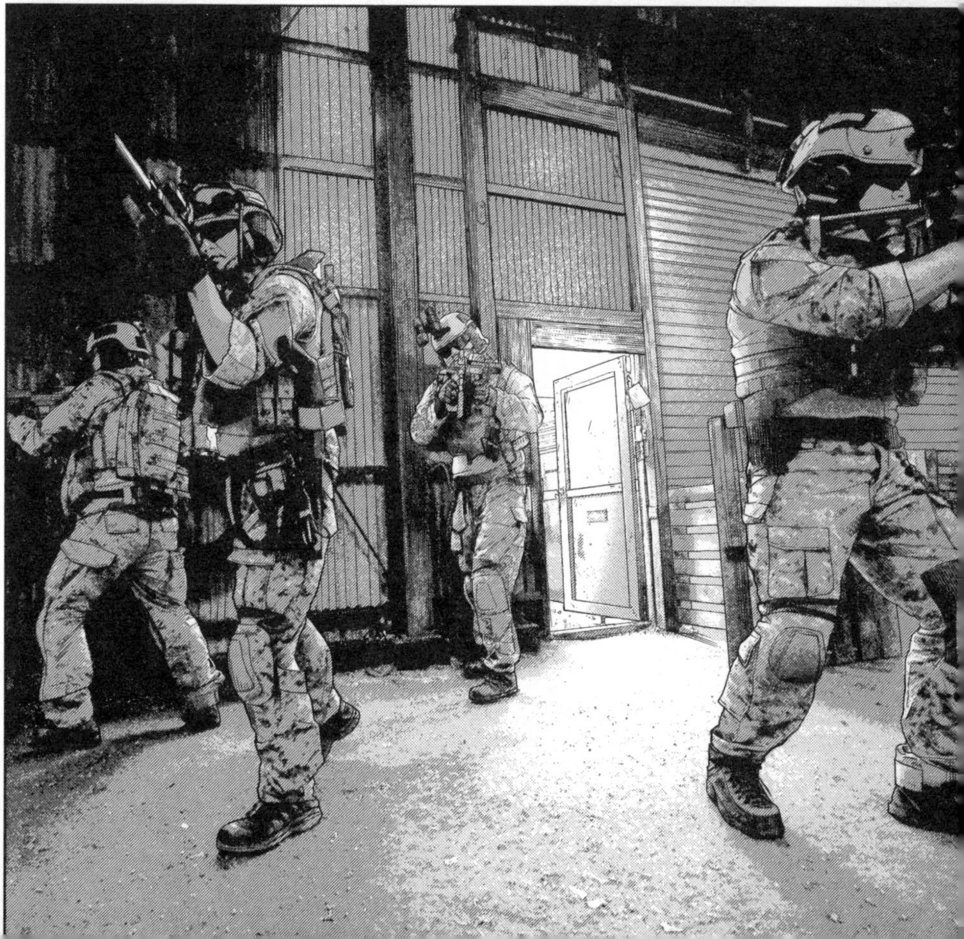

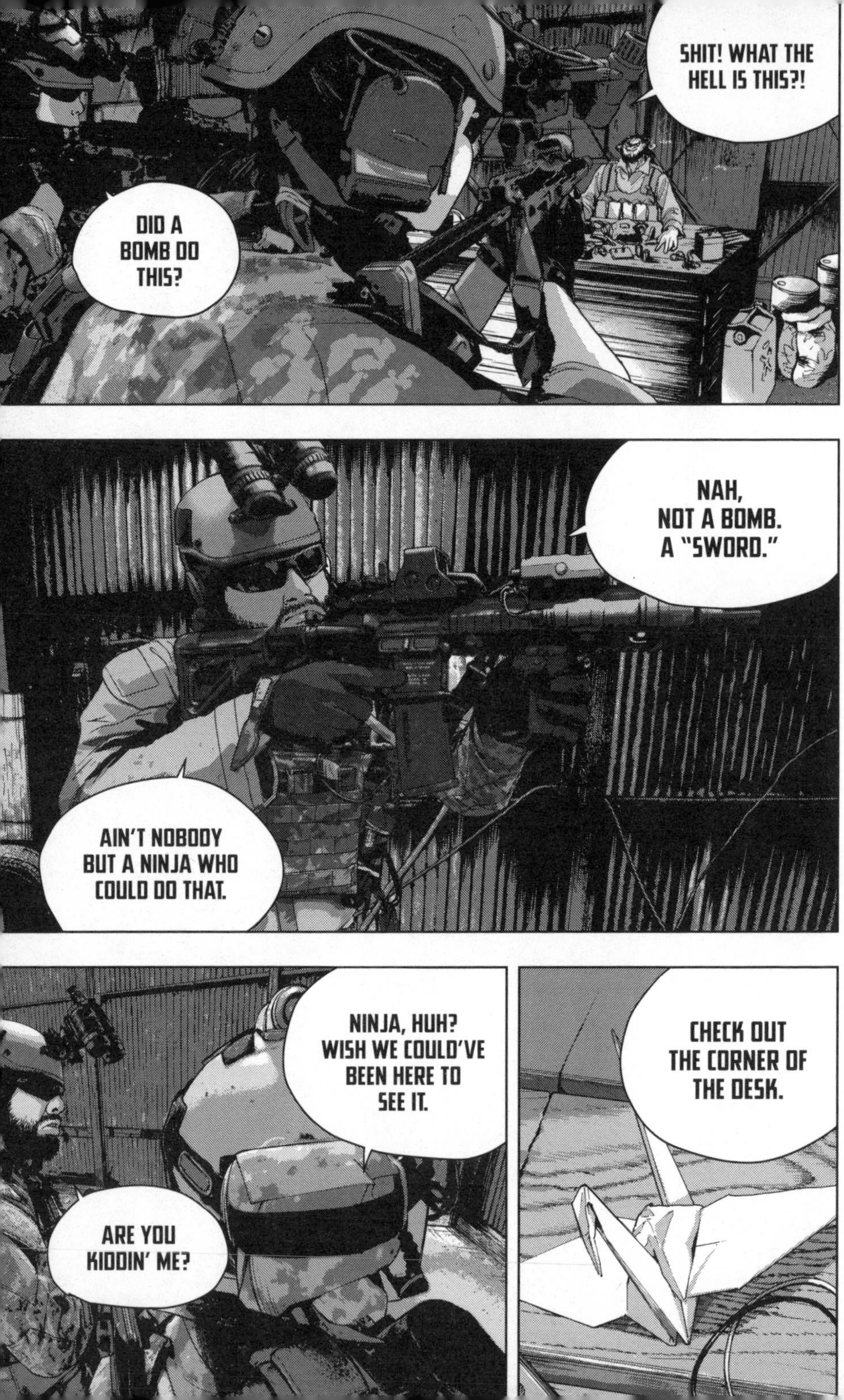
SHIT! WHAT THE HELL IS THIS?!
DID A BOMB DO THIS?
NAH, NOT A BOMB. A "SWORD."
AIN'T NOBODY BUT A NINJA WHO COULD DO THAT.
CHECK OUT THE CORNER OF THE DESK.
NINJA, HUH? WISH WE COULD'VE BEEN HERE TO SEE IT.
ARE YOU KIDDIN' ME?

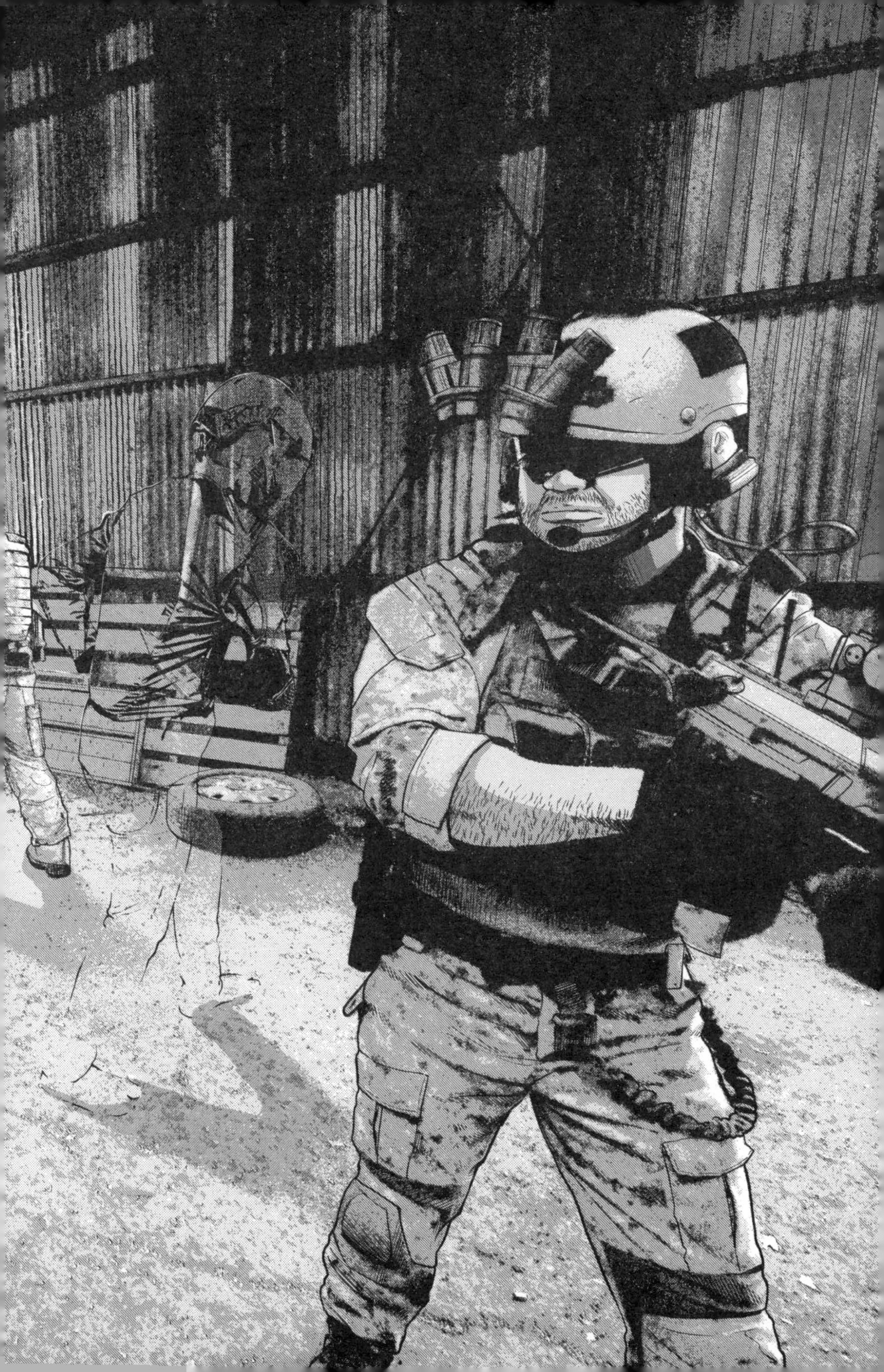

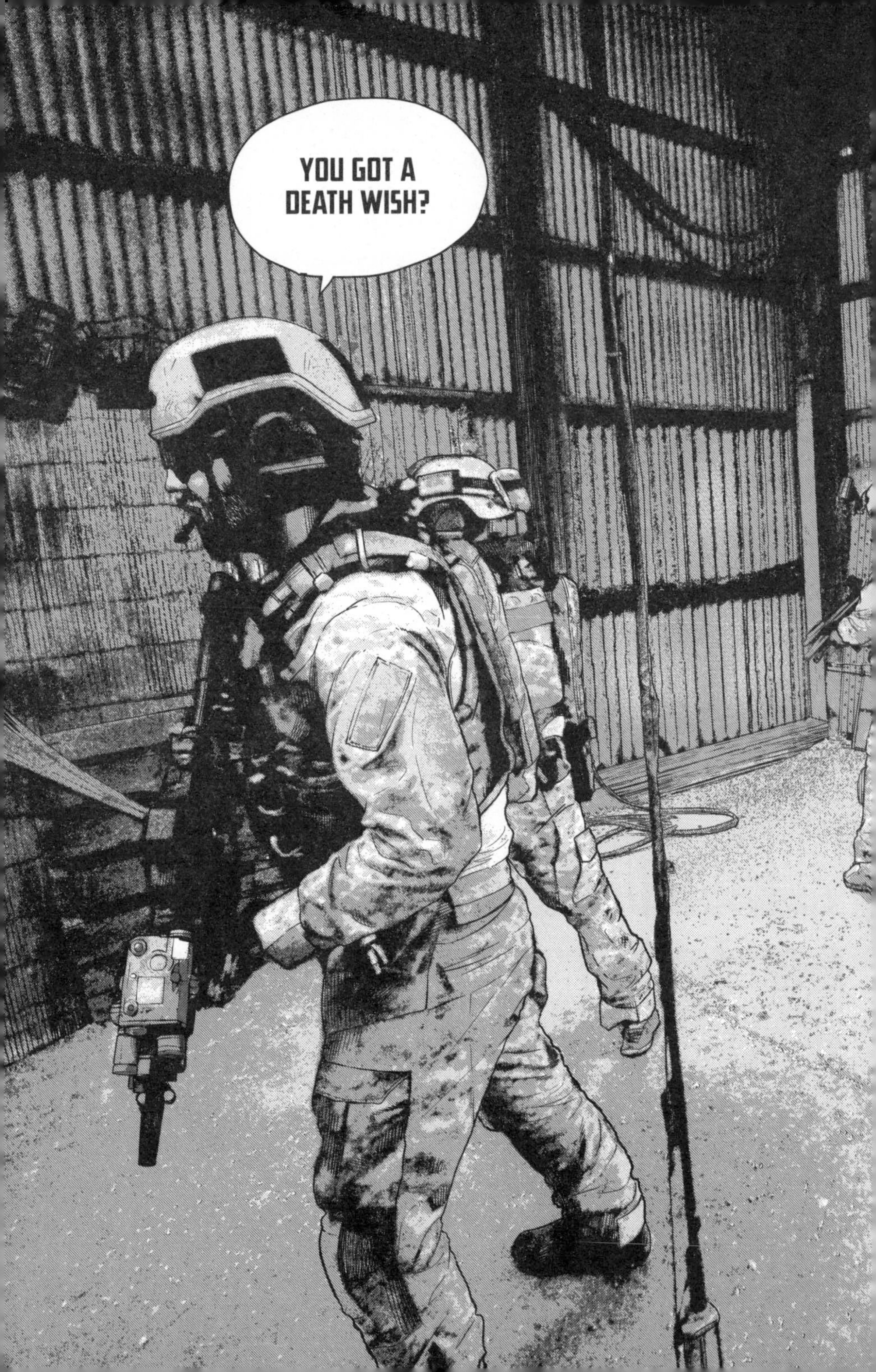
YOU GOT A DEATH WISH?

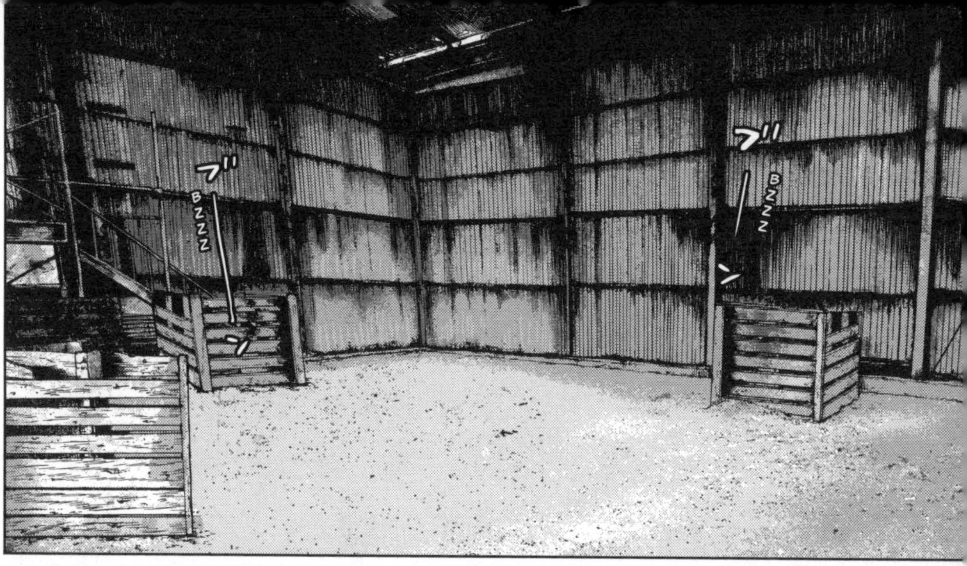
ブ
BZZZ
ッ
ブ
BZZZ
ッ

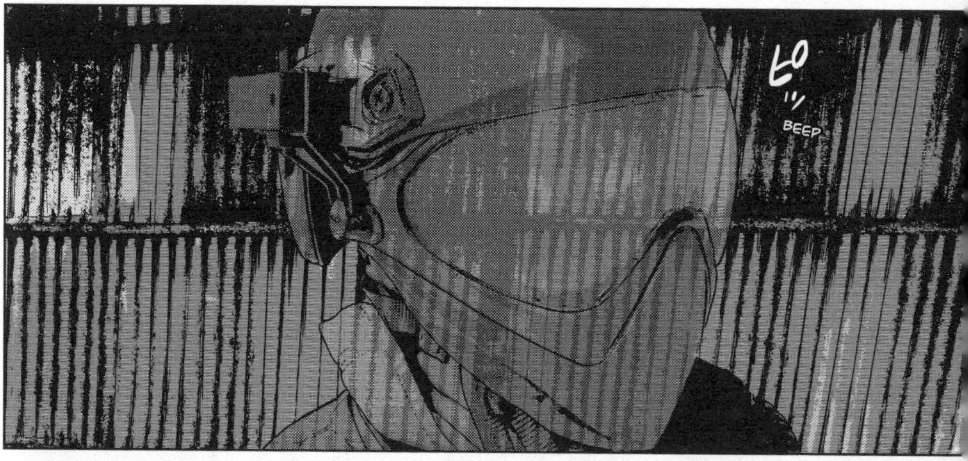
ピッ
BEEP

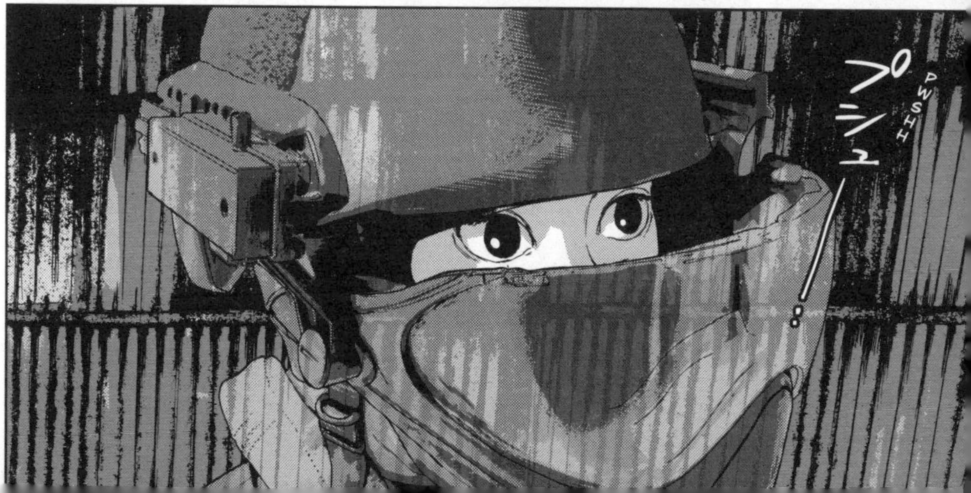
プシュ
PWSH

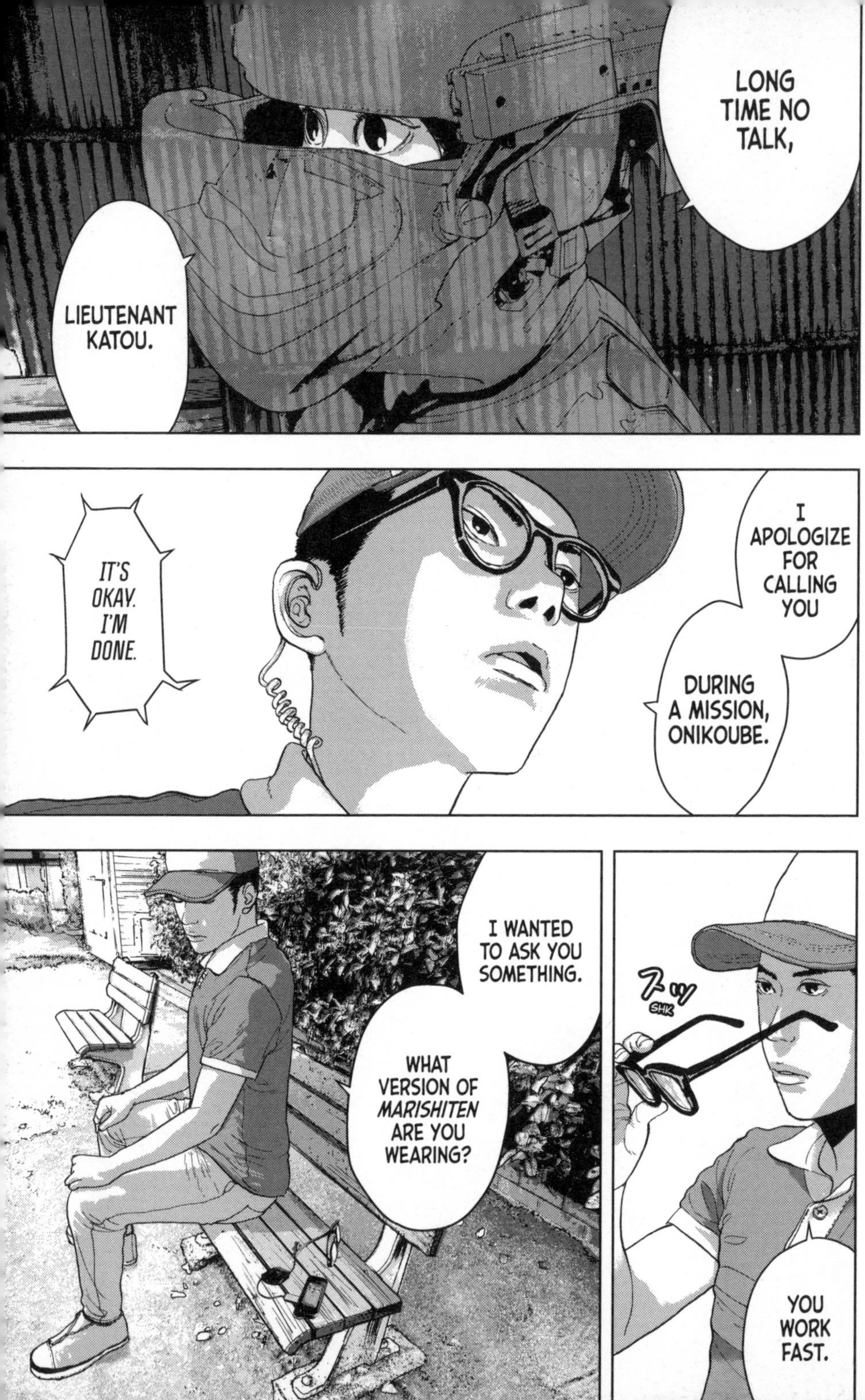
LONG TIME NO TALK,
LIEUTENANT KATOU.
I APOLOGIZE FOR CALLING YOU
DURING A MISSION, ONIKOUBE.
IT'S OKAY. I'M DONE.
フッ SHK
YOU WORK FAST.
I WANTED TO ASK YOU SOMETHING.
WHAT VERSION OF *MARISHITEN* ARE YOU WEARING?

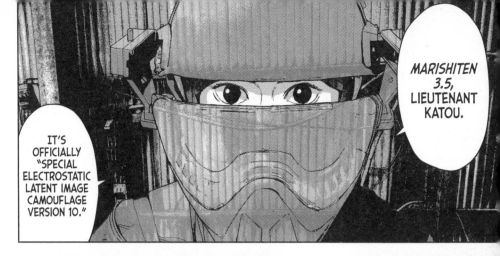

MARISHITEN 3.5, LIEUTENANT KATOU.

IT'S OFFICIALLY "SPECIAL ELECTROSTATIC LATENT IMAGE CAMOUFLAGE VERSION 10."

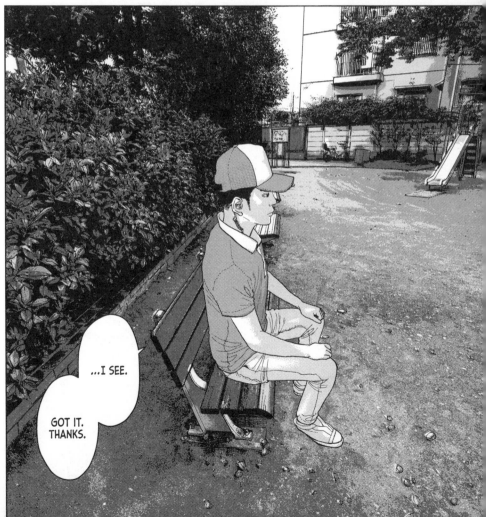

...I SEE.

GOT IT. THANKS.

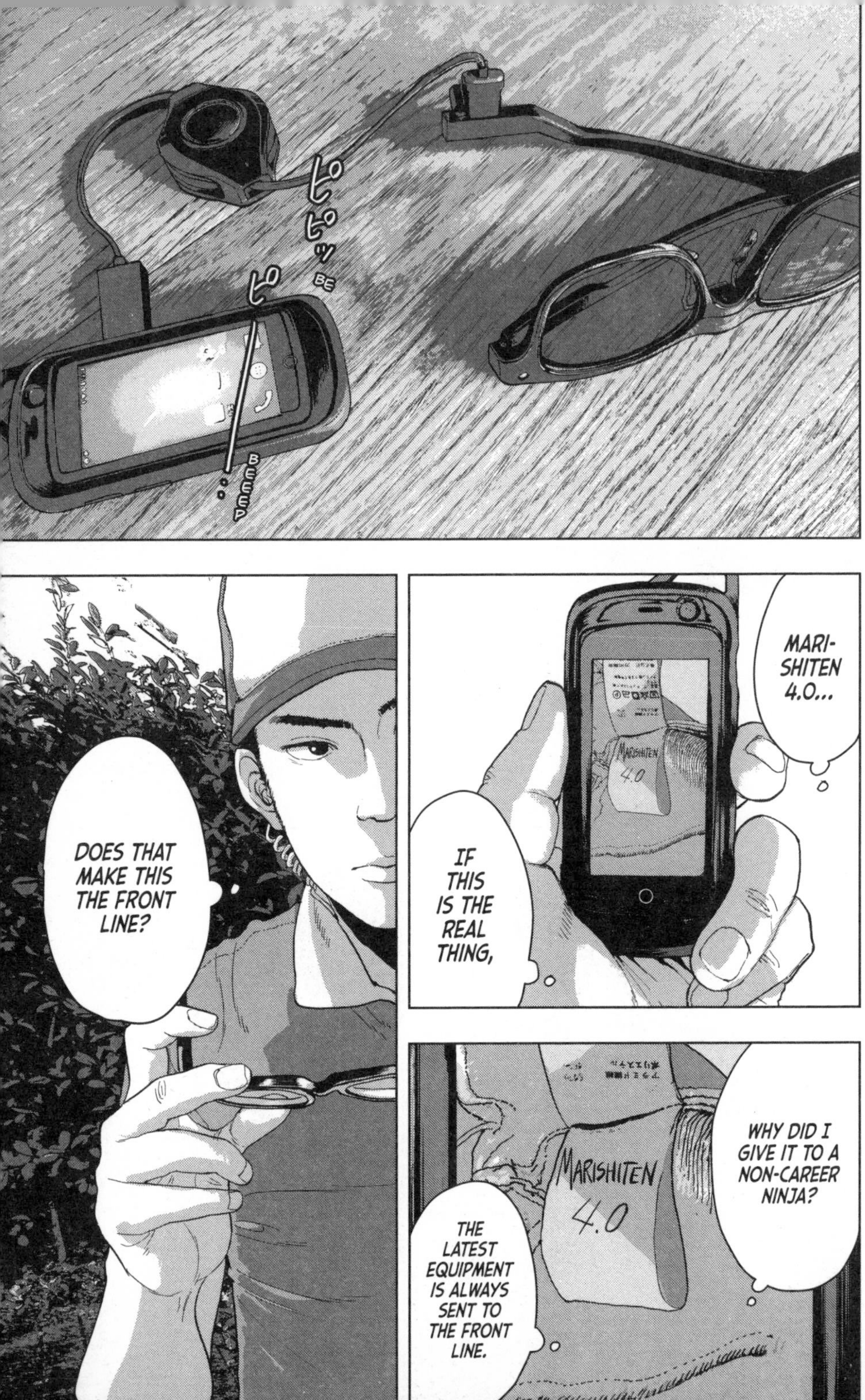
ピピピッ
BE
ピ
BEEEP
MARI-SHITEN 4.0...
IF THIS IS THE REAL THING,
MARISHITEN 4.0
WHY DID I GIVE IT TO A NON-CAREER NINJA?
THE LATEST EQUIPMENT IS ALWAYS SENT TO THE FRONT LINE.
DOES THAT MAKE THIS THE FRONT LINE?

THERE'S GOTTA BE

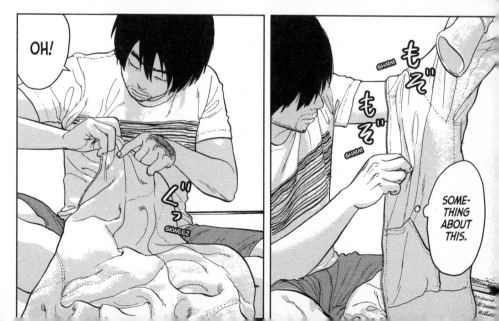

OH!

SKWEEZ

SHMM

SHMM

SOME-THING ABOUT THIS.

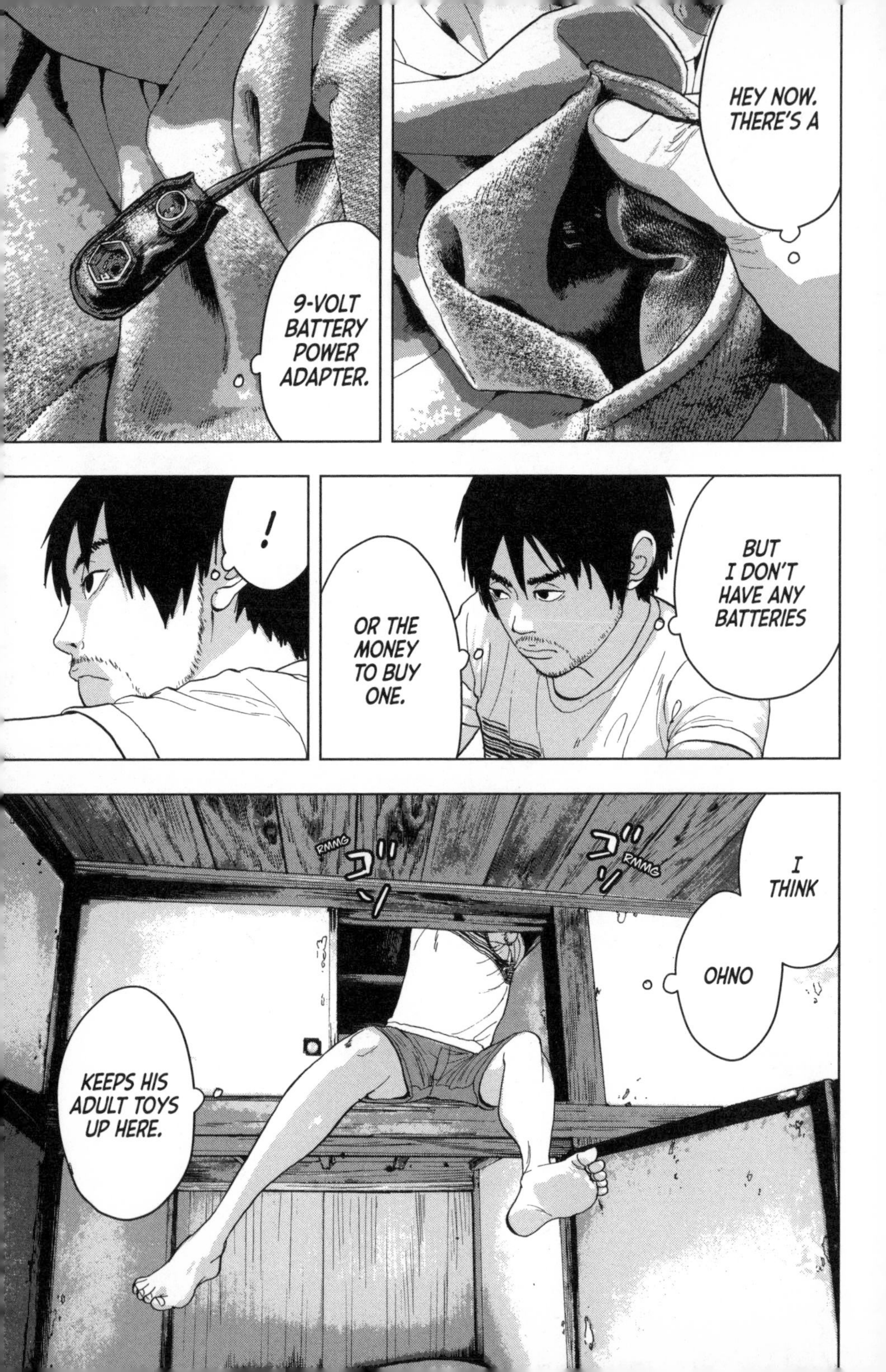
HEY NOW. THERE'S A
9-VOLT BATTERY POWER ADAPTER.
BUT I DON'T HAVE ANY BATTERIES
OR THE MONEY TO BUY ONE.
!
RMMG
RMMG
I THINK
OHNO
KEEPS HIS ADULT TOYS UP HERE.

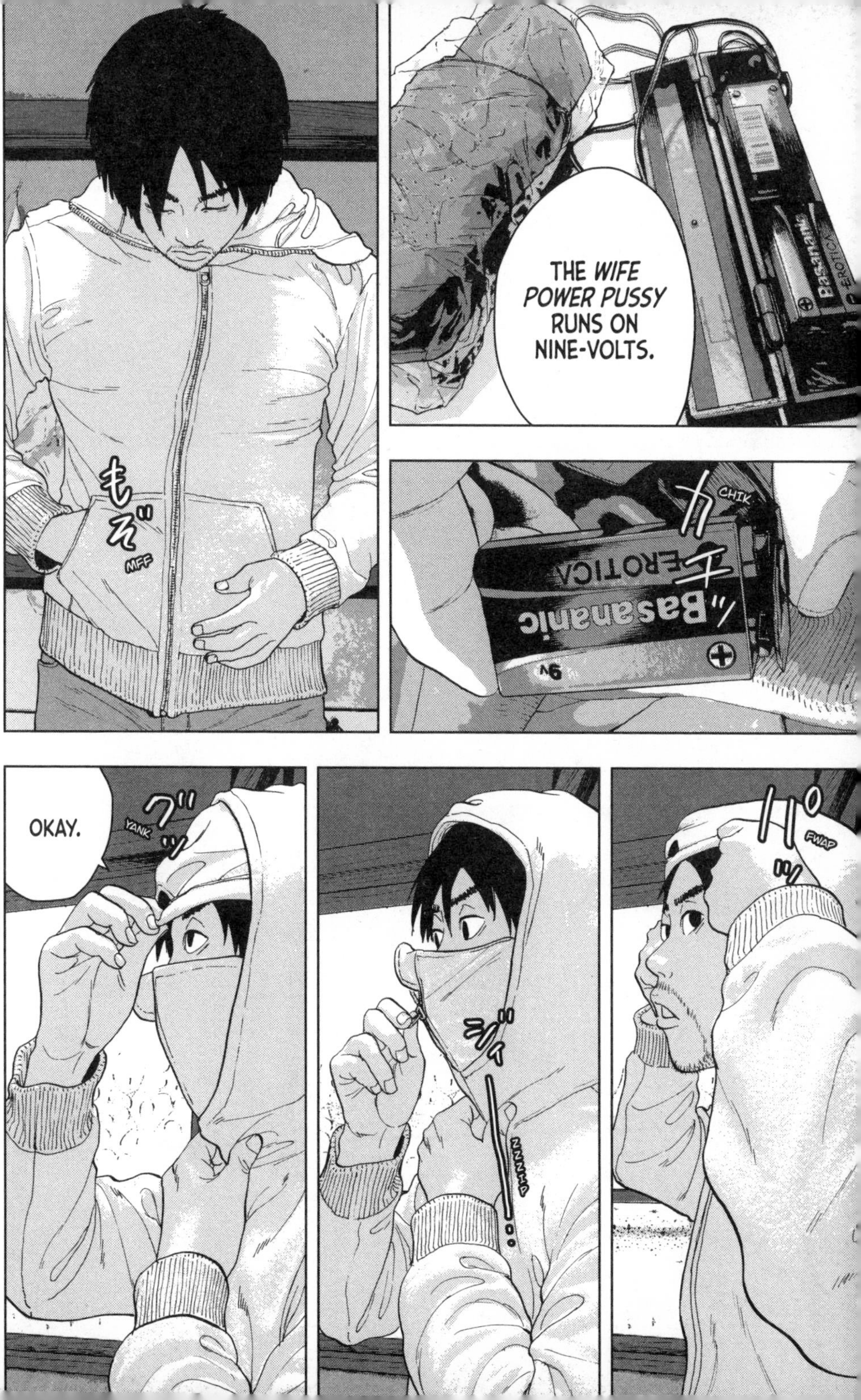
THE WIFE POWER PUSSY RUNS ON NINE-VOLTS.
Basananic EROTICA
カチッ
CHIK
Basananic EROTICA
9V
もぞ
MFF
パッ
FWAP
ジィーー
ZZZIP
OKAY.
グイッ
YANK

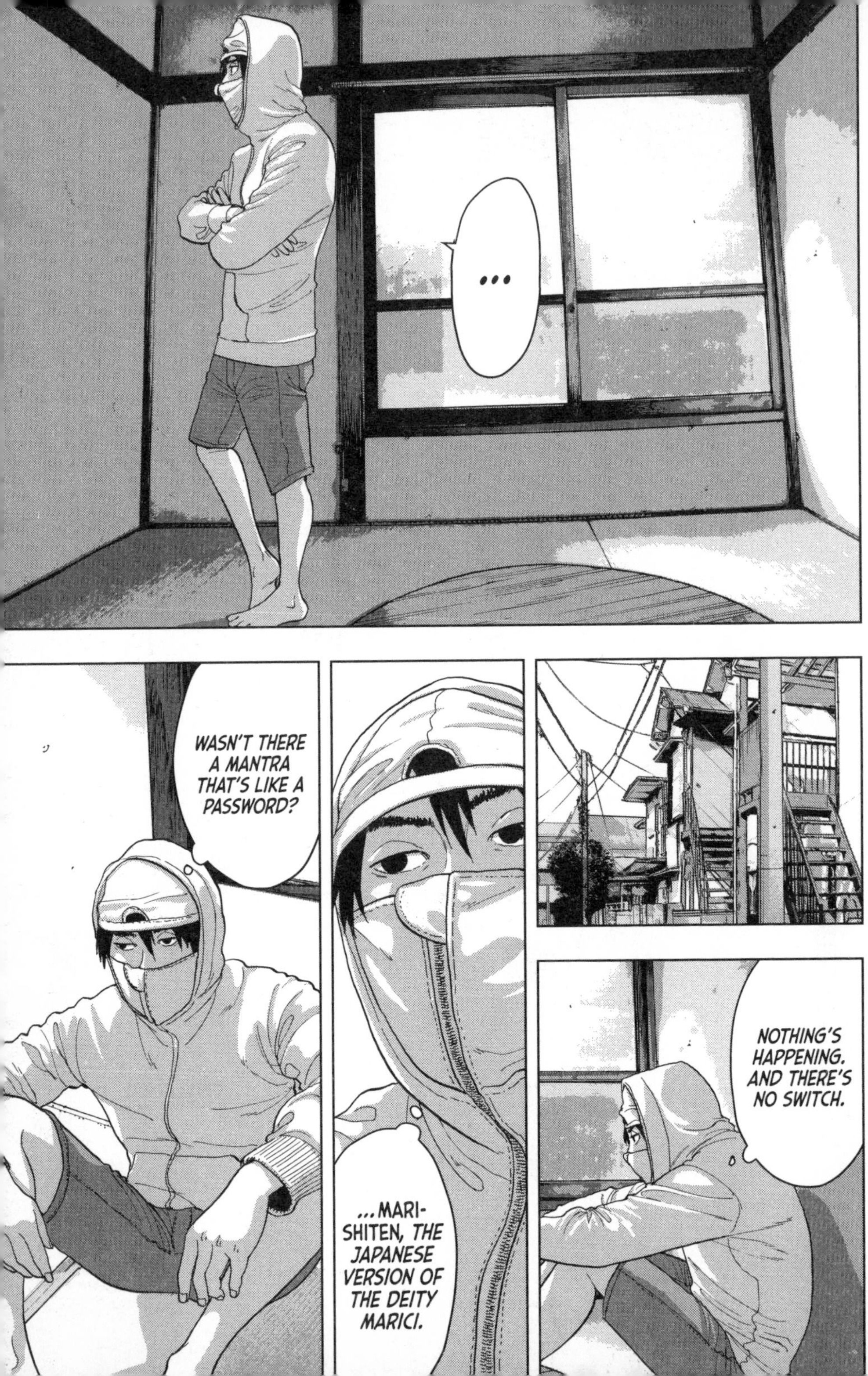
...
NOTHING'S HAPPENING. AND THERE'S NO SWITCH.
...MARI-SHITEN, THE JAPANESE VERSION OF THE DEITY MARICI.
WASN'T THERE A MANTRA THAT'S LIKE A PASSWORD?

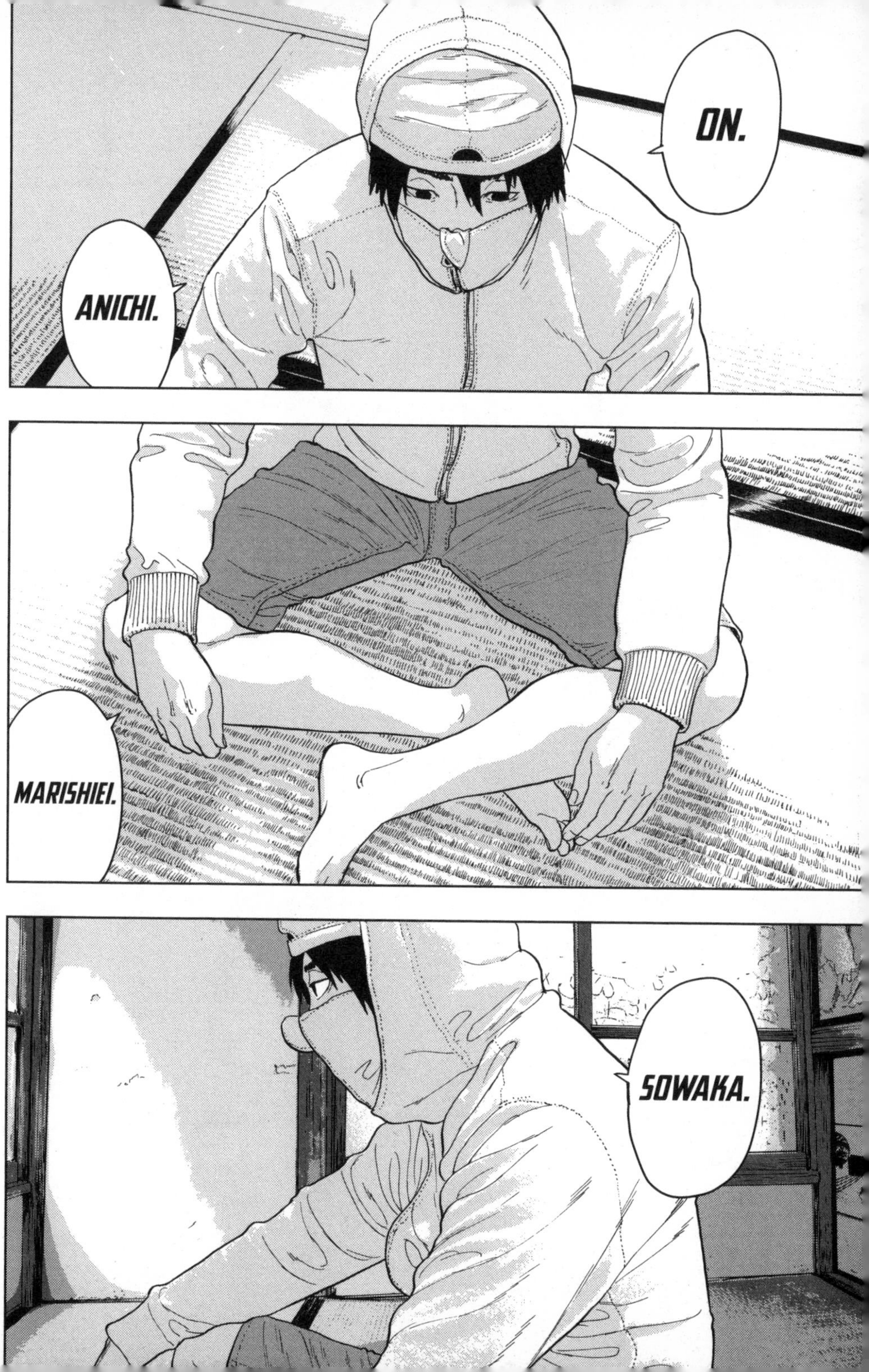
ON.
ANICHI.
MARISHIEI.
SOWAKA.

STILL NOTHING...

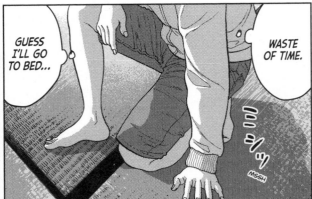

GUESS I'LL GO TO BED...

WASTE OF TIME.

MSSH

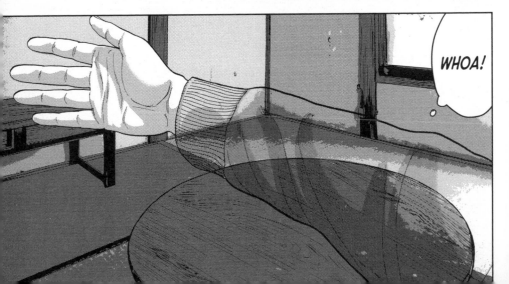

WHOA!

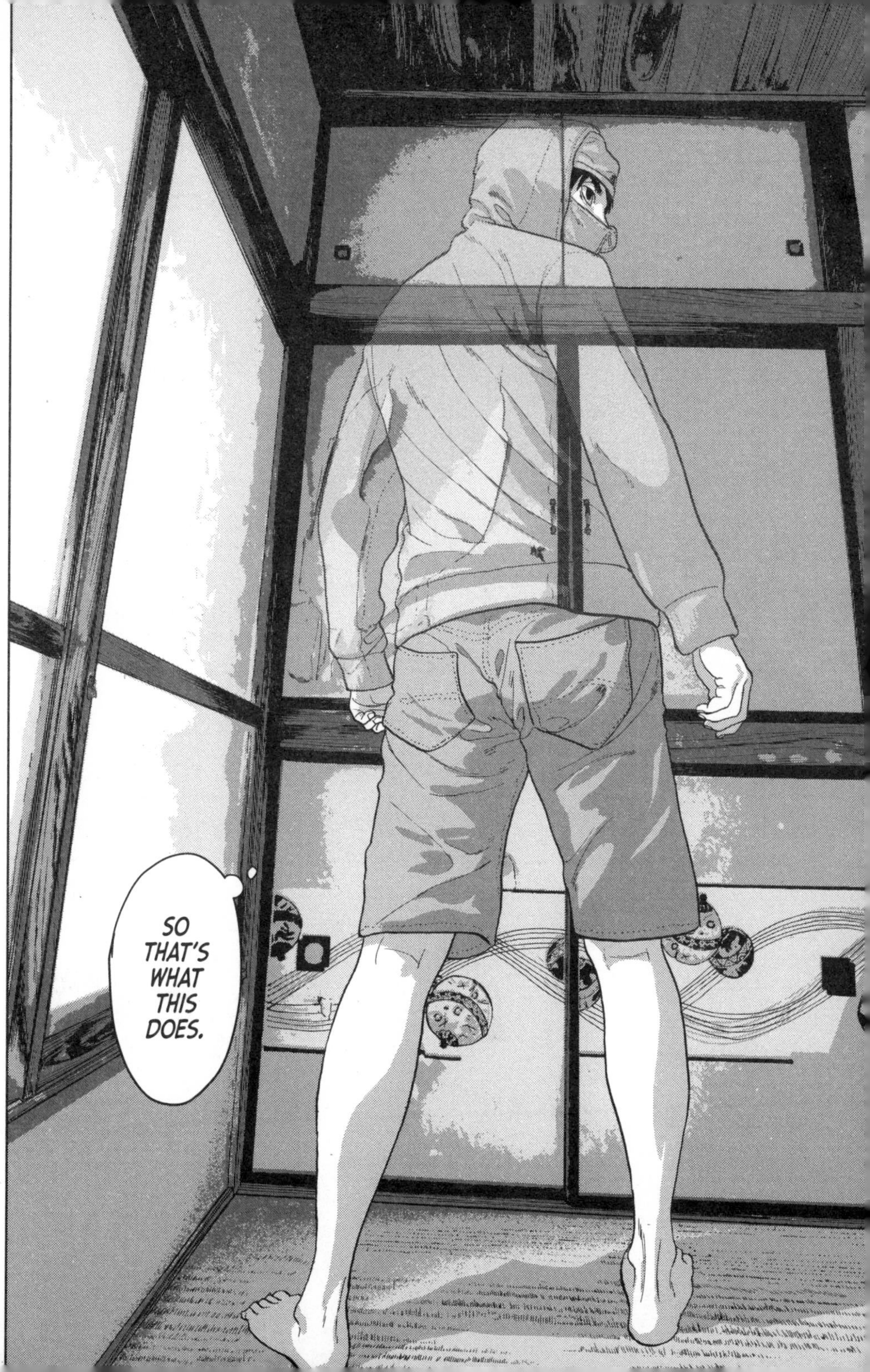
SO THAT'S WHAT THIS DOES.

POWERED BY
Dacha

STAFF
Ikka Matsuki
Kanae Tanaka
Ayumi Takamatsu
Momoko Takeda
Julie Okamoto
Miki Imai
Yoshito Kitakuni
Tatsuhiro Yasui
Hiromi Sato

SPECIAL THANKS TO
Kazunobu Gotou
MMR-Z
(Rico Tyndall, Leonidas-Z, Maru, sico, TP, taroybmx, Morizo)
Kenichi Tsuruoka
URBAN UNION
Matrix-AIDA
Yoshihito Aida
Satake Cutlery
ROCHE
ISTARI COMICS

UNDER NINJA

Volume 1

Translator:	Sheldon Drzka
Proofreading:	Patrick Sutton
Production:	Nicole Dochych
	Anthony Quintessenza

©2019 Kengo Hanazawa. All rights reserved.
First Published in Japan in 2019 by Kodansha Ltd., Tokyo.
Publication rights for this English edition arranged through Kodansha Ltd., Tokyo.

Published in English by Denpa, LLC., Portland, Oregon, 2022.

Originally published in Japanese as *Under Ninja* by Kodansha Ltd., 2019
Under Ninja first serialized in *Young Magazine*, Kodansha Ltd., 2018.

This is a work of fiction.

ISBN-13: 978-1-63442-992-4
Library of Congress Control Number: 2021952067
Printed in China

First Edition

Denpa, LLC.
625 NW 17th Ave
Portland, OR 97209
www.denpa.pub